ELECTRONIC SPEECH SYNTHESIS

Techniques, Technology and Applications

Geoff Bristow

McGRAW-HILL BOOK COMPANY
New York   St. Louis   San Francisco   Auckland
Bogotá   Hamburg   Johannesburg   London   Madrid
Mexico   Montreal   New Delhi   Panama   Paris
São Paulo   Singapore   Sydney   Tokyo   Toronto

Library of Congress Cataloging in Publication Data

Bristow, Geoff.
  Electronic speech synthesis.

  Includes bibliographies and index.
  1. Speech synthesis. I. Title.
TK7882.S65B75   1984   621.3819'5832   84-3943
ISBN 0-07-007912-9

1234567890 DOC/DOC 8987654

ISBN 0-07-007912-9

Printed and bound by R. R. Donnelley & Sons Company.

CONTENTS

iv *Contents*

FOREWORD

Speech research and speech technology is a field of great fascination and, therefore, inherently also of frustration. How many engineers have not entered the field with the high expectations that insight into computer technology, electronics, and high powered signal processing mathematics shall lead to the great break-though in speech synthesis or recognition? How many funding agencies have not put their hopes in the next two-year contract that they sponsor for turning out the ultimate product, after which it would be time for research to close down and for engineering and marketing to take over? I recall a comment from a US federal research funder some 25 years ago that 'speech research is like a huge pit — you can throw any amount of money into it and nothing comes out'.

Now, as evidenced by this book, VLSI techniques and technical developments in speech processing and synthesis have created a 'speech revolution'. The pit has given something in return, not ultimate solutions but an impressive growth of a new industry eagerly searching for and creating new markets. The pit may become a volcano and, if so, let's hope that it will not create a new pollution consisting of meagre quality synthetic speech prompting our daily activities.

A large amount of work is now put into the art of incorporating personality features in talking chips for video games, etc. In the future we will work less with copying specific individual voices and more with establishing general rules for speaker typology, situational and contextual variations. Synthesis by rule has not yet reached its limits of intelligibility and naturalness. Speech recognition is even further away from its ultimate goal: that of speaker-independent handling of connected speech.

The Japanese national programme for the 'fifth generation' of talking, speech understanding and translating computers represents a universal technological optimism. I would rather rephrase this challenge as the need for a fifth generation of speech scientists, an interdisciplinary body of engineers, linguists, psychologists, physiologists, etc., who have a common understanding of the task. The first speech revolution was the offspring of electronics. It is now up to a new generation to complete a second revolution, the advance of basic knowledge of speech, language and human communication which will ensure a much wider acceptance and use of speech synthesis and recognition techniques and enable the more advanced objectives of handicap aids.

Electronic Speech Synthesis should pave the way for this development. The introduction to speech synthesis theory, speech processing, linguistics and speaker performance is followed up by a massive and detailed survey of design modules, possible applications and human engineering aspects. The detailed inventory of an expanding market and its products not only serves those involved in development work but will also serve as a stimulant for more general research.

In summary, the book is primarily directed to speech technology engineers that need a broader outlook on their work and it has a definite profile centered around US technology. It does not pretend to cover the more basic research aspect but instead includes a wide range of useful references. Most of all it provides a very welcome interface between technology and the applied field. My congratulations to the contributors and editor for this impressive work.

Professor Gunnar Fant
Dept of Speech Communication
and Music Acoustics
Royal Institute of Technology
Sweden

PREFACE

Electronic Speech Synthesis is intended to be light enough for general reading and yet full enough to serve as a text book. For general reading, some chapters would be omitted, and the diagram shown in the Introduction gives a guide to a suitable skeleton reading plan. To help it achieve the status of text book I have aimed to identify the important topics and then match them with suitable authors, rather than *vice versa*, as is often the case in such compilations.

The contributions

Many of the authors are experts in their fields, and they have been given the daunting task of potting the essence of their subjects into ten or twenty pages. Somehow, they have managed it. For example, the excellent work by Wiktor Jassem and Francis Nolan is in every way a rigorous account of phonetics and phonology and assumes no basic linguistic knowledge on the part of the reader. Likewise John Makhoul has distilled the fundamentals of several powerful LPC techniques into a single chapter, in one of the most straightforward representations I have seen.

Nevertheless, I have taken the liberty in the LPC chapter of providing some stepping stones through the analysis by printing some of John's summarising sentences in bold type, and we have highlighted some of the more important equations. I apologise to those readers who sail through mathematical analyses such as this one without any help from the editor. As a justification I hope that the readership of this chapter will include a few of the people like me who might otherwise have lost confidence two equations from the end.

Many of the authors of the *Technology* section too are distinguished by being pioneers of their fields. For example, Forrest Mozer was the original inventor of the technique used in the National Digitalker (and which subsequently inspired many other similar methods). Richard Gagnon likewise is the designer of the technique used in the Votrax chips and John Stork pioneered much of the work which led to General Instruments' synthesis implementation. Similarly, Larry Brantingham was the designer of Texas Instruments' first LPC chip using algorithmic techniques developed by Gene Helms. In the same way, most of the authors of the sections on PCB modules are the actual designers of the modules they describe, and the authors of the *Applications* chapters include many pioneers in the use of synthetic speech in particular application areas.

The two introductory chapters on synthesis, *Voices of Men and Machines* by James Flanagan and on recognition, *Speech Recognition* by Michael Elphick, are in fact adaptations of previous articles (see acknowledgements). They were selected because they each gave a suitable overview of a broad and complex field. Dr Flanagan, for example, who is author of an early and highly respected foundation text, *Speech Analysis, Synthesis and Perception*, gives a complete introduction to synthesisers from a fascinating historical perspective through to the present day. Similarly, the technical contribution by Toshio Oura of the Nippon Electric Company is an adaptation of a recent technical paper, and two of the contributions by David Gilblom of Telesensory Speech Systems, *Choosing a Speaker* and *Making a Recording*, were constructed from a TSS hand-out.

Finally, one of the authors claims not to be an expert — at least not in this field directly. John Baddeley, an experienced actor and highly acclaimed *voice-over* artist, was dropped into the affray to offer some insight into the way we use our voices. John has worked much of late in recording for voice synthesis and I thank him for his bold and worthwhile entry into this otherwise technical book.

This book and its partners in the field

This book is in no way intended to borrow readership from the many excellent works which already exist on the subject of speech — in fact the reverse is true. The objective of *Electronic Speech Synthesis* is to combine between two covers an introduction to the specialised works which can be found scattered amongst library shelves and magazine racks. (In general the *Techniques* are found in library books and the *Technology* and *Applications* in the magazines!) Accordingly, at the end of most chapters there is a list of titles for suggested further reading, in addition to specific references made in the text. It is hoped that the reader will be stimulated to research widely after receiving a foundation from this book.

To achieve the stated objective, I have relied heavily on friends and contacts, and I would like to thank all the authors for their lively discussions as well as for their excellent contributions. I especially owe my gratitude to Gene Helms who gave me some good first contacts in California and Detroit. I am also indebted to Texas Instruments for providing the physical materials and support to engage myself on the book, and to my wife, Julia, for allowing my spare time to be consumed in this way. The manuscript was prepared with endless patience by Sue Bundock, without whom I would not have submitted it this decade.

Finally, let me apologise for referring from time to time to the reader or designer as *he*. No assumption is made about the sex of the reader.

Geoff Bristow

ACKNOWLEDGEMENTS

The following sections of the text were derived from previously published material, but have been adapted by the author or editor to fit into the context of the book. The permission of the original publisher is gratefully acknowledged:

(1) Chapter 4, *Voices of Men and Machines*, originally appeared in the *Journal of the Acoustical Society of America* (1972), **51**, 1375–1387.

(2) Chapter 7, *Speech Recognition*, originally appeared in *High Technology* magazine (Mar./Apr. 1982), 2(2), 71–78, under the title 'Unraveling the mysteries of speech recognition'.

(3) Sections 9.1–9.2, in chapter 9, *Chips using Time-domain Synthesis*, were derived from the same basic material as an article entitled 'Time-domain synthesis gives good-quality speech at very low data rates', which appeared in *Speech Technology* magazine (Sept/Oct 1982), 62–68.

AUTHORS' BIOGRAPHIES

Baddeley, John

Currently heavily involved in freelance voice recording for speech synthesis and media commercials, John has 30 years of experience in the dramatic arts. He has worked on radio, television and stage, in drama, comedy and musicals. He has toured extensively, and became popular as a 'voice-over artist' from about 1974, with the advent of commercial radio in Britain. (*chapter 2*)

Benbassat, Gerard

Currently a research project leader in Texas Instruments, France, Gerard was previously head of the speech processing research group, the *Companie Internationale des Telecommunications* at Paris. He received his MSEE in 1968 in Paris, after which he worked on computer-assisted instruction at the *Institut de Recherche en Informatique et Automatique* (IRIA). Before moving to the CIT he spent 4 years at Stanford University where he worked on LPC. (*section 18.1*)

Brantingham, Larry

Currently European Speech Strategy manager for Texas Instruments, based in Nice, France, Larry runs a research laboratory investigating phonetic coding, speech recognition and speech development tools. He holds twenty-five patents, fifteen of which are in speech and include the invention of the first single-chip LPC synthesiser. He received BSEE and MSEE degrees at the University of Arkansas, USA, and led the integrated circuit design team on the TMS5100 in Lubbock, Texas. (*section 10.1*)

Bristow, Dr Geoff

Currently Marketing Manager for the North European Semiconductor Division of Texas Instruments, Geoff has previously been responsible for the product marketing and engineering of TI's microcomputers, microsystems and speech products. His doctoral research project at Cambridge was on speech training aids for the deaf using computer colour graphics, and one of the portable aids he designed has subsequently been manufactured in volume. He has continued his involvement with this field as a director of a non-profit making concern, Cambridge Speech Research', which funds further speech research for the deaf out of royalties derived from the original speech aid. (*chapters 1, 14 and 21 and Editor*)

Brodersen, Prof. Bob

Currently Professor of Electrical Engineering and Computer Science at Berkeley, California, where he is engaged in research on the application of integrated circuits to digital signal processing, especially using analog sampled-data techniques. He holds a BS degree at California State Polytechnic in Electrical Engineering and Maths, and MS and PhD degrees from MIT. Before joining Berkeley he spent three years at Texas Instruments working on the application of Charged Coupled Devices for signal processing. He was elected an FIEEE in 1982. (*chapter 8*)

Buchwald, Prof. Jennifer

Currently Professor of Physiology at the University of California Los Angeles Medical Centre and a member of the Mental Retardation Centre, Jennifer holds a PhD in Physiology from the medical centres of the University of Minnesota and Tulane University. She is a member of the Brain Research Institute, UCLA, and she is also its Associate Director. (*section 18.2*)

Carterette, Prof. Edward

Currently Professor of Experimental Psychology and a member of the Brain Research Institute at the University of California, Los Angeles, Professor Carterette holds AB Degrees from the University of Chicago and Harvard University and a PhD from Indiana University. He was an NSF Fellow in Physics at the Royal Institute of Technology, Stockholm and Cambridge University, England. (*section 18.2*)

Costello, Joe

Currently manager of the Time Domain Speech Synthesis Development group of the National Semiconductor Corp., Santa Clara, California. Joe holds a BS in maths and physics at Harvey Mudd College and MS degrees in physics at Yale and Berkeley. He has worked in fibre optics for National, and in energy conservation at the Lawrence Berkeley Laboratory and has been involved with speech since May 1981. (*sections 9.1 and 9.2*)

Dilts, Mike

Currently senior software engineer in the Voice Engineering Group of Wang Laboratories Inc., Lowell, Massachusetts, Mike received a Bachelor of Linguistics degree at Berkeley in 1976, and an MA at Harvard in 1980. While continuing his research at Harvard he has been Speech Program Manager for the Texas Instruments' Regional Technology Centre at Boston, Massachusetts, before joining Wang in 1982. (*chapter 6*)

Durgavichs, Tom

Currently Speech Applications Manager at National Semiconductor Corp., Santa Clara, California, Tom is responsible for the development of new speech applications. He was formerly engaged in medical electronics at Analogic Corp, and at Hewlett-Packard Co, and holds BSEE and MSEE degrees from MIT. (*section 9.4*)

Edwards, Dr Gwyn

Currently Snr Applications Engineer at American Microsystems Inc., Santa Clara, California, in the telecommunications group, Gwyn holds a BSc and PhD at University College of North Wales, Bangor. He has worked in signal processing hardware design and applications since 1969, specialising in MOS LSI realisations of signal processing circuits. He is currently responsible for speech and signal processing devices. (*section 10.3*)

Elphick, Michael

Currently executive editor of *Computer Design* Magazine, based in Littleton, Massachusetts, Michael has also worked as an editor or contributor for several other US technical publications, including

Electronic Design, *Electronic Engineering Times* and *EDN*. Before becoming a journalist, he worked as a design engineer for EMI Electronics, Sperry and Dynamics Corporation of America. He holds a degree in Industrial Engineering from New York University and is a chartered engineer in the UK. (*chapter 7*)

Fallside, Dr Frank

Currently a reader in the Engineering Department of Cambridge University, England, Frank runs a research team engaged in the development of speech training aids for the deaf, synthetic speech output from concept, and other speech-related projects. His original PhD work was in control systems and he currently lectures in control engineering at Cambridge. He is an MIEE and Chartered Engineer, and a Fellow of Trinity Hall, Cambridge. (*chapter 17*)

Flanagan, Dr James

Currently Head of the Acoustics Research Department at Bell Laboratories, Murray Hill, New Jersey, Dr Flanagan is one of the pioneers of speech science. He is author of *Speech Analysis, Synthesis and Perception* (Springer-Verlag, 1972), is a Fellow of the IEEE and is a member of the Executive Council of the Acoustical Society of America. He has a BS degree at Mississippi State University and SM and ScD degrees at MIT, all in electrical engineering, and has been at Bell Laboratories since 1957. (*chapter 4*)

Fons, Katherine

Currently a speech scientist at the Votrax division of the Federal Screw Works, Troy, Mitchigan, Kathy holds a Masters Degree in Speech Technology and is involved in research on language processing systems. Her work at Votrax includes the development of consumer and industrial speech output devices, including text-to-speech translation processors. (*sections 11.2–11.4*)

Gagnon, Richard

Currently President of his own research and development firm, Gagnon Electronics Research Company, Richard has been engaged in the voice synthesis field for 12 years. He graduated from the University of Mitchigan in 1963 with degrees in Electrical Engineering and Mathematics, specialising in communications and circuit theory, and spent some time in biological research before moving into speech. Amongst his designs are the *VS* series of synthesisers employed by Votrax Inc. (*section 11.1*)

Gargagliano, Tim

Currently Senior Computer Engineer at the Votrax Division of the Federal Screw Works, Troy, Mitchigan, Tim has a Masters Degree in Computer Engineering and is responsible for development of text-to-speech translation processors. His experience covers language processing systems and speech output devices for the consumer and industrial markets. (*sections 11.2–11.4*)

Gilblom, David

Currently Sales Manager of Telesensory Speech Systems, Palo Alto, California, David has experience in sales, marketing and applications engineering for computer imaging systems and speech synthesis. He holds a BSEE Degree from the Case Western Reserve University (1968) and an MBA Degree from the University of Santa Clara (1979). His publications have included the topics of low-light-level television and text-to-speech synthesis. (*sections 12.4, 13.1 and 13.2*)

Gray, Tony

Currently Director of the Loughborough Primary Micro Project, at the Education Department of Loughborough University of Technology, England, Tony has been a qualified science teacher since 1968. He has spent most of his 12 years in school in arts education and working with children having special educational needs. He received an MA Degree at Hull University, where he began an interest in computing and its application to special education. (*chapter 15*)

Gunawardana, Raj

Currently Speech Systems Design Manager at Texas Instruments Ltd, Bedford, England, Raj has 7 years of design experience in speech and memory-related circuitry. He holds an MSc Degree from Birmingham University, and has a patent pending on an advanced graphics system. (*section 12.3*)

Helms, Dr Eugene

Currently Snr Vice President of operations at Voice Control Systems, Dallas, Texas, Gene has 10 years experience in the research and development of speech analysis and synthesis techniques and in speaker recognition systems. He holds a PhD in Electrical Engineering and amongst the devices he has designed is the TI 'Portable Analysis Synthesis System' for data preparation. (*sections 13.3 and 13.5*)

Jassem, Dr Wiktor

Currently head of the Acoustic Phonetics Research Unit at the Polish Academy of Sciences, Poznan, Poland, Wiktor specialises in phonetics and phonology. He has previously conducted research at Wroclaw University and Poznan University. He has many publications to his name, and is series editor for *Speech Analysis and Synthesis*, a set of volumes on acoustic phonetics published by the Polish Academy of Sciences. (*chapter 3*)

Makhoul, Dr John

Currently John is Principal Scientist at Bolt, Beranek and Newman, the Massachusetts acoustics consultancy, managing the Speech Signal Processing Department. He holds BE, MSc and PhD degrees in electrical engineering, which he received from the American University of Beirut (1964), the Ohio State University (1965) and MIT (1970), respectively. He has conducted research at BBN since receiving his PhD in 1970 and has become well known for his work and publications in various aspects of speech analysis, synthesis, compression, recognition and enhancement. (*chapter 5*)

Moller, Chris

Currently an independent design consultant in Bedfordshire, England, Chris was previously a design engineer in the Boston Regional Technology Centre of Texas Instruments, and Manager of the TI Regional Technology Centre at Bedford, England. He received an MA Degree in Electrical Sciences from Cambridge in 1976, and most of his design work has revolved around microcomputers and speech synthesis. (*sections 10.4 and 12.1*)

Mozer, Prof. Forrest

Currently a professor of physics at the University of California, Berkeley, Forrest has received a BS degree from the University of Nebraska, MS and PhD degrees from the California Institute of Technology, and a Guggenheim fellowship. He has taught at Berkeley since 1966, where amongst other things he has invented a time-domain method of speech synthesis, and previously worked in the Lockhead Missiles Co. and the US Aerospace Corporation. (*sections 9.1 and 9.2*)

Nolan, Dr Francis

Currently a lecturer in the Dept of Linguistics at Cambridge University, Francis teaches courses in phonology and instrumental phonetics. His PhD dissertation (Cambridge 1980) deals with the phonetics of speaker recognition, and his current research interests include speech production theories, and the synthesis of different voice qualities. (*chapters 3 and 20*)

Oura, Toshio

Currently supervisor of the special-purpose microcomputer department of the Nippon Electric Co. Ltd, Japan, Toshio has been engaged in MOS LSI design at NEC since 1970. He holds five patents and has worked with designs for calculators, video games and speech synthesis. He received a BS degree from Toyama University and is a member of the Institute of Electronics and Communications Engineers of Japan. (*section 9.3*)

Pfeifer, Dr Larry

Currently Vice President of Signal Technology Inc., Santa Barbara, California, Larry is responsible for the marketing of all the company's software products. He received a PhD Degree in Electrical Engineering from the University of California at Santa Barbara, and an MBA Degree at Pepperdine University, and was responsible for the development and implementation of automatic speech recognition software at the computer research laboratory of the University of California. From 1972, Larry spent 5 years with the Speech Communications Research Laboratory Inc. in Santa Barbara, California, where his posts included Principle Investigator and Associate Director of the Laboratory. He was responsible for the development of the ILS package, and joined STI at its inception in 1977. (*section 13.4*)

Roe, Peter

Currently a Systems Engineer with Texas Instruments, Bedford, England, Peter is working on the applications of microcomputers and speech synthesis in the telecommunications industry. He has a broad design background in telecommunications, including 7 years in Plessey Telecommunications and 7 years in the Communications Department of British Gas. He is a chartered engineer and corporate member of the IEE. (*chapter 16*)

Rush, Peter

Currently director of Triangle Digital Services, a speech consultancy in North London, Peter specialises in prototyping and the needs of the small OEM. He gained an MA in Electrical Sciences at Cambridge in 1966 before moving to Texas Instruments as a product engineer. He then spent 3 years in Italy working for General Instrument, and returned with GI to London where he was product manager for microcomputers until 1980. (*section 13.6*)

Shipley, Dr Carl

Currently research associate in physiology at the University of California, Los Angeles, Carl has an AB Degree in literature from the University of Arizona. He is also a member of the research staff at the Jet Propulsion Laboratories, California Institute of Technology, Pasadena. (*section 18.2*)

Stork, John E.

Currently president of the Speech Technology Corporation, Santa Maria, California, John obtained a BSEE at Standford University in 1949 and completed graduate programmes at the University of California, Los Angeles and Massachusetts Institute of Technology. After some design experience in Computer and Communications systems with TRW, and McDonnell Douglas, he moved into design consultancy in 1954, specialising in speech analysis and synthesis since 1968. In 1973 he founded the Speech Technology Corp. (*sections 10.2 and 12.2*)

Talbott, Marvin

Currently a senior member of the technical staff at the Corporate

Engineering Centre of Texas Instruments Inc., Dallas, Texas, Marvin has spent 14 years with TI involved with signal processing systems and computer architectural simulation. He received a BSEE Degree from Wichita State University, Kansas (1965), an MSEE from Syracuse University, New York (1968) and an MBA from the University of Dallas (1978). His recent inventions include the *Vocaid* voice communication aid for the disabled, on which he has a patent pending. (*chapter 19*)

Young, Dr Steve

Currently a lecturer at the University of Manchester Institute of Science and Technology, Steve holds an MA and PhD at Cambridge University. His doctoral research was in the new field of speech synthesis from concept, and he has continued these research interests at UMIST. (*chapter 17*)

To those who use technology
for the benefit of man

INTRODUCTION

This book is intended for anyone who wishes to understand *speech*, perhaps with a view to designing a system which talks. But first, what exactly do we mean by 'speech'?

During the last twenty years, speech research has been emerging as an inter-disciplinary subject in its own right. In that time, researchers at universities and commercial laboratories have developed techniques to allow computers to talk, requiring relatively small data storage requirements and offering excellent capabilities for instantaneous concatenation of phrases. These researchers were not purely engineers, though, or purely linguists — they found that they had to be a combination of the two. Some were linguists who learnt the elements of mathematics and the intricacies of computing, and some were electronic engineers who decided to expand their understanding of how we use our voices to communicate, and how we build spoken languages from the infinite variety of sounds we can produce.

Following the new understanding of the speech mechanism, and the emergence of suitable digital synthesis techniques, the true *speech revolution* could be said to have begun in about 1977 with the design of VLSI (Very Large Scale Integration) devices. The manufacture of such devices in high volumes, for prices of only a few dollars each, made talking products commercially as well as technically feasible. But while the technical side of adding speech synthesis to a system has been trivialised by 'chips' that can now be configured into a circuit using a simple data sheet, the necessity of cultivating *speech system designers* as interdisciplinary *linguist-engineers* still remains.

Electronic Speech Synthesis aims to cover concisely but completely all the fundamental subject matter which is a prerequisite to either speech research or the design of speaking products and systems. At the

1

same time it is hoped that all those involved in any way with synthetic speech — perhaps with project management or product planning, or as students of man–machine communications — will gain an appreciation of the capabilities of voice output and the pitfalls of which to beware.

The book is primarily aimed at the electronic engineer who wishes to become a speech scientist, although the linguist and generalist are also borne in mind. Accordingly no introduction to basic electronics is given, but the suggested reader's plan shown below indicates how some chapters (which assume a specific knowledge of electronics or mathematics) can be omitted without spoiling the flow of the argument for the non-technical reader. In particular, several of the introductory and summary chapters require no specialised academic or technical background, and the applications section should give an overall insight into the practical use of the new speech technology.

The text is divided into three parts, *Techniques*, *Technology* and *Applications*. Part I, *Techniques*, covers the basic concepts of speech communications and speech synthesis, and the techniques that were used for computer synthesis prior to the advent of dedicated silicon devices. The reader is introduced, in this section, to the versatility of the human voice and to the sounds of languages (and will note, for example, that the vowel sounds of English have very little to do with *a,e,i,o,u*!). He will become familiar with the basic tool of speech analysis, the spectrogram, and understand how the vocal tract can be modelled as an acoustic tube. If he feels mathematically inclined he can delve into a popular algorithmic technique of speech analysis and synthesis, *linear predictive coding*, which offers some fascinating and elegant conclusions. He is shown how synthetic speech can be derived *by rule* from simple text input, and finally, for background interest only, he is given an insight into a related and complementary field to synthesis — speech recognition.

Part II, *Technology*, illustrates how these same techniques (and others) have been exploited by designers of VLSI silicon circuits, and gives enough application detail to allow an electronic engineer to refer to data sheets alone and construct an electronic speech synthesis system. The section starts with an overview of the *state of the art*, and then discusses in detail the three main approaches — time domain synthesis, LPC, and a development of formant synthesis — as well as ready-built modules that use these techniques. However, these chapters are not intended to be an exhaustive survey of available speech synthesis devices, but rather the objective is to offer a technical summary of the types of product that exist. Before embarking on a particular project, the designer is invited to examine the VLSI market thoroughly. To this end, a list of companies known to be working in the area is given at the end of each chapter. Finally, following the theme that electronic design is only half the battle, the remainder of part II is devoted to the choice of vocabulary and speaker, data preparation, editing and the *human factors* aspects of a voice-output system.

Part III, *Applications*, is an assortment of selected examples of the use of speech synthesis in real projects, and a few ideas for the future. Some of the main application areas are surveyed, such as telecommunications, education and aids for the handicapped, and it is hoped that these will illustrate both the theory and the practical details that are offered in the first two parts of the book.

Reader's plan

Chapter	Short title	Prerequisite chapters	Non-technical interest in speech revolution	Casual interest in speech electronics	Training in speech systems design	Speech researcher looking for update
1	Speech Revolution	—	●	●	●	
2	Power of Speech	—	●	○	●	
3	Sounds and Languages	—		○	●	○
4	Voices of Men and Machines	—	●	●	●	
5	Linear Predictive Coding	4			●	○
6	Text-to-Speech	(3),4	●	●	●	○
7	Speech Recognition	—	○	●	●	○
8	Silicon and Speech	—		●	●	●
9	Time-domain Synthesis	4		○	●	●
10	Chips using LPC	4,(5)		○	●	●
11	Phonetic Synthesis	3,4		○	●	●
12	Ready-to-use systems	—		●	●	○
13	Data Preparation	—		●	●	●
14	Speech System Design	—	●	●	●	○
15	Speech in the Classroom	—	○	○	●	○
16	Speech in Telecomms	10		○	●	○
17	Speech and Complex Systems	—	○	○	●	●
18	LPC and Non-speech Sounds	5			●	●
19	Application Cookbook	(10)		●	●	○
20	Linguistics and Synthesis	3		○	●	●
21	Towards the Future	—	●	●	●	○

● = Strongly recommended reading plan.
○ = Optional extra reading plan.

PART 1
TECHNIQUES

CHAPTER 1

THE SPEECH REVOLUTION

Geoff Bristow

In this first chapter we discuss the history of speech synthesis technology and its likely style of use.

1.1 *The cause of the revolution*

As with the so-called *Microprocessor Revolution* of the last five years, in the *Speech Revolution* which is currently taking place no fundamental discoveries have been made about how machines can act, think or communicate. However, in both cases the cost and size of the electronic equipment involved have decreased steadily, and in the process have crossed various thresholds of feasibility for commercial applications. For example, it is now feasible to include computer control in a washing machine because a suitable microcomputer may only cost two dollars instead of the thousands of dollars the equivalent would have cost at the beginning of the last decade. Similarly, good synthetic speech from machines has been possible for about twenty years, but only with the use of minicomputers costing tens of thousands of dollars. The basis of the Speech Revolution is that the extra cost of adding speech output to a commercial product has now dropped below ten dollars, thanks to the use of silicon technology.

One of the first speech researchers was Alexander Graham Bell, who experimented with various analogues of speech waves as early as 1865. His work led to the invention of the telephone, for which he was awarded the Volta Prize in 1880, and the Bell Telephone Company has hosted one of the most important speech research laboratories up to the present day.

In 1940, at the Bell Laboratories, an apparatus was designed which allowed the spectrum of a speech wave to be analysed against time – the

Spectrograph. To understand the acoustic form of speech it is essential to study the complex changes that take place across the utterance, so this breakthrough meant that at last a piece of speech could be analytically described. A few years later, people began to develop apparatus which would *play back* speech from a simple spectrographic picture, as was done at the Haskins Laboratory in 1947. This could be regarded as the real beginning of speech synthesis technology, since the human voice was being analysed into a set of data and reconstructed at a later time.

By 1960 many academic institutions around the world shared techniques of synthesising human speech using minicomputers, storing only relatively small amounts of data – of the order of 10 000 binary digits for every second of speech. However, the expense of minicomputer systems and their related hardware prevented speech synthesis from becoming more than an experimental technology for large systems where a relatively large capital investment was feasible. For example, experiments were made with speaking telephone directories and aircraft timetables.

The techniques available at that time included derivatives of *Pulse Code Modulation* (PCM) – the method of regularly sampling a waveform and storing a digital representation of its amplitude – and *formant synthesis*, which uses filters to model the resonances of the vocal tract. Direct sampling techniques have been used widely in Telecommunications, mainly because they offer extremely high quality reproduction of any audio-band signal, and because the digital data are easy to store and manipulate in a computer. However, the data rate is high (for example, around 25 kbits/s for Delta Modulation – see fig. 1.1), which means that a simple synthesis system based on a sampled-data memory and Digital to Analog Converter (DAC) would only be able to store 5 seconds of speech in a 128 kbit ROM (Read Only Memory) or 2.5 seconds in 64 kbit RAM (Random Access Memory). In addition, PCM analyses and reconstructs a waveform taking account only of the bandwidth of that waveform, and the underlying structure of a signal such as speech is ignored. Accordingly, while complete messages can be reconstructed in this way, it is not possible to generate new phrases by recalling words from different parts of memory, *concatenating* them into new phases, (i.e. butting them together) and smoothing the intonation.

Formant Synthesis, on the other hand, offers the possibility of generation of speech from first principles, and it is therefore feasible either to reproduce a phrase as recorded by a human speaker, or even to synthesise a new utterance from theoretical parameters. The technique,

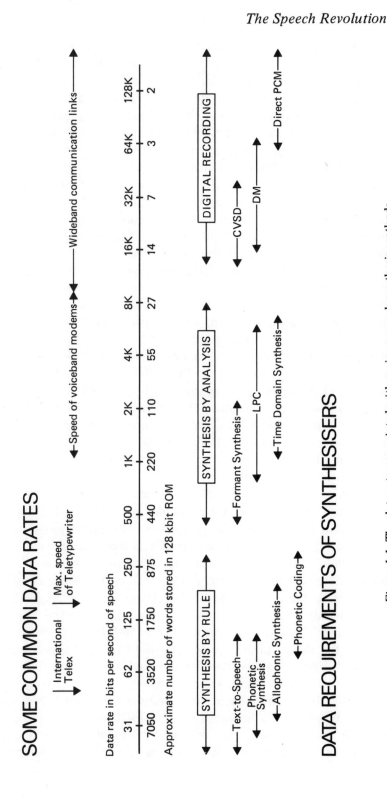

Figure 1.1 The data rates associated with various speech synthesis methods

which will be covered in greater detail in chapter 4, directly models the action of the human vocal tract, which is to excite a resonant cavity with pulses of air emitting from a tensed muscular closure. Clearly, then, formant synthesis is capable of combining sounds in the same way that the vocal tract can, and the data rate can be around 3 kbits/s without any special coding. So why did the speech revolution not begin when this was possible? Indeed, some excellent synthesis results were achieved (by John Holmes *et al.*, for example) as early as 1964. Simply, the cost was still too high. What is more, the next technological break-through was to be the unleashing of the vast power of digital integrated circuits, and formant synthesis is not inherently a digital technique – it requires multiple filters to represent the filtering action of the vocal mechanism, and so lends itself best to analog implementation.

In 1971 a new digital technique was developed for analysing and synthesising speech using computers. The method, known as *Linear Prediction*, was already known to other signal processing worlds, such as that of geophysical surveying, and a paper by Atal and Hanauer (1971) showed how it could be applied to speech. There followed a surge of academic activity (e.g. Itakura, 1972 and Markel, 1973), and it was demonstrated that Linear Predictive Coding (LPC) provided a much needed algorithmic technique of synthesis which was well suited to digital implementation. Its invention was timely, too, for exploitation on silicon; high density memory chips were just being designed and its low data rate (from around 800 to 5 kbits/s according to the coding method) would mean that up to 160 seconds of speech could be stored on a 128k ROM.

The start of the Speech Revolution could be said to have been in 1977. Around that time several consumer products started appearing on store shelves which took the public (and the industry) by surprise; not only did they speak long sentences relatively naturally, but they *cost less than $50*. Probably the first such product was a *Talking Calculator* designed by Telesensory Systems Inc., and this was followed shortly after by the *Speak 'n Spell* from Texas Instruments. Both these products included a dedicated chip set for the purpose and both were based on LPC. The TSI chip set formed a *digital signal processor* which performed the *direct* LPC algorithm, whilst the TI chip set included a dedicated single chip synthesiser employing a *lattice* filter (both methods are covered in detail in chapter 5).

After this initial activity, many companies entered the speech synthesis market, and although LPC remains the most popular tech-nique it is by no means the only one. Formant synthesis quickly reappeared in the form of a unique *phonetic synthesiser*, designed by

Votrax Inc. A phonetic synthesiser is a device which has the characteristics of a particular voice programmed inside it and which accepts phonetic commands, rather than accepting full voice data (see chapter 11). In addition, a completely new method was invented by Forrest Mozer and implemented by National Semiconductor Corp. on a chip. The so-called *Mozer method* is a time-domain technique which relies on the periodicity and redundancy in the speech waveform to achieve data compression (see chapter 9). Other related time-domain techniques (such as that described in section 9.3 from NEC) involve storing the shape of a full period of a range of speech waveforms, and playing back the appropriate waveform at the appropriate repetition rate (the same rate as the pulse of air through the vocal cords).

From this beginning, in the space of 5 years up to the time of writing, at least thirty companies have engaged in designing speech synthesisers on silicon wafers. The cost of an integrated circuit device which can emulate the human voice is down to less than $5 for the high volume user. Even including any subsidiary electronics (perhaps a microcomputer and a large ROM for speech data storage) a volume end-equipment manufacturer can make his product talk for a supplement of about $10 on his parts cost. In addition, the task of the circuit designer is no more complex for a speaking product than for any other electronic feature. He does not need to understand LPC to interface a synthesis chip to his bus, or to pass it any given data from a memory bank in his system. But in the choice of that data, there lies a whole new world of problems. Once again, one is reminded of the *Microprocessor Revolution* where the electronics suddenly became easy, and the engineer found himself treading the same path that the computer programmer had trodden a decade or so before.

1.2 *The nature of the revolution*

Why are we talking here of *revolution*? Why did the microprocessor cause a revolution and why will speech? The essence of the Microprocessor Revolution was not just that a change in technology affected the engineers' approach to design problems, but that the extra product features and system capabilities the engineer was able to invent with his new tools *radically changed the life-style* of the general public. Now, the capability of machines to communicate with men using the voice promises an even bigger change in the status of machines within society.

We have already seen a number of talking products appear on the market, and their reception has been mixed. We have seen talking typewriters and learning aids, calculators and watches, coffee machines, cash registers, cars and even books. Undoubtedly, the pattern of useage will change with the maturity of the technology, and when the public has had time to react to the new concept of vociferous machines. In the author's own opinion, we are likely to see a year or two of the exploitation of the novelty of speech, and then such useage will slowly disappear leaving a hard-core of serious application areas where speech is the very best communication medium to use. Machines will start their vocal lives, like young and insecure human beings, *talking too much*. As time goes on and their position in our lives becomes well accepted, they will talk less but be here to stay. For example, a washing machine which says *good morning* when it is turned on is conceivable as a *gimmick*, but very soon its speech will be modified to vocalise only when there is a malfunction or misuse of the machine.

However, speech communication means more to us than simply a way to pass messages from one to another. We judge people by their voices; we make assumptions about the intelligence of a new acquaintance, about the current mood of a person we know, about how interested he is in what we ourselves are saying, and so on. (The way we pass information of this sort is discussed in chapters 2,3,6 and 20.) How, then, does this affect machines? Are we likely to make assumptions about the *character* of a machine from the way it talks to us?

Although it may seem strange to have such a reference in a text book, we can gain some insight into this aspect of voice interaction with machines from science fiction films — or at least, our reaction to them. Probably the most famous talking-computer-film-star is *HAL* from *2001 – a Space Odyssey*.[1] Everything about HAL's synthetic speech is perfectly realisable with the technology described in this book (although his exceptionally accurate speech recognition is not — see chapter 7). We are now able to make a computer talk with any voice we choose, male or female. We can make it respond to one in a cheerful tone, or harsh, and indeed it can be programmed to change its apparent mood according to the temperature outside or the number of days before Christmas! And it could sound confident, or even a touch supercilious like HAL. Indeed, much of the menacing nature of HAL was due to the nature of his voice, rather than his antics. Would a film about a computer which took command of a space-ship and printed on a VDU '*I have taken control of this vehicle*' have been equally disturbing?

Even better examples of fascinating but realisable machines with character are to be found in Douglas Adams' popular book *The Hitch-Hiker's Guide to the Galaxy*. There is no behaviour exhibited by *Marvin, the depressed robot* which could not be programmed into a modern robot using current microcomputers and synthesis devices. Yet his character is unmistakable. Why then could one not envisage a member of the public buying one make of car rather than another, simply because it spoke like the sort of character he would like to be with? We already get very fond of our cars, even without speech; adding voice input and output to them is sure to increase our capability for liking them or hating them according to how we react to the character of the voice.

However, while the reader will be capable, upon completion of this book, of implementing any of the examples above, until he has done so they will remain science fiction. We cannot know for sure how the public is going to react to talking lifts or washing machines until we have tried it. The key lesson is that we are meddling with a powerful communication medium and we should be sure we know what we are doing. The speech system designer should aim to be a student of linguistics and of human behaviour more than of electronics, and he should spend more research time on field trials than on any other aspect of product development.

In the next twelve chapters the reader is presented with the information and background with which to start a speech system design. We will return in chapter 14 to the topic of field trials, and how to set about such a project.

Notes

1. 2001 – A Space Odyssey. Film directed by Stanley Kubrick: MGM Studios, Borehamwood, 1968. Published by Metro-Goldwyn Mayer Inc.

References

Adams, Douglas N. (1979) *The Hitch Hiker's Guide to the Galaxy*. London: Pan Books.

Atal, B.S. and Hanauer, S.L. (1971) 'Speech analysis and synthesis by linear prediction of the speech wave'. *J. Acoust. Soc. Amer.* **50**, 637–655.

Holmes, J.N., Mattingly, I.G., and Shearme, J.N. (1964) 'Speech synthesis by rule'. *Language and Speech* 7, 127–143.

Itakura, F. and Saito, S. (1972) 'On the optimum quantisation of feature parameters in the PARCOR speech synthesiser'. *Proc. 1972 Conf. Speech Commun. Process.* 434–437.

Markel, J.D., Gray, A.H., and Wakita, H. (1973) 'Linear prediction of speech – theory and practice'. *Speech Comm. Res. Lab. Monograph* **10**, 195.

CHAPTER 2

THE POWER OF SPEECH

John Baddeley

'You have no idea how interesting it is to take a human being and change her into a quite different human being by creating a new speech for her. It's filling up the deepest gulf that separates class from class and soul from soul.'

George Bernard Shaw, Pygmalion

In this chapter, an actor who has been involved with recordings for speech synthesis gives some insight into the nature of speech communication.

The endeavour to communicate with one's fellows is a prime function; it can both frustrate and delight. It takes time and effort. The desire to convey one's point of view, to relate one to another, is never ending. We need to share. There are many ways we express our feelings, through writing, music, drama; indeed by the use of our own bodies. Above all, however, the most powerful medium is speech. How well do we use this ability? By and large, rather poorly. In this brief chapter I would like to look at speech from the actor's stand point, unaffected by the scientific approach but purely from an emotional and instinctive aspect.

Both appearance and speech are influenced by the equipment one is born with and by social and geographical environment. It is the voice, however, that indicates one's situation far more than the body and it is the voice that displays character most boldly. Yet, this superb, sensitive organ is often used so badly, particularly by English speaking people. Rarely do we take advantage of more than a small subset of the games we can play on the sound of our sentences, unless we are trained to do so. But those who use their voices imaginatively win a better chance to interest, charm and influence others. The opportunity to gain position, power, popularity and indeed pleasure, is there to be taken. The difference between two equally qualified people as far as their success is concerned, can hinge on the voice and the way they use it. One has only to look back forty years to see the incredible influence of such people as Churchill and Hitler to realise what effect a great orator can have — for good or evil.

Those working in theatre and television, are obviously aware of the importance of voice and speech: in radio — and now in speech synthesis — where there is only the voice to convey every aspect of the character, even more so. The listener has to hear how the person 'looks'. Not only do dialect and emotions have to hold the audience's attention, but shades, tones and pacing must be used to capture them. The techniques used for recording for speech synthesis will have much in common with radio drama, TV and radio commercials, Audio Visual presentations and film dubbing. As far as advertising is concerned, voices are vital, for they are the hidden persuaders.

As we move fully into the age of voice synthesis, what effect will the chip have on man and his voice? It cannot be that it will take over, for surely it is impossible for synthetic reproduction, however brilliant, to supplant the real thing. As a back-up facility, on the other hand, the possibilities are without limit. In ten or twenty years time I am sure we will be talked to and instructed by electronic boxes, at almost every corner. However, having achieved the ability to produce a synthesised voice, what kind of voice will it be? The man in the street may imagine that it could sound like a dalek. It doesn't, or rather it needn't, because most synthesisers described in this book have the capability of 'soaking up' the characteristics of a phrase that make it sound human. The voices of daleks totally lack inflection and interest and so they sound mechanical — add an appropriate natural intonation from a professional speaker and the listener automatically makes the assumption that the voice is human, despite small imperfections in the individual sounds produced.

The power of the intonation — the *message on top of the words* — cannot be overestimated. The reader can probably think of at least six different ways of saying the simple word 'yes', each one conveying a different meaning, or to be used in a different situation. Some more elaborate examples of the way the meaning of words can be changed in this way will be found in chapter 6. One of the most fascinating groups to study for the use of the voice are politicians. Listen to the voice of a well-known parliamentarian now, and then to a recording of a speech or interview made ten years ago. Apart from the obvious change due to the ageing process, every mannerism they had before is magnified. Their voices bounce up and down as if whipping up enthusiasm with the sound waves. The same script read as a news item or as a children's story would be unlikely to persuade the house to vote a certain way. Here again, the actual words are only a small part of the information and feeling that is being pervayed by the voice.

Monotony in speech has to be avoided at all costs. I think this could be a great threat to the mechanically produced voice. If the sound is flat and not intonated the brain tends to reject it and therefore the information imparted will not be reacted to. Some voices have a range of no more than four notes – you hear them frequently being interviewed on radio and TV. Overall, the American voice seems to have a more limited range than the British voice, but I must admit that if there is too much intonation, this can be a problem for the unaccustomed ear as well. Nevertheless, monotony does limit acceptance of the message. It is interesting to talk to a cat or dog using inflection, colour, pitch, intensity, but using meaningless words. The animal will respond. Then speak to it in a monotone, but using meaningful words. Let the voice drone on and on, and you can actually make the animal fall asleep. Hence the comedian's maxim – *it's not so much the joke it's the way that you say it.*

The type of voice, too, has importance for particular audiences. Everyone hates being patronised. There can also be deep feelings of antipathy of one group to another. One nationality, region or race instructing another must be wary not to alienate. It may not be the agreeable thing to say, and may hopefully in the future change, but the truth is that who says what, to whom, and how, is very relevant. Therefore, with voice synthesis and its application, it is vital to choose a voice which is suitable for the likely listeners. An example of this is in Audio Visuals which are to be played to members of both management and shop floor; great care has to be taken in the selection of the voice that is used, in order not to annoy or distract one side or the other.

In fact, situations, as well as audiences, dictate the voice required. The sexy dark brown voice is interesting and can be delightful. But would you react or pay attention to a soothing French tone, or would you be lulled into a dream-like state so that you are unaware your brakes are failing? How would you react to a very cultured, layed-back voice telling you to 'abandon ship'? It is so easy to alienate and not achieve one's objective. I recall waiting at a bus-stop, standing next to a lady with a young child. When the bus arrived I said, 'after you madam', to which she replied, 'don't you madam me'. What could be offensive about those words? I sense it was something in my voice that irked her.

On first hearing a recording of your own voice the reaction is usually one of horror and disbelief. It appears higher than you imagine. This is caused not by the playback being too fast, but by the fact that you hear your own voice from within the head; as if it were inside a box: a similar sound as if speaking into cupped hands. This sense of horror is small compared to the apparent banality being spoken and the way it is being said. The voice sounds colourless and repetitive, and every sentence seems to be punctuated by *you know* or *OK* in an effort to get a point across. If the inexperienced speaker is given a script to read, it is usually stilted and unnatural. Will speech synthesis aim for correct speech or dare to be natural, warts and all? The model, again, needs to be the radio. We expect newscasters to be human and to exhibit warmth and compassion when emotional issues are discussed, but we cannot tolerate the broken, repetitive speech that would result from an announcer who was not totally happy with his script.

Voice synthesis has one great advantage over the announcer, though – there can be no mistakes! All will be clear and there is no possible chance of misunderstanding, unlike the human voice receiving its orders from the brain, which can on occasions get in a terrible twist. The well-known story of the BBC announcer who was worried over the pronunciation of the name 'Rimsky-Korsakov' illustrates the point. He read: *And now, a short piece by* (pause) *Rimsky Korsakov* (instant relief). *It is 'The Bum of the Flightle Bee'*. Synthetic announcements have no such dangers!

An exciting era lies ahead. The use of voice synthesis to augment the human voice so that there is more understanding between man and man, is a great step forward. At present some voices are more suitable than others, but I am sure that in the future any voice could be applied to the chip. Nevertheless, it is of paramount importance to train that speaker well, not only in elementary diction but in choosing the correct way to put across the message. It is not sufficient to specify the speech to be recorded for a system in words alone; there are many ways of saying a given script and the required impact and target audience must also be described to the speaker. With a talented speech editor, exceptional quality can be produced – it will then be possible to have a clear, authoritative and pleasing sound.

The synthesis chip is flexible and its application can cover a wide spectrum. Its use in the medical field would be incredibly beneficial, expecially for those who have lost the use of voice or eyes. Soon, I am sure, our kitchen, bathroom, TV, front door, back door, central heating system, car, office; will be talking to us. I sincerely hope that friends, relatives and colleagues will also be doing so.

As an actor, I look forward to reading the rest of this book with interest and some trepidation.

CHAPTER 3

SPEECH SOUNDS AND LANGUAGES

Wiktor Jassem and Francis Nolan

This chapter offers an introduction to phonetics and phonology; it should form basic reading for all students of the subject of speech.

3.1 *Basic attributes of speech*

When investigating speech, two rather different aspects of it can be focussed on: its physical characteristics; and the system which underlies it.

THE PHYSICAL ASPECT OF SPEECH
The physical characteristics are perhaps the more obvious aspect. Speech consists of a continuously changing complex sound wave linking the speaker's mouth and the hearer's ear. We can record and display an electrical analogue of this wave; we can (at least to some extent) sense the gestures of our own vocal organs, and see those of others, as speech is produced — these gestures all being directed towards creating aerodynamic and resonance conditions in the vocal tract appropriate to the generation of different sounds; and we can study the physical response of the ear to speech.

It might seem at first sight that someone interested in speech synthesis need only concern himself with the replication of the complex acoustic speech wave. But devices have long been available which can do this — they are called tape recorders. The new opportunities opened up by speech synthesis all depend on the ability to break down the speech wave into component elements, and recombine these elements to create new messages. The only kind of analysis and re-synthesis which is likely to lend itself to speech communication is one closely based on the human linguistic system underlying speech events.

SYSTEMS UNDERLYING SPEECH

The notion of a *system* underlying speech is less self-evident, but we can see its importance when we look at the flexibility of the vocal apparatus of a speaker. Figure 3.1 shows a schematic cross section through the head of a speaker seen from his left side. Many of the numbers, from 1 at the lips to 16 at the glottis, indicate different places at which the vocal tract can change its cross-sectional area, either to alter its resonance characteristics or actually to produce acoustic energy (the traditional phonetic terms corresponding to these places will be presented in section 3.2). Once we start considering the variable degrees of narrowing at each of these many *places of articulation*, and the possibilities for their simultaneous combination, it becomes apparent that the number of degrees of freedom of the vocal tract, and hence the number of acoustically different sounds it can produce, becomes vast. What speakers and listeners need for successful communication is a *system* imposed on this virtually in- finite range of acoustic effects – a system which selects a subset of sounds, and then organises these into a small number of functional *sound types* or sound classes basic to communication. This system is the *phonology* of a language. Different languages, of course, impose different phonological systems on the sound-producing potential of the vocal organs.

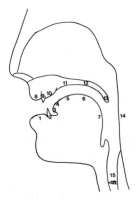

Figure 3.1 Mid-sagittal section through the speech organs. 1 lower lip, 2 lower incisor, 3 tongue-tip, 4 tongue-blade, 5 tongue-front, 6 tongue-back, 7 tongue-root, 8 upper lip, 9 upper incisor, 10 alveolar ridge, 11 hard palate, 12 velum, 13 uvula, 14 pharynx wall, 15 larynx, 16 vocal cords and glottis

The phonology of a language will permit a variety of different sounds – different in terms of their precise articulation and hence acoustic effect — to stand for or 'realise' any of its functional sound types or *phonemes*; for instance the point at which the tongue body makes a closure against the roof of the mouth for the *g* of *geese* and of *goose* will be different. In this case, as frequently, the difference stems from the fact that the vocal tract could not (even if this were perceptually desirable) jump discretely from one configuration to another, but rather blends its movements into a continuous flow; in this example, because of the different following vowel, the *g* of *geese* will be further forward on the roof of the mouth than that of *goose*. The part of phonology which deals with sound types or phonemes such as *g* (corresponding to a first approximation to the letters of alphabetic writing) may be termed *segmental* phonology; sections 3.5 to 3.7 will be principally concerned with segmental phonology.

Phonology, as introduced above, is part of the linguistic system a speaker knows, and is concerned importantly with lexical (word) identity: the phonology of English permits *g* to vary in particular contexts, but clearly not in such a way that the pronunciation of the *g* in the word *gay* would be confused with that of the *d* in the word *day*. There are, however, other ways in which speakers select acoustic features and exploit them for communicative effect. These conventional usages are considered to be a less central part of a language's system (and they are not, for instance, directly represented in writing), and are therefore sometimes called *para*linguistic features. Such conventional features include (in English at least) the use of a whispery voice to signal confidentiality, or of a wide pitch range (with specific pitch patterns) to indicate politeness. Notice that such effects characteristically extend over long stretches of speech and may even be used habitually by a speaker. Linguists have only recently come to view such features as within their domain of study, and since they are clearly less definable, certainly less categorical, than phonemes, they are as yet only partially understood. They will receive no more than this passing mention in this introduction to speech; but it should be borne in mind that they may become increasingly important if synthesis is to replicate the flexibility of human speech communication (see chapter 20 by Nolan below).

Intermediate between these least 'linguistic', least discrete. or categorical conventional uses of sound and the most 'linguistic', most discrete word-distinguishing phonemes of phonology come the *suprasegmental* aspects of speech — notably stress and intonation. Some suprasegmentals approach the categorical nature of the phonemes of segmental phonology — for instance shifting stress from the first to the second syllable of *digest* changes it from a noun to a verb, or changing the intonation from a basically falling to rising pitch on *it's raining* can change a statement into a question – but in general the way that suprasegmental phonology 'organises' the sound substance is less 'all-or-nothing' than in the case of segmental phonology. Nevertheless the suprasegmental phonology of a language is highly important for speech synthesis, for one reason because speech synthesised with acoustic effects not in accord with the system it imposes will sound at best odd, and at worst offensive and unintelligible. Suprasegmental phonology is dealt with in section 3.8. The domain of suprasegmental effects, as the name implies, is longer than a segment; they may extend over stretches from the size of a syllable up to quite long utterances.

PHYSICAL VERSUS PHONETIC DATA

If we return from the phonological and paralinguistic systems underlying speech to the physical event itself, we need to consider two interesting questions arising in the relation between the event, on the one hand, and on the other our impressions and phonetic analysis of it.

Firstly, let's imagine a child, a woman, and a man saying the vowel of the word *he*. Assuming that they all speak with an identical accent, it seems self-evident that they are all producing the 'same' vowel (and a trained phonetician would agree); but the problem emerges when their utterances are analysed acoustically. Vowel quality has been shown to depend on peaks (formants) in the acoustic spectrum; but in this example the absolute values in Hz of the formants will be very different (as might be expected given the different vocal tract sizes, hence resonances, of the three speakers). Yet human listeners are able to abstract away from these differences – to *normalise* across speakers – and hear the three acoustically different stimuli as *phonetically* the same. Phonetic description, then, also operates at this level where normalisation has taken place. Normalisation, of course, presents a major challenge for multi-speaker speech recognition devices.

Normalisation is also one of the reasons why, in the study of speech, it is vital to distinguish between, on the one hand, the *physical properties* of a speech event – its overall *intensity*, its frequency *spectrum*, its *duration*, and its *fundamental frequency* – and, on the other hand, the *perceptual attributes* it gives rise to (in a hearer) which correspond in a general but by no means simple way to these physical properties: its *loudness*, its *quality*, its *length*, and its *pitch*.

The second question arising from our impression of the physical event of speech has to do with *segmentation*. The *articulation* of an utterance involves virtually continuous movement by the organs of speech — in an x-ray film of a speaker, for instance, there is an absence of any succession of static postures which we might expect on the basis of our impression (reinforced by alphabetic writing) that speech consists of a series of different 'sounds'. Where then does our impression of *segmentation* arise from? Part of the answer may lie in the acoustic signal resulting from this continuous movement of the speech organs. Figure 3.2 shows a *spectrogram* of the phrase *speech we can see*: the spectrogram shows acoustic intensity as the relative blackness of the pattern, the *y* axis showing frequency between 0 and 8 kHz, and the utterance lasting approximately 1 second on the *x* (time) axis. This sort of spectral analysis reveals a considerable degree of segmentation. These segments we shall call *acoustic segments*.

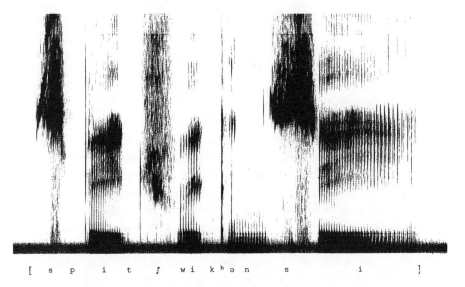

[s   p   i   t   ʃ   w i   kʰ ə n   s   i   ]

Figure 3.2 Spectrogram of the phrase *Speech we can see*

However our impression of segmentation is also dependent on our knowledge of phonology. That is, if we take the word *pin*, we perceive it to 'have' three segments because there are three and only three places at which we can make alterations that will change that word into another — *pin-bin*; *pin-pan*; *pin-pit*.

In some cases there will be a good correspondence between phonetic segments or *phones* arrived at this way, and the *acoustic segments* of the spectrogram — for instance in fig. 3.2 the [s] phones in the transcription correspond to single acoustic segments (consisting of random high frequency energy). The [p] of *speech*, however, has two acoustic segments: a silent interval (visible as a blank on the spectrogram) corresponding to the lip closure; and (visible as a single vertical spike before the regular vertical striations of [i]), the transient burst of energy, or *plosion*, caused by the release of air the instant the lips come apart.

Notice that it is conventional to write symbols corresponding to *phones* in square brackets – thus the two phones realising the letter *g* in *geese* and *goose* above could be written [g] and [g] respectively, where the plus sign with the [g] of *geese* indicates its more forward, or *advanced* tongue contact with the roof of the mouth. We can now look in more detail at the way in which phones are described in phonetics.

3.2 *The classification of phones*

In classifying segmental units phonetics has traditionally paid most attention to the way in which they are produced – that is, to their *articulation*. Perceptual criteria also play a part; and are more important in the description of the subset of phones called *vocoids*. The term vocoid may be explained as follows.

All phones involve the movement of air in the vocal tract, and its disturbance at some point to create acoustic energy. *Vocoids* are phones in which the airflow out through the vocal tract is central (along its mid-line) and is unimpeded; acoustic energy is created only by activity at the Larynx, while the oral (plus, sometimes, nasal) vocal tract acts as a variable resonating system to shape that acoustic energy. The letters corresponding to vocoids in the following words are italicised: f*i*sh, w*e*ld, *y*et, s*a*nd.

Any phone which does not satisfy the definition of a vocoid is a *contoid*. In contoids the airflow through the mouth may be blocked completely, as in *d*, *t*, *n* in the above examples; or may flow out not centrally but laterally – e.g. *l*, where it escapes around either side of the tongue; or may flow out centrally, but through such a narrow gap that turbulence and therefore acoustic energy is created at the narrowing – e.g. *f*, *sh*, *s*. Because contoids involve a blockage or narrowing at some point in the vocal tract, they are relatively easy to classify in terms of their articulation, and it is to this that we now turn.

THE CLASSIFICATION OF CONTOIDS
Figure 3.1 above shows, in cross section, the main speech organs. The numbers referring to the speech organs and locations in the vocal tract will be used in the discussion below so that areas under discussion can be located.

Some of the organs are mobile and active in the articulation of speech sounds, while others are immobile and passive. During the continuous process of speech articulation, some or all of the speech organs approach or actually achieve certain postures which are the *targets* of the movements – but rarely remain in any fixed position for long. For every phone there is one such target posture, and the articulatory classification of a phone is based on this.

Phones are classified on the following dimensions: (a) airstream mechanism; (b) direction of airflow; (c) type of constriction; (d) supra-glottal passage; (e) location of constriction; (f) phonation; and (g) force.

(a) *Airstream mechanism.* The production of any speech sound requires a movement of air. This movement is most usually initiated by the lungs; or, more rarely, by raising or lowering the (closed) glottis (16), or by moving the body of the tongue while the back of the tongue (6) is in contact with the velum (12). Accordingly, the airstream is *pulmonic, glottalic,* or *velaric.*

(b) *Direction of airflow.* The direction of the airflow may be *egressive* (outwards) or *ingressive* (inwards). The most usual combination of airstream mechanism and direction (and the only one used in the sound systems of western European languages) is *pulmonic egressive.*

(c) *Type of constriction.* When the articulators take or approach a posture, there is always at least one place along the vocal tract where its cross section is at a minimum. This narrowing is called a *constriction*; and if the passage is completely blocked, the sound is an occlusive or *stop* (e.g. the [p] of *speech*). If the passage is not blocked, yet sufficiently narrow for turbulence of the air to result, the sound is a *fricative* (e.g. the [s] of *speech*). If air passes unimpeded, the sound is a *non-frictional resonant* (e.g. the [l] of *leaf*, and of course all vocoids). Some active articulators (the tip of the tongue (3), and the uvula (13)) may be made to vibrate, and the corresponding sound is then *trilled* (cf. the stereotype [r] (tongue-tip trill) used by people mimicking Scottish pronunciation). If the active articulator hits a passive one, the sound is a *flap* (a tongue-tip flap occurs in many American English pronunciations of the middle sound in *better*).

(d) *Supraglottal passage.* Above the glottis, the air may pass through the mouth (oral cavity), the nose (nasal cavity), or both, and the sound is respectively *oral, nasal,* or *oro-nasal.* The opening to the nasal cavity is sealed by raising the *velum*, making a *velic* closure. If the air flows all the way along the mid-line of the vocal tract the sound is *central*; but if the oral cavity is blocked centrally (e.g. by the tongue-tip in the [l] of *leaf*) while air escapes at one or both sides the sound is *lateral*.

(e) *Location of constriction.* Contoids are classfied according to the location of their primary (narrowest) constriction. The default assumption is that a constriction is made between a passive articulator and the active articulator which lies opposite it when the ariculators are at rest. Locations are defined by naming the active and passive articulators involved; common terms are listed in table 3.1, together with the articulators as numbered in fig. 3.1 and an English example where possible — '*' indicates that not all speakers may use the particular articulation.

Table 3.1 Some common phonetic terms for location of constrictions, with the articulators involved (numbered as in fig. 3.1) and, where possible, familiar examples. '*' indicates that alternative articulations are used by some speakers

Label	Articulators	Example
bilabial	lower lip and upper lip (1 + 8)	*p*in
labio-dental	lower lip and upper incisors (1 + 9)	*f*in
apico-dental	tongue-tip and upper incisors (3 + 9)	*th*in
apico-alveolar	tongue-tip and alveolar ridge (3 + 10)	*t*in
lamino-alveolar	tongue-blade and alveolar ridge (4 + 10)	**s*in
palatal	tongue-front and hard palate (5 + 11)	**h*uge
velar	tongue-back and velum (6 + 12)	*g*oose
uvular	tongue-back and uvula (6 + 13)	[French] *r*ire
pharyngeal	tongue-root and pharynx wall (7 + 14)	————
glottal	vocal cords (16)	'be 'er'[1]

[1] As when *t* is 'dropped' (in fact replaced by a glottal stop) as in a Cockney pronunciation of *better*.

Of course these basic location labels may have to be qualified to deal with intermediate articulations, since the articulatory space is essentially continuous. For example a constriction made between *palatal* and *velar* is termed *prevelar* (geese). Occasionally an established label is unfortunate; for instance *palato-alveolar* for the *sh* of *shin* clearly cannot mean that the palate is actively articulating against the alveolar ridge — rather it refers to a constriction made with the tongue blade or tip near the join between palate and alveolar ridge, with some raising of the front of the tongue towards the palate.

Figure 3.3 shows the tongue positions and shapes for stops at four places of articulation: (i) bilabial, (ii) apico-alveolar, (iii) prevelar, (iv) velar.

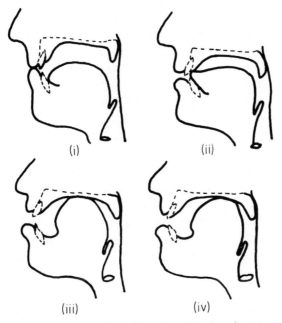

Figure 3.3 Shape of the speech organs for stops. The four locations of constriction are: (i) bilabial, (ii) apico-alveolar, (iii) prevelar, (iv) velar

Sometimes the default assumption (see above) about the active articulator involved does not apply — the active articulator moves away from its position of rest and the articulation is *displaced*. For instance the tongue-tip may curl up and back to the very back of the alveolar ridge (*postalveolar*) or even towards the hard palate (*retroflex*); for many English speakers the *r* of *red* will involve one of these possibilities.

If a simultaneous, but less narrow, constriction occurs, this is called a *secondary articulation*. The apico-alveolar or lamino-alveolar central occlusion of *l* may be accompanied by an approximation of the tongue-front to the palate (*palatalisation*) in *million*, and of the tongue-back towards the velum (*velarisation*) in *all*. A secondary articulation at the lips is called *labialisation*.

(f) *Phonation.* During the articulation of a phone, the glottis may be in one of several states, and the phones are classified according to the nature of the acoustic source, the *phonation*, at the glottis (16). If the glottis is basically closed but the vocal cords are vibrating as air flows through them, the sound is *voiced*; all the sounds in *landing* are voiced. If the vocal cords are not vibrating, the sound is voiceless; the *sh* and *ts* in *sheets* are voiceless. If the vocal cords are almost closed but not vibrating, allowing a high velocity turbulent airflow through a narrow gap, the sound is whispered; when the word *landing* is whispered, all its phones will be whispered; when *sheets* is whispered, the vocoid written *ee* will be whispered, but the other sounds remain voiceless.

(g) *Force*. Sometimes in a particular language a subset of the phones can be allocated to pairs where one member is produced with greater force (is *fortis*), the other with less force (is *lenis*). The initial phones in *sue* versus *zoo*, *toe* versus *doe*, exemplify fortis-lenis pairs.

Finally, we should note that sometimes a sequence of a stop phone and a fricative phone is called an *affricate*; affricates occur for instance at both start and end of the words *church*, *judge*. The term affricate is useful because this kind of sequence often functions as a single unit in the phonology of a language, and may develop historically from a stop phone.

THE DESCRIPTION OF VOCOIDS

Vocoids are generally less categorical than contoids. For instance, a contoid may be either a stop or a fricative — but nothing in between. Vocoids are described in three dimensions, and the distinctions along three dimensions tend to be gradual, or continuous. It is therefore preferable to speak of a description rather than a classification of vocoids.

There are four vocoids that are perceptually extreme. Their articulation is shown in fig. 3.4, in which a dot indicates the notional 'highest point of the tongue' which has been basic to traditional phonetic description of vocoids. The respective descriptions of this 'highest point' for the four vocoids, together with the phonetic symbols used, are (i) *close front* [i]; (ii) *open front* [a]; (iii) *open back* [ɑ]; and (iv) *close back* [u]. In addition to the tongue position, [i] has spread lips; and [u] has maximum lip-rounding — i.e. a very small area between the lips. (The terms *high* and *low* are sometimes used instead of *close* and *open*.) If the four articulations in fig. 3.4 are superimposed, the four 'highest points' may be joined to form a quadrilateral (see fig. 3.5(i)).

Four further reference points are defined in the following ways. Two front vocoids are defined between close front [i] and open front [a] such that the perceptual distance between [i] and [a] is divided into three equal steps: these extra vocoids are *half-close* front [e] and *half-open* front [ɛ]. Two back vocoids are defined between back open [ɑ] and back close [u], again so that the perceptual distance between [ɑ] and [u] is divided into three equal steps: the extra vocoids are

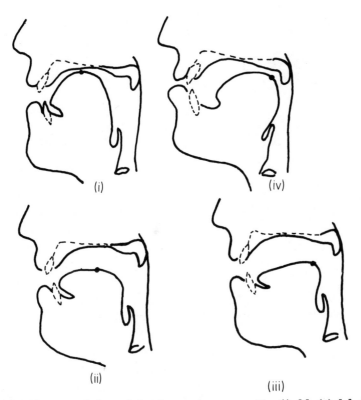

Figure 3.4 The articulation of the four extreme vocoids. (i) [i] (ii) [a] (iii) [*a*] (iv) [u]

half open back [ɔ], and *half-close* back [o], both of which have lip-rounding. See fig. 3.5(ii) for the position of these vocoids.

Each of the four 'degrees of opening' — close, half-close, half-open, open — has a particular degree of lip-rounding most naturally associated with it if the vocoid is rounded; thus the lip-rounding increases through the back rounded vocoids [ɔ], [o], [u]. A vocoid is described as 'over-rounded', or 'underrounded', if its rounding is more, or less, than naturally associated with its degree of opening.

The eight reference vocoids described and shown on the periphery of fig. 3.5(ii) are the eight *Primary Cardinal* vocoids defined by Daniel Jones (Jones, 1972: 311 ff.); they are widely used in phonetic description, the vocoids of languages being placed relative to them on the 'vocoid quadrilateral', as will be seen when English and American vocoids are described in section 3.7. A vocoid in a particular language is unlikely to coincide exactly with a Cardinal vocoid, because of the extreme (peripheral) nature of the latter. However the plotting of

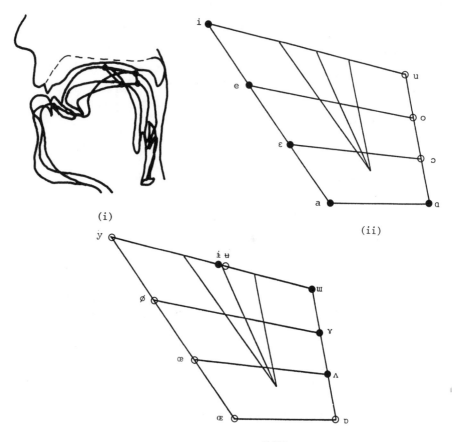

Figure 3.5 The vocoid quadrilateral. (i) Derivation of the quadrilateral from the highest point of the tongue in the four extreme vocoids, (ii) the eight primary Cardinal vocoids, (iii) the ten secondary Cardinal vocoids. Filled circles denote unrounded vocoids, open circles denote rounded vocoids

American and English vocoids in section 3.7 will help to give a guide to the Cardinal qualities. For the moment it is the principle of the descriptive system which is important.

A further eight *Secondary Cardinal* reference vocoids are defined by adding appropriate lip-rounding to the unrounded primary Cardinal vocoids, and removing it from the rounded ones. Two further close vowels, rounded and unrounded close *central* vocoids, are also defined. The symbols for these ten reference vocoids are shown in fig. 3.5(iii).

Vocoids, then, are described in terms of three parameters: on scales from *close* to *open*; from *front* through *central* to *back*; and from *unrounded* to *rounded*. Although these labels appear to be articulatory in nature, their articulatory implications are at best an approximation to, for example, what is revealed by x-rays; and it has been well argued that vocoid description is primarily perceptual and based on acoustic properties (e.g. Ladefoged, 1982: 201). Certainly accurate use of the vocoid framework outlined above is acquired principally through auditory training and imitation.

Vocoids may be produced with the velum lowered, giving an oro-nasal or *nasalised* vocoid (fig. 3.6(i)). Also, while the body of the tongue assumes the position for a vocoid the tongue-tip may simul-taneously curl up and back producing a *retroflex* vocoid (fig. 3.6(ii)).

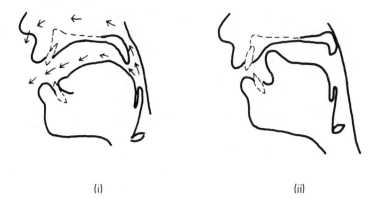

(i)   (ii)

Figure 3.6 Vocoids with secondary articulations. (i) A nasalised vocoid, (ii) a retro-flex vocoid

Many vocoids are not of static quality throughout their duration, but change from one to another perceptibly different. English has a number of such vocoids, called *diphthongs*, to be found (for most accents) in for example *by* and *how* (because of historical sound changes English spelling gives no accurate indication of pure versus diphthongal vocoids). To indicate diphthongs phonetically, two vocoid symbols are used — the first indicating the starting quality of the diphthong and the second the vocoid in the direction of which the quality changes. For English diphthongs two symbols are often used for the second element which indicate vocoids somewhat opened and centralised from [i] and [u] — respectively [ɪ] and [ʊ]. Thus *by* and *how* might be represented [baɪ] and [haʊ] (where the minus sign under the first element indicates a more retracted (hence centralised) quality than Cardinal [a].

For further information on traditional phonetic classification of phones see, for instance, O'Connor (1973), Ladefoged (1982), and Catford (1977).

3.3 *Syllable, vowel, consonant*

Generally speakers can decide how many syllables a word contains — *cat* has one, *catty* has two, and *catastrophic* four. At the phonetic level, the level of the phonetician's analysis of physical speech events, a reliable account of what a syllable is has proved elusive. However it is of interest in (at least) two respects.

Firstly, in terms of the sound system, the *phonology*, of a language, it allows statements to be made about the sequences in which phones may combine — that is, the *phonotactics* of the language. For instance, in English as many as three contoids in a row may precede a vocoid — e.g. *splay* — whilst in Japanese only one is permitted; in fact a speaker of Japanese hearing the word *splay* would almost certainly reanalyse it as having a vocoid after each of the three contoids, in order to make it correspond to the *syllable-structure* imposed by his language. Thus the syllable-structure CCCV (where, by convention, C stands for a phone acting as as syllable margin and V for a phone acting as a syllable peak — see below) is permitted in English, but not in Japanese, which permits no more than one contoid in syllable-initial position (CV).

Secondly, from the point of view of synthesis, we assume (section 3.1) that for synthesis to be capable of creating new messages, we have to break down the speech signal into component elements susceptible of different recombination. The syllable is one such element which may prove useful; it is intermediate in size between the word and the phone. If synthesis were based on a complete inventory of syllables, even though this would be quite large, new words could be added to the capability of the device through new combination of syllables, while many of the transitional problems associated with phone-concatenation would be avoided (see e.g. Fujimura and Lovins, 1978).

Although the structure of syllables differs from language to language, there are general properties of syllables common to different languages. A syllable will consist of a phone which constitutes the *peak* of the syllable by virtue of relatively great loudness (or duration); other phones which may, optionally, precede and follow the peak constitute the *margins* of the syllable.

Universally, vocoids are found most frequently functioning as syllable *peaks*, and *contoids* as syllable margins, as in the English word *cat*. Vocoids that form syllable peaks are *vowels*, and contoids that form syllable margins are *consonants*.

Many languages also have a limited number of vocoids which function as margins, such as the first sounds in *yet* and *wet*; these *nonsyllabic* vocoids are sometimes called 'semivowels'. If *yet* and *wet* are said very slowly, it will become clear that their first sounds are vocoids — in fact very like the vocoids of *he* and *who*.

Conversely, some relatively loud (usually voiced) contoids may function as syllable peaks, such as the lateral and nasal contoids in the second syllables of *little* and *mutton*.

The distinction between the pairs of labels *vocoid–contoid*, defined in terms of the physical properties of phones, and *vowel–consonant*, requiring reference to the function of phones within a syllable, was introduced by Pike (1943). Although the terminological distinction has not been universally adopted, it does avoid confusions. For instance, if the initial sounds in *yet* and *wet* are referred to (as in many works) as consonants, rather than non-syllabic vocoids, it is harder to understand why they are synthesised like vocoids.

3.4 *Phonetic transcription*

When writing speech sounds we need to use symbols that are directly related to phones. Languages' writing systems do not represent phones — some, like that of Chinese, give virtually no information about pronunciation; some, like English orthography, use letters in an idiosyncratic and inconsistent way relative to the pronunciation (as non-native learners are painfully aware); and even those writing systems which are often regarded as 'phonetic' (e.g. those of Spanish, and more clearly Finnish) do not indicate the *phones* of the language but rather the (much smaller number of) *phonemes*, units in the *phonological system*, which those phones 'realise'. This will be explained further in section 3.6.

A phonetic transcription is based on the principle that one phone is always represented by one symbol, and that that symbol always represents one phone. Given an inventory of symbols for phones, a phonetician should, in principle, be able to write down the phones of any language (familiar or unfamiliar), and communicate its pronunciation unambiguously to others familiar with the symbols.

Of the several inventories of symbols devised, the one developed by the International Phonetic Association (see *The Principles...*, 1949) has found widest acceptance and is adequate for most practical purposes, even if it is less than totally consistent with phonetic theory. It uses principally lower-case letters of the Roman alphabet, with additional symbols constructed, or borrowed from various sources. The symbols of the IPA alphabet are reproduced as table 3.2.

To refine the phonetic detail implied by letter symbols a large number of 'diacritics' which can be added to the letters are defined

Table 3.2

THE INTERNATIONAL PHONETIC ALPHABET

		Bilabial	Labiodental	Dental, Alveolar, or Post-alveolar	Retroflex	Palato-alveolar	Palatal
CONSONANTS (pulmonic air-stream mechanism)	Nasal	m	ɱ	n	ɳ		ɲ
	Plosive	p b		t d	ʈ ɖ		c ɟ
	(Median) Fricative	ɸ β	f v	θ ð s z	ʂ ʐ	ʃ ʒ	ç ʝ
	(Median) Approximant		ʋ	ɹ	ɻ		j
	Lateral Fricative			ɬ ɮ			
	Lateral (Approximant)			l	ɭ		ʎ
	Trill			r			
	Tap or Flap			ɾ	ɽ		
CONSONANTS (non-pulmonic air-stream)	Ejective	p'		t'			
	Implosive	ɓ		ɗ			
	(Median) Click	ʘ		ʇ ʗ			
	Lateral Click			ʖ			

DIACRITICS

- ₒ or . Voiceless ṇ ḍ
- ˇ Voiced ẓ ṭ
- ʰ Aspirated tʰ
- .. Breathy-voiced ḅ ạ
- ˌ Dental ṭ
- _ Labialized ṭ
- ⱼ Palatalized ṭ
- ˜ Velarized or Pharyngealized ɫ, ɨ
- ˌ Syllabic ṇ ḷ
- ˆ or ˌ Simultaneous sf (but see also under the heading Affricates)

- ˈ or . Raised eˈ, ẹ, e̥ w
- ˌ or ˌ Lowered eˌ, ẹ, e̞ ɐ
- ₊ Advanced u+, u̟
- ˗ or ˗ Retracted i̠, i-, ṯ
- ¨ Centralized ë
- ˜ Nasalized ã
- ˺, ˡ, ᴿ r-coloured aˡ
- : Long aː
- · Half-long a·
- ˘ Non-syllabic ŭ
- ˌ More rounded ɔ˕
- ˌ Less rounded y˕

OTHER SYMBOLS

- ɕ, ʑ Alveolo-palatal fricatives
- ʆ, ʓ Palatalized ʃ, ʒ
- ɼ Alveolar fricative trill
- ɺ Alveolar lateral flap
- ɧ Simultaneous ʃ and x
- ʃˢ Variety of ʃ resembling s, etc.
- ɪ = ɩ
- ʊ = ɷ
- ɜ = Variety of ə
- ɚ = r-coloured ə

(Revised to 1979)

Velar		Uvular		Labial-Palatal	Labial-Velar		Pharyngeal		Glottal	
	ŋ	ɴ								
k	g	q	ɢ		k͡p	g͡b			ʔ	
x	ɣ	χ	ʁ		ʍ		ħ	ʕ	h	ɦ
	ɰ			ɥ		w				
		ʀ								
		ʀ								
k'										
	g									

Front		Back	VOWELS	Front		Back	STRESS, TONE (PITCH)
i	ɨ	ɯ	*Close*	y	ʉ	u	' stress, placed at beginning of stressed syllable :
	ɪ				ʏ	ɵ	, secondary stress : ˉ high level pitch, high tone :
e		ɤ	*Half-close*	ø		o	_ low level : ´ high rising :
	ə				θ		ˏ low rising : ` high falling :
ɛ		ʌ	*Half-open*	œ		ɔ	ˌ low falling : ˆ rise-fall :
æ	ɐ						ˇ fall-rise.
a		ɑ	*Open*	ɶ		ɒ	AFFRICATES can be written as digraphs, as ligatures, or with slur
	Unrounded				*Rounded*		marks ; thus ts, tʃ, dʒ : ʦ tʃ ʤ : t͡s t͡ʃ d͡ʒ. c, ɟ may occasionally be used for tʃ, dʒ.

by the IPA, and shown at the foot of table 3.2. The most frequent diacritics are ~ (through a letter) — velarisation (e.g. [ɫ], indicating a velarised alveolar lateral as at the end of *fill*); ̪ (under a letter) — dental articulation (e.g. [n̪], a dental nasal stop as in *tenth*); ° (after a letter) — absence of plosion after a stop (e.g. [p°], an unexploded bilabial stop as in *upturned*); ˜ (over a letter) nasalisation (e.g. [ɛ̃], indicating an oro-nasal vocoid as in *men*, where the vocoid is nasalised under the influence of the adjacent nasal contoids); and _ (under a letter) retraction (e.g. [ɛ̱], indicating an open vocoid retracted from fully front, as might occur in *well* under the influence of the following velarised lateral).

3.5 *Phones and their distributions*

Given the vast number of articulatorily and perceptually distinguishable phones available it is clear that any one language will only use a subset of the total, defined by the phonology of the language as indicated in section 3.1. Not only do individual languages use but a small selection of the possible phones, but they also impose restrictions on their order of occurrence in utterances. The set of restrictions or rules applying to one particular phone defines that phone's *distribution* in the language.

   We can exemplify this notion of distribution by means of some of the phones of English; Standard Southern British English provides these examples, but they are paralleled in many other varieties including General American:

(a) [g̟] [k̟] only occur before front close or half-close vocoids, as in *geese, give; keen, Kim*; but not *goose, calm*, etc.
(b) [ɫ], a velarised alveolar lateral, only occurs before contoids, [w] (a non-syllabic vocoid), and utterance finally, as in *belt, always, well*; the lateral in *laugh* and *silly* is not velarised.
(c) [n̪], a dental nasal, only occurs before the dental fricatives [θ] and [ð] as in *tenth, run there*; whilst the alveolar nasal [n] occurs before the other contoids, and vocoids.

Notice that the rules governing the distribution of phones differ from language to language. For instance, Polish as well as English has [n] and [n̪]; but in Polish [n̪] occurs in all environments *except* before [tʃ] and [dʒ].

3.6 *The phoneme and phonemic transcription*

THE PHONEME
The phoneme is a pivotal concept in phonology. Its exact definition has

been much debated, but here we shall consider merely the basic insight as it helps our understanding of the system a language imposes on sound. Clear accounts of many of the various approaches to defining the phoneme can be found in e.g. Fischer-Jørgensen (1975).

The basic insight might be summed up as follows: for any language, a phonetician can discern many more different phones than there are units in the phonological system capable of distinguishing words. For instance, if we asked a phonetician to list all the lateral contoids which he could find in English words, he would list at least the following: [l], [l̥], [ɫ] and [ɫ̪]. Does this mean that we can find four different words in English which rhyme perfectly, apart from having those phones as their sole distinguishing segment? The answer of course is no, and the reason is that the *distribution* (see 3.5) of each of those phones is different. Thus, simplifying somewhat, and starting with those phones whose distribution is most restricted, [ɫ̪] (velarised dental) can occur only before [θ] or [ð] (e.g. *health*); [l̥] (devoiced alveolar) only after fortis stops (e.g. *play*, *clay*); [ɫ] (velarised alveolar) only before contoids (excepting [θ], [ð]) and silence; and [l] before vocoids.

In other words, any pair of those lateral phones is in *complementary distribution* - where one occurs, the other can't. Therefore there is no possibility, say, of distinguishing two English words [l]*ie* and [ɫ̪]*ie*, because the [ɫ̪] phone is just not permitted by the phonology of English to occur in that environment. All these lateral phones can be seen as variant realisations of a single underlying phonological unit, or *phoneme*, /l/ (phonemes are traditionally put in slants). We might schematise the situation of a phoneme and the phones which realise it — its *allophones* — thus:

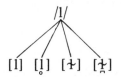

Applying the criterion of complementary distribution alone could actually give rise to some strange allocations of phones to phonemes. For instance, recall from 3.5 that dental [n̪] only occurs before [θ] and [ð], whilst alveolar [n] occurs in other environments. Thus, strictly, [n] is in a relationship of complementary distribution with [l], [l̥], and [ɫ]; while conversely [ɫ̪] is in complementary distribution with [n]. What then would be wrong with the following allocation of phones to phonemes?

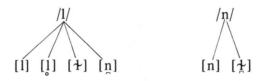

Well clearly this does not accord with the intuitions speakers have about their language; and these intuitions are reflected by using a criterion of *phonetic similarity* when allocating phones to phonemes. Phonetic similarity is sometimes hard to quantify, but here it is relatively easy to group the phones together, in an intuitively correct way, on the basis of their being lateral, or nasal:

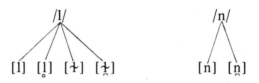

Sometimes phones which are not in complementary distribution are regarded as realisations of the same phoneme; this is the case when the two phones are used interchangeably by a speaker. For instance, saying the word *cap* at the end of an utterance a speaker might sometimes release the bilabial stop ([pʰ]), or instead leave his lips closed leaving an unexploded bilabial stop ([pº]). This makes no difference to the identity of the word – it is purely what is termed *free variation* – and so the criterion of *complementary distribution* is relaxed in this instance, and both are considered realisations of the /p/ phoneme.

Phonemes, then, are the underlying units which the phonological system of a language uses to distinguish words; and a phoneme is *realised* by phones which are in *complementary distribution* or *free variation*, and are *phonetically similar*.

PHONEMIC TRANSCRIPTION

A transcription recording only the phonemes of a language requires far fewer symbols than one which records its phones (even in moderate detail); furthermore it is largely in accord with a speaker's intuitions about his language – he is often unaware of the variety of phones realising any of his phonemes. An essentially phonemic transcription has been the main basis of alphabetic writing systems at the time they are devised for languages – though as their phonemic systems undergo change through time writing systems get 'out of date' and cease to be phonemic, which partly explains the remoteness of English spelling from a phonemic transcription.

On the other hand, a reader of phonemic transcription has to know the phonological rules governing the allophonic realisations of the various phonemes if he is to derive from it the pronunciation of an utterance. The same applies for speech synthesis: a phonemic transcription constitutes a convenient input code from the user's point of view; but if the synthesiser is to produce good quality speech from such a representation it needs to 'know' and implement the allophonic rules which specify the nature and distribution of phones.

The choice of symbols used in a phonemic transcription sometimes gives rise to confusion. Since a phonemic symbol such as /l/ is realised as a variety of phones, it follows that it cannot be equated with one exact phonetic quality. Similarly the choice of /i/ to symbolise the middle phoneme of *beet* should not be taken to mean that this phoneme is always, or indeed ever, realised by a phone which has exactly the quality of Primary Cardinal vocoid [i] — rather /i/ is used as a conveniently simple symbol which implies the approximate phonetic area within which the allophones of this phoneme are to be found.

3.7 *British and American pronunciation*

In a moment we shall have a look at the phoneme systems of British and American English, and compare the pronunciation of those varieties.

Given that the English of both Britain and America, let alone other parts of the English-speaking world, includes many different varieties of pronunciation, the problem always arises of which variety to describe. The variety of British English dealt with here might be termed, as above, Standard Southern British; or, to use rather loosely a term familiar in phonetics *Received Pronunciation (RP)*. An important defining characteristic of RP is that it does not associate the speaker with any particular geographical region within England (Wells, 1982:14); it constitutes a standard in the direction of which many speakers alter their pronunciation; and it is frequently heard, though less and less to the exclusion of other varieties, on the BBC. The variety of American English dealt with here has often been termed *General American (GA)*; it refers to the pronunciation (or more strictly, range of pronunciations) geographically most widespread in the USA, with the notable exceptions of New England and a large area of the South East.

Table 3.3 shows the system of non-syllabic phonemes of both RP and General American — on the whole, English pronunciation varies more in vowels than in the non-syllabic phonemes. It will be useful at this point to consider four ways in which accents can differ from each other. We might adopt here the labels of Wells (1982:72ff): *systemic, lexical-incidental, phonotactic,* and *realisational.*

Table 3.3 The non-syllabic phonemes of British (RP) and General American (GA) English. (/m/, /n/, /ŋ/, /l/ and /r/ may also function as syllable-peaks)

stops, affricates {	fortis	p		t	tʃ	k	
	lenis	b		d	dʒ	g	
fricatives {	fortis		f θ	s	ʃ		h
	lenis		v ð	z	ʒ		
nasals		m		n		ŋ	
lateral				l			
non-syllabic vocoids					r	j w	

/p/	pit, cap	bilabial fortis stop
/t/	tell, mat	alveolar fortis stop
/tʃ/	cheek, catch	palato-alveolar fortis affricate
/k/	cool, rock	velar fortis stop
/b/	bat, rib	bilabial lenis stop
/d/	door, rod	alveolar lenis stop
/dʒ/	just, bridge	palato-alveolar lenis affricate
/g/	girl, fig	velar lenis stop
/f/	fight, laugh	labio-dental fortis fricative
/θ/	thick, path	dental fortis fricative
/s/	sick, cross	alveolar fortis fricative
/ʃ/	shock, dish	palato-alveolar fortis affricate
/h/	hat, behind	glottal (fortis) fricative
/v/	veal, dove	labio-dental lenis fricative
/ð/	that, bathe	dental lenis fricative
/z/	zeal, rose	alveolar lenis fricative
/ʒ/	rouge, measure	palato-alveolar lenis fricative
/m/	mat, jam	bilabial nasal
/n/	nose, ban	alveolar nasal
/ŋ/	bang, singer	velar nasal
/l/	lead, call	alveolar lateral
/r/	ride; (GA only) fear	postalveolar or retroflex vocoid
/j/	yet, view (/vj. ./)	unrounded front close vocoid
/w/	wet, dwell	rounded back close vocoid

A *systemic* difference exists if the phonemic system of one variety has more or fewer phonemes than that of the other – in total, or in some subpart of the phonemic system (e.g. variety A could have one stop more, and one vowel fewer, than variety B; their total of phonemes would be the same, but a systemic difference would still exist). In fact some speakers of GA do differ *systemically* from RP speakers, in that they retain a distinction lost in RP between *wh* and *w*, phonemically /ʍ/ (a voiceless velarised bilabial fricative) and /w/ respectively, so that e.g. *whet* and *wet* are distinguished (there are however other ways of analysing this difference). Likewise, many non-RP varieties of English, in which *Ed* and *head* rhyme (i.e. where *h* is 'dropped'), lack the /h/ phoneme altogether.

Differences of *lexical-incidence* are ones where particular words contain different phonemes in the two varieties. For instance although GA and RP both have /h/ in words such as *hand* and *hurt*, the word *herb* begins with /h/ in RP but not (usually) in GA. Likewise /g/ occurs for many GA speakers in *suggest* − /səgdʒɛst/ − whilst this is never the case in RP − /sədʒɛst/.

Phonotactic differences have to do with the sequences in which phonemes can combine (see section 3.3 above). A fundamental difference between GA and RP is in the phonotactic distribution of /r/. In RP /r/ is only permitted to occur before vowels, so that in words like *car, card*, the *r* in the spelling is not pronounced. Instead, as we shall see, RP has rather more vowel phonemes (resulting, historically, where this non-pre-vowel /r/ has dropped). The difference in phonotactic distribution of /r/ produces one of the most noticeable impressionistic differences between RP and GA. South Eastern American accents, and those of New England, are in this respect more like RP.

Realisation differences concern the exact quality of the phones which realise the phonemes of the varieties under comparison. It is beyond the scope of this chapter to give the details of the phones of either variety, let alone compare them, and the reader requiring such information is referred to e.g. Gimson (1980) for RP; Bauer, Dienhart, Hartvigson, and Jakobsen (1980) for GA; and Wells (1982) for comprehensive comparisons of many accents of English. A few examples will illustrate realisational differences in the non-syllabic phonemes.

The allophones of /l/ have already been used to explain the concept of the phoneme (section 3.6). GA and RP agree broadly in their allophones of /l/, except that for many speakers of GA the allophone which occurs before vocoids (given as [l] above) may also be slightly velarised, so that the two *l*s in *leaf* and *feel* may not be as different as in RP. Secondly, the phones which realise the GA fortis stops tend to be less strongly articulated than their RP counterparts; thus the 'aspirated' phone realising /p/ before stressed syllables, [pʰ], which has a [h]-like release of air before the voicing of the vowel starts, has a rather shorter delay before voice onset in GA − while in some contexts before unstressed syllables /t/ may be weakened to such an extent that it ceases to be distinct from the lenis /d/ so that *writer, metal* are pronounced the same as *rider, medal*. Thirdly, /r/ is realised with a greater retroflex quality in GA than in RP. This is sometimes achieved articulatorily in GA by retroflexion of the tongue-tip (see section 3.2), but for other speakers by shortening and 'bunching' the tongue with the tip low in the mouth.

Table 3.4 (Adapted from Wells, 1982:117ff) British (RP) and General American (GA) English vowel phonemes with key words. '*' indicates words which differ between the two varieties by lexical incidence of phonemes (see text). '**' indicates words exhibiting differences in phonotactic distribution — due specifically to the restriction in RP of /r/ to pre-vowel positions. For phonetic quality, see figs 3.7 and 3.8

	RP	GA	
kit	ɪ	ɪ	*kit*
dress	ɛ	ɛ	*dress*
trap	æ	æ	*trap, *bath*
**lot*, **cloth*	ɒ		
strut	ʌ	ʌ	*strut*
foot	ʊ	ʊ	*foot*
a(ttain), (Chin)a	ə	ə	*a(ttain), (Chin)a*
fleece	i :	i	*fleece*
*palm, *bath, **start*	ɑ :	ɑ	*palm, *lot*
*thought, *force, **north*	ɔ :	ɔ	*thought, *cloth*
goose	u :	u	*goose*
***nurse*	ɜ :		
face	eɪ	eɪ	*face*
price	aɪ	aɪ	*price*
choice	ɔɪ	ɔɪ	*choice*
mouth	aʊ	aʊ	*mouth*
goat	əʊ	o	*goat*
***near*	ɪə	(ɪ + r	***near*)
***square*	ɛə	(ɛ + r	***square*)
***cure*	ʊə	(ʊ + r	***cure*)
		(ʌ + r	***nurse*)
		(ɑ + r	***start*)
		(o + r	***force*)
		(ɔ + r	***north*)

Vowel phonemes are shown in table 3.4. *Systemic* differences between RP and GA are immediately apparent from this list; for instance GA has no /ɒ/ phoneme distinct from the vowels both of *calm* and of *thought*. The phonotactic difference concerning /r/ results, as mentioned above, in changes in the vowel system: RP has an extra set of diphthongs in words like *near, square, cure*, where GA has sequences of vowel plus /r/; an extra pure vowel as in *nurse*; and there are what might be regarded as differences of *lexical incidence* whereby /ɑ:/ is found not only like its GA counterpart in words like *palm*, but also in words spelt with *ar* like *start*, and /ɔ:/ is found not only in *thought* but in words like *north* and *force* as well. Perhaps the clearest difference of *lexical incidence* is the one which gives words like *bath* /ɑ:/ in RP, and /æ/ in GA (and of course many northern varieties of British English).

Again, *realisational* differences cannot be treated in detail here, and the reader is referred to the works cited above. Figures 3.7 (for RP) and 3.8 for (GA) give an indication of the realisations of the vowel phonemes.

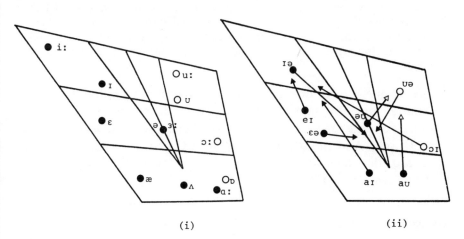

(i)   (ii)

Figure 3.7 The vowel phonemes of British (RP) English. (i) Pure vowels, (ii) diphthongs. Filled circles denote unrounded vowels, open circles denote rounded vowels. Arrows indicate the direction of change of diphthongs remaining or becoming unrounded, open arrows for diphthongs becoming rounded.

A few further comments need to be made on realisation. It will be noted that the RP pure vowels fall into pairs of 'long' and 'short' vowels, symbolised with and without a length mark (:) (e.g. the vowels of *seat* /i:/ and *sit* /ɪ/). Such durational differences are not so obvious in GA, hence the difference in symbolisation. Notice additionally that if a syllable is closed by a *fortis* phone, its vowel will be shortened considerably (by up to 50%) — compare how much shorter the vowel of *seat* is as against that of *seed*.

GA /o/ of *goat* is often diphthongised, as shown in fig. 3.8; the choice of a single symbol is swayed by the fact that its allophone

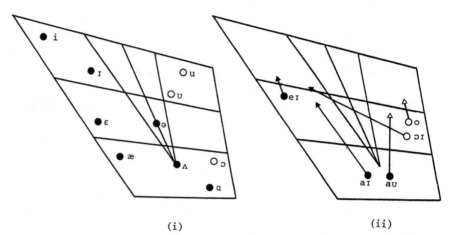

(i)　　　　　　　　　　(ii)

Figure 3.8 The vowel phonemes of General American (GA) English. (i) Pure vowels, (ii) diphthongs. Filled circles denote unrounded vowels, open circles denote rounded vowels. Arrows indicate the direction of change of diphthongs — filled arrows for diphthongs remaining unrounded, open arrows for diphthongs becoming rounded

before /r/ in e.g. *force* does not display this diphthongisation. (It should be pointed out also that some GA speakers do not have a distinction between /o/ and /ɔ/ before /r/ — so for them *force* and *north* have the same vowel.) And the sequence /ʌr/ as in GA *nurse* is usually realised by a retroflex half-open pure vocoid [ɝ] (cf. figure 3.6(ii)) rather than as a sequence of two sounds.

3.8 *Suprasegmentals*

The main linguistically relevant suprasegmental features involve variation along the perceptual dimension of *pitch, loudness,* and *length.*

With respect to the use of variations in these dimensions, languages may use them at the level of words, and at the level of syntactic units such as clauses and sentences. In much the same way that the segmental phonology of English organises phones into the phonemes which can distinguish words, so the suprasegmental phonology of a *tone language* like Chinese additionally organises variations in pitch, etc., into a limited number of word-distinguishing *tonemes.* Thus in Modern Standard Chinese the same sequence of phonemes /ba/ can represent four different words according to the pitch, loudness, and length assigned to the syllable: high level pitch /ˉba/ *eight*; high rising pitch /ˊba/ *to uproot*; low, long, fall-rise pitch /ˇba/ *to hold*; and high falling pitch /ˋba/ *a harrow* (Kratchovil, 1973).

However, although many of the world's languages use these parameters for making lexical distinctions, English and most other European languages do not; they reserve these suprasegmental parameters for changing the meaning of whole utterances rather than the identity of individual words. This use is called *intonation*. In English, for instance, the word *yes* can be spoken on a low rising pitch /ˌjɛs/ to sound encouraging; on a high falling pitch /ˈjɛs/ to convey confidence or assertiveness; on a low falling pitch /ˌjɛs/ to imply confirmation; on a high rising pitch /ˈjɛs/ as in a query; and with a falling-rising pitch /ˇjɛs/ to convey the speaker's reservations in agreeing.

There are several detailed descriptions of British English intonation, such as Jassem (1952a), Kingdon (1958), Crystal (1969), Halliday (1970), and O'Connor and Arnold (1973). American English intonation is described in Bauer, Dienhart, Hartvigson, and Jakobsen (1980:Ch.15) and a more theoretical treatment is to be found in Ladd (1980). Different traditions have grown up for the analysis of intonation, which sometimes obscure the similarity of the conclusions they arrive at; despite superficial differences, the works cited agree in analysing intonation in terms of contours rather than attempting to define pitch 'phonemes' parallel to segmental phonemes, which was common practice in earlier American analyses.

Some languages are more rhythmical than others. In those that are rhythmical, the degree of rhythmicality depends additionally on style, being greater in slow and careful speech. In a recent computer-aided analysis of English rhythm, it was found that Standard Southern British English (RP) has two kinds of suprasegmental units: one (termed *Narrow Rhythm Units*) exhibiting weak isochrony; the other (termed *Anacruses*) exhibiting no isochrony (Jassem, Hill and Witten, in press). *Isochrony* in general is a principle which equalises the overall duration of successive entities occurring in time. Weak isochrony means that this principle operates as a tendency rather than absolutely. An utterance may not include any anacrusis, but if it does, the anacrusis always precedes a narrow rhythm unit (which itself always begins with an accent).

Until the early fifties, the notion of linguistic stress in general and English stress in particular was almost unanimously taken to be related to articulatory effort (in production), to intensity (in the acoustic signal), or to loudness (in perception). But since then experimental research has shown this to be unrealistic and that stress, in English at least (and probably in most languages), depends on pitch and duration, and possibly also vowel quality. Some linguists and phoneticians have moved away from seeing 'stresses' ('word stress', 'sentence stress') as physical properties of utterances, and instead prefer to use the term stress to refer to the potential of a syllable of a word or phrase to be *accented* (cf. Jassem, 1952b; Gimson, 1956; Bolinger, 1958; Fry, 1958; and Jassem and Gibbon, 1980). *Accent* refers to combinations of values in the dimensions of pitch, duration, intensity and possibly vowel quality which cause certain syllables in utterances to be perceived as more prominent. Thus the speaker knows that given syllables in words and phrases have the *potential* to be accented (are stressed syllables); but in the realisation of the utterance only some will actually receive accents.

With the new insights in the area of English suprasegmentals, it is now possible to represent English speech by a transcription which is independent of grammar, showing phonological units (rather than syntactic units such as words), and which incorporates both segmental and suprasegmental information; for example:

#ðɪsɪzə↘strɪklɪ ·fəʊnə ·lɒdʒɪkl̩ trɑːn·skrɪpʃn̩ əvən·ɪŋglɪʃ ↘ʌtrəns#

This is a strictly phonological transcription of an English utterance.

There are two kinds of accent marks, showing pitch-plus-rhythm related accent (e.g.↘, ↘), versus merely rhythm related accent (·), as well as divisions between total rhythm units (spaces). An anacrusis is contained between the beginning of the utterance, or a space, and the next accent mark. The narrow rhythm unit is contained between an accent mark and the next space or the end of the utterance. The total rhythm unit is marked by two successive spaces, the beginning and end of the utterance counting as spaces.

With appropriate stored constants and contextual rules, such a transcription is, in principle, sufficient as an input into a computer programmed to synthesise spoken English. This prospect is explored further in chapters 4 and 6.

References

Bauer, L., Dienhart, J.M., Hartvigson, H.H. and Jakobsen, L.K. (1980) *American English Pronunciation*. Copenhagen: Gyldendal.

Bolinger, D. (1958) 'A theory of pitch accent in English'. *Word* **14**, 109–149.

Catford, J.C. (1977) *Fundamental Problems in Phonetics*. Edinburgh: Edinburgh University Press.

Crystal, D. (1969) *Prosodic Systems and Intonation in English*. London: Cambridge University Press.

Fischer-Jørgensen, E. (1975) *Trends in Phonological Theory*. Copenhagen: Akademisk.

Fry, D.B. (1958) 'Experiments in the perception of stress'. *Language and Speech*, **1**, 126–152.

Fujimura, O. and Lovins, J.B. (1978) 'Syllables as concatenative phonetic units'. In *Syllables and Segments* (eds Bell, A. and Hooper, J.B.). Amsterdam: North Holland.

Gimson, A.C. (1956) 'The linguistic relevance of stress in English'. *Zeitschrift für Phonetik und allgemeine Sprachwissenschaft* **9**, 143–149.

Gimson, A.C. (1980) *An Introduction to the Pronunciation of English.* 3rd edn. London: Edward Arnold.

Halliday, M.A.K. (1970) *A Course in Spoken English: Intonation.* London: Oxford University Press.

Jassem, W. (1952a) *Intonation of Conversational English.* Prace Wrocławskiego Towarzystwa Naukowego, No. 45.

Jassem, W. (1952b) 'Stress in modern English'. *Biuletyn Polskiego Towarzystwa Jezykoznawczego* **11**, 23–49.

Jassem, W. and Gibbon, D. (1980) 'Re-defining English accent and stress'. *Journal of the International Phonetic Association* **10**, 2–16.

Jassem, W., Hill, D.R., and Witten, I.H. (in press) 'Isochrony in English speech, its statistical validity and linguistic relevance'. In *Pattern, Process and Function in Discourse Phonology* (eds Gibbon, D. and Richter, H.). Berlin : De Gruyter.

Jones, D. (1972) *An Outline of English Phonetics.* 9th edn. Cambridge: Heffer.

Kingdon, R. (1958) *The Groundwork of English Intonation.* London: Longmans.

Kratchovil, P. (1973) 'Tone in Chinese'. In *Phonology* (Ed. Fudge, E. C.) Harmondsworth: Penguin.

Ladd, R. D. (1980) *The Structure of Intonational Meaning: Evidence from English.* Indiana University Press, USA.

Ladefoged, P. (1982) *A Course in Phonetics.* 2nd edn. New York: Harcourt, Brace, Jovanovich.

Morton, J. and Jassem, W. (1965) 'Acoustic correlates of stress'. *Language and Speech* **8**, 148–158.

O'Connor, J.D. (1973) *Phonetics.* Harmondsworth: Penguin.

O'Connor, J.D. and Arnold, G.F. (1973) *Intonation of Colloquial English.* 2nd edn. London: Longmans.

Pike, K.L. (1943) *Phonetics.* Ann Arbor: University of Michigan Press.

The Principles of the International Phonetic Association (1949) London: University College.

Wells, J.C. (1982) *Accents of English.* Cambridge: Cambridge University Press.

CHAPTER 4

VOICES OF MEN AND MACHINES

James Flanagan

In this chapter the basic techniques of voice synthesis are introduced from both acoustic and historic perspectives.

Through the developments of modern theory, the mechanism of human voice production is now well understood, although some of the non-linearities in vocal-cord vibration and in source-tract interaction remain to be studied and quantified. This acoustic understanding forms the basis for all present-day efforts in speech synthesis.[1]

In contrast, knowledge is incomplete about the relationships which dictate the ordered motions of the vocal system. Studies of speech *prosody*, relating to stress, pause, and pitch assignment, and studies of the dynamic properties of articulatory motions are all current topics of speech research.[2-5]

4.1 *The acoustic model of the vocal tract*

Acoustic understanding of voice production can be indicated with the help of fig. 4.1, a cross-sectional x-ray of a man's head, which will be familiar from chapter 3. From an acoustical point of view, the vocal tract proper is a non-uniform tube about 17 cm in length. It is terminated at one end by the vocal cords (or by the opening between them, the glottis) and at the other by the lips. The cross-sectional area of the tract is determined by placement of the lips, jaw, tongue, and velum, and can vary from zero (complete closure) to about 20 cm^2.

An ancillary cavity, the nasal tract, can be coupled to the vocal tract by the trap-door action of the velum. The nasal tract begins at the velum and terminates at the nostrils. In man, the cavity is about 12 cm long and has a volume of about 60 cm^3. During non-nasal sounds the velum seals off the nasal cavity and no sound is radiated from the nostrils.

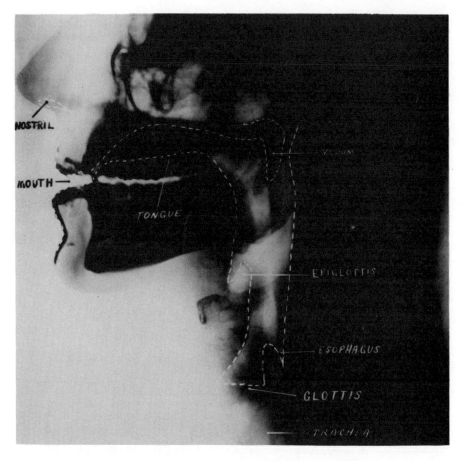

Figure 4.1 Sagittal-plane x-ray of the vocal system

Sound can be generated in the vocal system in three ways. *Voiced* sounds are produced by elevating the air pressure in the lungs, forcing a flow through the vocal-cord orifice (the glottis) and causing the cords to vibrate. The interrupted flow produces quasiperiodic, broad-spectrum pulses which excite the vocal tract. The physiological structure of the vocal cords, which produce this pulsive air flow, is shown in fig. 4.2. The vibrating ligaments of the vocal cords are about 18 mm long and the mean glottal opening is typically 5 mm².

Fricative sounds of speech are generated by forming a constriction at some point in the tract and forcing air through the constriction at a sufficiently high Reynolds' number to produce turbulence. A noise source of sound pressure is thereby created. *Plosive* sounds result from making a complete closure, again usually toward the front, building up pressure behind the closure, and abruptly releasing it. Fricative noise (or aspiration) typcially follows the transient release.

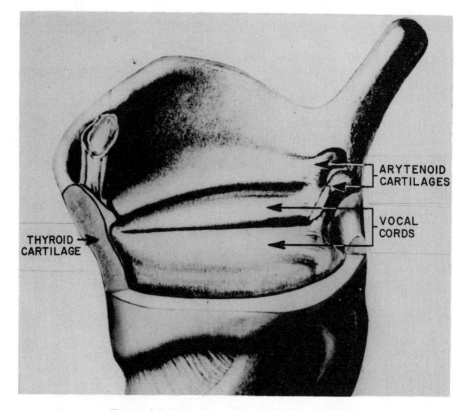

Figure 4.2 Schematic view of the human larynx

All these vocal sources – for periodic voiced sounds and for aperiodic voiceless sounds – are relatively broad in spectrum. The vocal system acts as a time-varying filter to impose its resonant characteristics on the sources.

Because of the relatively loose interaction between the vocal system and the sound sources, these can be approximately represented as linearly separable. In this form, their individual acoustic properties can be conveniently examined. Figure 4.3 (top) represents the vocal tract as a time-varying filter which is excited by broad-spectrum sources having relatively fixed characteristics. The sound radiated from the mouth $s(t)$ can, to a first approximation, be considered the convolution of the excitation source $g(t)$ and the transmission characteristic $h(t)$.

For voiced sounds, the excitation source is the acoustic volume velocity at the vocal cords. This is typically pulsive and periodic and has a line spectrum whose harmonics diminish in amplitude approximately as $1/f^2$ [sketched as $|G(f)|$ in fig. 4.3 (middle)]. The vocal-tract filter function [sketched as $|H(f)|$] has transmission poles

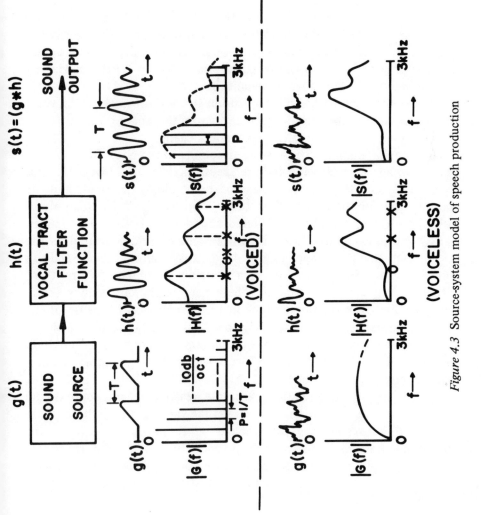

Figure 4.3 Source-system model of speech production

corresponding to the acoustic resonances (or *formants*) of the vocal tract. The tract length is comparable to the wavelength of sound at the frequencies of interest. Because the tract is essentially open at the mouth end and closed at the glottal end, its eigenfrequencies correspond roughly to the odd quarter-wave resonances of such a pipe. For a straight pipe of 17 cm length, the first three resonant frequencies are 500, 1500 and 2500 Hz.

For vowel sounds the pipe is excited at the glottal (vocal-cord) end, and it has no side-branch resonators. Its transmission consequently has only poles (shown by the x's). Nasal sounds typically exhibit an additional pole and zero in the frequency range below 3 kHz (shown by the dashed x-0). The output magnitude spectrum $|S(f)|$ is therefore a line spectrum which has imposed upon it the resonances of the vocal transmission. As the vocal tract takes on the shapes for different sounds, the frequencies of these resonances change.

In a similar manner, the unvoiced sounds are excited from a noise source which is relatively flat in spectrum [fig. 4.3 (lower)]. This source is typically positioned at some point along the tract, and the transmission function is, to first order, approximated by a couple of poles and a zero. Again the radiated sound reflects these resonances.

In continuous speech the formant resonances move around as the vocal tract changes shape. Figure 4.4 shows a sound spectrogram (a time–frequency–intensity plot) of a sentence in which the first three formant frequencies are traced. These parameters vary slowly (compared to the pressure fluctuations in the speech wave) because of the physical limitations on how quickly the vocal tract can change in shape. (That is, the tongue, jaw, lips, etc., have significant mass, and their accelerations are limited by the forces which the articulatory muscles can generate.)

On the basis of these relations, a simple, reasonable, and approximate model of speech generation includes a time-varying filter, whose resonances and antiresonances can change continuously to simulate the vocal-tract transmission, and whose excitation is derived from two kinds of signal sources: a periodic pulse generator of variable period to simulate voiced sounds, and a broad-band noise generator to simulate voiceless sounds.

4.2 *The evolution of speaking machines*

From earliest times man has sought to understand and duplicate the mechanism of the human voice. Fundamental understanding still motivates today's efforts, but in partnership with the important

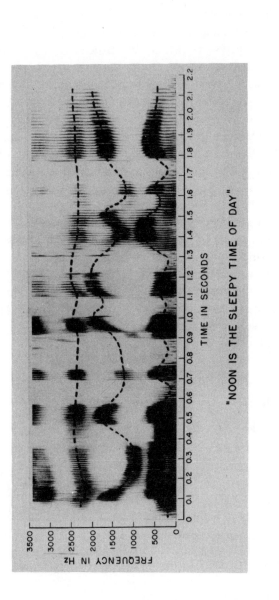

Figure 4.4 Sound spectrogram of a sentence showing the time variation of the first three vocal resonances, or formants

applications of voice answerback from computers and the efficient transmission of speech signals. Early attempts to imitate man's speech invariably took the form of mechanical devices. Modern efforts invariably develop in electrical terms.

Much treachery lies in trying to model nature verbatim, rather than in terms of underlying physical principles. However, while man has been notably unsuccessful in making flying machines which flap their wings like birds, he has been somewhat better at building mechanical contrivances which behave acoustically like the human vocal tract.

One of the earliest documented efforts at speech simulation was by Christian Gottlieb Kratzenstein. In the year 1779 the Imperial Academy of St Petersburg put the following questions as the subject of their annual prize. '(1) What is the nature and character of the sounds of the vowels a, e, i, o, u, (that make them) so different from one another? (2) Can an instrument be constructed like the *vox humana* pipes of an organ, which shall accurately express the sounds of the vowels?'

The winning solution was offered by Kratzenstein, who constructed a set of acoustic resonators similar in form and dimensions to the human mouth. He activated the resonators, shown in fig. 4.5, with a vibrating reed which, like the human vocal cords, interrupted an air stream. The resonators are said to have imitated 'with tolerable accuracy' the five vowels, but they provided little indication of the acoustic principles underlying vowel formation.

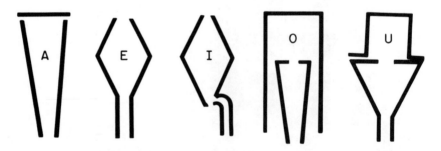

Figure 4.5 Kratzenstein's resonators for synthesis of vowel sounds. The resonators are actuated by blowing through a free, vibrating reed into the lower end. The I sound is produced simply by blowing into the lower pipe without a reed

A more successful imitation of vowel sounds and an imitation of many consonants was made about the same time by Wolfgang von Kempelen of Vienna.[6] His apparatus consisted of a conical resonator, like the bell of a clarinet, fitted with a reed which was enclosed in a box supplied with air from a bellows. A few years later – in 1791 –

von Kempelen constructed and demonstrated a more elaborate machine for generating connected utterances. Although the machine was ingenious and received considerable publicity, von Kempelen was not taken seriously by his scientific colleagues. The reason was that this truly brilliant gentleman had earlier perpetrated a deception in the form of a mechanical chess-playing machine. The principal 'mechanism' of the machine was the concealed, legless, excommander of the Polish regiment at Riga, named Worouski — a master chess player.

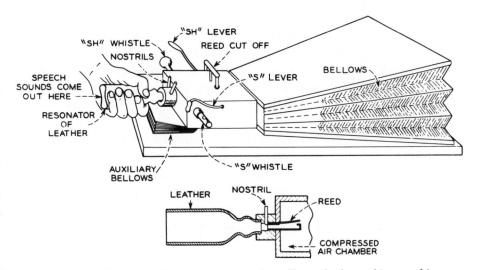

Figure 4.6 Wheatstone's reconstruction of von Kempelen's speaking machine

Von Kempelen's speaking machine, however, was a completely legitimate device.[7] It used a bellows to supply air to a reed which in turn, excited a single, hand-varied resonator that produced voiced sounds. Consonants, including nasals, were simulated by four separate constricted passages, controlled by the fingers of the other hand. An improved version of the machine, built by Sir Charles Wheatstone from von Kempelen's description, is shown in fig. 4.6.

Von Kempelen's efforts probably had a more far-reaching influence than is generally appreciated. During Alexander Graham Bell's boyhood in Edinburgh, Scotland (late 1800s), Bell had an opportunity to see the reproduction of von Kempelen's machine, which had been constructed by Wheatstone. He was greatly impressed with the device. With stimulation from his father (Alexander Melville Bell, an elocutionist like his own father), and his brother Melville's assistance, Bell set out to construct a speaking automation of his own.

Following their father's advice, the boys attempted to copy the vocal organs by making a cast from a human skull and molding the vocal parts in guttarpercha. The lips, tongue, palate, teeth, pharynx, and velum were represented. The lips were a framework of wire, covered with rubber which had been stuffed with cotton batting. Rubber cheeks enclosed the mouth cavity, and the tongue was simulated by wooden sections — likewise covered by a rubber skin and stuffed with batting. The parts were actuated by levers controlled from a keyboard. A larynx 'box' was constructed of tin and had a flexible tube for a windpipe. A vocal-cord orifice was made by stretching a slotted rubber sheet over tin supports.[8]

Bell says the device could be made to say vowels and nasals and could be manipulated to produce a few simple utterances (apparently well enough to attract the neighbours). It is interesting to speculate on how this background may later have been influential in creating US Patent No. 174, 465 dated 14 February 1876 — perhaps one of the most valuable in history.

Interest in mechanical analogues continues to the present day. The motivation is mainly to simulate and measure non-linear vocal effects. The latter are generally difficult to analyse computationally. One of the difficult parameters to measure in the real vocal tract is the location, intensity, spectrum, and internal impedance of the sound source for unvoiced sounds. One way of gaining knowledge about this source is with a mechanical analogue.

4.3 *The first electronic synthesisers*

The evolution of electronic technology caused interest in speech synthesis to assume a broader basis. Academic interest in the physiology and acoustics of speech production was supplemented by the potential for communicating at a distance. In modern terms, this takes the form of efficient digital encoding of speech information and the important applications of voice response from computers. Toward these ends the acoustic principles of speech production must be converted into electrical terms — much along the lines indicated in section 4.1 and in fig. 4.3.

One of the first electrical synthesisers which attempted to produce connected speech was the *Voder* (for Voice Operation Demonstrator).[9] Following the principles of source-tract separation, this device used electrical networks which could be selected by finger-actuated keys and whose resonances were similar to those of individual speech sounds. The device is shown in fig. 4.7.

The 'resonance control' box of the device contains ten contiguous bandpass filters which span the speech frequency range and are

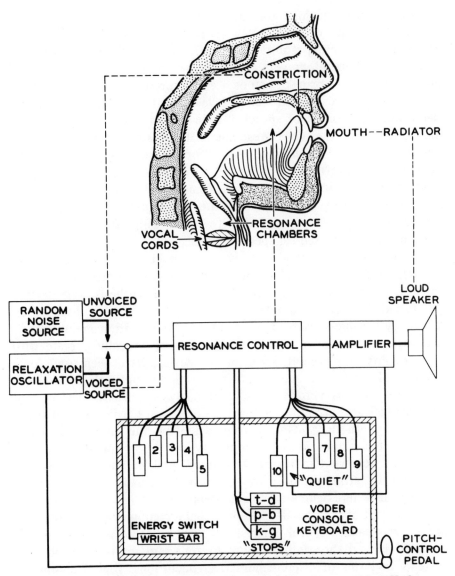

Figure 4.7 Schematic diagram of the electrical speaking machine, *Voder*

connected in parallel. All the frequency filters receive excitation from either the noise source or the buzz (relaxation) oscillator. The wrist bar selects the excitation source, and a foot pedal controls the pitch of the buzz oscillator. The outputs of the bandpass filters pass through potentiometer gain controls and are added. Ten finger keys operate the potentiometers. Three additional keys provide a transient excitation of selected filters to simulate stop-consonant sounds.

This speaking machine was demonstrated by trained operators at the World's Fairs of 1939 (New York) and 1940 (San Francisco). Although the training required was quite long (on the order of a year or more), the operators were able to 'play' the machines — literally as though they were organs or pianos — and to produce intelligible speech.

The Voder and related early developments led to other analog electronic synthesisers of speech. These ranged from analog circuitry that duplicated the vocal resonances to bilateral transmission-line simulations of the vocal tract. The efforts were largely characterised by two motivations: first, as before, a fundamental interest in speech production; and second, the new promise of highly efficient voice communication. In the latter case the techniques of speech analysis and speech synthesis pointed ways to conserve significantly the transmission bandwidth used for speech signals.

On the first count, good progress continued in understanding speech production. On the second count, complete band-compression systems, based upon the principles of speech analysis and synthesis, were devised and tested. The most notable of these was the Vocoder, invented by H. Dudley,[10] which spawned a subfield of communication engineering.[11] Although the Vocoder and its many relatives typically operate with some quality impairment, some of the devices have been used for a number of years for special communications applications. No civil telephone use has yet been made of analysis–synthesis devices, but bandsavings are accomplished in simpler ways with time-division switching methods.[12] One consideration in the use of analysis–synthesis techniques is the complexity of the terminal equipment needed to achieve bandsaving with good quality. Such processing is economically attractive only for expensive long-haul channels, or for applications where bandwidth is at a premium.

The advent of sampled-data theory, digital computers, and integrated circuits has caused speech analysis to take on some new dimensions. Sampled-data theory tells us how to represent continuous physical systems in terms of discrete numerical operations. Digital computers are able to perform the arithmetic of these operations fast and accurately, and are able to store large quantities of numbers — which can represent speech signals. Integrated circuitry allows us to build small, inexpensive, complex electrical components, among them the digital circuitry which makes computers.

Along with these developments, and with the emerging understanding of speech acoustics, the foci of fundamental and applied interests have shifted somewhat. On the fundamental side, linguistic and semantic problems of speech are coming under scrutiny through the power of digital machines.[2-5,13,14] On the applied side, an overwhelming motivation is to provide voices for computers.[15] Voice answer-back capability would open new possibilities for automatic information services, computer-based instruction, and simple inexpensive computer terminals. Further on the applied side, integrated digital circuitry makes complex processing for high-quality analysis–synthesis telephony more attractive, and applications to satellite communication, deep-space exploration, and mobile radiotelephone appear possibilities.[16]

4.4 *Digital synthesis techniques*

If computers could speak their answers, as well as print them on a typewriter or display them on an oscilloscope, their capabilities could be applied in new ways. Automatic information services — such as medical data, inventory accounting, travel information and the like — would only be as far away as the nearest telephone. In effect, the ordinary pushbutton telephone could become a computer terminal.

There are well-known techniques for pre-recording natural voice utterances and storing these messages in a computer memory.[17] For good results such messages can be used only in the context in which they were recorded. Therefore, if the computer is to speak with a large, sophisticated vocabulary, and if it is expected to use this vocabulary to form a wide variety of messages and contexts, the simple technique of pre-recorded natural speech is ruled out. Economical storage of large amounts of speech data, in a form flexible enough to generate arbitrary messages, implies a speech synthesis approach.[15]

Synthesis of a meaningful speech signal by a computer program requires a description, in some form, of the vocal-tract resonances corresponding to that speech signal. Following the source-system representation of the vocal tract, as described in fig. 4.3, leads to a digital synthesis system made up of the components shown in fig. 4.8. A random number generator simulates the source for voiceless sounds. Its variance is controlled as a function of time by the noise amplitude signal A_n.

Similarly, a counter is used to produce pulses at the pitch frequency P to simulate the vocal-cord source used for voiced sounds. Its amplitude is determined by the voicing intensity parameter A_v. These sources are filtered by a recursive filter whose coefficients are determined by the speech formants as they change with time. Three variable resonances, as shown in fig. 4.3, are typically used for voiced sounds, and a pole-zero combination for voiceless sounds. Digital-to-analog (D/A) conversion yields an audible output.

DIGITAL SYNTHESISER

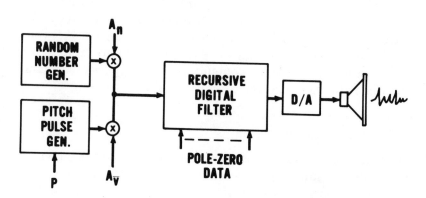

Figure 4.8 Digital circuit model of speech generation

The recursive digital filter generates quantised samples of the speech signal and it represents these samples by binary numbers. The filter can be implemented by discrete (digital) operation in a number of ways. An especially convenient approach is to represent the resonances and antiresonances individually by second-order difference equations.[1] The recursion relations for a single resonance and a single antiresonance are indicated in the upper and lower parts, respectively, of fig. 4.9. The time between samples is D, and the radian frequency and bandwidth of the resonance (or antiresonance) are ω and σ, respectively. These recursion relations can be realised by programmed instructions in the computer,[1] or they can be accomplished by special digital hardware[18] as will be discussed in Part 2 of this book.

The control functions which specify the resonances, antiresonances, and excitation of the filter must be supplied externally. A number of computer techniques can be used for obtaining these controls. Two are noted here. In one, called *formant analysis/synthesis*, the data are measured from natural speech utterances. In another, called *text synthesis*, the data are calculated from programmed knowledge of the speech process. A further recent method, *linear predictive coding*, is typically a member of the former category in that filter characteristics are derived from natural speech, although the formant frequencies may not be calculated explicitly.

Formant synthesis and text synthesis will be mentioned here and linear prediction will be covered in detail in chapter 5.

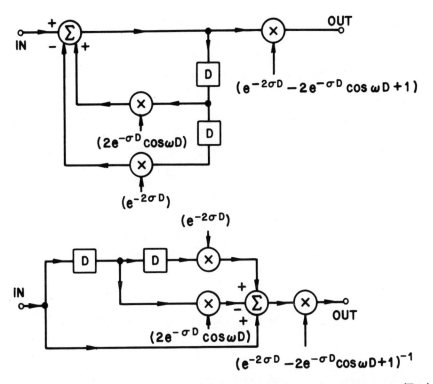

Figure 4.9 Recursive relations for digital approximation of a resonance. (Top) Sampled data approximation of a continuous simple resonance. (Bottom) Approximation of a simple antiresonance

FORMANT SYNTHESIS

The formant synthesis method depends upon a computer program that analyses natural speech to obtain the variation of three formants and the voice pitch. A typical output of this program is shown at the top of fig. 4.10.[19] These data, when provided to a synthesiser as in fig. 4.8, produce synthetic speech similar to the original natural utterance, as shown by the spectrograms in the lower part of fig. 4.10. Although this example is an all-voiced utterance, similar operations are applied for voiceless sounds.

In formant synthesis, economical storage and vocabulary flexibility are achieved by storing a library of formant-coded words. Individual, naturally uttered words are formant analysed, and their formant functions are stored. (The recorded bit rate for these data is 530 bits/sec, or 1/100 of that required to store the natural speech waveform.) When a given word sequence (message) is specified by an answer-back program, the computer accesses the formant functions in the prescribed

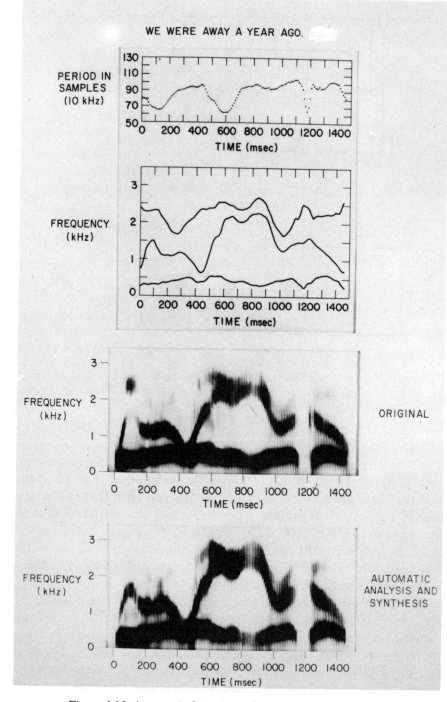

Figure 4.10 Automatic formant analysis and synthesis of speech

sequence. By a stored program it calculates the duration and the pitch inflection for each word in that prescribed context. It then calculates smooth transitions of the formant functions at the word boundaries to effect a realistic concatenation of the words. Finally, the computer issues the resulting control functions to a digital synthesiser.

Such a system was implemented for example at Bell Laboratories on a laboratory computer, as shown in fig. 4.11, as early as 1971.[20] In this case the synthesiser was a hardware digital filter, external to the computer. As a consequence, the synthesis operations ran about ten times faster than real time, hence one computer could serve ten external synthesisers. This system was applied experimentally to the automatic generation of seven-digit telephone numbers, and to the synthesis of spoken wire lists for the wiring of telephone circuits. A typical result of a digit synthesis produced by the system is shown in fig. 4.12.

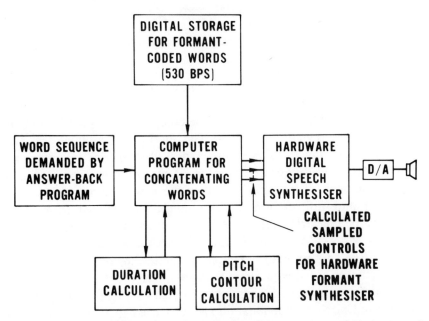

Figure 4.11 Bell Laboratories implementation of an experimental computer voice response system. A Honeywell DDP-516 laboratory computer is used for calculating the synthetic speech

TEXT SYNTHESIS

The storage economy and vocabulary flexibility achieved by formant synthesis appear attractive for 'medium-sized' vocabularies such as inventory reporting, flight information, and computer instruction. Voice readout of encyclopedic amounts of information requires even

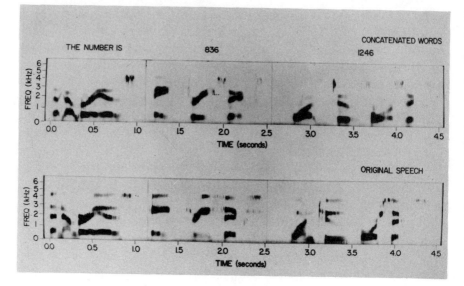

Figure 4.12 Synthesis of seven-digit telephone numbers from the computer system shown in fig. 4.11

more economy of storage, and hence a more elaborate synthesis system. *Text synthesis* is such.

In one approach to text synthesis, the computer stores a pronouncing dictionary, as shown in fig. 4.13. The dictionary contains for each entry just what one finds in ordinary desk dictionaries – a phonemic transcription of each word, indication of word stress, some rudimentary grammatical information (whether the word is a noun, adjective, verb, etc.) and information about endings and derived forms. The message to be converted into speech is supplied as the printed English text. Each word is looked up in the dictionary and the resulting information passed to a program which incorporates linguistic and syntactic rules for English. In this program a strategy for the stress and phrasing of each sentence is formed, pauses are inserted where necessary, and the duration and pitch of individual phonemes are assigned. The result is an output of discrete symbols representing the sequence of phonemes and their individual pitch and duration calculated for the prescribed context.[4] This symbol string represents a 2:1 or 3:1 expansion over the input discrete alphabetic symbols, and is illustrated in fig. 4.14.

The expanded symbol set constitutes 'commands' which are given to a dynamic (programmed) model of the vocal tract.[2] The model represents the shape of a man's vocal tract after the fashion shown in fig. 4.15. The seven articulatory parameters in this example define the shape of the vocal tract. They assume values dictated by the discrete

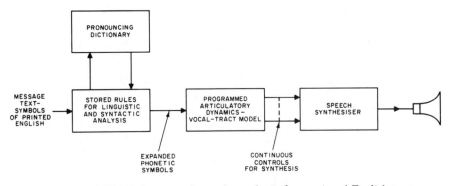

Figure 4.13 Block diagram of speech synthesis from printed English text

ENGLISH TEXT	SYNTAX AND PROSODIC RULES OUTPUT
the	4dh 4a
north	6n $4aw 2er 6th
wind	6w *qq51 4n 4d
and	4aa –n –d
the	–dh 4a
sun	6s *qq5uh 6n

Figure 4.14 Automatic conversion of printed English symbols into expanded phonetic symbols for text synthesis

symbol set, but in responding to these discrete commands they impose their own, physiologically realistic time constants. Periodically (typically at 100 per sec), the eigenfrequencies (or formants) of the model vocal tract are computed as the tract deforms, and the results, along with calculated excitation information, are issued to a hardware synthesiser of the type discussed previously.

In this scheme the machine synthesises the output speech with no recourse to any vestige of human speech. The storage economy and flexibility in synthesis approaches the order of 1000:1 when compared to a facsimile recording of the natural speech signal.

A typical output of this text synthesis system, also implemented in 1971 on a laboratory computer, is shown in fig. 4.16. As might be expected, the machine displays its own accent (which, incidentally, can be varied by changing the linguistic rules). While the naturalness of synthetic speech remains an issue, the intelligibility of text-to-voice synthesisers is beginning to be acceptable, and the state-of-the-art techniques will be described in full detail in chapter 6 and section 12.4

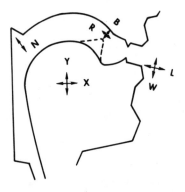

Figure 4.15 Articulatory model of human vocal tract. This vocal model, also programmed in a DDP-516 computer, is used for speech synthesis from printed text. The figure is identical to the computer scope display which shows the vocal motions during synthetic speaking

4.5 *Further reading*

This chapter has given an overview of the methods of modelling the vocal tract and synthesising the human voice. This understanding is basic to the rest of the book, but the details of acoustic modelling and the spectral characteristics of sounds will not be covered further. Accordingly, the reader who wishes to expand his fundamental knowledge in this area is referred to the following foundation texts in the subject:

Fant, G. (1960) *Acoustic Theory of Speech Production*. 's-Gravenhage: Mouton & Co.
Fant, G. (1973) *Speech Sounds and Features*. Cambridge, Mass: MIT Press.
Flanagan, J.L. (1972) *Speech Analysis, Synthesis and Perception*. 2nd edn. Berlin, Heidelberg, New York: Springer-Verlag.
Flanagan, J.L. and Rabiner, L.R. (Eds.) (1973) *Speech Synthesis*. Stroudsburg, PA: Dowden, Hutchinson and Ross.
Fry, D.B. (Ed.) (1976) *Acoustic Phonetics; A Course in Basic Readings*. Cambridge, England: Cambridge University Press.

DIGITAL PROCESSING OF SPEECH SIGNALS
After receiving a grounding in the acoustic and linguistic nature of speech signals, the reader may wish to find out more about the application of *digital signal processing* (DSP) in this area. The next chapter covers one of the most popular digital speech analysis methods, *linear*

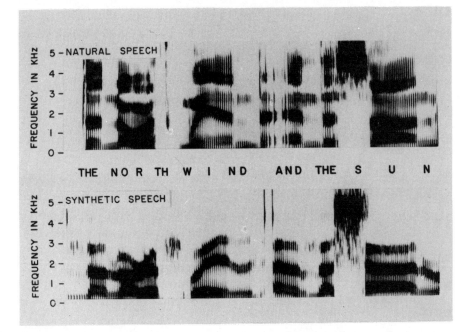

Figure 4.16 Spectrogram of speech synthesised from printed text. A comparison is made to a human utterance of the same sentence

predictive coding, but no further coverage of DSP will be given here. Accordingly, for a thorough treatment of such digital techniques, the reader is referred to the following texts:

Jayant, N.S. and Noll, P. (1983) *Digital Coding of Waveforms*. Englewood Cliffs, N.J.: Prentice-Hall (in press).

Markel, J.D. and Gray, A.H. (1976) *Linear Prediction of Speech*. Berlin, Heidelberg, New York: Springer-Verlag.

Oppenheimer, Alan V. and Schafter, Robert W. (1975) *Digital Signal Processing*, Englewood Cliffs, N.J.: Prentice-Hall.

Oppenheimer, Alan V. (Ed.) (1978) *Applications of Digital Signal Processing*, Englewood Cliffs, N.J.: Prentice-Hall.

Rabiner, Lawrence R. and Gold, Bernard (1975) *Theory and Applications of Digital Signal Processing*. Englewood Cliffs, N.J.: Prentice-Hall.

Rabiner, Lawrence R. and Schafer, R.W. (1978). *Digital Processing of Speech Signals*, Englewood Cliffs, N.J.: Prentice-Hall.

References

1. Flanagan, J.L. (1965, 2nd edn 1972) *Speech Analysis, Synthesis and Perception*. New York: Springer-Verlag.
2. Coker, C.H. (Aug. 1968) 'Speech synthesis with a parametric articulatory model', *Proc. Speech Symp., Kyoto, Japan* paper A-4.
3. Rabiner, L.R. (1968) 'Speech synthesis by rule: an acoustic domain approach', *Bell System Tech. J.* 47, 17–37.
4. Coker, C.H., Umeda, N., and Browman, C. (March 1971) 'Automatic synthesis from text', *Digest of IEEE Int. Commun. Conf., New York*.
5. Umeda, N. 'Linguistics and speech science', *Science* (in preparation).
6. Dudley, H. and Tarnoczy, T.H. (1950) 'The speaking machine of Wolfgang von Kempelen', *J. Acoust. Soc. Amer.* 22, 151–166.
7. Anon. (1871) 'Talking machines', *Sci. Amer.* 24, 32.
8. Bell, A.G. (1922) 'Prehistoric telephone days', *Nat. Geograph. Mag.* 41, 223–242.
9. Dudley, H., Riesz, R.R., and Watkins, S.A. (1939) 'A synthetic speaker', *J. Franklin Inst.* 227, 739–764.
10. Dudley, H. (1939) 'The Vocoder', *Bell Labs. Record* 17, 122–126.
11. Schroeder, M.R. (1966) 'Vocoders: analysis and synthesis of speech', *Proc. IEEE* 54, 720–734.
12. O'Neil, E.E. (1959) TASI, *Bell Labs. Record* 37, 83–87.
13. Cooper, F.S., Gaitenby, J.H., Mattingly, I.G., and Umeda, N.

(1969) 'Reading aids for the blind: a special case of machine-to-man communications', *IEEE Trans. Audio Electroacoust.* **AU-17**, 266–270.

14. Allen, J. (1968) 'Machine-to-man communication by speech part 2 : Synthesis of prosodic features of speech by rule', 1968, Spring Joint Computer Conf., Washington, DC, *AFIPS Proc.* **32**, 339–344.

15. Flanagan, J.L., Coker, C.H., Rabiner, L.R., Schafer, R.W., and Umeda, N. (1970) 'Synthetic voices for computers', *IEEE Spectrum* 7 (10), 22–45.

16. Flanagan, J.L. (Nov, 1970) 'Digital representation of speech signals', *BTL Symp. Digital Tech. Commun., Murray Hill, J.J.* 12–13.

17. These techniques are already in use for computer voice response.

18. Rabiner, L.R., Jackson, L.B., Schafer, R.W., and Coker, C.H. (Aug. 1971) 'Digital hardware for speech synthesis', *Proc. Int. Congr. Acoust., 7th Budapest, Hungary*.

19. Schafer, R.W. and Rabiner, L.R. (1970) 'System for automatic formant analysis of voiced speech', *J. Acoust. Soc. Amer.* **47**, 634–648.

20. Rabiner, L.R., Schafer, R.W., and Flanagan, J.L. (1971) 'Computer synthesis of speech by concatenation of formant-coded words', *Bell System Tech. J.* **50**, 1541–1558.

CHAPTER 5

LINEAR PREDICTIVE CODING

John Makhoul

In this analytical chapter we explore the fundamentals of the most popular digital analysis/synthesis technique – LPC

5.1 *Introduction*

In the early 1970s, within just a few years, linear predictive coding (LPC) became by far the most popular method for the digital analysis and synthesis of speech signals. In this chapter, we examine the basic methods and properties of linear predictive (LP) analysis and synthesis. The discussion will hopefully give the reader an appreciation of the time-domain and the frequency-domain aspects of linear prediction and some insights into its workings.

The chapter begins in section 5.2 with a description of the basic *all-pole* speech synthesis model upon which LP analysis is based. Although the most general LP model contains zeros as well as poles, we shall restrict our attention to the all-pole model since it is, practically speaking, the only model in serious use today. In section 5.3 we discuss various direct-form LP analysis methods and present the fundamental properties of linear prediction. Section 5.4 is devoted to the *lattice* analysis and synthesis methods of linear prediction. The unique advantages of lattice parameters lead in section 5.5 to a discussion of the quantization and coding of LPC parameters, including an exposition of the idea of variable-frame-rate analysis and coding. Also included is a brief presentation of the *vector quantisation* of LPC parameters, which is important for very low-rate speech coding. Finally, in section 5.6, we discuss the use of LPC in speech recognition.

5.2 *Basic synthesis model*

Figure 5.1 shows a schematic of the basic model used in LP synthesis. The model has two major components: a flat-spectrum excitation source and a spectral shaping filter $H(z)$. The excitation source generates a signal $u(n)$ with a flat spectral envelope, which is used to drive the filter $H(z)$ resulting in the synthetic speech signal $\hat{s}(n)$. Because the input to the filter $H(z)$ has a flat spectrum, the spectral envelope of the output signal $\hat{s}(n)$ will have the same shape as the spectrum of the filter $H(z)$. **Therefore, for speech synthesis, we endeavour to set the parameters of $H(z)$ on a time-varying basis such that its short-term spectrum is the same as the short-term speech spectral envelope we desire.**

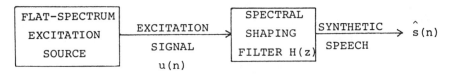

Figure 5.1 Basic speech synthesis model

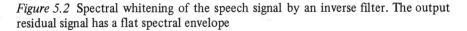

Figure 5.2 Spectral whitening of the speech signal by an inverse filter. The output residual signal has a flat spectral envelope

Given a particular speech signal $s(n)$, one can obtain its short-term spectral envelope by appropriate inverse filtering, as shown in fig. 5.2. The parameters of the inverse filter $A(z)$ are adjusted, as will be described in section 5.3, such that the residual signal $e(n)$ has a flat spectral envelope. In essence, $A(z)$ is a time-varying spectral whitening filter. If the excitation $u(n)$ in fig. 5.1 is set equal to the residual $e(n)$ and $H(z)$ is set equal to the inverse of $A(z)$, i.e. $H(z) = 1/A(z)$, then the synthetic signal $\hat{s}(n)$ will be equal to the original $s(n)$.

5.2.1 ALL-POLE MODEL

In LP analysis, [1-4] $A(z)$ is given by equation (5.1),

> **BASIC LP ALL-ZERO FILTER**
>
> $$A(z) = 1 + \sum_{k=1}^{p} a(k)z^{-k}$$

(5.1)

where $\{a(k), 1 \leqslant k \leqslant p\}$ are known as the *predictor coefficients*, and z^{-1} is the *unit delay operator*. The residual $e(n)$ is then given by

$$e(n) = s(n) + \sum_{k=1}^{p} a(k)s(n-k)$$

(5.2)

Equation (5.2) can be transformed into a synthesis equation by re-writing it as

$$s(n) = -\sum_{k=1}^{p} a(k)s(n-k) + e(n)$$

(5.3)

If we set

$$\tilde{s}(n) = -\sum_{k=1}^{p} a(k)s(n-k)$$

(5.4)

as the predicted value of $s(n)$ from the previous p samples, then

$$e(n) = s(n) - \tilde{s}(n)$$

(5.5)

can be viewed as the *prediction error*.

Analogous to (5.3), the synthetic signal $\hat{s}(n)$ can be computed from equation (5.6),

> **LP SYNTHESIS EQUATION**
>
> $$\hat{s}(n) = -\sum_{k=1}^{p} a(k)\hat{s}(n-k) + Gu(n)$$

(5.6)

where G is a gain factor. It is clear from (5.3) and (5.6) that if $Gu(n)$ is set equal to $e(n)$, the synthetic signal $\hat{s}(n)$ will be identical to the speech signal $s(n)$. The synthesis equation (5.6) is known as *direct-form synthesis*, following digital signal processing terminology.[5] In section 5.4, we will discuss a different form of synthesis : lattice synthesis.

In the z domain, the transfer function represented by (5.6) is given by equation (5.7),

BASIC LP ALL-POLE FILTER

$$H(z) = \frac{\hat{S}(z)}{U(z)} = \frac{G}{A(z)} = \frac{G}{1 + \displaystyle\sum_{k=1}^{p} a(k)z^{-k}} \qquad (5.7)$$

where $\hat{S}(z)$ and $U(z)$ are the z transforms of $\hat{s}(n)$ and $u(n)$, respectively. Of interest below will be the autocorrelation $\hat{R}(i)$ of the impulse response of $H(z)$ which can be shown[1,2] to obey the following equations

$$\hat{R}(0) = -\sum_{k=1}^{p} a(k)\hat{R}(k) + G^2 \qquad (5.8)$$

$$\hat{R}(i) = -\sum_{k=1}^{p} a(k)\hat{R}(i-k), \qquad 1 \leqslant |i| \leqslant \infty \qquad (5.9)$$

The same equations apply if the input to $H(z)$ is a white noise source with unit power instead of a unit impulse.

5.2.2 SOURCE MODEL

The major problem in using $e(n)$ as the excitation signal in practice is the large number of bits required to store it. For example, at a sampling rate of 10 kHz, if one quantised each sample to one bit only, the required storage would be 10 000 bits/s, which for many commercial applications would be prohibitive. One effective solution to this problem has been to model the excitation as coming from one of two sources: a pulse source (buzz) or a noise source (hiss).

The most general form of a pulse source is the impulse response of an all-pass filter. The simplest and most popular form is the single impulse. When the pulse source produces a sequence of pulses separated by a pitch period, it is known as a buzz source, and is used to synthesise *voiced* sounds.

The noise or hiss source is a white noise source that can be simply a random number generator producing random sample values with a flat spectral envelope. A noise source is used to synthesise *unvoiced* or fricated sounds.

While most sounds can be generated by either a pulse source or a noise source, there are some sounds, such as the voiced fricatives [z] and [v], that are best synthesised by a combination of the two sources. If such a mixed-source model is used, the speech is found to be more natural sounding.[6]

Coding the parameters of the source model described above requires on the order of a few hundred bits/s only. The resulting speech quality is not quite as natural as using the residual signal for the excitation, but the vast reduction in bit rate more than offsets the loss in speech quality for many applications.

5.3 *Direct-form analysis*

In direct-form analysis, the predictor coefficients $\{a(k)\}$ are computed as the result of the minimisation of the energy in the residual $e(n)$. This computation must be performed on a short-term basis so as to follow the speech dynamics. Below we describe two methods of effecting the short-term aspect of the computation: by windowing either the speech signal or the residual signal.

5.3.1 DATA WINDOWING

In this method, the speech signal $s(n)$ is first multiplied by a *data window* $w(n)$ before it is inverse filtered. The most popular data windows are finite in extent. Thus we form

$$x(n) = \begin{cases} w(n)s(n), & 0 \leqslant n \leqslant N-1 \\ 0, & \text{otherwise} \end{cases} \tag{5.10}$$

where we have assumed that the window is zero outside the interval $0 \leqslant n \leqslant N-1$. The *window width N* is usually set to correspond to 20–30 ms for short-term analysis. The most popular data windows used in speech analysis are the Hamming and Hanning windows,[7] both raised cosine types of windows.

The residual signal whose energy is to be minimised is obtained by passing $x(n)$ through the filter $A(z)$. The residual energy is given by

$$E = \sum_{n=-\infty}^{\infty} e_x^2(n) = \sum_{n=-\infty}^{\infty} \left[x(n) + \sum_{k=1}^{p} a(k)x(n-k) \right]^2 \tag{5.11}$$

where $e_x(n)$ is the residual corresponding to the windowed signal $x(n)$. E is also the total squared error in predicting $x(n)$ from its past. **The coefficients $\{a(k)\}$ that minimise E are obtained by setting the partial derivative of E with respect to each of the coefficients $a(k)$ to zero.** The result is the normal equations (5.12), where equation (5.13) is the autocorrelation of the windowed signal $x(n)$. Equations (5.12) are p linear equations in p unknowns, which can be solved to obtain the desired predictor coefficients. This method is often called

---

AUTOCORRELATION METHOD

$$\sum_{k=1}^{p} a(k)R(i-k) = -R(i), \qquad 1 \leqslant i \leqslant p \tag{5.12}$$

$$R(i) = \sum_{n=-\infty}^{\infty} x(n)x(n-i) = \sum_{n=i}^{N-1} x(n)x(n-i), \qquad 0 \leqslant i \leqslant p \tag{5.13}$$

---

the *autocorrelation method* because the coefficients $R(i-k)$ in (5.12) are the autocorrelation coefficients of the signal.

The minimum residual energy E_p is obtained by substituting (5.12) in (5.11)

$$E_p = R(0) + \sum_{k=1}^{p} a(k)R(k) \tag{5.14}$$

E_p is also known as the minimum total squared error, or simply the minimum prediction error. For synthesis, if we set the gain of the filter $H(z)$ such that

$$G^2 = E_p \tag{5.15}$$

one can show by comparing (5.14) to (5.8) and (5.12) to (5.9) that

$$\hat{R}(i) = R(i), \qquad 0 \leqslant i \leqslant p \tag{5.16}$$

or the first $p + 1$ autocorrelation coefficients of the windowed signal and the synthetic signal are equal. In particular, having $\hat{R}(0) = R(0)$ means the energy in the synthetic signal is equal to the energy in the original windowed signal.

5.3.2 RESIDUAL WINDOWING
In this case, the energy to be minimised is given by

$$E = \sum_{n=-\infty}^{\infty} w_e(n)e^2(n) \tag{5.17}$$

where $e(n)$ is the residual in (5.2) and $w_e(n)$ is a window that weights the residual. Minimising (5.17) with respect to $\{a(k)\}$ results in the normal equations (5.18),

---

COVARIANCE METHOD (1)

$$\sum_{k=1}^{p} a(k)R(i,k) = -R(0,i), \qquad 1 \leqslant i \leqslant p \tag{5.18}$$

where

$$R(i,k) = \sum_{n=-\infty}^{\infty} w_e(n)s(n-i)s(n-k) \tag{5.19}$$

The most popular residual window is the rectangular window

$$w_e(n) = \begin{cases} 1, & p \leqslant n \leqslant N-1 \\ 0, & \text{otherwise} \end{cases} \tag{5.20}$$

in which case (5.19) reduces to equations (5.21).

COVARIANCE METHOD (2)

$$R(i,k) = \sum_{n=p}^{N-1} s(n-i)s(n-k), \qquad 0 \leqslant i, k \leqslant p \tag{5.21}$$

(Note that while a rectangular window is not acceptable as a data window for best results, it is perfectly acceptable as a residual window.) Since $R(i,k)$ provides an estimate of the covariance of the signal $s(n)$, this method is sometimes called the *covariance method*. Equations (5.18) are p linear equations in p unknowns, which can be solved for the predictor coefficients.

Substituting (5.18) in (5.17), we obtain the minimum residual energy or the minimum prediction error

$$E_p = R(0,0) + \sum_{k=1}^{p} a(k)R(0,k) \tag{5.22}$$

In (5.21), note that $s(n)$ must be known in the range $0 \leqslant n \leqslant N-1$, just like in the autocorrelation method, but the equations to be solved in the two methods are different.

5.3.3 COMPUTATION OF PREDICTOR COEFFICIENTS
The solution of (5.12) or (5.18) for the predictor coefficients can be obtained using any of the familiar methods for solving a set of linear equations. Because the matrix of coefficient values in both sets of equations are symmetric and usually positive definite, the equations

can be solved efficiently by the square-root or Cholesky decomposition method. The computation of the autocorrelation or covariance co-efficients requires on the order of pN operations, which can dominate the total computation time if $N \gg p$, as is often the case.

Further reductions in storage and computation can be obtained in solving (5.12) because of its special form. The autocorrelation matrix $R(i-k)$ is not only symmetric but also Toeplitz, i.e. the elements along any diagonal are identical. **For this special case, Levison[8] and then Durbin[9] developed an efficient recursive solution that solved for the optimal predictors of successive order.** The procedure is as follows:

LEVINSON-DURBIN RECURSIVE METHOD

$$E_0 = R(0)$$
$$\text{For} \quad m = 1, 2, \ldots, p$$

$$K_m = -[R(m) + \sum_{k=1}^{m-1} a_{m-1}(k)R(m-k)]/E_{m-1} \quad (5.23)$$

$$a_m(m) = K_m$$
$$a_m(k) = a_{m-1}(k) + K_m a_{m-1}(m-k), \quad 1 \leqslant k \leqslant m-1 \quad (5.24)$$

$$E_m = (1 - K_m^2)E_{m-1} \quad (5.25)$$

The coefficients $\{a_m(k), \quad 1 \leqslant k \leqslant m\}$ are the predictor coefficients for the optimal mth order predictor. The final solution is given by the co-efficients $a_p(k)$, $\{1 \leqslant k \leqslant p\}$.

From (5.25) one can write

$$E_m = R(0) \prod_{i=1}^{m} (1 - K_i^2) \quad (5.26)$$

The minimum error E_m has to decrease as the predictor order in-creases, otherwise one would not increase the order. From (5.26) this means that we must have:

CONDITION FOR STABILITY OF ALL-POLE FILTER

$$|K_m| < 1, \quad 1 \leqslant m \leqslant p \quad (5.27)$$

The intermediate quantities K_m are known as the reflection coefficients (see section 5.4). In the statistical literature, in autoregressive modelling, the negatives of K_m are known as *partial correlation* (PARCOR) *co-efficients*. Equation (5.27) can be shown to be a necessary and sufficient condition for the all-pole filter $H(z)$ to be stable, i.e. all poles are inside the unit circle. Filter stability is very important in speech synthesis, because an unstable filter can lead to 'pops' and 'clicks' in the synthetic signal. If $|K_p|=1$, then all the poles will be *on* the unit circle, which is an unstable condition.

Dividing E_p in (5.26) by the energy $R(0)$ of the signal, we obtain the *normalised minimum error*

$$V_p = \frac{E_p}{R(0)} = \prod_{m=1}^{p}(1-K_m^2) \tag{5.28}$$

From (5.27) and (5.28), we have

$$0 < V_p \leqslant 1 \tag{5.29}$$

If any $|K_m|=1$, we see that the error is zero, which means that the signal is perfectly predictable. For a windowed signal, this condition is impossible to achieve unless the signal is identically zero elsewhere.

In the covariance method, filter stability is not guaranteed. To test whether a particular predictor solution will lead to a stable filter or not, one can derive from (5.24) a backward recursion that computes the K_m from the $a(k)$:

CALCULATION OF REFLECTION COEFFICIENTS FROM PREDICTOR COEFFICIENTS

$$\begin{aligned}
a_p(k) &= a(k), \qquad 1 \leqslant k \leqslant p \\
K_m &= a_p(p) \\
\text{For } m &= p, p-1, \ldots, 2 \\
a_{m-1}(i) &= \frac{a_m(i) - K_m a_m(m-i)}{1 - K_m^2}, \qquad 1 \leqslant i \leqslant m-1 \\
K_{m-1} &= a_{m-1}(m-1)
\end{aligned} \tag{5.30}$$

If all the K_m obey (5.27), then the corresponding $H(z)$ is stable, otherwise it is not.

5.3.4 SPECTRAL PROPERTIES

In this subsection we shall discuss some of the salient spectral properties of all-pole modelling. Our attention will be directed to the autocorrelation method only, since it is difficult to present an exact frequency-domain derivation of the covariance method.

From (5.11) and using Parseval's theorem, one can show that

$$E = \frac{1}{2\pi}\int_{-\pi}^{\pi} P(\omega)|A(e^{j\omega})|^2 \, d\omega \tag{5.31}$$

where

$$P(\omega) = |X(e^{j\omega})|^2 = |\sum_{n=0}^{N-1} x(n)e^{-j\omega n}|^2 \qquad (5.32)$$

is the power spectrum of the windowed signal $x(n)$. If we define the spectrum of $H(z)$ as

$$\hat{P}(\omega) = |H(e^{j\omega})|^2 = G^2/|A(e^{j\omega})|^2 \qquad (5.33)$$

then we have

$$E = \frac{G^2}{2\pi} \int_{-\pi}^{\pi} \frac{P(\omega)}{\hat{P}(\omega)} \, d\omega \qquad (5.34)$$

Therefore, minimising the total error E is equivalent to minimising the integrated ratio of the signal spectrum to its approximation $\hat{P}(\omega)$ Because the contributions to the total error are determined by the ratio of the two spectra, the matching process should perform uniformly over the whole frequency range. Also, since the contribution to the total error is more significant when $P(\omega) > \hat{P}(\omega)$, than when $P(\omega) < \hat{P}(\omega)$, we conclude that, on the average, one would expect a better fit of $\hat{P}(\omega)$ to $P(\omega)$ where $P(\omega) > \hat{P}(\omega)$ than where $P(\omega) < \hat{P}(\omega)$. **This property ensures that, for a quasiperiodic signal, the approximation of $\hat{P}(\omega)$ to $P(\omega)$ is far superior at the harmonics than between harmonics.** These properties are apparent in fig. 5.3 which shows the spectrum of a windowed vowel waveform, modelled by a fourteen-pole spectrum.

One reason that linear prediction does a good job in modelling speech spectra is because most speech sounds consist largely of vocal-tract resonances, which are well modelled by poles. Another reason is that human auditory perception is more sensitive to the location of resonances than of antiresonances or zeros, and therefore a process that models resonances well should result in good speech quality.

In female speech, the spectral harmonics are separated by about twice as much as for male speech, because female pitch is about twice male pitch. Therefore, the vocal-tract resonances are not as obvious on the spectrum as for male speech. **Because LP modelling tends to follow the harmonics, the error in modelling spectral resonances for females is much higher than for males.**[10] This may be a major reason why, in general, LPC does not sound as good for female speech. To date, there are no clear-cut solutions to this problem. Naturally, the problem is even worse for children's speech because of the much higher pitch frequency.

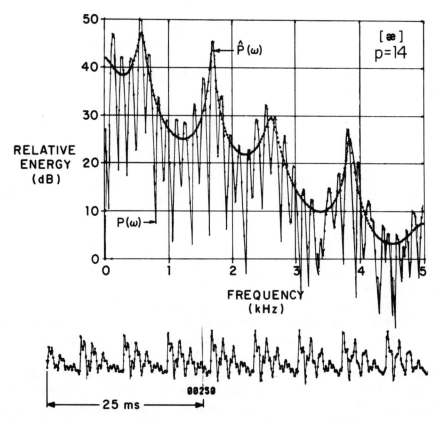

Figure 5.3 Comparison of LP spectrum with actual spectrum. $P(\omega)$ is the spectrum of 25 ms of the vowel in the word 'bat', after windowing it by a Hamming window. $\hat{P}(\omega)$ is the spectrum of a fourteen-pole linear prediction model of spectrum $P(\omega)$

5.4 *Lattice analysis/synthesis*

While direct-form LP analysis/synthesis of speech has been very popular in computer implementation, lattice synthesis has been the most popular method of LP synthesis in commercial synthesis chips. In this section we present the basic lattice structures for analysis and synthesis and discuss some of the advantages of the lattice structures. One of the major advantages of lattice analysis is that filter stability can be guaranteed with finite wordlength (FWL) computations.

5.4.1 LATTICE STRUCTURES[11-14]

Figure 5.4 shows the basic two-multiplier all-zero lattice introduced by Itakura and Saito.[11] The all-zero lattice can be thought of as a physical realisation of the Levinson–Durbin recursion represented

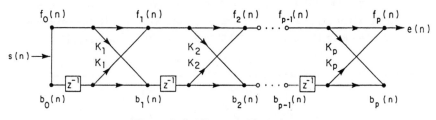

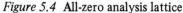

Figure 5.4 All-zero analysis lattice

by (5.24). From fig. 5.4 one can write the following relations:

RECURSIVE RELATIONS OF ALL-ZERO ANALYSIS LATTICE

$$f_0(n) = b_0(n) = s(n) \tag{5.35}$$

$$f_m(n) = f_{m-1}(n) + K_m b_{m-1}(n-1) \tag{5.36}$$

$$b_m(n) = K_m f_{m-1}(n) + b_{m-1}(n-1) \tag{5.37}$$

---

where $s(n)$ is the input signal, $f_m(n)$ is the 'forward' residual at stage m, $b_m(n)$ is the 'backward' residual, and $e(n) = f_p(n)$ is the output residual. The transfer function between input and output is $A(z)$ given by (5.1). In general, the impulse response of the all-zero filter realised between the input $s(n)$ and the output of the mth stage $f_m(n)$ is given by the mth-order forward predictor $\{a_m(k), \; 0 \leqslant k \leqslant m\}$, as in (5.24). In fact, one can show from (5.35)–(5.37) and (5.24) that

$$f_m(n) = \sum_{k=0}^{m} a_m(k) s(n-k), \qquad a_m(0) = 1 \tag{5.38}$$

Similarly, one can show that

$$b_m(n) = \sum_{k=0}^{m} a_m(m-k) s(n-k) \tag{5.39}$$

That is, the impulse response between the input and $b_m(n)$ is given by the reverse or backward predictor $\{a_m(m-k), \; 0 \leqslant k \leqslant m\}$.

The all-pole lattice filter structure can be obtained from the all-zero structure by simply rewriting (5.36) as

---

RECURSIVE RELATIONS OF ALL-POLE SYNTHESIS LATTICE

$$f_{m-1}(n) = f_m(n) - K_m b_{m-1}(n-1) \tag{5.40}$$

$$b_m(n) = K_m f_{m-1}(n) + b_{m-1}(n-1) \tag{5.37}$$

Equations (5.37) and (5.40) now form the two recursive relations for the all-pole structure, shown in fig. 5.5. The transfer function between the input $u(n)$ and the output $\hat{s}(n)$ can be shown to be $1/A(z)$.

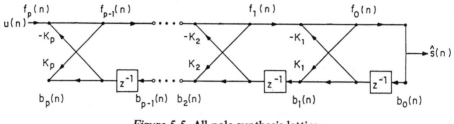

Figure 5.5 All-pole synthesis lattice

The structure in fig. 5.5 can be viewed as a model of a lossless acoustic tube with p sections of equal length but different areas A_m.[2,4] The coefficient K_m is then the reflection coefficient between sections m and $m-1$:

$$K_m = \frac{Z_m - Z_{m-1}}{Z_m + Z_{m-1}} = \frac{A_{m-1} - A_m}{A_{m-1} + A_m} \tag{5.41}$$

where Z_m is the characteristic impedance of the mth section. From (5.41), one can write

> **RELATIONSHIP BETWEEN REFLECTION COEFFICIENTS AND AREA RATIOS**
>
> $$\frac{A_{m-1}}{A_m} = \frac{1+K_m}{1-K_m}$$

$$\tag{5.42}$$

There have been some attempts to relate the area ratios represented by (5.42) to those of the actual human vocal tract.[15] While under certain conditions such a relation may be found, the problem of recovering the vocal-tract cross-sectional area from the speech signal alone is inherently an indeterminate problem.[16] In our view, it is best to think of the K_m as the reflection coefficients of an idealized acoustic tube, or alternatively as simply another parametric representation of an all-pole or all-zero model.

5.4.2 LATTICE ANALYSIS
A pth order all-pole model of a signal $s(n)$ can be obtained by inverse filtering $s(n)$ using the all-zero lattice in fig. 5.4 and finding those coefficients K_m that minimise the output residual energy. In general, the problem of determining the values of K_m that minimise the output energy is a non-linear problem. However, for the special case when the

input signal is windowed or is known for all time, the pth-order global minimisation problem can be solved as a sequence of p first-order local minimisation problems, one at each stage.[14] The procedure is given below.

Data windowing

Let F_m and B_m be the total energy of the forward and backward residual, respectively, at the output of stage m. Then, from (5.36) we have

$$F_m = \sum_n f_m^2(n)$$
$$= F_{m-1} + 2K_m \sum_n f_{m-1}(n) b_{m-1}(n-1) + K_m^2 B_{m-1} \tag{5.43}$$

where the summation over n is for all time. One can show that, if the signal is windowed, the energies of the forward and backward residuals are equal at each stage

$$F_m = B_m \tag{5.44}$$

Defining

PARCOR COEFFICIENTS

$$r_{m-1} = \frac{\sum_n f_{m-1}(n) b_{m-1}(n-1)}{\sqrt{\sum_n f_{m-1}^2(n) \sum_n b_{m-1}^2(n-1)}} \tag{5.45}$$

as the correlation coefficient between $f_{m-1}(n)$ and $b_{m-1}(n-1)$, and using (5.44) one has from (5.43):

$$F_m = (1 + 2r_{m-1} K_m + K_m^2) F_{m-1} \tag{5.46}$$

Setting the partial derivative of F_m with respect to K_m to zero, we obtain the result that the value of K_m that minimises F_m is given by

$$K_m = -r_{m-1} \tag{5.47}$$

or K_m is equal to the negative of the correlation between the input forward and backward residuals to stage m. These coefficients, r_m, are known in the statistical literature as the partial correlation coefficients. r_m is the partial correlation between $s(n)$ and $s(n+m)$ holding $s(n+1), \ldots, s(n+m-1)$ fixed. From (5.46) and (5.47) we also see that

$$F_m = (1 - K_m^2) F_{m-1}$$

which is the same as (5.25) in the Levinson–Durbin recursion. One can also show that (5.47) is identical to (5.23).

Since K_m is equal to a correlation coefficient, it must be less than one in magnitude. This is, of course, the same condition we obtained in the autocorrelation method. In fact, we have seen above that **lattice analysis is essentially a realisation of the Levinson–Durbin recursion, but without computing the predictor coefficients explicitly.** Actually, the Levinson–Durbin recursion can be implemented directly using the lattice if one uses the autocorrelation coefficients as the input to the lattice.[17] In particular, if we set

$$s(n) = \begin{cases} 0, & n < 0 \\ R(n), & n \geqslant 0 \end{cases} \tag{5.48}$$

in fig. 5.4, then we have from (5.38) and (5.39)

$$f_{m-1}(m) = \sum_{k=0}^{m-1} a_{m-1}(k)\, R(m-k)$$

$$b_{m-1}(m-1) = \sum_{k=0}^{m-1} a_{m-1}(m-1-k)\, R(m-1-k)$$

$$= \sum_{k=0}^{m-1} a_{m-1}(k)\, R(k) = E_{m-1}$$

Therefore, from (5.23) we have

CALCULATION OF K_m WHEN $R(n)$ IS INPUT TO THE LATTICE
$K_m = -\dfrac{f_{m-1}(m)}{b_{m-1}(m-1)}$

$$\tag{5.49}$$

This means that K_m can be computed by feeding the autocorrelation through the all-zero lattice as a signal. The value of K_1 is computed from (5.49) at time $n = 1$ at the inputs to stage 1, and, in general, the value of K_m is computed at $n = m$ from the inputs to stage m. This method avoids the computation of the predictor coefficients explicitly and has some very good properties for FWL implementations.[18]

Residual Windowing
We have seen in direct-form analysis that if the residual is windowed instead of the signal, the resulting all-pole filter is not guaranteed to be stable. Using the lattice, we shall see that, with residual windowing, one can guarantee a stable filter if the sum of the forward and backward residual energies is minimised at each stage.

Let the quantity to be minimised be given by

$$E_m = \sum_{n=-\infty}^{\infty} w_e(n) [f_m^2(n) + b_m^2(n)] \tag{5.50}$$

The result of minimising (5.50) with respect to K_m is:

$$K_m = -\frac{\sum_n w_e(n) f_{m-1}(n) b_{m-1}(n-1)}{\sum_n w_e(n) [f_{m-1}^2(n) + b_{m-1}^2(n-1)]/2} \tag{5.51}$$

One can show that $|K_m| \leqslant 1$ in (5.51) for non-negative $w_e(n)$. Equation (5.51) can be seen as an approximation to the correlation coefficient given in (5.45). Actually, Itakura used (5.51) as a short-term approximation to the partial correlation. In his work, Itakura[11] used the response of a single-pole filter as the weighting $w_e(n)$, while Burg[19] used a rectangular window.

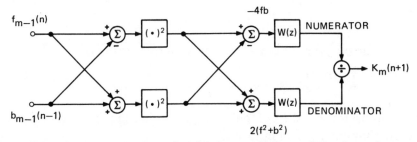

Figure 5.6 Adaptive estimation of reflection coefficients. Only the mth stage is shown; other stages have an identical structure

Equation (5.51) may be implemented adaptively as shown in fig. 5.6.[20] In this figure, given $f_{m-1}(n)$ and $b_{m-1}(n-1)$, **we can compute an estimate of K_m to be used at time $n+1$. In this way, we obtain a value of K_m at each time instant.** $W(z)$ in fig. 5.6 is a filter whose impulse response is the weighting window $w_e(n)$. If we write (5.51) as

> **ADAPTIVE ESTIMATION OF REFLECTION COEFFICIENTS (1)**
>
> $$K_m(n+1) = -\frac{C_m(n)}{D_m(n)}$$

$$\tag{5.52}$$

then if

$$W(z) = \frac{1}{1-\beta z^{-1}}, \qquad 0 \leqslant \beta \leqslant 1 \tag{5.53}$$

we have

ADAPTIVE ESTIMATION OF REFLECTION COEFFICIENTS (2)

$$C_m(n) = \beta C_m(n-1) + f_{m-1}(n)b_{m-1}(n-1) \qquad (5.54)$$

$$D_m(n) = \beta D_m(n-1) + [f_{m-1}^2(n) + b_{m-1}^2(n-1)]/2 \qquad (5.55)$$

Therefore, $K_m(n+1)$ can be computed adaptively with few computations. Equations similar to (5.54) and (5.55) can be written for multiple-pole weighting filters. Experimentally, it has been found that a double- or triple-pole weighting filter produces better speech quality than single-pole filters. For a multiple-pole filter

$$W(z) = \frac{1}{(1-\beta z^{-1})^M}, \qquad M = 1,2,3 \qquad (5.56)$$

it was found[20] that, for best speech quality, the value of β should be set to

WEIGHTING-FILTER PARAMETER FOR ADAPTIVE ESTIMATION

$$\beta \simeq 1-100MT \qquad (5.57)$$

where M is the number of poles in the weighting filter and T is the speech sampling interval in seconds.

If the computation of K_m is to be performed on a frame-by-frame basis rather than adaptively, there exist efficient ways of performing the computations in (5.51) which utilise the covariance of the input directly.[13]

There exist other lattice-type analysis methods in the literature[21] which have been shown to perform well for certain applications. However, those methods tend to be more complicated, are expensive computationally, and have not been shown to produce any perceptible difference in speech applications.

5.5 *Coding of LPC parameters*

In LPC transmission of speech or in playback of LPC speech, it is often very important to minimise the number of bits used to code the LP parameters. Below we present a number of LP representations and discuss their coding properties.

5.5.1 DIFFERENT REPRESENTATIONS

We have seen above that **the LP predictor may be specified uniquely by either the autocorrelation coefficients, predictor coefficients, or reflection coefficients.** Other unique representations include cepstral coefficients, selected spectral values, and the poles of $H(z)$. Previously, we have argued that the reflection coefficients or a simple transformation thereof have excellent properties for scalar quantisation of LP parameters. The most popular transformation is perhaps the *log-area-ratio* transformation[22,23]

$$L_m = \tfrac{1}{2} \log \frac{1 + K_m}{1 - K_m} = \tanh^{-1} K_m \qquad (5.58)$$

so called because of (5.42). Another transformation is[23,24]

$$J_m = \sin^{-1} K_m \qquad (5.59)$$

Both transformations expand the region near $|K_m| = 1$ because small changes in the value of K_m in that region cause relatively large changes in the spectrum. For coding purposes, one quantises either L_m or J_m uniformly. **The number of bits used to quantise each coefficient depends on the range of values for that coefficient. Typically, K_1, K_2 and K_3 are accorded the largest number of bits.**

A different set of coefficients has been proposed by Itakura,[25] which is claimed to have superior quantisation properties. This coding scheme transforms the set of p poles *inside* the unit circle to a set of p poles *on* the unit circle. In this manner, the new poles become automatically ordered by frequency (i.e. position on the unit circle), and hence one can collect the statistics needed for efficient coding. The new poles are actually computed from two polynomials that are obtained easily from the original LP polynomial. Let the LP polynomial of order p be given by (5.1). The LP polynomial of order $p+1$ is given by

$$A_{p+1}(z) = A_p(z) + K_{p+1} z^{-(p+1)} A_p(z^{-1}) \qquad (5.60)$$

where K_{p+1} is to be specified. The method consists of setting K_{p+1} to either $+1$ or -1, resulting in two polynomials:

$$A_{p+1}^{+}(z) = A_p(z) + z^{-(p+1)} A_p(z^{-1}) \qquad (5.61)$$

$$A_{p+1}^{-}(z) = A_p(z) - z^{-(p+1)} A_p(z^{-1})$$ (5.62)

The coefficients of $A^+(z)$ and $A^-(z)$ are thus obtained from the coefficients of $A_p(z)$ by simple additions and subtractions. The two new polynomials are guaranteed to have their poles interleaved *on* the unit circle. The resulting representation in terms of poles on the unit circle has been termed by Itakura as a 'line spectrum' representation. (The actual implementation involves the root computation for two transformed polynomials, each having $p/2$ roots on the real line between -1 and 1, which is much simpler than computing the $p+1$ complex roots of each of the two polynomials.) At the synthesis end, $A_p(z)$ is computed from (5.61) and (5.62) by simple addition

$$A_p(z) = [A_{p+1}^{+}(z) + A_{p+1}^{-}(z)]/2$$ (5.63)

Itakura has claimed that his line spectral representation has superior coding and interpolation properties. Interpolation is needed during synthesis if the parameters are transmitted less often than every 10 ms. Typically, LP parameters are transmitted every 20 ms, but the synthesis updates the all-pole filter parameters every 10 ms for smoother speech quality. The interpolated parameters are often obtained as the average of the two neighbouring sets of transmitted LP parameters.

5.5.2 VARIABLE FRAME RATE

Because speech consists of a number of quasi steady states connected by relatively fast transitions, one can save on parameter storage by coding LP parameters less often when the speech is changing slowly. This concept of variable frame rate (VFR)[26] has been used successfully to maximise speech quality at a given average bit rate. Typically, one detects the changes in parameters from one frame to another and transmits only if there is a significant change. Fairly good speech quality has been obtained at bit rates close to 1000 bits/s.

5.5.3 VECTOR QUANTISATION

To maintain good speech quality at bit rates much lower than 1000 bits/s, one must resort to vector quantisation of LP parameters.[27,28] In vector quantisation, one considers the LP parameters as a vector in p-dimensional space. If B bits are available per frame, one divides the space into 2^B regions or clusters and finds for each frame the region that contains each particular LP vector. The vector is then quantised to the centre of that region, computed using some distance measure.

One popular distance measure is the Itakura–Saito distance[3,29] defined by:

$$d_1(\mathbf{a}_x, \mathbf{a}_y) = \frac{\mathbf{a}_y^T \mathbf{R}_x \mathbf{a}_y}{\mathbf{a}_x^T \mathbf{R}_x \mathbf{a}_x} \qquad (5.64)$$

where

$$\mathbf{a}_x = [1\, a_x(1)a_x(2)\ldots a_x(p)]^T, \quad \mathbf{a}_y = [1\, a_y(1)a_y(2)\ldots a_y(p)]^T,$$

and $\mathbf{R}_x$ is the autocorrelation matrix whose corresponding optimal predictor is given by $\mathbf{a}_x$. Note that the denominator in (5.64) is equal to the minimum residual energy. The distance measure in (5.64) is not a metric; in particular it is not symmetric, i.e. $d(\mathbf{a}_x, \mathbf{a}_y) \neq d(\mathbf{a}_y, \mathbf{a}_x)$. The measure can be made symmetric, but the distance computation doubles. Another simple distance measure that is a metric is the Euclidean distance between log-area-ratios

$$d_2(\mathbf{L}_x, \mathbf{L}_y) = \|\mathbf{L}_x - \mathbf{L}_y\|^2 \qquad (5.65)$$

where $\mathbf{L}_x$ and $\mathbf{L}_y$ are vectors of log-area-ratios and $\|\cdot\|$ denotes the Euclidean norm. Experimentally, we have found that the speech quality is the same whether one uses d_1 or d_2 as the distance measure.

Having chosen a distance measure, one divides the p-dimensional space into 2^B regions. This is done by one of several established pattern recognition clustering algorithms.[30] Each region is then represented by its centre of mass, c_i, $1 \leqslant i \leqslant 2^B$. Given an input parameter vector, one then quantises it to that vector c_i that is closest to it, using the chosen distance measure. If $B = 10$ bits, there are 1024 distance calculations to be made for each frame. One can reduce the number of computations by dividing up the parameter space in a binary fashion. That is, the space is divided first into two regions, then each region is divided into two, etc. In this fashion, one needs to make only $2B$ distance computations per frame (or 20 distances per frame for our example). This vast reduction in computation is gained at the expense of a larger quantisation error. However, for real-time speech coding, such a trade off may be necessary. In our experience, with binary coding we lose about 0.5 bits per frame when compared to optimal coding. **When compared with optimal scalar quantisation, vector quantisation at 10 bits gave similar results to scalar quantisation using 15 bits.** This 5-bit gain is achieved at an increase in computations and a substantial increase in storage. Note that one needs at least 2^B vectors to be stored for vector quantisation purposes. This storage requirement renders vector quantisation impractical for large values of B.

Another issue of concern in vector quantisation is the amount of speech data needed for the training or clustering operation. A general rule of thumb is that one needs about fifty vectors per cluster, so that the resulting clusters are reliable. For $B = 10$ bits, one requires about 17 minutes of speech, assuming 20 ms frames. For every additional bit, the amount of training data needed is doubled. One could, of course, use fewer sample vectors per cluster, but then the speech quality will not be uniform for all sounds or across speakers.

Using data from a single speaker, good speech quality and intelligibility has been achieved at 400 bits/s with vector quantisation.[28] Further reductions in bit rate are possible using *segment quantisation*, where the vector to be quantised includes several frames of speech.[31]

5.6 *Linear prediction in speech recognition*[32]

One of the principal tools in the automatic recognition of speech has been the use of the short-term power spectrum. The spectrum has been used in different ways to achieve the desired recognition. Spectral 'template matching', where a new spectrum is classified (i.e. recognised) by matching it against a stored set of templates, has been a very simple, widely used and often effective method of recognition. Other recognition systems have attempted to extract salient features of the spectrum and then compare those features against stored values. Examples of such features include formants (resonances of the vocal tract), antiformants, regions of maximum energy concentration, regions of maximum spectral slope, spectral dynamic range, etc. The choice of which type or types of analysis to employ in a particular recognition system is often a function of ease of implementation, cost, speed, accuracy of recognition, scope of the recognition problem, and also knowledge of the acoustics of speech and speech production.

Given a set of LP parameters, a spectrum $\hat{P}(\omega)$ defined in (5.33) can be computed at all frequencies. This model spectrum can be viewed as a smooth version of the speech short-term spectrum. Starting from such a spectrum, one could then use any of the many traditional methods to do speech recognition. However, certain LP parameter representations allow for simple distance measures that can be used if one plans to use the template matching approach to speech recognition.[29,33] We have already mentioned the Itakura–Saito distance and the Euclidean distance on log-area-ratios; both distance measures have been used effectively in speech recognition tasks. Another popular distance measure for speech recognition is the Euclidean distance used with cepstral coefficients. Given a set of predictor coefficients, the cepstrum $c(n)$, which is the Fourier transform of the log spectrum, can be computed iteratively from

$$c(n) = a(n) - \sum_{k=1}^{n-1} \frac{k}{n} c(k) a(n-k), \qquad 1 \leqslant n \leqslant p \tag{5.66}$$

One can then use either $c(n)$ or $nc(n)$ as basis coefficients for recognition.

References

1. Makhoul, J. (1975) 'Linear prediction: A tutorial review'. *Proc. IEEE* **63**, 561–580.
2. Atal, B.S. and Hanauer, S.L. (1971) 'Speech analysis and synthesis by linear prediction of the speech wave'. *J. Acoust. Soc. Amer.* **50**, 637–655.
3. Itakura, F. and Saito, S. (1970) 'A statistical method for estimation of speech spectral density and formant frequencies'. *Electron. Commun. Japan* **53**-A, 36–43.
4. Markel, J.D. and Gray, A.H., Jr. (1976) *Linear Prediction of Speech*. New York: Springer-Verlag.
5. Oppenheim, A.V. and Schafer, R.W. (1975) *Digital Signal Processing*. Englewood Cliffs, N.J.: Prentice-Hall.
6. Makhoul, J., Viswanathan, R., Schwartz, R., and Huggins, A W.F. (1978) 'A mixed-source model for speech compression and synthesis'. *J. Acoust. Soc. Amer.* **64**, 1577–1581.
7. Harris, F.J. (1978) 'On the use of windows for harmonic analysis with the discrete Fourier transform'. *Proc. IEEE* **66**, 51–83.
8. Levinson, N. (1947) 'The Wiener RMS (root mean square) error criterion in filter design and prediction'. *J. Math. Phys.* **25**, 261–278. Also Appendix B, in Wiener, N. (1949) *Extrapolation, Interpolation and Smoothing of Stationary Time Series*. Cambridge, Mass.: MIT Press.
9. Durbin, J. (1959) 'Efficient estimation of parameters in moving-average models'. *Biometrika* **46**, 306–316.
10. Reddy, D.R. (Ed.) (1975) *Speech Recognition*. New York: Academic Press. Atal, B.S. Linear prediction of speech – recent advances with applications to speech analysis', 221–230.
11. Itakura, F. and Saito, S. (1971) 'Digital filtering techniques for speech analysis and synthesis'. *Conference Record, 7th Int. Congr. Acoustics*, paper 25-C-1.
12. Gray, A.H., Jr. and Markel, J.D. (1973) 'Digital lattice and ladder filter synthesis'. *IEEE Trans. Audio and Electroacoustics* **AU-21**,

491–500. Also Gray, A.H., Jr. and Markel, J.D. (1975) 'A normalized digital filter structure'. *IEEE Trans. Acoustics, Speech, and Signal Processing* **ASSP-23**, 268–277.

13. Makhoul, J. (1977) 'Stable and efficient lattice methods for linear prediction'. *IEEE Trans. Acoustics, Speech, and Signal Processing* **ASSP-25**, 423–428.

14. Makhoul, J. (1978) 'A class of all-zero lattice digital filters: properties and applications'. *IEEE Trans. Acoustics, Speech, and Signal Processing* **ASSP-26**, 304–314.

15. Wakita, H. (1973) 'Direct estimation of the vocal tract shape by inverse filtering of acoustic speech waveforms'. *IEEE Trans. Audio and Electroacoustics* **AU-21**, 417–427. Also, chapter 4 of reference 4.

16. Sondhi, M.M. (1979) 'Estimation of vocal-tract areas: The need for acoustical measurements'. *IEEE Trans. Acoustics, Speech, and Signal Processing* **ASSP-27**, 268–273.

17. LeRoux, J. and Gueguen, C. (1977) 'A fixed point computation of partial correlation coefficients'. *IEEE Trans. Acoustics, Speech, and Signal Processing* **ASSP-25**, 257–259.

18. Rajasekaran, P.K. and Hansen, J.C. (1982) 'Finite word length effects of the LeRoux–Gueguen algorithm in computing reflection coefficients'. *Proceedings of the IEEE International Conference on Acoustics, Speech, and Signal Processing, Paris, France*, 1286–1290.

19. Burg, J. (1975) *Maximum Entropy Spectral Analysis*. PhD. dissertation, Stanford Univ., Stanford, CA.

20. Makhoul, J. and Cosell, L.K. (1981) 'Adaptive lattice analysis of speech'. *IEEE Trans. Acoustics, Speech, and Signal Processing* **ASSP-29**, 654–659.

21. Friedlander, B. (1982) 'Lattice filters for adaptive processing'. *Proc. IEEE* **70**, 829–867.

22. Viswanathan, R. and Makhoul, J. (1975) 'Quantization properties of transmission parameters in linear predictive systems'. *IEEE Trans. Acoustics, Speech, and Signal Processing* **ASSP-23**, 309–321.

23. Tohkura, Y. and Itakura, F. (1979) 'Spectral sensitivity analysis of PARCOR parameters for speech data compression'. *IEEE Trans. Acoustics, Speech, and Signal Processing* **ASSP-27**, 273–280.

24. Gray, A.H., Jr., Gray, R.M., and Markel, J.D. (1977) 'Comparison of optimal quantizations of speech reflection coefficients'. *IEEE Trans. Acoustics, Speech, and Signal Processing* **ASSP-25**, 9–23.

25. Itakura, F. (1975) Line spectrum representation of linear predictor coefficients of speech signal'. *Trans. Comm. Speech Research*

(Acoustical Society of Japan), No. S75–34 (*in Japanese*). Also see House, A. (ed.) (1981) *Proceedings of a symposium on Acoustic Phonetics and Speech Modeling.* Princeton, New Jersey : Institute for Defence Analyses. Fujisaki, H. 'Review of some Japanese work at Electrocommunication Laboratories (Nippon Telephone and Telegraph Company) on speech analysis–synthesis using pseudo-formants', paper F6.

26. Viswanathan, V.R., Makhoul, J., Schwartz, R.M., and Huggins, A.W.F. (1982) 'Variable frame rate transmission : A review of methodology and application to narrow-band LPC speech coding'. *IEEE Trans. Communications* **COM-30**, 674–686.

27. Buzo, A., Gray, A.H., Jr., Gray, R.M., and Markel, J.D. (1980) Speech coding based upon vector quantization'. *IEEE Trans. Acoustics, Speech, and Signal Processing* **ASSP-28**, 562–574.

28. Roucos, S., Schwartz, R., and Makhoul, J. (1982) 'Vector quantization for very-low-rate coding of speech'. *Proceedings of IEEE GLOBECOM-82*, Miami, F.L.

29. Itakura, F. (1975) 'Minimum prediction residual principle applied to speech recognition'. *IEEE Trans. Acoustics, Speech, and Signal Processing* **ASSP-23**, 67–72.

30. Anderberg, M.R. (1973) *Clustering Analysis for Applications.* New York: Academic Press.

31. Roucos, S., Schwartz, R., and Makhoul, J. (1982) 'Segment quantization for very-low-rate speech coding'. *Proceedings of the IEEE International Conference on Acoustics, Speech, and Signal Processing, Paris, France*, 1565–1568.

32. Reddy, D.R. (Ed.) (1975) *Speech Recognition.* New York : Academic Press. Makhoul, J. 'Linear prediction in automatic speech recognition', 181–220.

33. Myers, C.S. and Rabiner, L.R. (1981) 'A level building dynamic time warping algorithm for connected word recognition'. *IEEE Trans. Acoustics, Speech, and Signal Processing* **ASSP-29**, 284–297.

CHAPTER 6

TEXT TO SPEECH

Michael Dilts

In this chapter some of the elements of phonology are restated and used to work through a practical example of text-to-speech.

6.1 *Preliminaries*

In reviewing the various waveform analysis techniques currently available for commercial use it is necessary to bear in mind that language is itself a system for encoding and transmitting information. While a spoken message can indeed be characterised by reference to the properties of the associated acoustic signal, the content of the message is quite independent of the shape of its waveform. In fact, as is illustrated by the article you are reading at this very moment, words can be understood without ever being realised as sound.

Language conveys meaning by stringing together discrete symbolic units at several concurrent levels. Sequences of sounds form words, words are organised into phrases, and phrases are assembled into sentences. The combination of these units is governed at each level by a set of principles or *rules* which are, like the actual units themselves, language-specific. The science of linguistics provides rigorous methods for identifying these principles and representing them in a formal manner.

Regardless of which voice output technology is employed in a particular system, the multi-level structure of the linguistic message supports a number of possible strategies for their storage and retrieval. Suppose, for the sake of an example, that a vending machine application requires synthesis of the following sentence: *Please deposit thirty-five pence.* One option would be to analyse the message in its entirety and reference it as a single block of data. It could also be broken apart into two phrases *Please deposit . . .* and *. . . thirty-five pence*, or into five individual words which would then be called up one after the other to speak the full sentence: *please, deposit, thirty, five, pence*. Some of the words could even be decomposed into prefixes, suffixes, and roots which appear in other words as well:

DEPOSIT = DE- (DE-TECT, DE-RIVE) + POSIT

THIRTY = THIR- (THIR-TEEN) + -TY (TWEN-TY)

The most radical alternative would be to encode a set of sounds from which words and parts of words may be patched together as needed.

Application of the last option to a vocabulary of sufficient size would eventually yield a complete inventory of phonetic building blocks from which any English word could be constructed. Such an inventory, combined with algorithms for selecting sounds and stringing them together on the basis of ordinary English spelling, would eliminate the necessity for further waveform analysis. The result would be a system capable of synthesising words and phrases from arbitrary text input, *Text-to-Speech*.

6.2 *Segment storage strategies*

SENTENCE STORAGE

Each of the encoding strategies outlined above has advantages and disadvantages which render it more or less suitable for a given application. Analysis at the sentence level usually has as its starting point a live speaker whose voice is recorded with the desired inflection and 'personality' (friendly, authoritative, soothing, etc.) and then processed to derive a matrix of parameters from which the original utterance may be reconstructed. This 'play-back' function is no different in essence from traditional analog recording, but is compatible with digital circuitry and is achieved at data rates as low as 700–2400 bits per second of stored speech. Because it preserves the intonational patterns of the human speaker intact, sentence storage offers the highest level of *naturalness* currently possible for synthetic speech.

WORD AND PHRASE STORAGE

Most real-life applications require greater flexibility than is available from a sentence-based system. Returning to our hypothetical talking vending machine, a real design would most likely have to accommodate products costing more or less than thirty-five pence, as well as price increases due to inflation. Even with the assumption that prices will always be divisible by five and will never exceed ninety-five pence, it would obviously be an inefficient use of memory space to store a separate sentence for every possible combination of coins:

(1) Please deposit five pence.
(2) Please deposit ten pence.
(3) Please deposit fifteen pence.

    .

    .

    .

(19) Please deposit ninety-five pence.

(Total word count = 84)

Storing the repeated phrase *Please deposit. . .* only once reduces the number of words to be stored from 84 to 48 but a word-level approach is even more economical, requiring a total of 14 items:

(1) Please	(6) Twenty	(11) Seventy
(2) Deposit	(7) Thirty	(12) Eighty
(3) Five	(8) Forty	(13) Ninety
(4) Ten	(9) Fifty	(14) Pence
(5) Fifteen	(10) Sixty	

The phrase-level and word-level strategies need not, of course, be mutually exclusive. In this particular example we could retain *Please deposit. . .* as a phrase and generate the remainder of each message from individual words. This not only costs nothing in terms of word count, but frees up memory that would otherwise be dedicated to address storage.

Contextual variation
Dissection of sentences into words and phrases is not as straightforward a process as the simplicity of the above example might suggest. In natural speech, words blend together as a continuous stream of sound. Neighbouring words influence one another, especially when they occur within the same syntactic unit. The second syllable of *twenty*, for example, is shortened considerably before another number. The final /t/ of *deposit* will tend to merge completely with the initial /t/ of *ten* or *twenty*, but will sound like a /d/ before the beginning vowel of *eighty*.

Another problem is that in English, at least, variation in intonation and duration provide important clues about *syntactic structure*, as well as indicating where a speaker wishes to place emphasis. Consider, for example a sentence like *The boy hit the ball*. As indicated by the final full-stop (period), it is a declarative sentence, a statement of fact. If the sentence were read aloud, a native speaker of English would indicate this by introducing a steady fall in pitch throughout the utterance, so that *ball* would reach a level much lower than that of *boy*. Reversing the order of the two words without changing their pitch would produce a rising intonation contour and change the statement into a question: *The ball hit the boy?* Slapping together words and phrases from different sentences recorded at different times can also result in a choppy, 'sing-song' effect, since the pitch and duration of the words will not necessarily match.

Where the total range of syntactic variation from message to message can be determined in advance, as with our vending machine, contextual variation of the type described above may be accounted for by processing and storing multiple versions of each word. Memory size, however, will not always accommodate redundancy on this scale. In such cases, and in those cases where syntax is not fixed, the only alternative is to ignore context altogether and opt for 'neutral' inflection, which usually results in a completely flat (i.e. monotone) intonation contour. Naturally, the resulting speech will sound 'machine-like' and artificial rather than human, although the individual words may be perfectly intelligible.

STORING PARTS OF WORDS

The problem of contextual variation becomes more acute at the sub-word level. Addition of the plural suffix to a set of nouns increases the total number of words which can be generated by that set by a factor of two (somewhat less than two if 'irregular' plurals like *geese, children*, etc., are involved). The situation, however, is somewhat less straightforward than conventional spelling might suggest. In the word *days*, for example, the plural suffix is written with the letter *s*, but pronounced as a /z/-sound, and in *glasses* or *lashes* a vowel is inserted before the /z/. Selection of one of these three versions of the plural suffix for a particular word is not arbitrary, but depends upon the final sound present in the singular. After /p/, /t/, /k/, /f/, and /θ/ (*th* as in *month*), the /s/-sound occurs. A vowel is inserted after /s/, /ʃ/ (*sh*), /tʃ/ (*ch*) and /dʒ/ (the 'soft' g-sound as in *messages*). Plain /z/ occurs everywhere else.

In order to generate the correct plural forms of regular nouns, then, it is not only necessary to store all three variants of the suffix, but to know when and where to use each of them, i.e. to implement the linguistic rule which governs their distribution. Complications of this type are quite common in English. The suffix which forms the past tense of 'regular' verbs, spelled *-ed*, is also realised in three different ways: /t/ as in *baked*, vowel plus /d/ as in *dated*, and /d/ as in *flagged*. The prefix *pro-* can have a 'long' vowel (*pronoun*), a 'short' vowel (*proverb*), and a reduced vowel (*pronunciation*). Somewhat more obvious are the changes undergone by the negative prefix *in-*, as in *intractable*, which is spelled (and pronounced) *im-* before /p/, /b/, and /m/ (*impossible, imbalance, immoral*). A third version of the prefix which is not reflected in the spelling can be heard in words like *incredible*, where *in-* is pronounced as if it were *ing-*.

Even when the correct variant of a prefix or suffix has been selected, there remains the problem of matching its intonation to that of the word to which it is attached. Discontinuities from word to word detract from a sentence's *naturalness*. Occurring within a word, they impact on *intelligibility* as well.

CONSTRUCTIVE SYNTHESIS

The advantage of going a step beyond building words from word-elements and attempting to assemble the word-elements themselves from a set of stored speech sounds is that one is then no longer limited to a fixed vocabulary. Provided with access to a complete phonetic inventory, one can theoretically synthesise any word in a given language. While it is customary to contrast the sound-based approach, so-called *Constructive Synthesis*, with all other encoding strategies, usually lumped together under the term *Synthesis-by-Analysis*, it should be obvious from the above discussion that this distinction is somewhat artificial. Words can be constructed' from word-elements; sentences and phrases can be 'constructed' from words. At the same time, analysed speech is the direct or indirect source for any phonetic inventory. The essential differences lie in the number of elements stored and in the amount of linguistic information which must be incorporated into the stringing algorithms.

Just as words and word-elements are influenced by the contexts in which they appear, speech sounds are influenced by surrounding sounds, as well as by word and phrase boundaries. The total number of possible sound-combinations is quite large, and real-life implementations tend to ignore some or all of the inner details of contextual variation in assembling a phonetic inventory. Unless it is limited to the generation of isolated words, a complete Constructive Synthesis system will not only require the logic necessary for selection and concatenation of speech sounds but must also take account of the same environmental effects at the word and sentence level encountered by other strategies. Even when the principles involved are well understood, which is not always the case, it is often impractical to apply all relevant linguistic knowledge due to limitations in memory capacity and hardware capability. If the system is to be made accessible to users untrained in phonetic transcription, procedures must also be provided for automatically deriving from ordinary text input a list of the sounds to be drawn from the phonetic inventory. This adds to the processing burden and contributes yet another layer of complexity – another opportunity for errors to be introduced.

The quality of speech generated by Constructive Synthesis varies widely from system to system, depending on the size of the phonetic inventory, the complexity of the stringing algorithms, and the levels at which linguistic information is applied. While an intelligibility rate of up to 99%, as measured for isolated words by the *Modified Rhyme Test*, has been claimed for some systems,[1] none has yet proven capable of anything which could be described as 'natural' speech. Whether attributed with an obscure foreign accent, or accused of being 'robotic', the currently implementable systems appear to be in no imminent danger of being mistaken for a live native speaker, much less for a specific speaker. However, recent product offerings have shown that constructive synthesis can be perfectly adequate for many applications (see section 12.4).

EVALUATION OF APPROACHES
The problem of selecting a synthesis approach for a specific application can be expressed in terms of a trade-off between the two basic factors of overall speech *quality* (including *naturalness* as well as *intelligibility*) and *flexibility*. 'Flexibility' in this sense refers to a system's capacity for generating different messages from a finite set of stored data. As flexibility increases, quality decreases. For applications involving a relatively limited number of messages and a fixed vocabulary, storage of words and phrases requires no sacrifice in quality provided that context is properly accounted for. If the synthetic voice must have a particular personality or be recognised as that of a celebrity, Synthesis-by-Analysis is really the only option. The same applies to telecom applications where the consumer expects to hear a human voice.

The *sound*-based constructive approach is appropriate, on the other hand, when the necessity for storing an extremely large vocabulary outweighs any consideration for what the synthetic voice sounds like. This holds true, of course, for many applications: talking books, talking computer terminals, aids for the speech-handicapped (including victims of cerebral palsy, laryngectomy patients) etc. Further discussion of the quality trade-off for different applications is given in chapter 14.

6.3 *Building a text-to-speech system*

As intimated in the previous section, the automatic conversion of arbitrary text input to voice output, often referred to as *Synthesis-by-Rule*, actually involves two separate tasks. The first consists of accepting a sequence of characters, identifying the phonetic components of the required message, and extracting information about its syntactic structure. The output of this stage, then, will be an intermediate string of symbols representing sound-units and boundaries between words, phrases, and sentences. The second part of the process is to match the symbols up with items stored in the phonetic inventory, link them together, and send the resulting coded waveform to a voice output device for decoding.

PHONETIC SYMBOLS

The first task, that of *text interpretation*, is not necessarily a trivial one. The spelling system (or *orthography*) of present-day English, for example, is an awkward and unwieldy affair, as any veteran of grammar-school spelling tests would agree. Convention has failed to keep pace with the rate of phonetic change, so that English not only makes contrasts which are no longer necessary (e.g. *y* in *fly* vs *ie* in *tie*), but also neglects many contrasts which are linguistically meaningful (e.g. *th* in *thin* vs *th* in *then*). A notorious but instructive illustration of these shortcomings comes to us from George Bernard Shaw, who used the letters *ghoti* to spell *fish* – from *gh* as in *cough*, *o* as in *women*, and *ti* as in *nation*.

Because of such inadequacies, which are present to some degree in the writing systems of other languages but seem to be epitomised in that of English, students of natural language have devised a special set of phonetic symbols. These symbols, known as the *International Phonetic Alphabet*, (IPA) allow the unambiguous representation of speech sounds and have the further advantage of being applicable to any language in the world. The IPA is based upon a scientific classification of sounds according to the configurations assumed by the tongue, teeth, lips, etc., during their production. A detailed account of the features used in phonetic classification was supplied in chapter 3 and the system of symbols developed there will be used throughout this text.

PHONEMES

From the set of all the sounds which the human vocal tract is capable of producing, each language uses only a rather limited number to produce contrasts in meaning. For example, English recognises /b/ and

/d/ as distinctive sound-units, so that native speakers perceive a difference between pairs like *big* and *dig*. Because a difference is heard, these
words can be used to represent different concepts. Linguists have
attempted to explain the mechanism by which human beings encode
meaning into sound and decode sound into meaning by hypothesising
the existence of intermediary units called *phonemes*. Phonemes are
abstract units which are assumed to operate in the psychological
rather than in the physical domain – they cannot be pronounced.

In spite of their abstractness, phonemes are defined in terms of
features which characterise real sounds. In a sense, they are sounds
for which only the most important features have been specified and
the rest left to be filled in later. Consequently, it is possible to represent
phonemes by means of IPA symbols, as was defined in tables 3.3 and
3.4 for English. Remember also that in order to distinguish them from
actual sounds, phonemic symbols are customarily enclosed within slanted
lines (/ /). Square brackets ([ ]) are reserved for pronounceable symbols.

ALLOPHONES
Sounds, like sound itself, cannot occur in a vacuum. There is always
context to be reckoned with, even if the context is silence. As phonemes
are generated one by one during normal speech production, each of
them tends to take on some characteristics of other phonemes in the
immediate vicinity. In informal conversation, for example, a phrase
like *Did you eat yet?* ends up sounding more like *Didja eachett?* (Note
that this *General American* phrase may be transcribed phonetically
as /dɪdʒə itʃɛt/ – see chapter 3). This transformation goes more or
less unnoticed by the average speaker of English, because phonetic
adjustments of this type are compensated for automatically. Linguists
believe that it is possible to identify for each language of the world a
finite set of rules approximating those which native speakers uncon-
sciously employ.

The *phonological rule*, then, is the mechanism by which the precise
phonetic characteristics of a phoneme are 'filled in' for a specific context. The actual sound (or *phone*) produced by operation of a rule
is called an *allophone* of the phoneme in question. Since their identity
is predictable from context, given a properly formulated rule set,
allophones cannot be used to make contrasts in meaning. It is at the
phonemic level that variation is unpredictable and that information is
conveyed. Approaching the problem from a somewhat different angle,
it is possible to define a phoneme as a collection of allophones. Under
this interpretation, the function of the rule set is to select the allophone
which is appropriate to a particular phonetic context.

Allophonic alternation

Listen carefully to the [t] sounds in the words *top* and *stop*. They are not the same. The [t] in *top* is followed by what seems to be a rush of air before the vowel sound begins. This feature, known as *aspiration*, is absent after the [t] in *stop*. Yet, to the native speaker of English, these very different types of [t] are perceptually the same sound. They are allophones of the phoneme /t/. Additional allophones of /t/ include the final, unreleased [t] in *pot*, the word-medial, lightly aspirated [t] in *batter* and unreleased [t] before a consonant, as in *motley*.

The /k/ phoneme in English not only has aspirated and unaspirated variants, but is also influenced by a following vowel. Pronounce the following words one after the other: *keep, cup, coop*. You should feel the point of contact between the back of your tongue and the roof of your mouth move further back for each successive /k/-sound. This movement may appear to be quite subtle, but to a speaker of Russian, for example, the difference between [k] in *keep* and [k] in *cup* would be as significant as that between /k/ and /t/.

Vowels are also subject to allophonic alternation. In most varieties of English, all vowels tend to be shorter before voiceless consonants like /p/, /t/, and /k/ than before their voiced counterparts, /b/, /d/, /g/. Before nasal consonants, /m/, /n/, /ŋ/, anticipation of future articulatory requirements leads to a slight nasalisation of vowel sounds. In English, nasality in vowels is an allophonic rather than a phonemic feature and therefore goes unnoticed. The situation is different in French, where nasalisation alone can signal a contrast in meaning: cf. French *mot* 'word' vs *mon* 'my'.

SPELLING RULES

The rule concept turns out to be a useful one for text interpretation as well as phoneme-to-allophone mapping. While spelling has only loose, primarily historical connections with phonetic reality, its purpose is, after all, to represent a linguistic message. Consider the familiar maxim *i before e except after c*, which is nothing less than a rule disguised as doggerel verse. Unfortunately, the vagaries of English spelling are capable of eluding any rule set, no matter how well formulated. It is ironic that some of the most common words in the language contain blatant violations of the general principles. In order to take advantage of what regularities English orthography does possess without wreaking havoc upon the pronunciation of such items, it is necessary to compile a list of the significant exceptions, specifying the correct phoneme composition for each so that the rule set may be by-passed when necessary.

SYNTAX PARSING

Further obstacles to the development of a rule set for interpreting English spelling are provided by pairs of words which are spelled the same but pronounced differently — for example, *lead* (*Lead* us not into temptation.) vs *lead* (the metal) or *live* (*Live* and let *live*) vs *live* (A *live* programme). The only real solution to this problem would be to devise an algorithm capable of determining the syntactic structure of a given sentence and assigning each word to its proper grammatical category, so that *lead* number one is classified as a verb and *lead* number two as a noun or adjective. Unfortunately, automatic text *parsers* are not only computationally expensive but are also notoriously unreliable, even for relatively simple sentences. Without access to the meanings of the words, it is nearly impossible to find a structural difference between *I don't want to eat this morning* and *I don't want to eat this mouldy cheese*. The most sophisticated parser available would be stumped by the ambiguity of a typical newspaper headline: *Beating Witness Provides Names!* We must therefore be content to let statistics be our guide in deciding which rules to apply to *lead* or *live*. Unless the target system is a good-sized mini-computer, it is safest to restrict the parsing function to the identification of major boundaries, most of which will already be indicated in the text by standard punctuation marks.

FUNCTIONAL COMPONENTS

The outlines of a possible Text-to-Speech system based on linguistic principles should now come into sharper focus. The initial translation of text characters to sound-units can be accomplished by a set of rules which convert letters to phonemes based upon their immediate environment within a word. This rule set must be augmented by a 'dictionary' which associates exceptional text strings with appropriate phoneme strings. A simple strategy for identifying word boundaries would involve replacing spaces, commas, full-stops (periods), etc., with phonetic symbols which are then part of the input to subsequent rule sets (see fig. 6.1).

It would obviously be inefficient to have separate entries in the *exceptions dictionary* for words like *live, lived, living*, which are formed by adding suffixes to the same root. If these words are broken down into their component parts, or *morphemes*, only a single entry *liv-* is necessary, since final *-e*, *-ed*, and *-ing* will be interpreted correctly by the general rules. Such a *morpheme stripping* function is also useful for the specification of rule contexts.

Yet another function to be included in the text interpretation component of our Text-to-Speech system is the expansion of abbreviations

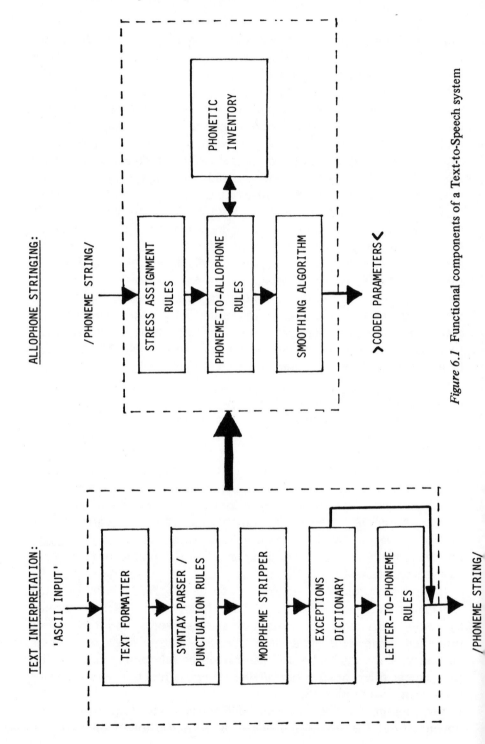

Figure 6.1 Functional components of a Text-to-Speech system

and special symbols. We may take such short-cuts as *Mr, Mrs, Dr*, for granted, but our rule set cannot. Pound or dollar signs, decimal points, plus and minus signs — all of these are frequently encountered in running text and must somehow be converted to spoken form. This can be accomplished by simply including such items in the exceptions dictionary or by implementing a text formatting module which will convert *MR* to *MISTER* at the text level before submitting the string to the next rule set.

Within the second major component of the generalised system we are constructing, a set of smaller functional units may likewise be defined. Based on the intermediate phonetic representation supplied by the text interpretation component, a string of allophones must be selected. In other words, we need a set of *phoneme-to-allophone rules*. Allophonic variation in English vowels is determined by syllabic stress as well as by the identity of neighbouring phonemes. Placement of stress is conditioned to a large degree by word structure and it is possible to develop a set of *stress assignment rules* applying at the phoneme level and preceding the phoneme-to-allophone rules. In a real application, an allophone string will most likely consist of a table of vectors into a set of stored parameters derived from speech waveform analysis. Before passing a set of parameters to a voice output device for synthesis, it is usually necessary to provide interpolation logic so that the transitions from one allophone to the next will be relatively smooth.

6.4 *Inside a rule set*

FORMAL CONVENTIONS

The way in which a rule set is actually implemented will largely depend on the programming language used, the data structures chosen by the program, and the hardware available on the target system. The initial specification of the rules can be facilitated by application of a well-defined set of formal conventions developed by linguists for just this purpose. Consider, for example, the following statement:

$$A \Rightarrow B / X \_ Y$$

Here 'A' represents the input and 'B' the output of a rule. The arrow indicates the direction of the process and may be translated into prose as *is replaced by* or *becomes*. The material to the right of the slash mark identifies the context in which the rule applies. Specifically, 'X' represents the left environment and 'Y' the right environment.

ADDITIONAL SYMBOLS

To describe completely the rule sets outlined in the previous section, it will be necessary to make use of a set of phonetic symbols covering the full range of allophonic variation. In addition to the phoneme symbol /t/, for example, we need [T″] (initial aspirated /t/), [T] (unaspirated /t/), [T#] (final, unreleased /t/), [T′] (medial aspirated /t/) and [T*] (unreleased /t/ before a consonant). For the purpose of convenience and efficiency, we will also want to introduce a set of *cover symbols* at both the textual and the phonemic levels. Cover symbols make it possible to collapse rules which operate on the same input and generate the same output in similar environments. For example, using the symbol /<V1>/ to represent any vowel phoneme makes it quite simple to write a rule selecting the allophone [T′] when /t/ is followed by a vowel:

$$ /t/ \Rightarrow [T'] \quad /\_/<V1>/ $$

The alternative would be to write a separate rule for each vowel

$$ /t/ \Rightarrow [T'] \quad / \quad \_/i/ $$
$$ /t/ \Rightarrow [T'] \quad / \quad \_/ɪ/ $$
$$ /t/ \Rightarrow [T'] \quad / \quad \_/ɛ/ \quad (etc.) $$

Some cover symbols are shown in table 6.1.

Table 6.1 Cover symbol definition table

Cover symbols for text characters:

(1)	<V1> =	'A', 'E', 'I', 'O', 'U'
(2)	<V2> =	<V1>, <V1><V1>, <V1><V1><V1>, <V1><V1><V1><V1>
(3)	<C1> =	'B', 'C', 'D', 'F', 'G', 'H', 'J', 'K', 'L', 'M', 'N', 'P', 'Q', 'R', 'S', 'T', 'V', 'W', 'Z', 'PH', 'SH', 'TH', 'CH'
(4)	<C2> =	<C1>, <C1><C1>, <C1><C1><C1>, <C1><C1><C1><C1>, 'X'
(5)	<F/S> =	'F', 'S'
(6)	<+/#> =	'+', '#'

Cover symbols for phoneme symbols (following table 3.4 for RP English):

(1)	/<V1>/ =	/i:/, /ɪ/, /ɛ/, /æ/, /a:/, /ɒ/, /ʌ/, /ɔ:/, /ə/, /ʊ/, /u:/, /ɜ:/, /eɪ/, /aɪ/, /ɔɪ/, /aʊ/, /əʊ/, /ɪə/, /ɛə/, /ʊə/
(2)	/<Y/W>/ =	/j/, /w/
(3)	/<#>/ =	/#/, /# #/

Another helpful convention is the use of parentheses to indicate optional elements in the rule environment. Thus, if we want the above rule to apply whether or not /r/ intervenes between /t/ and the vowel, we can write the rule as follows:

$$/t/ \Rightarrow [T'] \quad / \quad \_(/r/)/<V1>/$$

A SAMPLE DERIVATION

In order to illustrate exactly how a rule set works, a miniature Text-to-Speech system has been presented in its entirety in table 6.2. This system consists of a simplified *punctuation interpreter* and a *morpheme stripper* limited to the identification of noun and verb endings. Next comes a partial list of exceptions, starting with the letter *T*, followed by letter-to-phoneme rules for the character *T*. The final stages include phoneme-to-allophone rules for the phoneme /t/ and *pause insertion rules*. (Stress assignment rules have been omitted in the interest of brevity.) Let us examine in detail the effect each of these modules has upon the following input string: *THREE TRAINS RATTLED INTO THE STATION*.

The first step is the conversion of spaces between words to '#' and of the full stop (period) to '##'. (We will also want to invoke a convention by which any input string is prefixed by '#'.) The morpheme stripper will insert '+' before the final *S* of *TRAINS*, the *D* of *RATTLED* and the *ING* of *STOPPING*. We now have the following string as input to the exceptions dictionary:

'# *THREE*#*TRAIN*+*S*#*RATTLE*+*D*#*INTO*#*THE*#*STATION*##'

Failing to find *THREE* listed as an exception, we proceed to the letter-to-phoneme rules, where pass-through rules convert the text symbols '#', '+' and '##' to phonemic symbols /#/, /+/, /##/. The *TH* of *THREE* does not fit the context for Rule 5, so the more general Rule 6, applies. *TRAIN* also falls through the exceptions dictionary, and, faling to find a match among any of the *T* rule contexts, is subject to the default Rule 14. The first *T* of *RATTLE* is deleted by Rule 3. The right environment of the second *T* is the correct one for Rule 2, but the match fails for the left environment, and the default rule again applies. Rule 14 also affects the *T* in *INTO*. *THE* is listed in the exceptions dictionary, and requires no letter-to-phoneme rules. The first *T* in *STATION* is accounted for by Rule 14, but *TI* is replaced by /ʃ/ before *O*. Assuming that the letter-to-phoneme rules for the remaining characters are correctly formulated, the resulting phoneme string will be:

Table 6.2 A miniature Text-to-Speech system

I. Punctuation rules (simplified)

(1)	' '	⇒	'#'
(2)	','	⇒	'#'
(3)	'.'	⇒	'# #'

II. Morpheme stripper (simplified)

(1) 'ED'   ⇒   'E + D'   / <C1><V2><C2> __ '#'
(2) 'ES'   ⇒   'E + S'   / <C1><V2><C2> — '#'
(3) 'S'   ⇒   '+ S'   / <C1><V2><C2> (') __ '#'
(4) 'ING' ⇒   '+ ING'   / <C1><V2><C2> __ '#'

III. Exceptions dictionary (partial)

(1) 'THAN'   ⇒ / ð _ æ _ n/   / '#' __ '#'
(2) 'THAT'   ⇒ / ð _ æ _ t/   / '#' __ '#'
(3) 'THE'   ⇒ / ð _ i:/   / '#' __ '#'
(4) 'THEIR'   ⇒ / ð _ɛə/   / '#' __ '#'
(5) 'THEM'   ⇒ / ð _ɛ_ m/   / '#' __ '#'
(6) 'THERE'   ⇒ / ð _ɛə/   / '#' __ '#'
(7) 'THESE'   ⇒ / ð _ i: _z/   / '#' __ '#'
(8) 'THEY'   ⇒ / ð _ eɪ/   / '#' __ '#'
(9) 'THEY'RE' ⇒ / ð _ɛə/   / '#' __ '#'
(10) 'THIS'   ⇒ / ð _ɪ _ s/   / '#' __ '#'
(11) 'THOSE' ⇒ / ð _ əu _ z/ / '#' __ '#'
(12) 'THOUGH' ⇒ / ð _əu /   / '#' __ '#'
(13) 'THUS'   ⇒ / ð _ ʌ _ s/   / '#' __ '#'

IV. Letter-to-phoneme rules for 'T'   *Examples*

(1) 'T' ⇒ //   / <V1><F/S> __ 'EN' <+/#>   listen
(2) 'T' ⇒ //   / 'S' __ 'LE' <+/#>   whistle
(3) 'T' ⇒ //   / __ 'T'   little
(4) 'T' ⇒ //   / __ 'CH'   watch
(5) 'TH' ⇒ /ð /   / __ 'E' <+/#>   the
(6) 'TH' ⇒ /θ/   / ELSEWHERE   thumb
(7) 'TI' ⇒ /tʃ/   / 'S' __ <V1> 'N'   Christian (GA)
(8) 'TI' ⇒ /ʃ/   / __ 'A'   initial
(9) 'TI' ⇒ /ʃ/   / __ 'EN'   patient
(10) 'TI' ⇒ /ʃ/   / __ 'O'   nation
(11) 'T' ⇒ /tʃ/   / __ 'UA'   actual
(12) 'T' ⇒ /tʃ/   / __ 'UR' <V1>   nature
(13) 'T' ⇒ /ti:/ / '#' __ '#'   t
(14) 'T' ⇒ /t/   / ELSEWHERE   tan

cont'd....

Table 6.2 (cont.)

V. Phoneme-to-allophone rules for /T/   *Examples*

   (1) /t/ ⇒ [T]   / /s/ __ (/r/)/<V1>/   steam, steam
   (2) /t/ ⇒ [T]   / /s/ __ /j/   student (RP)
   (3) /t/ .⇒ [T″]   / /<#>/ __ (/r/)/<V1>/   tree, tea
   (4) /t/ ⇒ [T″]   / /<#>/ __ /<Y/W>/   twenty
   (5) /t/ ⇒ [T′]   / __ (/r/)/<V1>/   intrude, into
   (6) /t/ ⇒ [T′]   / __ /<Y/W>/   between
   (7) /t/ ⇒ [T#]   / __ /<#>/   it
   (8) /t/ ⇒ [T*]   / ELSEWHERE   outside

VI. Pause insertion rules

   (1) /# #/   ⇒   [PS2]   (= LONGER PAUSE)
   (2) /#/   ⇒   [PS1]   (= SHORTER PAUSE)
   (3) /+/   ⇒   []

/#_θ_r_i:_#_t_r_eɪ_n_+_z_#_r_æ_t_ə_l_+_d_#_
ɪ_n_t_u:_#_ð_ə_#_s_t_eɪ_ʃ_ə_n_#_#/

The first instance of /t/ in the intermediate output string occurs at the beginning of a word before /r/ followed by a vowel and thus satisfies the environment for phoneme-to-allophone Rule 3. The /t/'s of /r_æ_ t_ə_l/ and /ɪ_n_t_u:/, which precede vowels but are not word-initial, meet. the more general requirements of Rule 5. Note that it is not necessary to specify a left environment for 5 because 3 has already 'trapped' all the cases where it does not apply. This progression from particular to more general conditioning environments is characteristic of ordered rule sets.[2] The last /t/ in our string occurs after /s/ and before a vowel, and Rule 1 correctly selects the unaspirated allophone [T]. Additional phoneme-to-allophone rules, together with the pause insertion rules specified in table 6.2, will produce a final output string something like. this:

   [PS1 _TH_R(Y)_′I:(#)_PS1_T″_R(-V)_′EI(N)_N_Z#_PS1_
   R(V)_′AE_T′_<@L_D#_PS1_′I(N)_T′_<U:(#)_PS1_DH_
   @_PS1_S*_T_′EI_SH_@N(#)_PS2]

where, for example, TH, I:(#), EI(N), N, Z#, AE, <@L, D# are allophones of the phonemes /θ/, /i:/, /eɪ/, /n/, /z/, /æ/, /l/, /d/ and R(Y), R(-V) and R(V) are all allophones of /r/, and so on.

6.5 *Future directions for improved quality*

As was pointed out in section 6.2, synthesis-by-rule has a major drawback: the resulting speech, while certainly intelligible on a word-by-word basis, tends to be perceived as 'mechanical' and 'non-human'. In order to make machines sound more like people, future Text-to-Speech systems will need to devote more attention to phonetic detail in linking allophones together. More importantly, rule sets will have to take better account of the subtleties of intonation and rhythm, the so-called *prosodic* features of language by which human speakers maintain our interest and direct our attention.

TRANSITIONS

At the phonetic level, the problem with isolating and recombining a set of discrete pieces of sound should by now be obvious. A real vocal tract does not change shape abruptly for each phoneme. Instead, tongue, lips, and teeth are in constant motion, gliding smoothly from one articulatory position to another. The result is that it is next to impossible to pinpoint precisely where one allophone leaves off and the next begins. Analysis of frequency spectra only emphasises this fact, revealing that a good part of any speech waveform consists of transitions between sets of *target* configurations. On a spectrogram, these transitions are clearly visible in the trajectories of the primary resonant frequencies of vowels and resonant consonants (the *formants*).

Many Text-to-Speech systems attempt to incorporate the effects of transitions into their smoothing algorithms by inserting interpolated sets of parameters between contiguous allophones. This approach may be sufficient for the relatively slow transitions from vowel to vowel, but where the rapid changes associated with consonants occur, important acoustic cues may be slurred over or lost completely. For this reason, some researchers have experimented with encoding *trans-allophonic* units which include the transitions – either *diphones*, which are combinations of two allophones, or *demi-syllables*, which contain a consonant or consonant cluster plus half of a vowel. An alternative approach would be to store sub-allophonic units, i.e. parts of allophones. For instance, one could divide up a given vowel allophone into an *onset*, a *centre value*, and an *off-glide*. The onset and off-glide would be determined by the surrounding phonemes, while the centre value would depend on syllabic stress, etc. About 450 such units would be required for English.

PROSODY

The role of intonation in English is by no means limited to distinguishing questions from statements. As illustrated in fig. 6.2, where an overall pitch contour is indicated by superscript lines in accordance

1)   ´JANE ARRIVES AT ´HEATHROW TO´NIGHT.

(Tonight as opposed to next Wednesday.)

2)   ´JANE ARRIVES AT ´HEATHROW TO´NIGHT.

(Heathrow as opposed to Gatwick.)

3)   ´JANE ARRIVES AT ´HEATHROW TO´NIGHT.

(Jane as opposed to Aunt Mary.)

4)   ´JANE ARRIVES AT ´HEATHROW TO´NIGHT?

(Are you sure it´s not next Wednesday?)

5)   ´JANE ARRIVES AT ´HEATHROW TO´NIGHT?

(I´m sure she told me Gatwick.)

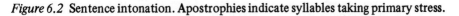

6)   ´JANE ARRIVES AT ´HEATHROW TO´NIGHT?

(You mean Aunt Mary´s not coming after all?)

Figure 6.2 Sentence intonation. Apostrophies indicate syllables taking primary stress.

with IPA convention, a five-word sentence can have six different readings (or more). The fact that linguists have tended to neglect such phenomena in describing the grammatical system of English is due to the traditional view that, in this particular language, prosodic features are extrinsic to information content and serve primarily to allow speakers to express emotion or indicate the relative importance of individual words. More recent research has demonstrated that some pitch fluctuations are correlated with syntactic boundaries, suggesting that intonation may provide important cues for sentence processing.[3] Such studies have also provided the basis for attempts to define rule sets capable of generating pitch contours for English sentences.[4] The duration of pauses between units as well as that of the units themselves has also been shown to be phonologically relevant.[5] For example, syllables tend to be relatively shorter in polysyllabic words, but are lengthened at word and phrase boundaries. While much more work is necessary before our understanding of prosody comes close to matching what we know about other aspects of linguistic behaviour, advances in computer-aided analysis make it possible to predict rapid progress in this field during the next decade.

6.6 *Further reading*

In this chapter, the fundamentals of text-to-speech system design have been covered, but no reference has been made to products which can be found on the market already offering this capability. Such printed circuit board products are discussed in section 12.4, and a short list of companies known to be working in the area is presented at the end of chapter 12.

However, the reader with an interest in the inner workings of such systems, as presented here, should refer to the following useful collection of papers:

Flanagan, J.L. and Rabiner, L.R. (Eds), (1973) 'Speech synthesis by rule', Part 5 of *Speech Synthesis*. Stroudsburg, PA: Dowden, Hutchinson & Ross.

Notes

1. In particular for Speech Incorporated's *Klattalk* system. High scores were also obtained by the related *MITALK* system. Cf. Pisoni, D.B. and Hunnicutt, S. (1980) 'Perceptual evaluation of MITALK', *IEEE ICASSP-80*, 574–582; Pisoni, D.B. (1982) 'Perceptual evaluations of voice response systems'. Paper presented at the Workshop on Standardisation of Speech I/0 Technology, National Bureau of Standards, Gaithersburg, Maryland, March 18-19.
2. Note that the second /t/ would turn out quite differently in American English,

where /t/ and /d/ between vowels both result in a light 'tap' of the tongue against the ridge behind the teeth rather than a full-fledged stop.
3. For example, Cooper, W.E. and Sorensen, J.M. (1981) *Fundamental Frequency in Sentence Production*. New York: Springer-Verlag.
4. Extremely interesting is the unpublished doctoral thesis of Breckenridge Pierre-humbert, J. (1980) *The Phonology and Phonetics of English Intonation*. MIT.
5. *Klattalk* is one of the few systems which makes a serious effort to account for segment duration. Cf. Klatt, D.H. (1979) 'Synthesis by rule of segmental durations in English sentences'. In *Frontiers of Speech Communication Research* (Eds Linblom, B. and Ohman, S.). New York: Academic Press.

References

Allen, J., *et al.* (1979) 'MITalk-79: The MIT Text-to-Speech system'. In *Speech Communication Papers Presented at the 97th Meeting of the Acoustical Society of America* (Eds Wolf, J.J. and Klatt, D.H.). New York: Acoustical Society of America.

Brightman, T. (20 Aug. 1981) 'Speech-synthesiser software generated from text or speech'. *Electronic Design* pp. 108–112.

Chomsky, N. and Halle, M. (1968) *The Sound Pattern of English*. New York: Harper and Row.

Gargagliano, T.A. and Fons, K. (10 Feb. 1981) 'Text translator builds vocabulary for speech chip'. *Electronics* pp. 118–121.

Gimson, A.C. (1980) *An Introduction to the Pronunciation of English*. 3rd edn. London: Oxford University Press.

Halle, M. and Keyser, S.J. (1971) *English Stress*. New York: Harper and Row.

Hunnicutt, S. (1976) 'Phonological rules for a Text-to-Speech system'. *American Journal of Computational Linguistics Microfiche* 57.

Klatt, D.H. (1982) 'The Klattalk Text-to-Speech system'. *IEEE ICASSP-82*, pp. 34–37. 'Review of the Science and Technology of Speech Synthesis'. Paper presented at the annual meetings of the Committee on Hearing, Bioacoustics, and Biomechanics of the National Research Council, November 13–14, 1981.

Ladefoged, Peter (1975) *A Course in Phonetics*. New York: Harcourt Brace Jovanovich.

Lin, K.-S. and Goudie, K. (10 Feb. 1981) 'Software rules give personal computer word power'. *Electronics* pp. 122–125.

Smith, W. and Crook, S.B. (25 June 1981) 'Phonemes, allophones, and LPC team to synthesise speech', *Electronic Design* pp. 121–127.

Wickey, D.O. (11 June 1981) 'Synthesiser chip translates LPC to speech economically'. *Electronic Design* pp.213–218.

Wijk, A. (1966) *Rules of Pronunciation for the English Language*. London: Oxford University Press.

CHAPTER 7

SPEECH RECOGNITION

Michael Elphick

Although the bulk of this book is devoted, as its title implies, to speech synthesis, no instructive work on the field of speech would be complete without an overview of speech recognition. This chapter aims to give the reader an understanding of the methods, difficulties, and state-of-the-art of recognition that will serve as a useful background for his work in synthesis.

7.1 *Background*

Progress in speech recognition seems disappointingly slow by comparison to speech synthesis. The performance of commercial speech recognition machines sometimes ranks closer to that of well-trained dogs than of people. Inexpensive machines, costing less than $1000, can recognise a small set of single-word commands from one or a few speakers, after a few minutes of training. But only a few commercial machines can recognise continuous speech, and they have vocabularies of less than a thousand words and prices of more than $10 000.

Considering the inherent difficulty of speech recognition, it may be unfair, after all, to compare a machine (which typically gets less than an hour of training) with a human (who gets a lifetime of training in spelling, grammar, logic, literature, and other intellectual pursuits – many of which can provide important contextual clues to word recognition). Because verbal communication is inextricably intertwined with human intellect, matching the human speech-recognition capabilities would require duplicating the capabilities of the human brain – an impossibility given today's technology. Indeed, advanced speech recognition by machines borders on artificial intelligence, a discipline still in its infancy.

Extracting verbal messages from the sound stream in which they are encoded is a formidable task in itself. Speech patterns vary from speaker to speaker because of such differences as physiology, sex, age, geographic origin, and education. A word, syllable, or other speech element may vary in loudness, pronunciation rate, and stress, depending on its function in a sentence and a speaker's psychological state. Quite different sound patterns may represent the same word, while different words may sound very similar – especially if the speech has been distorted by background noises, echoes, transmission medium limitations, and other interference sources that plague electronic equipment. Compounding these problems is the fact that individual elements, such as words or phonemes, tend to lose their identity in continuous speech, making them difficult to isolate (see chapters 3 and 6).

Because the general problem is so difficult, most research has concentrated on solving specific tasks, such as *speaker-dependent* recognition of isolated words or continuous speech with a small vocabulary. Fortunately, many practical applications exist for limited recognition. Isolated word recognition, for example, is adequate for logging freight destinations in warehouses or identifying and counting items for inventory control. Factories can use word recognisers for programming numerically controlled machine tools by voice entry and for dictating the results of quality-control measurements to a computer.

Isolated-word recognition also side-steps the problem of segmenting continuous speech. For this reason, the development of such machines has received great emphasis and has led to the emergence of low-cost commercial systems. Recently, research has accelerated because speech-recognition technology has started to show commercial promise. It has been predicted, for example, that the market for speech-recognition products will grow to $1 billion by 1990.[1]

Even though word-recognition machines vary greatly in detail, they all use the same basic recognition process. A spoken word is converted into an electrical signal by a microphone; the signal is processed to extract a set of identifying features; the features are then compared to a library of templates representing the machine s vocabulary. A word is recognised if it matches one of the templates stored in the machine's memory.

The stored *reference templates* are created either in a laboratory or by using the recognition machine itself in a special training mode. During training, a speaker repeats each word several times to enable the machine to compute an average template for that word and that speaker (or class of speakers). For laboratory experiments, soundproof rooms are used to avoid errors due to background noise, echo, and other sources. Commercial systems operating in offices and warehouses usually employ noise-cancelling microphones, mounted on headsets to fix the distance to the speaker. *Speaker-independent* systems also need a set of stored templates, but here the attempt is to choose the templates to be applicable to any speaker with a similar accent. However, the vocabulary size has to be considerably smaller than that available in speaker-dependent systems.

7.2 *Feature extraction*

The analysis stage of speech recognition consists of extracting identifying characteristics from the electrical analog of the speech signal generated by a microphone. When viewed in the time domain (as on an oscilloscope), speech signals look extremely complex and reveal no readily identifiable characteristics that distinguish one speech sound from another. Speech signals are much more readily analysed in the frequency domain, where a signal's amplitude is examined as a function of frequency. This is because each speech element has a characteristic spectral signature, as evidenced in *spectrograms* (see chapters 3 and 4). A trained observer can use spectrograms to identify and distinguish speech sounds. (In fact, 'voiceprints' have been used as the basis for electronic security systems intended to prevent unauthorised access to buildings and other restricted areas.) A spectrogram reveals the bar patterns of pulsating sounds from the vibrating vocal cords, the blurred aperiodic traces made by fricative sounds (such as /f/), or the clearly defined areas mapped out by the vocal-tract resonances (*formant frequencies*) for vowel sounds.

Word-recognition systems employ various strategies of extracting spectral information from speech sounds. Such strategies minimise the computer processing needed to analyse speech sounds and the computer storage needed to store sounds and reference templates. They do, however, entail a trade-off. Simplifying the sounds by discarding irrelevant information can lower a machine's cost or increase its vocabulary size and response speed. Over-simplification can lead to a loss of recognition accuracy. The trick is to find a suitable compromise for a particular application.

The simplest and cheapest way to convert a speech signal into the frequency domain is to count the number of times per second the signal changes algebraic sign, using a circuit known as a *zero-crossing detector* (see fig. 7.1). This gives a rough measure of the dominant frequency, or pitch, of a speech signal. Experimenters have used inexpensive recognition machines based on a zero-crossing technique

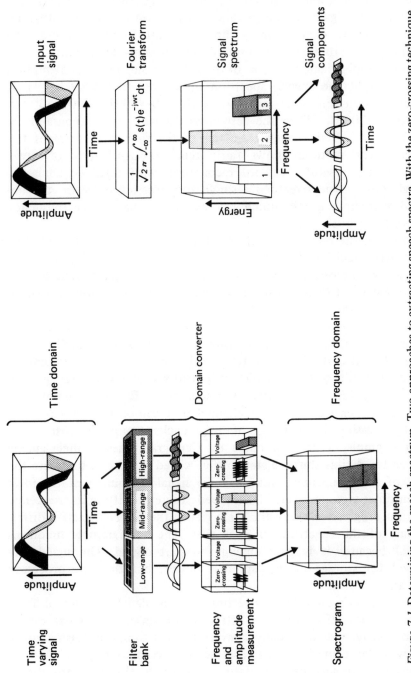

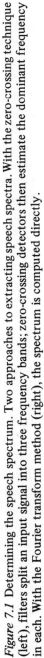

Figure 7.1 Determining the speech spectrum. Two approaches to extracting speech spectra. With the zero-crossing technique (left), filters split an input signal into three frequency bands; zero-crossing detectors then estimate the dominant frequency in each. With the Fourier transform method (right), the spectrum is computed directly.

to input a tiny vocabulary of simple commands to microcomputers. However, this method is not very discriminating, since it measures only the dominant signal frequency and does so only crudely. Most researchers believe that at least three formant frequencies must be identified to discriminate vowel sounds with reasonable certainty.

A more sophisticated version of the zero-crossing technique employs filters to split the speech spectrum into three frequency bands. A typical division might be into the bands 200–900 Hz, 800–2500 Hz, and 2000–3200 Hz. Then the zero-crossings are counted separately in each band to obtain rough estimates of the first three formant frequencies. The method allows fairly reliable classification of vowel sounds and is useful for word recognition with small vocabularies. Though more expensive than a single zero-crossing detector, the improved technique is still much less expensive than other frequency analysis techniques.

Increasing the number of filters – typically to sixteen or thirty-two – improves precision. In fact, this *filter-bank* technique eliminates the need for zero-crossing detection because any energy passed by the filters must be at or near the centre fequencies of the filter passbands, which are known.

Filter banks, however, are costly. Fortunately, escalating filter costs can be avoided. One way is to filter a speech signal digitally, using *digital filter* circuits. Digital filters can be cheaper and more compact than analog filters for complex applications like voice recognition because they can be integrated on silicon chips. But even digital filter banks are expensive. A sixteen-channel unit can cost $180. However, digital processing allows the use of design tricks to minimise cost.

For example, a product made by Centigram uses a single analog filter and a digital shift-register buffer, called a *spinner*, to create the effect of a sixteen-filter bank. A voice signal is 'spun' past the filter sixteen times at successively higher speeds, thereby shifting its frequency spectrum progressively upward. As a result, the filter extracts a different part of the spectrum on each pass. The Centigram technique is unusual because it is part analog and part digital. The signals are digitised for storage in the 'spinner' buffer, but they are processed by an analog filter.

Digital filtering entails converting speech signals to digital form before filtering. However, this often makes sense, since most speech recognition systems eventually convert a signal to digital form anyway to allow the information to be processed by a computer.

Digital processing can be used to eliminate the need for digital filtering altogether. For example, Fourier spectral analysis by computers has become very popular as the result of the development in the '60s of a computationally efficient version of the Fourier transform, called the *fast Fourier transform (FFT)*. The FFT makes it possible to compute rapidly and directly the amount of energy present in a speech signal at each frequency and its relative phase as a function of time – in other words, its spectrum. However, use of the Fourier transform still requires a fairly powerful computer or signal processing chip (see section 10.3).

As lip reading illustrates, speech can be recognised from the position of the organs used to produce it. In fact, some researchers argue that analysis of the state of the speech organs at any given instant would lead to more reliable speech recognition than direct analysis of speech sounds. This argument motivates another approach to speech recognition based on speech synthesis. Essentially, this method analyses a speech waveform to extract the information that would be needed to enable a speech synthesiser to reproduce the waveform. The synthesis information – rather than spectral information – is then used in template matching.

A virtue of this approach is that techniques for deriving speech synthesiser parameters from human speech have already been developed for use in producing the vocabularies of commercial synthesisers. One such technique is *linear predictive coding* (LPC) which was described in detail in chapter 5. LPC predicts the amplitude of a speech waveform at a given moment from a weighted average (linear combination) of its amplitudes at a small number of previous instants. LPC is especially appropriate for speech recognition because it is based on a simple acoustic model of the human vocal tract that emphasises the formant structure of speech, which is important for recognition. The heavy computation required to extract LPC coefficients has prevented its use in commercial recognisers. This is changing, however, with the emergence of inexpensive, high-performance microcomputers.

7.3 *Template matching in word recognition*

After analysis, speech signals must be compared to reference templates before they can be recognised. This matching operation presents a major stumbling block to successful speech recognition. One difficulty is in isolating the speech elements to be matched. For example, a word recogniser that allows very short gaps between words to accommodate rapid-fire speech could be fooled into mistaking syllables for words, and *vice versa*. A solution to this problem is to analyse words in units smaller than a word. Even when the basic unit is a complete word, the word must be subdivided into time intervals so that the changing speech sounds can be tracked throughout the word. Threshold Technology's Quik-talk system (see fig. 7.2), which recognises speech at rates exceeding 180 words per minute, breaks a word down into sixteen time segments; from each segment it extracts thirty-two spectral components using a thirty-two-channel filter bank. The system makes an initial estimate of word boundaries based on the occurrence of one of thirty-two acoustic features; the estimate is then refined by analysing the speech for the occurrence of other features.

Figure 7.2   The *Quicktalk* system used for data entry in inventory control (Reproduced by permission of Threshold Technology)

Another difficulty with template matching is that speech elements are rarely the same length as the templates they are supposed to match. A word can be drawled or spoken crisply, depending on the speaker and the circumstances. This is true even when the speaker is the same person who recorded the original template. Varying the pronunciation rate can also change the relative distances between identifying features in a speech element.

Low-cost word-recognition systems handle this problem by adjusting all templates and words to be matched to a standard length, typically by omitting or interpolating time segments. Systems that require greater matching accuracy use techniques collectively known as *dynamic programming* to warp a template so that its features are aligned as accurately as possible with those of the word to be matched. (Dynamic programming is a mathematical technique; it should not be confused with computer programming.)

Nippon Electric's *DP-100* continuous-speech recognition system, for example, successively associates slices of an input word with slices of a template, compressing and stretching the slices to minimise a distance measure of fit between the input and template. This procedure, called 'non-linear time-warping', is repeated with other templates, and the resulting distance measures are compared. The match having the lowest distance score is the one with the highest probability of being correct.

PERFORMANCE OF WORD RECOGNISERS

How accurate are the various analysis and template-matching techniques? A recent study[2] showed that the range of accuracy and cost was extremely large — from, for example, a $500 machine from Scott Instruments that used a zero-crossing analysis technique and had a 12.6 percent error rate, to a $66 000 machine from Verbex, which displayed a 0.2 percent error rate.

The accuracy of *speaker-dependent* word-recognition machines — matching or exceeding human performance in similar conditions — leaves little room for improvement. Indeed, the state-of-the-art has reached the point of diminishing returns. Any improvement in accuracy would be too small to justify the additional cost.

Word recognition's next break through will most likely be a dramatic cost reduction. Machines comparable in performance to those now costing $20 000 or more will soon be available for a few thousand dollars. Semiconductor technology can drive down the price for speech recognition just as it has for other kinds of electronic systems. The low-cost Interstate machine, with its respectable performance, illustrates this trend — which is likely to accelerate as growing markets and continuing circuit integration yield manufacturing economies. In addition, semiconductor companies, already supplying speech synthesis circuits, are showing increasing interest in speech recognition as the market's size becomes evident.

7.4 *Continuous-speech recognition*

Although word-recognition systems are adequate for some applications, there are many potential applications that will require continuous-speech recognition. For example, speech recognition could be used to allow unskilled people to operate sophisticated computer systems, such as patent database systems. Such applications, however, require that a system recognise entire phrases and sentences.

Continuous-speech systems share some basic similarities with word-recognition systems. For one, they employ the same basic recognition process of extracting spectral signatures from speech signals and comparing them to templates. In addition, most use words as their basic recognition element.

With continuous-speech systems, however, isolating words from the speech stream presents a difficult problem. For one thing, words tend to run together — especially in rapid speech. For example, *What do you want?* might become *Waddayahwant?* Such word blurring makes it difficult for a machine to separate words for identification. Also, the *coarticulation* of adjacent words or syllables can modify their sounds (*what do* becomes *wadda*), increasing still further the number of sound patterns a word-recognition machine must identify.

Two basic approaches to the segmentation problem are being tried in experimental systems — neither of them very satisfactory. One method attempts to pinpoint segment boundaries by analysing the speech signal for significant features, such as a burst of energy, an abrupt transition, or a pause. The other technique works by trial and error. A template is slid along a waveform to find the best possible match.

Some continuous-speech systems neatly avoid the problem of determining word boundaries by treating any sequence of speech sounds between two pauses as a recognition unit. Even fast talkers usually pause noticeably at the end of a sentence or long phrase — if only to catch their breath. The larger units also allow a machine to use context as an aid to recognition. For example, a sentence-recognition machine could recognise from the context that the *wadda* portion of *Waddayah-want?* means *what do* and not *water*. A machine working with smaller units would get into serious difficulties. Such systems do have a drawback, however. The approach entails storing templates not only for words but for phrases and sentences as well. For example, a system that needs to recognise *What do you want?* may have to store a template for *Waddayahwant?* as well as templates for *what, do, you,* and *want.* In addition, analysis of the larger units requires enormous processing power.

FINITE-STATE GRAMMARS

The next step in contexual recognition, which requires greater program complexity but less template storage space, is to test words to see if they fit grammatically with preceding words in a sentence. In fact, human word recognition frequently employs this kind of 'educated guesswork'. For example, a human knows that the next word in a sentence beginning *The cat sat on the. . .* is more likely to be *mat* than *gnat.* Thus even if the word sounded like *gnat,* a human listener might pick *mat,* while a machine would pick *gnat* — unless, of course, it were trained to recognise the incongruity of a cat sitting on a gnat.

Machines do employ — albeit primitively — such contextual techniques. Some continuous-speech systems, for instance, employ primitive grammars, called *finite-state grammars,* that specify what types of words are allowed to precede or follow other types of words. The method uses a word's context to constrain the possible number of identifications, increasing the probability of correct identification.

A language's grammar specifies the word combinations in which a given word can appear. Formal language theory has yielded precise and computationally efficient grammars for describing the artificial languages used in speech-recognition systems. (Unfortunately, theorists have yet to develop comparably rigorous descriptions of natural languages.) Because these grammars are well adapted to computer processing, they enable recognition systems to use context efficiently as a recognition aid.

A formal grammar used on some systems describes every possible sentence in its language via a state diagram (see fig. 7.3). Each path through the diagram represents a valid sentence. When processing a sentence, the system goes through the diagram, assigning probabilities to each state transition. The probabilities are then multiplied for each path to obtain the probabilities of possible sentence matches; the path with the highest cumulative probability is selected as the recognised sentence. This procedure, in effect, uses context as a recognition aid. For example, a poor word match might be chosen over a better one if it results in a sentence with a higher probability of correctness.

Finite-state grammars improve recognition efficiency by streamlining template matching. A recogniser does not have to match a sound pattern against every template — only those allowed by the grammar for a given transition.

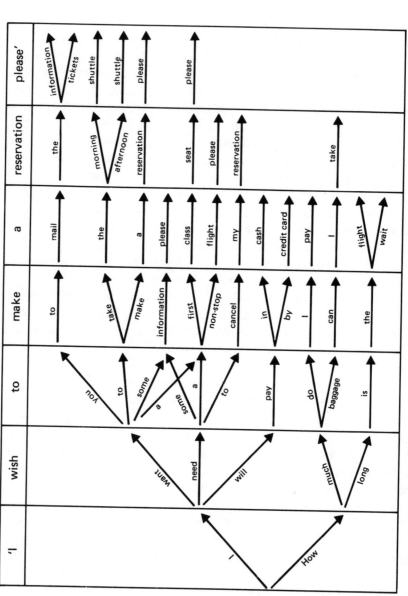

Figure 7.3 A typical grammar for speech recognition system. This state diagram represents sentences that might be encountered by a speech recogniser used to handle airline reservations. State diagrams for actual systems would be far more elaborate

A finite-state grammar also allows accurate continuous-speech recognition without prohibitively expensive recognition procedures for speech sounds, and similar strategies of contextual analysis can be employed for sequences of phonemes within words as for sequences of words within phrases. Unfortunately, however, because of the limitation of computer hardware, the grammars permit only a very restricted number of word combinations compared to the virtually unlimited number of phrases and sentences allowed by natural language grammars. This is probably where the major advances in the forthcoming decade will appear.

PERFORMANCE OF CONTINUOUS-SPEECH RECOGNISERS
How well do today's continuous-speech systems perform? Answering this question entails first deciding what an adequate performance measure is. Vocabulary size alone, for example, can be a misleading indicator of a continuous-speech system's performance. A system with a large vocabulary might be capable of recognising only a small number of phrases or sentences because of a restrictive grammar. Indeed, it would be trivial to build a system with a 1000-word vocabulary, if the words could only be combined in one way.

For this reason, the performance of continuous-speech systems is usually measured by the complexity of the languages that they recognise. Information theory provides a rigorous quantitative measure of a language's complexity, called *perplexity*, which roughly equals the average number of alternative words that can follow any given word in the language (average branching factor).

In perplexity and vocabulary size, the most powerful continuous-speech system in existence at the time of writing is an IBM research system that reliably recognises an English-based artificial language having a vocabulary of 1000 words and a perplexity of twenty-five words. This language falls far short of natural English, which has a vocabulary of more than 300 000 words and a perplexity of fifty words. Moreover, the IBM system does not offer realtime performance. Recognition of a six-second sentence takes 20 minutes of computer analysis, and the cost of the system would be prohibitive in practical applications.

The low performance of existing continuous-speech systems might be adequate for some applications. An airline reservations terminal, for example, might need only a limited and specialised vocabulary (flight numbers, airport names, etc.), although it would have to be speaker-independent to allow use by the general public. Other applications, however, clearly require much higher performance — especially in the area of vocabulary size. For example, it is questionable whether a user would be content with an automatic dictation machine having only a 1000-word vocabulary and low accuracy, although he or she might not demand real-time response or speaker-independence.

FUTURE TRENDS

Improving the performance of continuous-speech systems, however, will not be easy. As vocabulary size increases, for example, so does the amount of template storage required to accommodate the vocabulary. A system capable of recognising the entire English vocabulary would have to store and retrieve some 300 000 templates, which even using speech compression would be prohibitively expensive and slow with today's computer technology. For this reason, many researchers believe that practical large-vocabulary machines will be forced to use smaller speech elements as recognition units — specifically *phonemes*, (see chapter 3). The sound systems of natural languages are generally made up of less than a hundred phonemes. Thus a phoneme-recognition machine would require only a small amount of template storage, yet could recognise a virtually unlimited vocabulary.

But recognising phonemes reliably is much more difficult than recognising words because there is a higher incidence of coarticulation and other sound-modifying phonomena. Therefore, with phoneme recognition, the need for contextual techniques to help sharpen recognition is much greater than for word recognition, causing the heavy research emphasis in this area.

Interactive operation is a technique that could be used to boost recognition accuracy. A machine that synthesises as well as recognises speech could request a user to repeat or confirm an unclear word. An experimental continuous-speech system built by Bell Labs to handle airline reservations operates in this manner, although its vocabulary numbers only 127 words.

Clearly, continuous-speech systems have a long way to go before they become suitable for practical use. Vocabularies have to be expanded at least tenfold, and speeds expanded over a hundredfold. Also machines must handle the perplexity of natural languages and become essentially speaker-independent. Furthermore, to penetrate the really large markets, costs must drop to below $100 — far below the cost of mainframe-based research systems.

Progress in computer hardware is fairly certain. The parallel architectures and associative memories needed for speech recognition are already being developed. So, too, are faster and denser integrated circuits. But the electronic engineers will not be able to meet the goals alone. There must be continuing research in areas such as the physiology of hearing, the psychology of learning, and the structure of natural languages. The real breakthroughs, however, will probably come from artificial intelligence research in continuous learning and self-optimisation. The future speech recognition machines will be able to learn throughout their lifetimes – just as people do.

7.5 *Further reading*

The area of speech recognition is changing fast, and a book that is primarily about synthesis can only hope to give a flavour of the approaches employed and difficulties encountered in the field. At the time of reading there will probably be many more companies providing recognition products than at the time of writing, but we offer here a short list of some of the companies that, to the editor's knowledge, had OEM products on the market in 1982:

> Auricle Inc. Cupertino, California
> Bridgeport Textron, Horsham, Pennsylvania
> Centigram Corp., Sunnyvale, California
> Covox Co., Eugene, Origon
> Heuristics Inc., Sunnyvale, California
> Hycom Inc., Irvine, California
> Infovox, Stockholm, Sweden
> Intel Corp., Santa Clara, California
> Interstate Electronics, Anaheim, California
> Logica, London, England
> Marconi Avionics, Rochester, England
> Mimic Electronics Co., Acton, Massachusetts
> Nippon Electric Co. Ltd, Kawasaki, Japan
> Scott Instruments, Denton, Texas
> Technology Service Corp., Santa Monica, California
> Texas Instruments Ltd, Dallas, Texas
> Threshold Technology, Delran, New Jersey
> Verbex, Bedford, Massachussets
> Voicetek, Goletta, California
> Votan, Fremant, California
> Weitek Corp., Santa Clara, California

In addition, a recent IRD report[3] lists many companies that it speculates to be conducting significant research in recognition and which may announce products during 1983. These include Fujitsu in Japan; Philips, Siemens, and Thompson CSF in mainland Europe; and a group of ten companies in the UK, organised in a 'recognition club' by the National Physical Laboratory (including Plessey, Ferranti, and Quest Automation).

Finally, whilst information on OEM products available at any given time can be obtained from these companies, for the reader who would like to delve a little deeper into the techniques of Speech Recognition the following book will be of great value:

Lea, Wayne, A. (1980) *Trends in Speech Recognition.* Englewood Cliffs, N.J.: Prentice-Hall.

Notes

1. Market predictions by SRI International, Menlo Park, California.
2. Comparative Survey conducted by George Doddington and Tom Schalk of the Central Research Laboratories of Texas Instruments Inc., Dallas, and published in *IEEE Spectrum*, Sept. 81 in an article entitled 'Speech recognition: Turning theory into practice', pp. 26-32.
3. *European Speech Recognition and Synthesis Markets*, Report no. 515, International Resource Development, Norwalk, Connecticut.

PART 2

TECHNOLOGY

CHAPTER 8

COMBINING SILICON AND SPEECH

Bob Brodersen

The speech synthesis chips described in this section of the book demonstrate the wide variety of competing approaches that are available. A brief survey of the basic design trade-offs which resulted in this wide variety of chips will be given in this introductory chapter, followed by some predictions of how the exponentially increasing density of integrated circuit technology will affect future chip designs.

The major design decisions which must be made by the chip designer can be grouped into three interdependent categories:

(a) The type of fabrication technology — High performance state-of-the-art vs. low performance and inexpensive
(b) Complexity of the algorithm — Complex low bandwidth algorithms vs. simpler but higher bandwidth
(c) Chip architecture — General purpose vs special purpose

8.1 *Fabrication technology*

The considerations which go into deciding the appropriate technology for a special function chip such as a speech synthesiser are different from those that are used in high volume general-purpose chips such as microprocessors and memory. The relatively small size of the market for special function chips does not allow the continuing redesign to exploit the newest fabrication technology. In addition the effect of the architectural and algorithmic decisions can easily be more important than the improvements obtained by the speed and density advantages of an advanced technology. The speech synthesis chip designer must make his technology decision based on such factors as

131

present availability, the reliability of future availability, the cost of fabrication, and compatibility with special circuits, such as high density ROMs (for vocabulary storage) and analog circuits such as D/A converters. If the synthesis chip is made to execute only a single algorithm, then as demonstrated by the first Texas Instruments synthesis chips (see section 10.1, Brantingham) an early 1970's technology (PMOS) is adequate to meet the performance requirements of LPC speech synthesis if an appropriate architecture is used.

It is likely that system houses with speech expertise will become more involved in the chip design, because of the importance of system level considerations (algorithms and application-dependent circuitry). An example of this is the Votrax chip (see section 11.2, Fons and Gargagliano), in which the phonemic synthesis algorithms proprietary to Votrax were integrated by an IC design house and fabricated at a 'foundry'. A foundry is a company that will fabricate the designs of outside customers. The processes available at foundries are generally several years behind the state of the art, so as in the case of the Texas Instruments chip, an algorithm-specific architecture and an efficient circuit technique must be used to overcome the low performance of the technology (metal gate CMOS in the case of Votrax).

8.2 *Algorithms*

The primary motivation of the use of sophisticated algorithms in most of the speech synthesis chips is the reduction of bandwidth (bits/s), which allows a lower cost system since the memory requirements for a given amount of speech can be substantially reduced. However, this bandwidth reduction does not come without its costs. The naturalness and intelligibility of low bandwidth speech (< 2 kbits/s) is degraded for all algorithms. It is only a question of the degree of degradation for a given bandwidth, which fuels the controversy over which algorithm is best. As more sophisticated algorithms are used to reduce the bandwidth, the increased processing requires more silicon area, offsetting some of the gains in memory size. Finally, the analysis task of encoding the speech can become extremely difficult and time consuming for the very low bandwidth systems, and can only be performed by experts. This is very disconcerting to many customers who would like to have the ability to develop their own vocabularies.

A potential solution to all of these difficulties may lie in the inexorable increase in the density of IC technology. In several years, when today's most advanced state-of-the-art technology becomes available (and cost effective) for speech synthesis chips, the need for extremely low bandwidth coding will diminish, since even now there are 1 Mbit ROM chips available. At bandwidths above 10–20 kbits/s, very high quality speech can be obtained using straightforward waveform coding techniques (CVSD, ADPCM), which do not require a speech model. These methods are extremely easy to encode and in fact the encoding and decoding can both be integrated onto a chip, for applications such as voice mail. The quality of these synthesisers is significantly better than the low bandwidth systems and can be expected to capture an increasing amount of the market as IC technology progresses.

Several of the chips to be described in the next few chapters demonstrate some interesting design decisions with respect to the algorithms and the technology available for their implementation. The NEC chip (see section 9.3, Oura) has enough flexibility to implement high bandwidth waveform coding algorithms as well as their 'Variable Sampling Rate Speech Segment Synthesis Method' which can encode at rates below 1 kbit/s. Since they only have 64 kbits of ROM on the chip the usefulness of the higher bandwidth schemes is questionable at this time, but this chip is likely a portent of the future.

The approach used by National (see section 9.2, Costello and Mozer) avoids the problem of using excessive amounts of silicon area to implement a complex algorithm, by using a simple 2-bit digital-to-analog converter, which requires very little silicon area. They use an extremely complicated analysis procedure, which is described in section 9.2, in order to obtain a sufficiently low bandwidth, for a reasonable size vocabulary to be integrated using presently available ROM technology.

The complexity of the algorithm on the Votrax chip makes it expensive, so that it is unsuitable for many consumer applications. It is, however, able to synthesise phonemes directly and with a little software able to synthesise from text. Though the speech quality is marginal for many words, the ability to synthesise an unlimited vocabulary is unique amongst single chip products.

8.3 *Architectures*

Most of the discussion so far has been on chips which make use of special-purpose architectures, that have been optimised for an algorithm or class of related algorithms. Most of the recent general-purpose digital signal processing chips, which include the AMI 28211 (see section 10.3, Edwards), the NEC 7720 and the TI 320, have the ability to implement even the most complex of synthesis algorithms by simply programming the chip. In general, these devices are not economically competitive with the special-purpose synthesisers, since not only is the chip itself more expensive, but for a complete speech system they need additional circuitry such as interfacing chips (glue logic), D/A converters and vocabulary ROM. Probably the best use of the general-purpose chips is in prototyping, in order to determine the optimal system configuration before designing a special-purpose chip to implement the function efficiently.

The line between general-purpose and special-purpose chips is not clear. As mentioned above, the NEC synthesiser can execute a number of related algorithms, so that it lies somewhere between the general-purpose AMI signal processor and the algorithm specific chips of TI, Votrax and National. The architectures of the general-purpose digital signal processors are basically very similar – a microcomputer with an array multiplier. However, no such uniformity holds for the special-purpose chips. The architectures of each of the special-purpose chips described in the following sections are each very different. They range from the use of a pipelining (section 10.1), switched-capacitor analog circuits (section 11.2), and one which has conventional bus architecture but has a D/A converter and a large ROM (section 9.3).

8.4 *Future trends*

The clear direction for the fabrication technology of future synthesis chips is CMOS, since this appears to be the direction that the microprocessor and memory development is headed. As the fabrication technology is scaled to smaller dimensions, the already low power dissipation of CMOS will be reduced even further (e.g. Toshiba has presented data on a CMOS LPC synthesiser chip with power dissipation of less than 1 mW). It is clear that the power dissipation of these future chips will be totally dominated by the audio transducer.

Scaling will also reduce the area of the computational circuitry, so that future synthesis chips will be mostly memory (even now the NEC chip is almost 2/3 memory). If it is assumed that the doubling of circuit complexity every year and a half continues to the year 1990, then 8 Mbit ROMS should be available. This would allow 500 seconds of speech at 16 kbits/s. As discussed earlier, this capability will obviate the need for sophisticated bandwidth compression algorithms. Though this will be a loss in sophistication (at least to the digital signal processing theorist), the increased quality should result in significantly greater acceptance of voice I/O in the marketplace.

CHAPTER 9

CHIPS USING TIME-DOMAIN SYNTHESIS

Joe Costello and Forrest Mozer (9.1, 9.2),
Toshio Oura (9.3), Tom Durgavichs (9.4)

In this chapter we explore two techniques of time-domain synthesis, which were developed specifically with silicon implementation in mind.

9.1 *Time- vs frequency-domain synthesis*

Frequency-domain synthesis schemes are based on modelling human speech as the combination of a small number of source excitations (e.g. vocal-cord oscillations and turbulent air) and a much larger variety of output filter states (representations of the resonance states of the vocal tract). Data compression is achieved through storing the vocal-tract excitation and filter parameters in place of the original waveform. Relatively complex integrated circuit hardware (a many-pole analog or digital filter) transforms these stored frequency-domain parameters into a time-domain audio signal with a time-varying frequency spectrum which approximates the spectrum of the original speech waveform. Frequency-domain synthesis is the classic approach to the problem. It has been actively investigated by many research groups for several decades.

By contrast, in time-domain synthesis, the quantities stored in the speech memory are compressed representations of a waveform as a function of time. The action of the synthesiser is simply to unpack these stored time-domain waveforms to produce an output speech signal. As a result, the large-scale integrated circuits required for time-domain synthesis are simpler than those for frequency-domain synthesis since no hardware is needed to convert the stored data from the frequency domain to the time domain (i.e. no filter is necessary). The revolutionary aspect of the time-domain technique is not the hardware implementation but rather the analysis that enables speech waveforms to be stored in such a highly compressed form.

Because time-domain speech synthesis is a young technology, rapid improvements in both speech quality and bit rate have been and should continue to be made. The first technique that will be discussed below was developed by Prof. Forrest Mozer of the University of California, Berkeley, and is currently being implemented in integrated circuit form by the National Semiconductor Corporation. The second is a recent development of a similar technique, offered by the Nippon Electric Company.

One common misconception about time-domain synthesis is that the goal is to reproduce or approximate the original speech waveform with a smaller number of bits than would be required by using a straight-forward digital representation of the waveform. The goal is, in fact, to produce a *synthetic* time-domain waveform that is represented by a very small number of bits, but that may not necessarily bear any resemblance to the original time-domain waveform, even though the ear perceives the original and synthesised waveforms as nearly the same. This is illustrated in figs 9.1 and 9.2 for the *Mozer method*. The left-hand side of each figure is a segment of the original time-domain waveform taken from the spoken word *zone*, and the right-hand side is the synthesised equivalent. There is almost no visual similarity between the two waveforms and yet they sound very nearly the same.

The basic methodology employed by the time-domain technique is to extract from the original time-domain waveform that information which the human ear uses to distinguish a sound (the short-term power spectrum); then, using the degrees of freedom provided by the remaining information (the short-term phase) a waveform is chosen that can be represented by very few bits, and yet sounds very much like the original waveform. The figures also illustrate the data compression that is achieved in this process. Features of particular note are the long silent sections of the synthesised waveform (represented by constant amplitude levels), the small number of discrete amplitude levels, and the waveform symmetry properties.

The human ear is primarily sensitive to the power spectrum of the incoming audio signal and only secondarily sensitive to the relative phases of the component frequencies. Both time- and frequency-domain synthesis techniques are grounded in this observation; however, the two techniques exploit it in a very different manner. The frequency-domain technique ignores the phase information and finds the best possible fit to the signal power spectrum, given a limited number of frequency parameters. On the other hand, the time-domain techniques have the flexibility to start with a time-domain waveform whose power spectrum closely resembles that of the original waveform, and the phases of the component frequencies can then be selected such that the resulting time-domain waveform can be represented by a very small number of bits. Of the methods described in this chapter, the *Mozer* method uses this capability and the NEC technique, *Speech Segment Synthesis*, does not.

9.2 *The Mozer method*

SEGMENTATION OF THE SPEECH WAVEFORM

In the analysis section of the Mozer technique, the speech waveform is divided into fundamental segments called analysis periods. For voiced waveforms the analysis period is equal to the period of the vocal-cord oscillation (fig. 9.2(a) illustrates two such periods), while for unvoiced waveforms the analysis period is taken to be a fixed number of input samples, usually 256. The first step is to decimate each analysis period – that is to say replace each analysis period with a smaller fixed number of samples – while preserving the power spectrum of the original waveform. Fixing the number of samples per analysis period makes the digital analysis and reconstruction of the signal much simpler, and also yields a reduction in data rate.

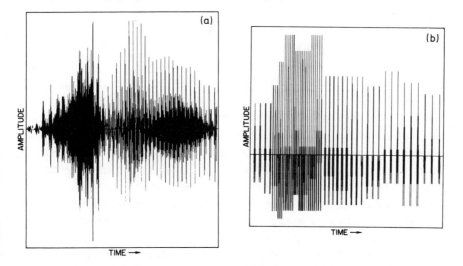

Figure 9.1 Spoken word 'zone'. (a) Digitised, (b) synthesised

The reduction in the number of digitisations per analysis period may or may not be accompanied by a decrease in the playout clock frequency at which samples are sent to a digital-to-analog converter for the generation of the analog speech wave. In either case, a computational

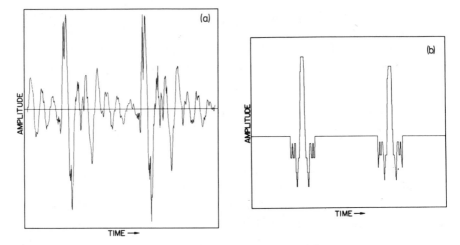

Figure 9.2 Two periods of the raw (a) and synthetic (b) waveforms of fig. 9.1

procedure guarantees preservation of that part of the power spectrum below the Nyquist frequency during the process of decreasing the number of samples and changing the clock frequency, in order to preserve the formant frequencies. In different implementations, the number of samples per analysis period has been selected between 16 and 256.

VOICED WAVEFORM COMPRESSION
Pitch control
Playing back a constant number of samples per analysis period at a fixed clock rate would yield pitch periods of constant duration and thus a completely monotone speech output. In order to reproduce the pitch contour of the original speech signal, either the playback frequency or the number of samples per period must be varied. In the most recent product offering from National Semiconductor, for example, both the number of samples per analysis period and the playout clock frequency are allowed a small number of values, and finer pitch control is made by adding a variable number of silent samples to the beginning of each synthesised pitch period. The number of silent samples to be added to each pitch period is stored in memory along with other necessary control information and the speech data itself.

The synthesised waveform of fig. 9.1(b) illustrates this method of pitch control. The distance between successive peaks varies throughout the waveform, even though there are thirty-two data samples associated with each peak and the playout clock frequency is constant. The changes in peak-to-peak distances (i.e. the pitch) are accomplished solely by the addition of a variable amount of silence. In the first third of the waveform, the peaks are relatively close, and the peak-to-peak distance gradually lengthens over the last two-thirds of the waveform. This is interpreted by the ear as a high initial pitch followed by a gradually decreasing pitch, corresponding to the word being heard with a falling intonation.

This method of pitch control enables one to adjust easily the pitch of an entire word, or sentence, without adding large amounts of additional data to the speech memory. Changing the pitch only involves changing the number of silent samples associated with each pitch period, so generating a word or phrase with new intonation simply requires changing the length of silence for each period. Changing the silence length of a series of periods is a simple operation, and, as a result, a user with a fairly simple development system will be able to produce high quality phrases with appropriate inflections, starting from a vocabulary of stored single words.

Amplitude scaling
Given a set of fixed length periods and an associated table of silent lengths which adjust the pitch, the next stage is to reduce the data required for each period. The first step is to scale the amplitude. From period to period, speech amplitude changes scale and a 12-bit sampling resolution of a raw speech waveform is necessary to preserve the accuracy of low amplitude periods while at the same time capturing high amplitude peaks. However, within a single period the 12-bit accuracy is not required. This fact is exploited by using 3 bits to set the overall amplitude of a period. These 3 bits are used to control the gain of an amplifier that resides on-board the speech synthesiser chip. This represents a 25% reduction in data rate since the 3 bits that give overall amplitude are stored once per pitch period instead of being added to each data point.

Phase adjusting
A discrete Fourier transform is then performed on each pitch period to produce a set of amplitudes and phases for the component frequencies in that period. If, for example, there are 128 sample points in the pitch period, the Fourier analysis produces sixty-four amplitudes and sixty-four phases. As discussed above, the amplitudes of these component frequencies have the greatest influence on speech quality and intelligibility while the sixty-four phases play only a minor role. This flexibility in the values of the phases is exploited in time-domain

synthesis by treating the phases as free parameters which are varied in order to produce a waveform that may be represented by much less data than 128 12-bit samples per period.

One data compression strategy consists of choosing the phases such that the time-domain waveforms are symmetric about the centre of each period. Since this symmetry requires cosine waveforms for each Fourier component, the phase angles must all be either 0 or 180 degrees. In fig. 9.3, these two phases are shown for each of the three lowest Fourier harmonic frequencies of a period, and it is clear that the sum of these waves plus those corresponding to all the higher frequency components will produce a resultant waveform that is also symmetric about the mid-point of the period.

Figure 9.4(a) shows the amplitude of a period of speech as a function of time. Figure 9.4(b) shows this period when one possible set of phases having values of 0 or 180 degrees is chosen. It must be emphasised that the power spectra of waveforms (a) and (b) in fig. 9.4 are identical, so the two periods sound the same to the human ear. Since each of the sixty-four Fourier components can independently have either of the two possible symmetric phases, 0 or 180 degrees, there are 2^{64} (approximately 10^{19}) possible waveforms that can be generated from waveform 9.4(a). All of these waveforms will be symmetric about their centre point and they will sound the same.

In the following sections, methods of data compression will be discussed that require searching through these symmetric waveforms to find examples having specific attributes. If a computer program analysed these 10^{19} waveforms at the rate of ten per second, it would take the age of the universe to study all of the waveforms generated from one pitch period of speech! Accordingly some very efficient algorithms for searching through the waveforms are required.

Choosing symmetric waveforms yields a factor of two compression in data since only the first half of the original data samples must be stored — the second half of any period being just the mirror image of the first half. This symmetry in the synthetic waveform is best seen in fig. 9.2(b).

Half-period zeroing

In fig. 9.4(b), there is much less power in the first and last quarters of the pitch period than there is in the middle half. The *half-period zeroing* comression technique consists of finding, from among the 10^{19} symmetric waveforms, those that have very little power in the first and last quarters of the pitch period, and replacing these low power portions by a constant amplitude level. This is illustrated by fig. 9.4(c),

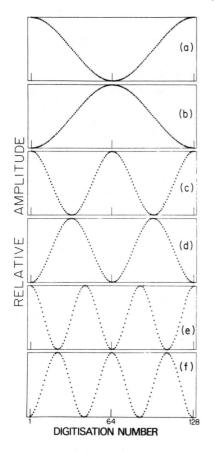

Figure 9.3 Two symmetric phases for each of three frequencies

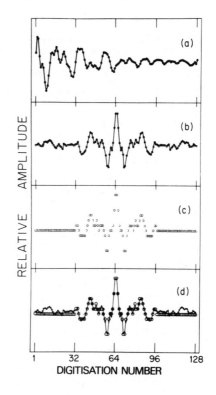

Figure 9.4 Data compression or a voiced waveform by phrase adjustment. (a) Single pitch period of a raw voiced waveform, (b) a symmetric waveform with same power spectrum as (a), (c) the waveform further quantised and zeroed where the power is small, (d) comparison of 2-bit quantised synthetic waveform with that of part (b)

in which the half-period zeroing results in a further factor of two reduction in data rate. This reduction is achieved with little degradation of quality since symmetric waveforms having little power in the first and last quarters can always be found among the essentially infinite number of candidates. As an example, the waveform in fig. 9.4 has less than 7% of its power in the first and last quarters.

Two-bit levels

Simultaneously while the symmetric waveforms are examined for those having low power in the first and last quarters, they are searched for waveforms whose amplitudes cluster around a small number of levels. Thus, for example, if the amplitudes of a waveform were to cluster around, say, sixteen levels, then instead of storing 12 bits for each sample, only 4 bits would be necessary. This is, in fact, generally possible and allows a representation of each data point by 2 bits instead of 12. Such clustering is illustrated in fig. 9.4(d) where the actual 12-bit waveform of part (b) is represented by black dots and the restricted level approximation is represented by open circles. In this case, the open circles are produced from 2 bits of delta-modulated information per digitisation.

Even though the points cluster around a restricted set of levels, the important question is how close the actual data points are to the allowed levels. On the average, in fig. 9.4(d), the 12-bit data points differ from the chosen 2-bit levels by less than one-sixth of the difference between the levels. Thus, each of these 2-bit levels possesses nearly 5 bits of accuracy as a result of the freedom in choosing phases. To this 5-bit accuracy, one can add the 3-bit amplitude multiplication factor associated with each pitch period to obtain an 8-bit effective resolution for only two bits of storage.

While the example in fig. 9.4 utilises 2-bit delta-modulated compressed data, it is also possible to use 2-bit non-delta-modulated waveforms allowing only four amplitude levels. This is a simpler scheme and, in addition, it improves the high frequency performance of the system. Successive synthesisers made by National Semiconductor have used both the 2-bit delta modulation scheme, and the 2-bit absolute levels. The synthetic waveforms of figs. 9.1 and 9.2 contain sixteen amplitude levels and are created from 4 bits of absolute amplitude data for each digitisation. Both 2-bit and 4-bit waveforms are available with National's latest synthesiser.

Pitch period reptition

Further compression of the stored data required for a word is made possible by repetitively using the already very compressed data in each pitch period. Instead of storing data for every pitch period and playing each of them once, every nth period may be stored and repeated n times on playback. This reduction in stored data is possible because the power spectrum changes very slowly from pitch period to pitch period. A good illustration of this fact is given in fig. 9.2(a) where it can be seen that consecutive periods differ very little from one to the next. As a result, in the synthetic waveform of fig. 9.1(b), each pitch period is repeated three times.

Repeating pitch periods in most situations not only reduces the data rate, but also improves sound quality. When every pitch period is played, the phases of the component frequencies change from period to period. The ear interprets this rapidly changing phase as a scratchy background noise. This is an example of a secondary effect of phase on the quality of speech. The repetition of periods keeps the phase at a given frequency constant over a longer period of time and, thus reduces the phase noise.

This completes the list of techniques used to reduce the data stored for a given pitch period of voiced speech. To summarise, the methods include:

(a) storing a smaller number of fixed samples per period than a raw sampled waveform;
(b) storing an overall gain for an entire period, reducing the number of bits required for each sample;
(c) adjusting the phases of the component frequencies to produce a waveform that (i) is symmetric, (ii) has very low power in the first and fourth quarters enabling half-period zeroing and (iii) has sampled amplitudes clustered around a restricted number of levels that allow a 2-bit or 4-bit representation of each amplitude; and
(d) pitch period repetition.

UNVOICED WAVEFORM COMPRESSION
Time-domain compression techniques applicable to unvoiced waveforms differ somewhat from those used on voiced waveforms because of the different power spectra of the two types. Compression techniques such as half-period zeroing introduce low frequency noise that is masked by the relatively high power at low frequencies in voiced waveforms, but that produces significant degradation in the quality of unvoiced waveforms because they contain relatively little power at low frequencies.

Phase adjusting
Unvoiced waveforms may be compressed in the same way as voiced waveforms by taking advantage of the fact that the major information content in a speech waveform resides in its power spectrum and not in the phases of its Fourier components. The somewhat different approach for unvoiced waveforms will be illustrated with reference to the example shown in fig. 9.5(a), which contains 128 samples digitised to

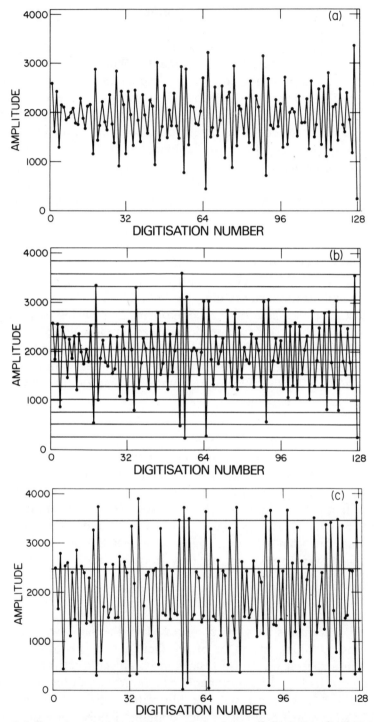

Figure 9.5 Data compression of an unvoiced waveform using level matching. (a) Raw unvoiced waveform, (b) 4-bit level matching, (c) 2-bit level matching

12-bit accuracy. The sixty-four phases obtained by Fourier analysis of this signal may be changed arbitrarily without changing the intelligibility of the speech, even though such a change causes the waveform to look very different to fig. 9.5(a).

In fig. 9.5(b), one of the possible variations is plotted, selected because it has the interesting property that its 128 digitisations tend to cluster about the sixteen amplitude levels denoted by the sixteen horizontal lines. Thus the amplitudes of the waveform in fig. 9.5(b) may be reasonably represented by 4 bits. In this way a compression factor of three is achieved. Similarly, in fig. 9.5(c) another possible waveform is shown which can also be obtained from that of fig. 9.5(a) by adjustment of its sixty-four phases. However, in this case, only four levels, and therefore 2 bits, are required for an adequate description, allowing a compression factor of six.

Segment repetition
Just as in the case of voiced speech, the power spectrum of unvoiced waveforms changes on a time scale of many tens of milliseconds. The duration of one analysis segment of unvoiced speech is, on the other hand, only 10 ms, so a saving could be made if segments of the unvoiced waveform were stored in the memory at 50 ms intervals throughout the waveform. The time-domain synthesiser could then produce a waveform that sounded like the original by playing each 10 ms segment five times before playing the following segment. If it worked, such a scheme would produce a data compression factor of five in the same way that the period repetition scheme enabled data compression for voiced speech. This scheme, however, does not work for unvoiced speech because the multiple repetition of the same segment produces a distinct buzz at the repetition frequency. The buzz is often sufficient to render unintelligible not only the phoneme of interest, but several words in its vicinity.

The buzz is caused by the spurious harmonic content introduced at the segment repetition frequency. For voiced periods, this low frequency harmonic is interpreted by the human ear as the pitch of the speech; but for unvoiced speech there is no corresponding spectral feature.

In order to eliminate the buzz in an unvoiced repetition scheme, one must remove the periodicity in the playback. The following three facts are useful in developing such a scheme:

(a) the power spectrum of the waveform determines its sound;
(b) the power spectrum of the waveform segment played backwards is the same as that when the segment is played forwards;

(c) the power spectrum of a part of the segment of the waveform is, on average, the same as that of the entire segment.

One solution based on these concepts involves sequentially playing different segments of the unvoiced synthetic period forwards and backwards. This maintains the power spectrum of the original unvoiced waveform without introducing erroneous low frequency harmonics due to periodic repetition. In this way, one could achieve the hypothetical compression factor of five by, say, playing the segment, then playing it backwards, then playing the last two-thirds of the segment, then playing the first two-thirds, then playing the middle two-thirds backwards, then playing the last half, and, finally, playing the first half backwards. The factor of five increased duration is achieved without repetitively playing any segment. Hence, little, if any, buzz sound or other audible distraction is produced.

A particular method of compressing the unvoiced waveform of fig. 9.6(a) by a factor of four is illustrated by fig. 9.6(b) which is constructed from digitisations 1 to 32 of the waveform. The digitisations are played out in the sequence 1 to 32, then 32 to 1, then 17 to 32, then 1 to 16, then 16 to 1, and finally, 32 to 17. This method of repetition is easily implemented with digital logic and its quasi-randomness is sufficient to minimise degradation in the quality of the unvoiced sound. A similar technique has been implemented in National's newest synthesiser, significantly reducing the storage required for unvoiced speech.

SUMMARY

Using the time-domain data compression techniques described above, it is possible to achieve data rates of around 1000 bits/s, as demonstrated by National Semiconductor's latest synthesisers. The complexity of the technique is contained within the analysis routines that generate the data compressions described in this paper. The synthetic waveforms produced by these routines are then dissected to enable efficient storage in ROMs. The speech synthesiser itself is basically a decoder which unpacks the information stored in ROM in order to produce the correct output waveforms. As a result, these synthesisers do not contain on-board filters or look-up ROM as do LPC devices. In addition, the recent advances in time-domain synthesis reported here mean that bit rate as well as speech quality is similar to that of LPC.

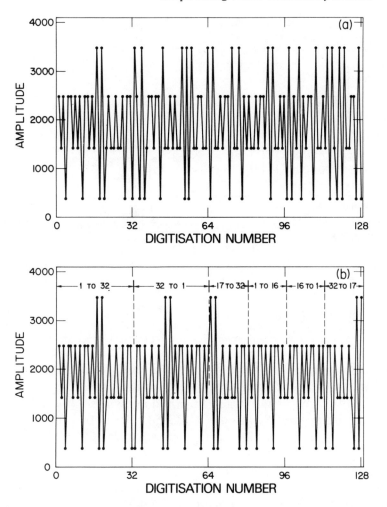

Figure 9.6 Data compression of an unvoiced waveform by segment repetition. (a) 2-bit unvoiced waveform, (b) synthesised waveform using segment repetition

9.3 *Speech segment synthesis*

In this section an alternative method of time-domain synthesis will be described in which idealised speech segments are stored in memory and read out every pitch period. This technique has much in common with the Mozer technique and is representative of the methods used by several manufacturers. However, as an example a device manufactured by the Nippon Electric Company will be described here.

The device chosen is a single-chip 8-bit *Sound Synthesis Micro-computer* (SSM), the μPD1776C, containing 64 kbits of on-chip

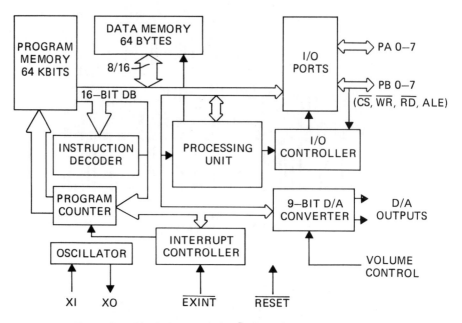

Figure 9.7 Block diagram of sound synthesis microcomputer

program memory (ROM) and 64 bytes of data memory (RAM). The SSM can synthesise high quality speech, musical sounds and imitation sounds with a low bit rate using a method known as *Variable Sampling Rate Speech Segment Synthesis* (VSRSSS). The μPD1776C is, in fact, a member of a family of SSM devices, known as the μPD1770 series.

THE SOUND SYNTHESIS MICROCOMPUTER

Figure 9.7 shows a block diagram of the SSM. It has a set of 182 instructions which mostly execute in one machine cycle (1.33 μs). To facilitate the high speed processing required of a microcomputer approach to synthesis the word length of the ROM is 16 bit. In the ROM, the program for the sound synthesis, and all the speech data are stored.

Thirty-two bytes of the 64-byte RAM are accessible directly and can be used to store table addresses as 16-bit Pair Registers, or used as temporary memory for speech parameters. The rest of the on-chip RAM can be used as an eight-level stack register and can be addressed in either 16-bit or 8-bit units. The processing unit contains an 8-bit special ALU (Arithmetic/Logic Unit), as well as multiplication registers, a quasi-random noise generator and other logic. In addition to the general functions of an ordinary ALU, the processing unit can execute a high speed multiply between a speech segment and suitable envelope data.

To enable the SSM to be used in the read-out of speech segments, there is an on-board interrupt controller which determines the sampling rate. The interrupt controller contains an 8-bit timer and 9-bit binary counter and the timer periodically generates a *tone interrupt* signal determined by a divide ratio. The minimum period of the tone interrupt is identical to sixty-four times one machine cycle. Two kinds of interrupt signals are generated from the binary counter; one is a *noise interrupt*, selected as one of four periods (of 32, 64, 256 or 512 times the machine cycle), while the other is a *timed interrupt* of 512 machine cycles. An external interrupt may also be generated by the *EXINT* line. These interrupts are enabled by the *Mode Register* and only one of them may be accepted at one time.

The on-chip 9-bit D/A converter can drive directly a 32–64 ohm speaker at 200 mW output power, and the maximum output power can be varied by the volume control line. This D/A converter can supply sound signals with up to 23.4 kHz sampling rate, as generated by the VSRSSS method.

There are also two multi-purpose 9-bit I/O ports, which have four modes determined by the mode register. The *PB* port can be set to receive control signals from other microcomputers, or can be set to supply signals to peripherals by software, so that the SSM can control them. The SSM can receive and transmit byte-wide data through the PA port connected to an external data bus. It can also interface to a key-matrix directly and/or drive display devices as a stand alone micro-computer. The PB port is TTL and key-matrix compatible, and the PA port is TTL compatible, allowing the SSM to be applied to various systems. Figure 9.8 shows an example of a single-chip system and fig. 9.9 shows an example of a multi-chip system.

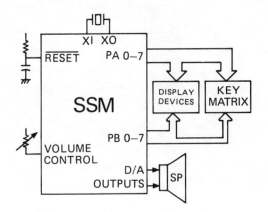

Figure 9.8 Example of single-chip system

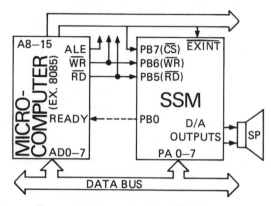

Figure 9.9 Example of multi-chip system

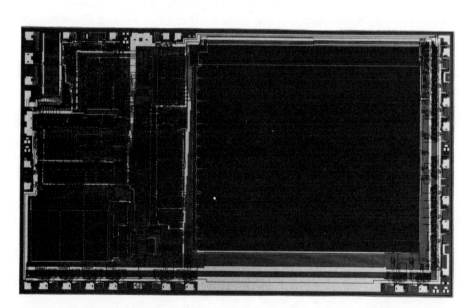

Figure 9.10 Photomicrograph of the SSM μPD1776C. (Reproduced by permission of the Nippon Electric Co. Ltd)

Figure 9.10 shows a photomicrograph of the SSM chip. It is fabricated by an N-channel MOS process, contains 47 000 transistors and has a die size of 4.83 mm × 8.09 mm (246 mil square). It can operate with a single power supply of +4.5 to +6.6 V with a 6 MHz clock. In operation, the power dissipation is 450 mW, but on stand-by, it is down to 50 μW. It is housed in 28-pin plastic DIP.

THE VSRSS METHOD

Figure 9.11 shows the Variable Sampling Rate Speech Segment Synthesis method. The ROM contains the software for speech synthesis, speech segments normalised for amplitude and time, envelope data, pitch data and sequence data. The *Normalised Speech Segments* (NSS), envelope data and pitch data are read from the ROM in order, in accordance with the sequence data. The sampling rate of the NSS is varied by the pitch data, namely the divide ratio. The processing unit multiplies the NSS data and the envelope data every sample, and supplies multiplied data to the D/A converter. The shape of the envelope and the pitch can be freely varied along the time axis by changing the appropriate parameters, and the amplitude of the envelope can also be varied, as can the number of times that the NSS data are repeated. The sequence data table can contain commands of *subroutine call*, *jump* and *return* for the current table, as well as *initial set*, *change* and *rest*.

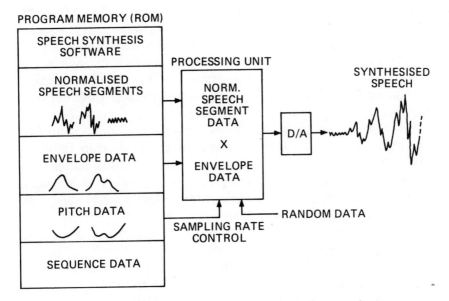

Figure 9.11 Variable sampling rate speech segment synthesis

As the SSM can synthesise speech by varying the amplitude and pitch of the NSS, and changing the NSS, and as it can repeat speech data sequences using subroutines, the data compression is higher than for many other speech synthesisers. It is capable of synthesising 90 seconds of high quality female speech with a bit rate of about 700 bits/s, or about 50 seconds of male speech. The SSM can also synthesise music and imitation sounds, even during the execution of a main program for control or numerical computation. Also, although the device has only been shown here operating with the VSRSSS method (for which it was designed), it is also capable of implementing other speech synthesis techniques, such as *Fixed Sampling Rate Speech Segment Synthesis* (FSRSSS), *ADPCM, DPCM, ADM, DM* and *PCM*. The only changes required to alter the synthesis method, or the speech to be uttered, will be in the software ROM.

ACKNOWLEDGEMENT
The author of this section wishes to thank M. Sakai, M. Endo, H. Aoyama, I. Fujitaka, T. Mukawa, E. Sugimoto, F. Tsukuda and N. Miyake for their helpful support.

9.4 *Designing with time-domain chips*

Following the introduction to the principles of time-domain synthesis that has been given in this chapter so far, in this section we will demonstrate how such integrated circuit devices may be used in a few simple configurations. By way of example, the *Digitalker* chip set manufactured by the National Semiconductor Corporation will be described here. However, it is not the intention to provide full and working circuit diagrams, but rather an illustration of the use of such chips so that the reader may refer to the up-to-date literature from the chosen manufacturer when creating his own design.

The Digitalker speech synthesis system consists of an *N*-channel MOS integrated circuit, the *MM54104* speech processor chip (SPC), and speech ROMs that, when used with an external filter, amplifier and speaker, produce a system which generates synthetic speech including the natural inflection and emphasis of the original speech. Male, female and children's voices can be synthesised.

Speech ROMs contain data that has been generated by a complex program on a large computer, as described in section 9.2. The ROMs may be standard MOS-type ROMs, electrically programmable ROMs (EPROMs) or electrically erasable ROMs (EEROMs).

The SPC interfaces directly to the speech ROMs via a 14-bit address bus and an 8-bit data bus. The speech ROMs contain the compressed speech data as well as the frequency and amplitude data required for speech output. Up to 128 kbits of speech data can be accessed directly by the SPC. With external hardware for address decoding an unlimited amount of speech data can be added.

In order to speak a word or phrase an 8-bit data word is applied to the SPC switch inputs (*SW8–SW1*) and a strobe signal is connected to *WR*. The SPC will fetch data from the speech ROMs and output the speech waveform to the external filter and amplifier. While the SPC is executing a speech sequence the *INT* line is held low and then goes high when the sequence is complete.

Figure 9.12 shows the minimum configuration using a switch interface, although an 8-bit data word from a microprocessor could be substituted.

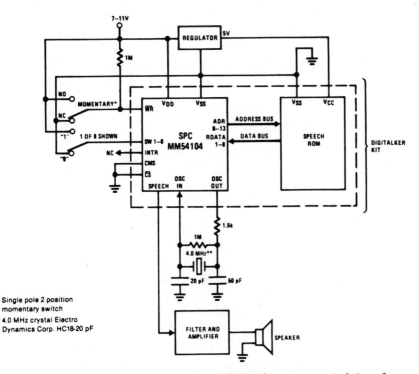

Figure 9.12 Minimum configuration of the MM54104, using a switch interface

The output of Digitalker consists of a 2- or 4-bit DAC output waveform that is filtered and amplified. The desired frequency response of the amplifier, filter and speaker are shown in fig. 9.13, and an active filter configuration that implements this response is shown in fig. 9.14.

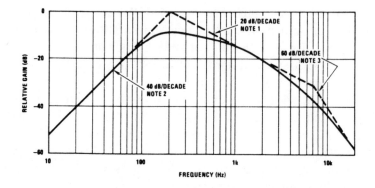

FREQUENCY (Hz)

Note 1: This curve is the desired response of the entire audio system including speaker. Minimum response is a low pass filter with a cutoff frequency of 200 Hz. For an audio system with a natural cutoff frequency around 200 Hz, this filter can be eliminated. This cutoff frequency may be tuned for the particular voice being synthesized. For a low pitched male voice it may be 100 Hz, while for a high pitched female or child's voice it might be 300 Hz.

Note 2: This is optional filtering that can be eliminated by proper selection of the speaker. If this 2 pole response is electronically produced, it should be adjusted as described in Note 1.

Note 3: This is optional filtering that can be eliminated for simpler systems. The acceptable range for this cutoff frequency is 6000 Hz–8000 Hz.

Figure 9.13 Frequency response of combined amplifier and speaker

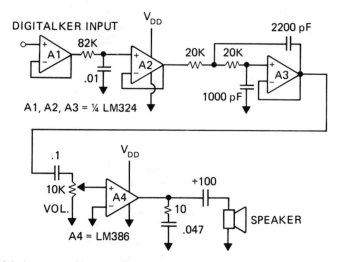

Figure 9.14 An active filter configuration, providing the frequency response shown in fig. 9.13

As shown by the above examples the Digitalker speech processor chip handles the entire data transfer from ROM and the reconstruction of the speech waveform, freeing the host microprocessor from that chore. All that is necessary for the host processor to do is transfer the

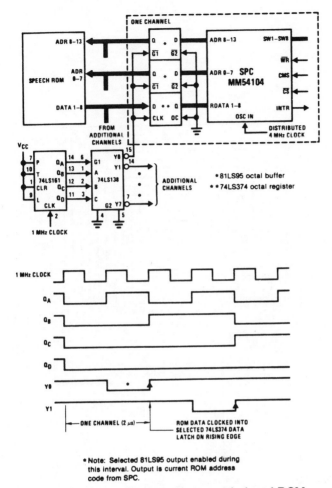

Figure 9.15 Multi-channel synthesiser with shared ROM space

8-bit address of the word or phrase to be spoken and wait for the *INT*/ line to go high at the end of the speech sequence, or use the *INT*/ line to interrupt the processor when the speech sequence is finished.

In some applications it is desired to have only one set of speech ROMs and have multiple SPCs access this ROM set. A group of products that might use this feature are voice response telephone answering equipment, telephone call announcement systems and electronic bank tellers. The circuit in fig. 9.15 will accomplish this.

The speech ROM is shared by eight SPCs, with each SPC channel scanned once each 16 μs as shown. During each channel period of 2 μs, an SPC output address is presented to the ROM address input port via

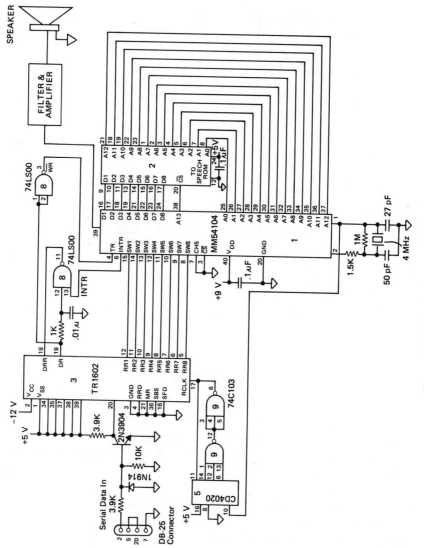

Figure 9.16 Synthesiser with RS232 interface

a pair of octal bus drivers. After 1 μs, the data from the ROM is clocked into the channel's octal data latch, the output of which is connected to the SPC ROM data input port. The remaining 1 μs of each channel cycle is provided for bus settling time.

Although the Digitalker normally is addressed with 8-bit parallel data, the circuit in fig. 9.16 will allow Digitalker to be addressed via an RS-232C serial link at 300 baud. The *TR1602* is an asynchronous receiver–transmitter chip that converts the serial data received to a parallel format and strobes the *WR/* line on the SPC to initiate the speech sequence. The TR1602 clock is derived by counting down from the Digitalker crystal oscillator.

9.5 *Further reading*

Only two time-domain synthesis techniques have been described in this chapter. However, many companies use similar methods which also involve segmentation of the speech waveform in the time domain, and still more are using developments of PCM such as *Adaptive Delta Modulation* and *Continuously Variable Slope Delta Modulation.*

It is hoped that the reader will have gained sufficient background at this point to be able to design a time-domain speech synthesis circuit using data sheets alone, and may now contact the manufacturers directly for details of devices that are currently available. There are many such manufacturers, and a list in a book of this sort must necessarily be incomplete, but as a guideline here are a few companies that, to the editor's knowledge, were offering time-domain synthesis chips in 1982:

> ITT Semiconductors, Kent, England
> Motorola Corp., Austin, Texas
> National Semiconductor Corp., Santa Clara, California
> Nippon Electric Co. Ltd, Kawasaki, Japan
> OKI Semiconductor Inc., Japan
> Sharp Corp., Nava, Japan
> Sony, Japan
> Telesensory Systems Inc., Palo Alto, California
> Texas Instruments, Dallas, Texas
> Toshiba Corp., Kawasaki, Japan

CHAPTER 10

CHIPS USING
LINEAR PREDICTIVE CODING

Larry Brantingham (10.1), John Stork (10.2),
Gwyn Edwards (10.3), Chris Moller (10.4)

In this chapter we discuss the implementation on large-scale integrated circuits of the linear predictive coding techniques shown in chapter 5. Three levels of dedication of the silicon to speech synthesis are demonstrated – as illustrated by devices from Texas Instruments Ltd, General Instrument Corp., and American Microsystems Inc. – followed by some circuit design examples.

10.1 *LPC using dedicated LSI chips*

LPC SYNTHESIS ARCHITECTURES

As noted in part 1 of this book, and in particular in chapter 5, linear predictive coding is one of several vocal-tract modelling techniques which are employed to produce synthetic speech. As was shown in fig. 5.1, it comprises an *excitation source* and a *time-varying filter*, and it is now convenient to include an overall *gain correction*. The use of a high-order all-pole filter distinguishes LPC from other vocal-tract modelling techniques such as formant synthesis.

The function of the *excitation source* is to emulate the periodic sound pressure variation resulting from the vocal-cord vibration as well as the noise produced by the rush of air past constrictions in the vocal tract during the production of sibilants and fricatives. The *time-varying filter* represents the action of the vocal-tract transfer function on the acoustical excitation. Such action produces several resonances (formants) in the speech spectrum and it is the position and movement of these which carries much of the information contained in speech. The ability of an LPC filter to accurately model the vocal-tract transfer function depends on several factors, most of which in turn affect the design of the synthesis device as will be described in this section. Finally, the overall *output energy* of the synthesiser is the product of the varying filter gain, the excitation energy, and the adjustment gain transmitted with the excitation and filter control data.

LSI IMPLEMENTATION

An integrated circuit LPC synthesiser can take many forms, depending chiefly on how much speed the manufacturing process allows the designer to trade for device area. In the extreme case where speed exceeds need by a large margin, the synthesis function may be performed by a microprocessor-like programmable structure. The TI *TMS320*, NEC *7720*, AMI *S28211* and others illustrate the case. However, speed at this level is presently very expensive, so all production synthesis devices have utilised specialised architectures to arrive at a minimum cost compromise between speed and device size. The TI *TMS5100* will serve as an example.

The TMS5100 has clearly defined logic blocks which correlate directly with the idealised form of an LPC synthesiser. There are an excitation block, a filter block, and a control and data acquisition interface. Since this is a digital implementation, there is also a digital-to-analog conversion section. Figure 10.1 identifies these sections on a photo-micrograph of the device.

The excitation section comprises a 13 bit pseudo-random shift counter to produce a random sequence of $+/-0.5$ for unvoiced excitation, and a period counter addressing a stored digitised waveform to represent the periodic voiced excitation. The stored waveform is repeated once each pitch period and is very carefully defined to have a flat spectrum so that all spectral shaping can be relegated to the digital filter section. Very simple logic allows the selection of voiced or unvoiced excitation.

Of the several mathematical options for implementing the filter, the so-called *two-multiply* version of the lattice structure has become the most commonly used method in integrated circuit LPC realisations. The two-multiply filter and its acoustical tube analogue are shown in fig. 10.2 (see also fig. 5.5 for its derivation).

The popularity of this approach is due in part to its suitability to fixed-point arithmetic and to its guaranteed stability (see chapter 5). Other important considerations are that such a filter can be designed to perform its operations with a minimum of intermediate storage and with a maximum of order in its arithmetic sequences, both features being important in determining the final size, and therefore cost, of integrated circuits. The filter must perform $2N$ operations of the type $C = AX + B$ for each output sample. For the TSM5100, the filter order

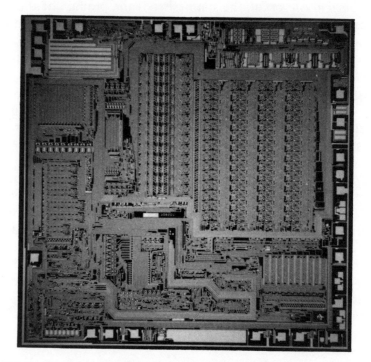

Figure 10.1   Photomicrograph of the TMS5100 LPC synthesiser, showing the functional blocks. (Reproduced by permission of Texas Instruments Ltd)

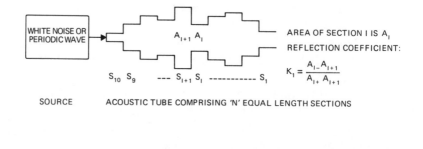

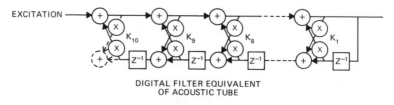

Figure 10.2

N is ten and the sample period is 125 μs, thus 160 000 10-bit by 14-bit multiply-accumulates must take place each second. To achieve this rate of computation it is necessary to *pipeline* the operations – that is, to begin a new operation before the previous one(s) are completed. The well-ordered sequences of the lattice structure are put to good use and eight operations are simultaneously in progress in the filter block.

In a practical synthesis system, the rate at which the filter control parameters are replaced is constrained to a fairly low value (40–50 Hz) to maintain a low data rate requirement. An *update* (or *frame*) *rate* in this range is adequate to model the general evolution of the vocal tract, but would produce a harshness in the voice quality. To reduce that effect, most synthesisers incorporate logic to smooth or interpolate the filter and excitation control parameters between updates. The TMS5100 has a separate logic block which, adhering to the concept of pipelining, uses two single bit adders and a variable delay line to interpolate the twelve parameters one at a time, eight times per frame. This very small amount of logic is thereby able to handle about 7700 10-bit additions and half that number of binary scalings each second.

COMPROMISES

Speech coding in itself is a compromise between reduction of data and accuracy of voice reproduction and the implementation in LSI only modifies the constraints slightly. At the present state of the semiconductor art, it is safe to say that a purpose-designed circuit could implement all features necessary to allow an LPC synthesiser to produce virtually recording quality speech while maintaining a cost suitable for consumer products.

However, for the last 5% of quality, and for applications related to speech but which have more severe requirements (e.g. music), the compromises begin to reappear. The following areas are the most important:

Filter order and sampling rate
Sampling rate directly determines the output bandwidth of the system. For speech, there is very little to be gained in going beyond 10 kHz sampling rate, but there are rare occasions when up to 14 kHz could be used. An increase in the sampling frequency itself of this magnitude could be accepted without circuit costs increase but unfortunately, a concomitant increase in filter order of about *two poles per kHz of bandwidth* means that the real increase in operating frequency must approximate the square of the sample rate factor. For music, with its 20 kHz bandwidth, filter order need not keep pace, but nonetheless

the problem is even greater than for speech. A sampling rate of 10 or 12 kHz and twelfth-order filter are typical compromises for today's technology.

Excitation accuracy

Excitation accuracy has two parts: *pitch accuracy* and *spectral accuracy*. The second is perhaps the simpler to solve, but has an interaction with the dynamic range of the filter which makes it desirable that the stored excitation waveform be variable length appropriate to pitch. This is difficult to solve and is usually ignored. Pitch accuracy has been traditionally bounded by the use of an integral number of samples to define the pitch period. At higher pitch levels, as in womens' voices, such a quantisation becomes rather coarse. To ameliorate the problem it is necessary to emulate an *oversampled* excitation function and this requires considerable enlargement of the excitation function storage area in most systems. Oversampling of the function is therefore often minimised or omitted.

Digital-to-analog converter and output filter

One of the most important contributions to distortion in synthetic speech is the digital-to-analog converter and, to a lesser extent, the low-pass output filter which is necessary in every sampled data system. Speech requires as a minimum a 12-bit dynamic range, though precision need not be 12 bits. These constraints form the basis of the μ- and A-law logarithmic coding conventions used in the telecommunications industry. The ability to put such a device on a monolithic circuit has only recently come about and still requires large amounts of device area. Similarly, the switched capacitor filtering techniques needed to provide an on-chip output filter have only recently become available and require that relatively expensive manufacturing processes be used. Though rather prosaic beside the sophisticated digital processing concepts in the rest of the circuit, these two elements put an effective limit on the attainable quality.

Other compromises that were essential with the very first attempts at synthesiser design are having less effect as semiconductor technology progresses and will not be mentioned here. In fact, it is now generally agreed that the speech modelling state of the art is the limiting factor in the design of new speech synthesis products.

10.2 *LPC using semi-dedicated digital filter chips*

SEMI-DEDICATED ARCHITECTURE

For a simpler design and mechanised test than required by 'two-multiply' lattice implementations, as well as for use in signal processing other than speech synthesis, a synthesiser chip can be configured using a single second-order digital filter section. Such a chip is the *SP0250* manufactured by General Instrument Corp., in which the filter is combined with a long *data in process* register, so that it may be time-multiplexed to realise any all-pole transfer function up to twelfth order at a data rate of 10 000 samples per second.[1-3]

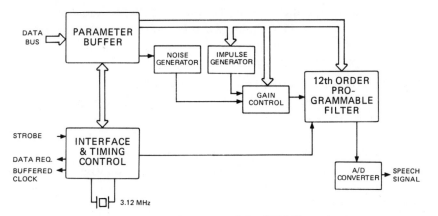

Figure 10.3 Major functions of the SP0250 synthesiser

The main features of the SP0250 architecture are shown in fig. 10.3. In speech synthesis applications, the filter is energised either by an on-chip impulse generator or on-chip pseudo-random noise generator. The impulse rate is selected by an external 8-bit code, and the amplitude of the impulse and noise sources is adjusted by an 8-bit code in exponent-magnitude form to provide more than 50 dB dynamic range. Filter output samples are converted with 7-bit accuracy to an audio signal by pulse-width modulation. Such a digital-to-analog converter is particularly simple and reliable, using no linear devices or voltage reference. The output signal is recovered with a simple (external) low-pass filter.

The control codes and 8-bit (sign + magnitude) coefficients are transmitted to the synthesiser as a sequence of 15 bytes. A data request signal from the synthesiser remains active until all 15 bytes have been received. Double internal buffering is used so that immediately after receiving an initial frame (15 bytes) the next frame may be requested and independently registered. Thus for many microprocessors, the SP0250 data request may be regarded as a relatively low priority interrupt. Typical speech production requires a data transfer time of 150 μs at intervals of 40 ms.

In section 12.2 two simple OEM boards are described which illustrate how this synthesiser is used in a simple hardware design. However, two features are of special interest for more sophisticated designs: Firstly, the SP0250 provides a serial, twos-complement coding of the output samples. By using an external register and synchronising signal (also supplied by the chip), audio conversion accuracy of 10 to 14 bits may be obtained. Secondly, an external, parallel, twos-complement input may be used in place of the internal excitation functions. External excitation is useful for coded predictor residuals and for abitrary signal processing. A synchronising signal is available for this application, and the external signal may also be scaled by the internal amplitude control.

LP CODING FOR SECOND-ORDER FILTER SECTIONS

While direct control of individual second-order filter sections has direct application to formant-coded speech, and particularly to synthesis-by-rule, it is important to understand how a cascade of second-order sections is used for linear prediction synthesis.

As demonstrated in chapter 5, linear prediction coefficients derived from short-term autocorrelation analysis of speech signals can be represented by the *predictor polynomial* (equation 5.1):[4]

$$A(z) = 1 + \sum_{k=1}^{p} a(k)z^{-k} \qquad (5.1)$$

A steady-state system transfer function for the analysed signal can then be stated as:

$$H(z) = \frac{G}{A(z)}, \qquad (5.7)$$

and from this representation it is clear that the $a(k)$s are the coefficients of a recursive direct digital filter of order p. A direct filter may be represented with complete equivalence by a cascade of lower-order sections, and in particular an even-order direct filter by a series of second-order sections. It is known that stable and accurate second-order sections are realised using much shorter coefficients than required for the equivalent direct filter[5] – a design principle of this style of synthesiser.

Arithmetically, second-order coefficients are obtained by finding the roots of the predictor polynomial. A commonly used numeric algorithm, *Bairstow's method*, in fact resolves the second-order factors of the polynomial.

Each second-order section generally represents a complex pole-pair in the z plane of the form:

$$II_2(z) = \frac{g}{(z^{-1} - p)(z^{-1} - p^*)} = \frac{g'}{1 - 2Pz^{-1} + Qz^{-2}}$$

where P is the abscissa of pole locations and Q is the square of the radius vector to either pole. Thus the second-order factors of the predictor polynomial may be expressed in either polar or cartesian form and readily converted to second-order filter coefficients. In factoring the predictor polynomial it is often found that there are one or more pairs of real roots. These may be represented in equivalent second-order form by:

$$H_2(z) = \frac{g}{(z^{-1} - a)(z^{-1} - b)} = \frac{g'}{1 - Az^{-1} + Bz^{-2}}$$

where the filter coefficients $A = a + b$ and $B = ab$.

When representing the coefficients as 8-bit or smaller values, care must be taken that the quantised values represent stable transfer functions for either the complex or real-axis pairs. This is easily accomplished numerically in programs which format the synthesiser data and will take into account a translation table – internal to the synthesiser – that allows greater precision for poles close to the unit circle or at extreme frequencies. A secondary consideration is that of filter overflow (exceeding the 18-bit range of *data in process* available for each filter term) which is partially dependent on the order in which coefficient pairs are assigned. A practical way to test overflow during off-line creation of fixed vocabularies is to incorporate a software model of the synthesiser in the data formatting programs.

10.3 *LPC using digital signal processors*

PROGRAMMABLE SIGNAL PROCESSORS VERSUS DEDICATED
SYNTHESISERS

Programmable *digital signal processing* (DSP) circuits that can be used for speech synthesis have recently become available. The architectures of such devices are usually organised to enable efficient implementation of DSP algorithms, which typically involve considerable multiplication and accumulation. Speech synthesis algorithms, including LPC, are in this category.

Most programmable DSP chips, however, contain features that are not required for speech synthesis, since they are of necessity general-purpose devices. For example, LPC synthesis requires very little variable data storage (RAM), typically less than sixty-four words, whereas a programmable DSP chip may have up to 256 words of RAM. Therefore, DSP chips are inevitably more expensive than dedicated speech synthesisers. Thus it may not be obvious to the reader why a programmable DSP chip (that must, after all, be programmed) should be considered when a speech synthesiser can be purchased off the shelf. The answer is that if a synthesiser that meets all the requirements is available, then that is usually the best solution. However, there are applications where the synthesiser chips on the market fail to satisfy the system requirements in one or more ways. This may be the result of technical reasons (such as incompatibility with existing speech data bases) or subjective reasons (such as inadequate speech quality). In either case it will be necessary to consider the alternative methods of realising a synthesiser. Few practical means are available, and a programmable DSP chip will invariably be the best.

One of the advantages of the DSP chip is that it allows the user to choose his own algorithm, data rates, and so on. DSP chips are especially appropriate in cases where a specific algorithm, not available in standard synthesisers, needs to be implemented. This will allow the user to realise systems with special features, such as variable speed and variable pitch, or with a selectable quality/data rate trade-off. Any algorithm, LPC or otherwise, can then be chosen. DSP chips are very powerful devices, and that power can be used to great advantage once the DSP chip solution is chosen. In large, expensive systems, for example, the extra cost of the DSP chip will be negligible, but the unique features it can add to the system can be very valuable. Another possibility is that the DSP chip may also be used to realise some other function, either simultaneously or in a time-shared mode. Examples of such functions include the front end of a speech recognition or analysis system, or *tone synthesis* and detection in communications systems. In many such cases the overall system may then be more cost effective than if the two functions had been realised separately with a speech synthesiser chip and additional circuitry for the second function.

The DSP chip can be used to synthesise speech using any of the common algorithms, including LPC, Formant synthesis, Adaptive Delta Pulse Code Modulation, etc. Although the choice of algorithm will be dictated entirely by other factors, the use of a DSP chip for LPC synthesis will be the only one considered here.

A TYPICAL LPC IMPLEMENTATION

The basic structure of an LPC synthesiser, including the lattice filter, was presented in section 10.1. Although other variations of the LPC algorithm can be implemented with a DSP chip, we will consider this implementation since the reader is assumed to be acquainted with it, and since it is probably the most commonly used structure. Other structures are presented in chapter 5, and the interested reader should refer to that chapter for more information.

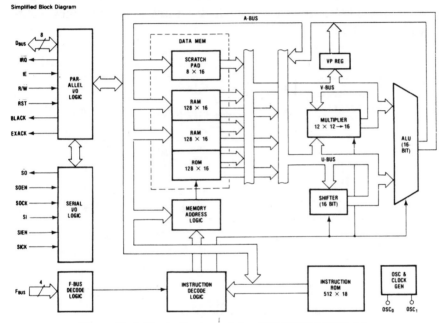

Figure 10.4 Block diagram of the AMI S28211 DSP chip

For the purpose of a short example, a programmable DSP chip designed and manufactured by American Microcircuits Inc., the *S28211*, will be described. The architecture of this chip is shown in fig. 10.4. The microprocessor-like structure will be immediately obvious to some readers, as will the many variations from the typical microprocessor architecture. In particular, the *multiple buses* (to eliminate bus sharing between signals, in order to minimise delays), and the *single-cycle parallel multiplier*, pipelined with the ALU/accumulator, are commonly used in DSP chips, but not in conventional microprocessors. Signal processing is usually a real-time operation, and these features all help to increase the throughput of the device.

The chip has many other features that help to make it an efficient signal processor, including a 256 word data RAM with two output ports that can both be read in a single instruction cycle, and two index registers that can be incremented simultaneously, allowing tracked addressing of two separate address groups in the memory. The software also differs from a conventional microprocessor since it has two sets of operators, one exclusively for the Arithmetic/Logic Unit (ALU). Every instruction executes two operators, one from each set, and all instructions are executed in a single 250 ns instruction cycle.

Applying this general-purpose signal processing power to speech synthesis is then a trivial software task — a ten-stage lattice filter routine for LPC is only eighteen instructions long and takes eighty-one cycles (24.3 μs) to execute.

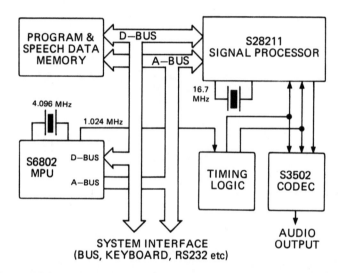

Figure 10.5 A synthesiser implementation using the S28211 DSP chip

A speech synthesiser circuit using the S28211 DSP is shown in fig. 10.5. The system shown is controlled by an *S6802* microprocessor (MPU), although this could equally be a different micro- or even a mini- or mainframe computer. The 28211 is operated as a memory mapped peripheral occupying sixteen addresses. The remaining address lines (A15–A4 in this case) are decoded to provide a strobe each time it is addressed. The output signal is brought out on the serial port of the DSP and converted into an audio signal with a PCM (Pulse Coded Modulation) *codec* chip. The *S3502* does this as well as executing the smoothing filter function. The clock and strobe signals are both derived very simply by dividing down the 1.024 MHz microprocessor clock. The reason for using the codec as a digital-to-analog converter (DAC) is that the codec has a dynamic range equal to a 12-bit linear DAC, but at a much lower cost. The digital input to the codec, however, is not linearly encoded, but is in the logarithmically compressed form known as the *MU-255 law*, used in digital telecommunication systems. The S28211 converts the linear signal generated internally to this code in a thirty-five instruction routine, taking approximately 10.5 μs to execute.

The software required to make a synthesiser with a DSP consists of two parts: the *synthesiser program* itself, executed by the DSP, and the *control program*, executed by the control processor. These two need to be designed concurrently, although they can be developed separately. An LPC synthesis program for the S28211 was written at AMI, and shown to work very well. It showed that the DSP could be programmed to execute the synthesis function and still have room in its memories to enable it to be programmed to execute other functions as well, although it would not be able to execute both functions simultaneously in real time without special optimisation. The program used was actually a translation of a Fortran program that executed the same function on a large computer. The entire code was 237 instructions long, and took approximately 100 μs to execute. The user of such a program on a DSP chip is rewarded with the ultimate flexibility, allowing the synthesiser to operate with many optional features, including independently variable pitch and speed. However the trade-off is higher chip cost compared to dedicated but restricted synthesiser chips.

10.4 *Designing with LPC chips*

Following the introduction to the common structures of LPC-based speech synthesis devices, the reader will now be shown some basic methods of designing an electronic circuit incorporating such a device.

SYNTHESIS SYSTEM CONFIGURATION

The simplest theoretical configuration of *VLSI* synthesis circuitry is a single chip, containing the synthesis logic, a ROM for the speech data to be stored in, and sufficient interface logic to permit the system to be activated by a number of contact closures. At the time of writing (November '82), existing systems have not been integrated to this extent, though it is likely that integrated circuits will be produced which are configured in this way, for extremely low-cost applications. A single chip without intelligence does, however, impose some restrictions on system design. Without a microprocessor, (or one integrated into the single-chip solution), there is no capacity for generation of complex phrases from a single key-closure, except by storing the whole phrase *verbatim*. For example, a talking elevator might require storage of eight complete phrases, each with the word *floor* in it, with consequent waste of ROM space.

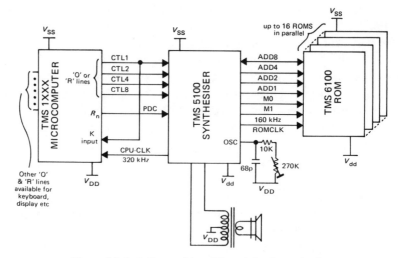

Figure 10.6 A three-chip self-contained synthesiser

Intelligence can be added to the system using a dedicated single-chip microcomputer, or by driving a synthesiser with a standard microprocessor bus. A typical general-purpose configuration is a three-chip set, comprising a *synthesiser*, a *ROM* and a *single-chip microcomputer*, as shown in fig. 10.6. (This is essentially the configuration used in Texas Instruments' *Speak & Spell*, and subsequent products.) The microcomputer generates the signals to activate the synthesiser, and also typically implements all the other functions of the product, for example, scanning a multiplexed display and keyboard. The three-chip solution is a very powerful and cost-effective solution when production volumes are large (say above 5000 units/year), but it is impractical for smaller volumes, due to the need to *mask* the program and speech data into ROM. For lower volumes, and where a microprocessor is already present in the system to which speech is to be added, the speech synthesiser may be interfaced to the bus in the same way as any other peripheral device.

Micro-based system considerations
Assuming that the system has a microprocessor driving the synthesiser, there remains a choice of where the speech data is to reside. Some

synthesisers, like TI's *TMS5220*, can either accept data from the system data bus, or from a low-cost serial-access ROM connected directly to the synthesiser (see fig. 10.7). The latter option not only saves money, but also relieves the bus of the requirement to carry the data, and uses less space in the system memory map. Conversely, putting data on the microprocessor bus allows the data to be in RAM or EPROM, and also gives the software the power to modify the data 'on the fly', for example to change the pitch contour. Of course this alternative requires more intervention by the microprocessor, but even so, a typical figure of 1–4% of total processing power is all that is likely to be required for the data transfer.

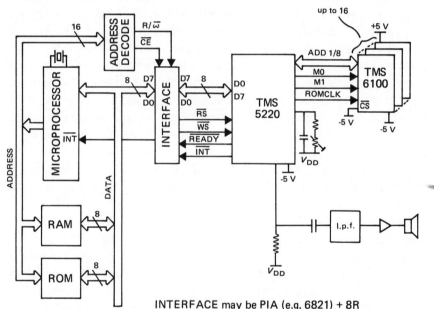

INTERFACE may be PIA (e.g. 6821) + 8R
or 74LS646 + LS74 + LS00 + 8R

Figure 10.7 A synthesiser configuration using both serial and parallel data transfer

HARDWARE REQUIREMENTS
In order to describe the hardware interface requirements of LPC chips, the Texas Instruments' family of *PMOS* synthesisers shall serve as an example.

Latching the data
Since PMOS technology runs internally at a relatively slow clock rate, devices in this family require about $30\,\mu s$ to accept data from the system, and take a similar time to provide data themselves. This is a

long time in bus terms, and during a write cycle the data must be held stable. It may be possible to latch the data using microprocessor wait states, or by reconfiguring the bus as a port, but both these solutions prevent the microprocessor from doing anything else while it is waiting. If this is a problem, or the processor does not have these features, a bi-directional latch will be needed. A minimum cost solution uses two *SN74LS373* octal latches connected back-to-back, with an *SN74LS74* to do the handshaking. A minimum-parts-count solution uses an *MC6821* PIA (Peripheral Interface Adaptor) connected directly to the synthesiser.

System clocks

The lowest-cost clock generator for a synthesiser uses the internal clock oscillator with an external capacitor and resistor as the frequency-determining components. Limitations of this scheme are that the frequency varies appreciably with supply voltage (a problem with battery-powered designs), and precision capacitors are expensive. A preset variable resistor will probably prove necessary. An alternative (though slightly more expensive) solution is to use a *ceramic resonator*. These are less expensive than quartz crystals, for frequencies below 1 MHz, and their stability is more than adequate in this context. Yet another solution is to extract a suitable waveform from elsewhere in the system, though note that most clock oscillator pins are not TTL-compatible when used as logic inputs, and an interface may be needed.

Audio output

Although a few synthesisers provide enough milliwatts to drive a small loudspeaker, in most cases the power will be inadequate, and an amplifier IC will be needed. These are quite inexpensive and simple to use, and may only require a couple of additional components. The synthesiser output consists of a series of voltages. Typically, the voltage is updated 8000 times/second. This produces an additional 8 kHz component in the output waveform, and worse, sidebands of that with the speech output. If this is left in, the effect is to add a whistle and an undesirable fuzziness to the output, and, as it has a different spectrum from human speech, it will contravene regulations if fed into the telephone system. For both these reasons, filtering is recommended before amplification, except in the most cost-critical applications. A fifth-order *Butterworth* filter is suggested; beyond that the improvement is barely audible.

Printed circuit layout

It is often overlooked that a synthesiser, like a DAC or ADC, is a mixed analog/digital part, and as such it needs to have its circuitry laid out with particular care to keep noise levels to a minimum. A ground plane is recommended, with output signals routed well away from the data buses. Note which pin the audio output is referenced to, and where possible feed the audio into one input of a differential amplifier, with the other input a.c. coupled to the reference. The other source of noise is the power rails, and attention should be paid to decoupling these perhaps better than usual, to minimise this source of noise.

SOFTWARE

Address vectors

The simplest way to make a synthesiser say a word is to tell it the *starting address* of the data. For a small number of words this is quite adequate. Consider, though, the common requirement to say a digit, in the range 0–9, based on the binary value in a register. This would have to be done by code to implement the equivalent of:

```
ZERO  =  1302H:ONE = 134DH:TWO = 137FH: THREE
         = 13A2H: (etc)
IF A  =  0 THEN ADDRESS = ZERO
IF A  =  1 THEN ADDRESS = ONE
       .        .
       .        .
       .        .
       .        .
IF A  =  9 THEN ADDRESS = NINE
SPEAK (ADDRESS)
```

This is clearly very wasteful of code. A *vector table* on the other hand, consists of a list of addresses of the starts of the speech data for each word. Each address vector is the same length (usually two bytes long). To simplify the problem above, we would arrange that the first few locations of the ROM contained:

Addr	Contents
0000	1302
0002	134D
0004	137F
0006	13A2 (etc.)

The necessary code to say a digit would then just be

SPEAK (@(A*2))

(where '@' means 'fetch the data from this address').

The '@' function may either be implemented by using the *READ-AND-BRANCH* command in the synthesiser, or by the microprocessor. For an 8-bit processor using BASIC, and with all data on the system bus, the program would be:

SPEAK (256*PEEK(A*2)+ PEEK(A*2+ 1))

It should be emphasised that speech data is just like any other data to the microprocessor; it may make good sense to merge it with other word-related data in the system (for example, spelling data or linked lists for phrases), and a vector structure makes this quite easy to implement.

Use of FIFO to reconcile data rates
The frames of speech data, although used at a regular rate (40/second for TI chips), are of variable length, and so the bit-rate will be a function of the data and will vary with time. Although it is theoretically possible for the processor to calculate when the synthesiser needs another byte, this is unwieldy in practice. Thus, when speaking data provided by the microprocessor, a *FIFO* (first-in-first-out) buffer is used to allow for discrepancies. This FIFO may be integrated into the synthesiser. Status-bits are provided to indicate to the processor whether the FIFO is less than half-full, and needs topping up, and whether it is empty. All the processor then needs to do is to ensure that the FIFO never becomes empty while the synthesiser is speaking.

Interrupt or polled operation?
The amount of time required to speak a given phrase will be unknown to the microprocessor. Frequently, it is necessary to know when the synthesiser has finished speaking (for example, if it is to speak another word immediately afterwards). Additionally, if the speech data is coming from the processor, the status of the FIFO will need to be monitored. The simplest way to achieve this is for the processor to continuously check the status register in the synthesiser. This does, however, occupy the processor for appreciable amounts of time. A more elegant solution is for the synthesiser to generate an interrupt when attention is required, which can then be serviced by the processor to take whatever action is necessary. This frees the processor to do other tasks in the interim.

Unpacking of data
In order to minimise the storage requirement for speech data, only the minimum number of bits is used for each parameter. This means

that data do not occupy a byte per parameter, but are packed into the bytes bit by bit. A 5-bit parameter might, for example, reside in the two most significant bits of the next. (Bits are packed *least-to-most significant* in TI synthesisers.) Hence, to detect a stopcode in the data, the program must keep track of where the parameter starts within the byte. To actually manipulate the data, (for example to change the pitch), software must be written to unpack the data into individual parameters, and to pack it again before speaking. This might typically involve about 150 bytes of code.

10.5 *Further reading*

There is a large number of companies manufacturing speech synthesis devices employing a variation of the LPC technique, and the list is growing fast.

The general introduction to this broad family of products which has been given in this chapter should be sufficient to allow the reader to approach manufacturers directly about LPC devices available at the time of reading, and to design directly from a current data sheet.

As a guideline, here is a list of some of the manufacturers who in 1982, to the editor's knowledge, offered synthesisers based on LPC or a variant.

American Microsystems Inc., Santa Clara, California
Fujitsu, Japan
General Instrument Corp., Hicksville, New York
Hitachi Ltd, Tokyo, Japan
Intermetall Gmbh, Freiburg, W. Germany
Matsushita, Japan
Mitsubishi, Japan
Nippon Electric Co. Ltd, Kawasaki, Japan
Panasonic, Secaucus, New Jersey
Sanyo, Japan
Suwa–Seikosha, Japan
Telesensory Systems Inc., Palo Alto, California
Texas Instruments Inc., Dallas, Texas
Toshiba Corp., Kawasaki, Japan

References

1. Vetter, D., Stork, J., Skoge, K., and Ahrens, P. (April 1981) 'LPC speech IC using a 12-pole cascade digital filter'. *Proc. 1981 IEEE Int. Conf. on Acoustics, Speech, and Signal Proc.*

2. Stork, J.E. *US Patent* No. 4 296 279, 20 October 1981.
3. Jackson, L.B., Kaiser, J.F., and McDonald, H.S., (Sept. 1968) 'An approch to the implementation of digital filters'. *IEEE Trans. Audio and Electroacoustics*, **AU-16**, No. 3.
4. Rabiner, L.R. and Schafer, R.W. (1978) *Digital Processing of Speech Signals*. Englewood Cliffs, N.J.: Prentice-Hall, Inc.
5. Rabiner, L.R. and Gold, B. (1975) *Theory and Application of Digital Signal Processing*, Englewood Cliffs, N.J.: Prentice-Hall, Inc.

CHAPTER 11

PHONETIC SYNTHESIS

Richard Gagnon (11.1),
Kathryn Fons and Tim Gargagliano (11.2–11.4)

In this chapter we examine one of the best known silicon implementations of formant synthesis, the SC-01 phonetic synthesiser chip from Votrax Inc. Other recent formant devices employ similar synthesis methods, although phonetic conversion on-chip is currently unique to Votrax. The subject is introduced with a description of the PCB synthesiser module on which the SC-01 was modelled.

11.1 *Phonetic synthesis using analog filters*

First, what is phonetic synthesis? It is the process of simulating human speech at the phonetic level. This is accomplished with a device called a *phonetic voice synthesiser* which accepts a variety of digital phonetic input commands and from these commands produces intelligible synthetic speech with virtually an unlimited vocabulary. The big advantage this type of synthesis offers is complete freedom in choice of possible output utterances. Other types of synthesisers require to be fed with data representing the utterances, rather than simply a phonetic code. Phonetic synthesisers are therefore inherently suitable for text-to-speech systems because they can be driven directly by text-to-phonetic converters, as discussed in chapter 6.

Another possibility is a *phonemic synthesiser* which would accept straight phoneme inputs. However, such a device would need to be much more complicated in order to produce the same output quality and would probably never sound as good as the phonetic synthesiser. With only phoneme inputs driving it the phonemic synthesiser would have to perform many more computations to determine just how to pronounce each phoneme. The same phoneme in different contexts takes on numerous different forms and the phonemic synthesiser would have to calculate which form was needed in each case. The phonetic synthesiser, on the other hand, depends on external inputs which must be chosen with care to produce properly pronounced speech.

To get maximum performance from the phonetic synthesiser, the phonetic codes for each word or phrase must be developed manually in most cases. This should not be viewed as excessively burdensome. Once a word has been so coded it need not be repeated. If an electronic system was putting words on a CRT terminal or a printer instead of over a loudspeaker, the spelling of all possible words would have to be entered manually in the first place anyway. The phonetic codes to produce an utterance require perhaps only 20% more memory than is required to store the letters to spell the utterance.

The phonetic synthesiser described in this section is the model *VS6* manufactured by Votrax of Troy, Michigan (see figure 11.1). It accepts sixty-four *phonetic input codes* along with four inflection or *pitch codes*. It contains a phonetic parameter generator which derives a frequency domain vocal-tract model which is composed of a cascaded array of tuneable analog filters driven by voiced and unvoiced sources.

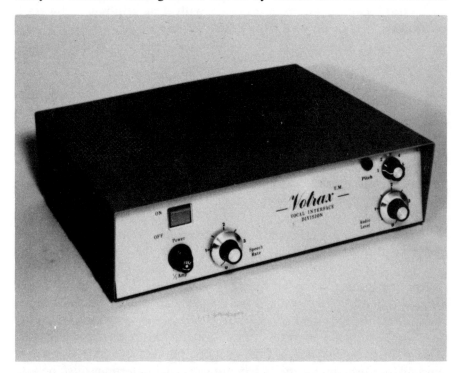

Figure 11.1 Votrax model VS6 voice synthesiser. Note the *Speech rate* control at lower left, *Audio level* control at lower right and *Pitch* control at upper right. (Photograph by permission of Votrax of Troy, Michigan, USA)

Each phonetic command consists of one byte (8 bits) of data. Six of the bits determine which of sixty-four phonetic sounds will be produced and the remaining 2 bits determine which of four pitch and inflection levels will be generated. Some of the phonetic inputs are phonemes such as /m/ and /n/ while other inputs are allophones of the same phoneme which differ in stress, duration, and dynamic features such as [O], [O1], and [O2]. A complete listing of the VS6 allophone set is given in table 11.1.

Figure 11.2 shows the block diagram of the synthesiser. The phonetic input commands go to the input buffer which may be an RS-232 interface, a TTL parallel interface, or whatever type of standard interface is suitable for the application. The buffer is necessary to provide the synthesiser with continuous phonetic data, thus relieving the host system of this burden. The six allophone-selection bits drive the address inputs of the *allophone parameter ROM* (read only memory) which generates all the static parameters needed by the synthesiser. The dynamic features of these parameters are generated by the *articulation generators*. The ROM generates sixteen parameters as shown in table 11.2.

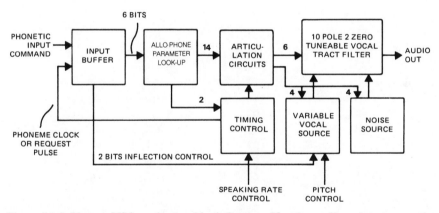

Figure 11.2 Votrax VS6 synthesiser block diagram. Numbers adjacent to connecting lines indicate number of parameters at these points

The allophone timing and transition rate parameters drive the timing control. The other fourteen parameters are filtered and/or delayed in the articulation generators where all the transitions and dynamics are formed. These generators are made up of tuneable low-pass analog-active filters and delay elements. The first seven ROM parameters are filtered by the slow-acting second-order low-pass filters. The eleventh through the fourteenth ROM parameters are delayed and then filtered by the faster second-order low-pass filters. The vocal amplitude (ninth

Table 11.1 VS6/SC-01 phoneme conversion chart (see tables 3.3 and 3.4 for a list of 'GA' phoneme symbols as used in the 'parent phoneme' column)

Hex code	Allophone symbol	Duration (ms)	Example word	Parent phoneme
00	EH3	59	jackEt	/ɛ/
01	EH2	71	Enlist	/ɛ/
02	EH1	121	hEAvy	/ɛ/
03	PA0	47	-PAUSE-	—
04	DT	47	buTTer	/d/
05	A2	71	enAble	/eɪ/
06	A1	103	mAde	/eɪ/
07	ZH	90	meaSure	/ʒ/
08	AH2	71	hOnest	/ɔ/
09	I3	55	inhibIt	/ɪ/
0A	I2	80	Inhibit	/ɪ/
0B	I1	121	inhIbit	/ɪ/
0C	M	103	Mat	/m/
0D	N	80	suN	/n/
0E	B	71	Bag	/b/
0F	V	71	Van	/v/
10	CH*	71	Chip	/tʃ/
11	SH	121	SHop	/ʃ/
12	Z	71	Zoo	/z/
13	AW1	146	AWful	/ɔ/
14	NG	121	thiNG	/ŋ/
15	AH1	146	fAther	/a/
16	OO1	103	lOOking	/ʊ/
17	OO	185	bOOk	/ʊ/
18	L	103	Land	/l/
19	K	80	Kitten	/k/
1A	J†	47	JuDGe	/dʒ/
1B	H	71	Hello	/h/
1C	G	71	Get	/g/
1D	F	103	Fast	/f/
1E	D	55	paiD	/d/
1F	S	90	paSS	/s/
20	A	185	mAId	/eɪ/
21	AY	65	mAId	/eɪ/
22	Y1	80	Yard	/j/
23	UH3	47	missIOn	/ə/
24	AH	250	gOt	/ɔ/
25	P	103	Past	/p/
26	O	185	mOre	/ɔ/
27	I	185	pIn	/ɪ/

cont'd....

Hex code	Allophone symbol	Duration (ms)	Example word	Parent phoneme
28	U	185	tUne	/u/
29	Y	103	anY	/i/
2A	T	71	Tap	/t/
2B	R	90	Red	/r/
2C	E	185	mEEt	/i/
2D	W	80	Win	/w/
2E	AE	185	dAd	/æ/
2F	AE1	103	After	/a/
30	AW2	90	sAlty	/ɔ/
31	UH2	71	sUspect	/ʌ/
32	UH1	103	About	/ə/
33	UH	185	cUp	/ʌ/
34	O2	80	fOr	/ɔ/
35	O1	121	abOArd	/ɔ/
36	IU	59	yOU	/u/
37	U1	90	yOU	/u/
38	V	80	THe	/ð/
39	TH	71	THing	/θ/
3A	ER	146	bIRd	/ə/
3B	EH	185	gEt	/ɛ/
3C	E1	121	bEfore	/i/
3D	AW	250	cAll	/ɔ/
3E	PA1	185	-PAUSE-	—
3F	STOP	47	-STOP-	—

Note: Durations listed will vary depending on the Master Clock Frequency.
*[T] must precede [CH] to produce /tʃ/ sound.
†[D] must precede [J] to produce /dʒ/ sound.

ROM parameter) gets similar treatment but with its own delay parameters. All of the timing and articulation functions are proportionately
varied by the speech rate control on the front panel of the device.

The vocal-tract filter model is an analog filter network which is
tuned with duty cycles derived from the outputs of the articulation
circuits. Excitation for the filter comes from the *variable-frequency
vocal source* and from the *fricative noise source*. The vocal source is
an analog oscillator whose frequency is varied by a low-pass filter
which is driven by the inflection bits of each phonetic input command.
The fricative source is a pseudo-random digital noise generator whose
sequence repetition rate is too slow to be audible. During voiced
fricative consonants the noise source is modulated by the vocal-source

oscillator frequency just as it is in the human vocal system. This feature gives the voiced fricatives their characteristic 'buzzy' quality.

The vocal-tract filter block diagram is shown in fig. 11.3.

Each of the filter blocks is a second-order tuneable filter. The *nasal notch resonator* places a notch or depression in the frequency spectrum and is normally active during nasal consonants and during the transitions going into and out of these phonemes. In addition to the stages shown in fig. 11.3, the two excitation sources have tuneable filters on their outputs which alter the excitation driving the vocal-tract filter. The fricative noise source passes through the *fricative bandpass filter* and then through the *fricative low-pass filter* to shape its spectral structure before injection into the vocal tract. The vocal source passes through the *spectral contour filter* which gives a controlled amount of high frequency attenuation to voiced sounds prior to injection into the vocal tract.

Table 11.2 Parameters output by phoneme parameter ROM of the VS6 synthesiser

Parameter	Destination
First formant frequency	Vocal-tract model, F1 stage
Second formant frequency	Vocal-tract model, F2 stage
Third formant frequency	Vocal-tract model, F3 stage
Nasal closure	Vocal-tract model, nasal resonator
Nasal frequency	Vocal-tract model, nasal resonator
Fricative frequency	Fricative source bandpass filter
Fricative low-pass	Fricative source low-pass filter
Phoneme timing	Phoneme timer
Vocal amplitude	Vocal-source injection
Vocal delay	Vocal amplitude parameter delay
Vocal spectral contour	Vocal spectral contour filter
Closure	Vocal and fricative injection
Second formant bandwidth	Vocal-tract model, F2 stage
Fricative amplitude	Fricative source injection
Closure delay	Closure parameter delay circuit
Transition rate	Articulation and timing circuits

In summary it is interesting to note that phonetic synthesis involves both analog and digital processes. Initially phonemes or allophones are digital entities. Their translation into acoustic reality involves a complex blending of variables which are ultimately converted into analog parameters, which in turn control a voice model in order to produce the desired analog audio signal.

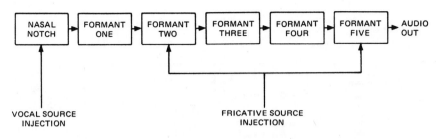

Figure 11.3 Votrax VS6 vocal-tract filter block diagram

11.2 *Designing with a phonetic synthesiser*

Following the general introduction to the make-up of a phonetic synthesiser given in section 11.1, in this section we will describe the use in a circuit of the *SC-01* single-chip phonetic-input formant synthesiser manufactured by Votrax Inc. of Troy, Michigan. The SC-01 has many similarities to the VS series of synthesisers, having been developed from them in the early 1970s. The main difference, of course, is that the SC-01 is a low power CMOS device packaged in a twenty-two pin DIP, whereas the VS series was generally made of several boards of MSI devices, loaded in a 19″ rack.

THE SC-01 DEVICE

There are two sections in the SC-01, the *vocal tract* and the *allophone controller* (see fig. 11.4). The vocal tract is a set of variable filters which are excited by periodic and/or aperiodic signals. It is based upon analog filter design. Switched capacitance networks are used to create a broad range of resistances required in the filter design. This permits the vocal tract to be realised in a very small area of silicon.

Keeping the vocal tract small is important in order to allow the allophone control circuitry to be included on the same piece of silicon. This controller is not a trivial part of the SC-01 circuitry. An allophone has both static and dynamic properties that must be handled by the allophone controller. Static properties are defined in a look-up type device. Dynamic properties require continuous calculations to be performed on parameters being fed to the vocal tract and timing circuits. It is the dynamic properties that present the most complexity in allophone controller implementation. Fortunately this complexity is hidden to devices external to the SC-01. Both static and dynamic aspects of an allophone are automatically handled internally.

Using a 6-bit allophone code, the SC-01 produces enough allophones to synthesise virtually any English-based word. Its allophone set is very

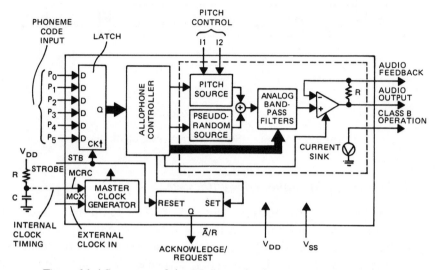

Figure 11.4 Structure of the SC-01 single-chip phonetic synthesiser

similar to that of the Votrax VS-6 synthesiser (see table 11.1). The SC-01 voice is sometimes described as sounding 'robotic'. What this usually refers to is the lack of natural sounding stress overlaying the speech output. This is not a shortcoming of phonetic synthesis in general, but more due to the minimised design of the SC-01 to meet size and cost constraints of mass production. However, like the rapid evolution that microprocessor technology went through, future generations of LSI phonetic synthesisers will have increased performance and incorporate new features to produce very natural-sounding synthetic speech.

INTERFACE CONSIDERATIONS

An SC-01 will function well in nearly any type of microprocessor system. Its lean data requirement presents an insignificant demand on a processor. This permits non-speech related tasks to be performed simultaneously with speech. A typical configuration would have the SC-01 connected directly to the data bus of the processor (see fig. 11.5). Only the lower 6 bits are required to supply an allophone code. Optionally two additional bits (I1, I2) may be externally latched to exercise the pitch. These two signals are recommended for use on a word or phrase basis because they change instantly. If used on allophone basis the results are sometimes undesirable.

Data transfers are handled with a simple handshake scheme. A decoded write pulse must be connected to the *STB* (STROBE) input to latch an allophone code at the appropriate time. The *A/R* (ACKNOWL-EDGEMENT/REQUEST) line goes high to request a new allophone code and low to acknowledge that it has been strobed in. This will occur every 50–250 ms depending upon the phoneme selected. If interrupts are used, the *ACK/REQ* output can be connected to the lowest priority available. If interrupts are not used then this signal should be scanned periodically. Another alternative would be to ignore this signal, since it is only a timing indicator, and use software timing. In this way it is possible to produce variable speech rate under software control.

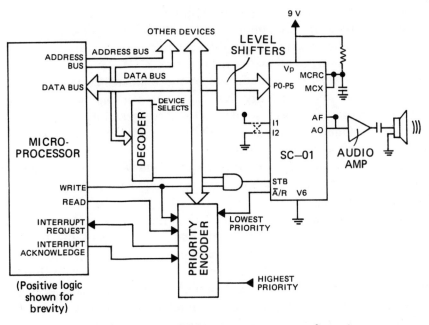

Figure 11.5 A basic SC-01 microprocessor configuration

A master clock frequency must be supplied to the SC-01, or else the onboard oscillator may be used with a resistor-capacitor connected. All signals inside the SC-01 are slaved off the master clock. By varying its frequency it is possible to achieve a variety of voice and sound effects.

All that remains to make the SC-01 speak is to supply a sequence of allophone codes. Procedures for developing allophone sequences are described below.

11.3 *Phonetic programming*

If speech is viewed as an acoustic coding system for language, then an allophone (speech sound) represents a single component used to construct an item (sound, syllable, word, phrase, etc.) within that system. The Votrax synthesisers generate the static and dynamic features of these components electronically in such a way that the task of creating synthetic speech for a language can be as simple as stringing the characters together to write the language. The SC-01 synthesiser chip is directed to produce speech via two methods. *Manual Phonetic Programming* (direct selection of phonemes for sequencing) and *Automatic Phonetic Programming* (phoneme selection via text-to-speech rules). The Manual method requires that the programmer has some background in basic phonetics as well as some knowledge of the Votrax phonetic system. (Note that chapter 3 of this book gives an adequate grounding in phonetics for this task.)

There are sixty-four components in the standard Votrax allophone repertoire. Of these, twenty-five represent consonant sounds and thirty-six represent vowel sounds. The three remaining components generate no-sound conditions essential for creating pause states within a sequence of allophones. Although the reference dialect for SC-01 pronunciation is *Middle American English*, the VS series does include synthesisers that generate allophones specific to other languages (e.g. French, Spanish, etc.)

A note is required about the 'no-sound' components. They are grouped with the sound-emitting allophones because of the function they perform. A no-sound state (pause) provides a space into which the previous phoneme's frequencies may transition (fade out or abruptly halt). These no-sound states are subject to the same selection procedures as phonemes and, thus, are often referred to as *pause phonemes*.

The *Votrax Phonetic Alphabet* is used to represent the allophones generated by all Votrax synthesisers, including the SC-01 chip. This alphabet is an alphanumeric symbol system equatable to other phonetic alphabets such as the International Phonetic Alphabet (IPA) (see table 3.2). Table 11.1 lists each symbol along with an example word in American English to illustrate the use and/or pronunciation of the sound represented, and for convenience all the allophones are cross-referenced to the phoneme of table 3.3 or 3.4 to which they belong. Numbers are used in conjunction with letters in this system to indicate a pronunciation variation of the target phoneme represented by the letters: e.g. [EH] is a short $/\varepsilon/$ vowel; [EH3] is the fastest duration allophone of [EH]; and [Y1] is a constricted and short pronunciation

Table 11.3 Diphthong chart

ASCII combination	Allophone combination	Example words
Fai , F!)	A1-AY-Y	gAme, mAId, dAY
U i , U)	AH1-EH3-Y	tIme, skY, gUY
cHi , #H)	UH3-AH2-Y	fight, mice
Ucw, U#7	AH1-UH3-U1	cOW, clOUd
cHw, #H7	UH3-AH2-U1	hOUse, abOUt
uw , 57	O1-U1	bOAt, nOte
uci , 5#)	O1-UH3-Y	tOY, nOIse
bvw , "67	Y1-IU-U1	YOU, mUsic

of the [Y]. These shorter-duration allophones are used to create the diphthongs as noted in Table 11.3. Other uses will become more evident as examples are observed.

Manual Phonetic Programming may be accomplished in stages utilising the phonetic system described above. The basic sounds in a word must first be identified then transcribed into an appropriate phonetic sequence using the Votrax Phonetic Alphabet (the allophone sequences in chapter 6 follow a similar style).

```
e.g.  cat     3 sounds   K AE T
      both    3 sounds   B O TH
      five    4 sounds   F AH E V
      starve  5 sounds   S T AH R V
```

When this sequence of *phonemes* (note that no allophonic variation has been included yet) is drawn from the synthesiser, the 'basic phonetic program' created may, or may not, auditorially meet personal intelligibility standards. If the latter is true, the phoneme sequence must be adjusted.

The second stage in the manual procedures is to identify where in the phoneme sequence an adjustment must occur. In some cases a simple substitution of one phoneme for another can be made to satisfy the listener. In other cases the vowel phoneme(s) require either lengthening or shortening to accommodate more precisely the syllabic environment, rhythm needs, etc. — that is, to be replaced by another allophone of the same phoneme. The vowel allophones are frequently used to assist with this type of adjustment.

```
e.g.  cat     K AE T      K AE1 AE1 T
      both    B O TH      B O1 U1 TH
      five    F AH E V     F AH1 EH3 E1 V
      starve  S T AH R V   S T AH1 UH3 R V
```

'Fine tuning' the phoneme sequence is the last stage of the programming procedure. Here, adjustments are made for creating special speech effects, like creating the pronunciations unique to a dialect or for producing language effects which require over-articulated pronunciations with extended durations.

e.g. you all   Y AH1 AW2 O2 UH3 L
      (i.e. yawl)

e.g. charge!   T CH AH1 AH1 AH1 AH2 UH2 R D J J

Allophone sequences for words produced in isolation are different from those for continuous speech. They tend to reflect more precise pronunciations with longer vowel durations. Often an isolated program will contain both a long duration phoneme and its shorter duration allophone.

e.g. the   THV UH1 UH1
      first   F ER R S T
      train   T R A1 AY Y N
      station S T A1 AY SH UH2 N

Continuous speech would have the vowel durations of some words/syllables short in order to shift the emphasis for the resulting language on to another word/syllable. Note how the allophone sequences for the examples above are changed to accommodate the new environment:

e.g. The FIRST train station...
      THV UH1 F ER R S T PA1 PA1 T R A1 Y N S T A2 AY SH
      UH3 N...

The flexibility offered by the allophone approach to synthesising speech may further be exemplified in the sequence below where, with some allophone sequence adjustment, the emphasis is placed on the third word instead of the second as above.

e.g. The first TRAIN station...
      THV UH1 F R R S T PA1 PA1 T R A2 A2 AY Y N N S T A2
      AY SH UH3 N...

There is a difficulty factor related to phonetic sequencing. Creating speech with allophones is directly related to the programmer's familiarity with phonetics as well as with how they will be auditorially realised. The time required to proceed through the programming stages has the potential of being very extensive even for the more accomplished phonetician. For this reason, *Automatic Phonetic Programming* is desirable. A set of text-to-speech translation rules developed for the

SC01 synthesiser, and used in conjunction with its hardware, eliminates stage 1 of the manual process. Words may be presented for translation in their orthographic form to produce basic allophone sequences

e.g. Three trains rattled into the station.
    TH R E1 Y . . . T R A1 AY Y N Z . . . PA1 PA 1 . . . R AE1 EH3
    T UH3 L D . . . PA1 . . . I1 I3 N T IU U1 . . . THV UH1 UH3 . . .
    S T A1 Y SH UH3 N

Stage 2 is reduced to an occasional spelling adjustment process to elicit more desirable pronunciations.

The Votrax rules for selection of phonemes are based on American English grammar rules (and follow the lines outlined in chapter 6). The general function is much like that which a human speaker might perform. Each letter, or letter group, in a word is scanned to determine the environment in which it currently exists. A decision is then made as to which sound the synthesiser will produce to translate the letter(s). Certain letters, when occurring in a specific environment, have pronunciations other than their standard. One classic example is the 't' in the word 'nation'. A rule exists to translate the 't' as an /ʃ/ instead of a plosive /t/. Similarly, the synthesiser will produce the [UH3] vowel for the 'io' combination when it occurs between a 't' and an 'n'. There are some words with letter sequences that defy the pronunciation rules totally. These are usually English words based in another language. They would have their own translation rules.

Automatic and manual phonetic programming are often combined, retaining the stage 3 processes. This maintains the flexibility of allophone usage. An example of such a mixture, using our sample sentence, would present both text for translation and phonetic data for the synthesiser:

e.g. Three trains /PA1 PA1 R AE1 EH3 D UH3 L D PA1 I2 N T IU
    U1 THV UH3 S T A1 Y SH UH3 N/

11.4 *Applications*

The SC-01 is best used in applications with restricted memory or large vocabulary needs. Six to eight bytes are required to store the allophone codes for a typical word. A 250 word vocabulary can be contained in as little as 2000 bytes. This is well within the internal ROM capacity of many single chip microcomputers available today.

Some fixed vocabulary applications could benefit if each unit could be customised with personal or specialised vocabulary. A unit can be configured in production with a standard vocabulary. An empty ROM socket would allow a user to augment the standard vocabulary with names or absent words. The SC-01 is well suited for such a product due to its user programmability. A reasonable personal vocabulary for the SC-01 could be placed into a common EPROM or other field programmable device. An example of this application would be a product designed for speech prothesis. A non-verbal user would surely want the names and vital information of friends and relatives contained in the unit's speech repetoire.

In applications involving general-purpose computers, phoneme sequences can sometimes be stored and manipulated directly in a high level language. It is not necessary to have a resident standard vocabulary in such cases because the vocabulary is loaded along with the program from a mass storage device. This permits complete vocabulary customisation and only those words used will consume memory.

Text-to-speech translator products are possible using the SC-01. Several have been developed for the personal computer market as general-purpose speech synthesisers. These units appear like a printer to the computer. Text or phoneme strings can be turned into speech using simple output commands such as *PRINT*. Even a novice programmer can include a customised vocabulary in a program with a text-to-speech synthesiser.

Like other speech technologies the SC-01 can be applied to situations where a man–machine interface is required. Some applications, however, might require a speech technology which reconstructs a signal extracted from a human source. The low data rate and vocabulary flexibility of the SC-01 must be weighed against it's 'robotic' voice when trying to utilise it in any application.

11.5 *Further reading*

The exact technique which has been described in this chapter is unique to Votrax Inc. of Troy, Michigan. However, the actual synthesis model used in this Phonetic Synthesiser is an adaptation of the formant synthesis method described in chapter 4.

Other semiconductor manufacturers have also adopted formant synthesis for their LSI and VLSI implementations, and as a guide here are some such companies that were known to the editor in 1982. (Unless otherwise specified, the companies offered a dedicated LSI or VLSI device):

Intel Corp. (using the 2920), Santa Clara, California

Nippon Electric Co. Ltd, (using the 7752), Kawasaki, Japan
Philips, Eindhoven, Holland
Votrax Inc., Troy, Michigan

CHAPTER 12

READY-TO-USE SPEECH SYSTEMS

Chris Moller (12.1), John Stork (12.2),
Raj Gunawardana (12.3), David Gilblom (12.4)

In this chapter we explore some different types of printed circuit board products which can be bought, ready-made, from many suppliers. Examples are discussed under four broad categories: Evaluation modules, for easy experimentation; OEM Boards, for low-cost incorporation into products; programmable speech systems, for solving any voice response problem; and text-to-speech modules, for large vocabulary systems.

12.1 *Evaluation modules*

WHAT IS AN EVALUATION MODULE?
Evaluation modules are small, low-cost speaking systems, with little or no built-in intelligence. They typically have a small vocabulary, and no capability for concatenation of phrases. However, they contain all that is necessary for a minimum-configuration speaking system, and should be supplied *ready-to-speak*.

When would an evaluation module be used?
At the conception of a project, much deliberation will occur about the extent to which speech can contribute to the product design, and even whether the product should speak at all (see chapter 14). The decision depends on a whole composite of human, as well as technological, questions. The only valid way to establish the answers to the human questions is to try the system out on a sample audience. As this clearly should happen at an early stage in the project, before too much money has been spent, the electronic system design will not have been done. Nevertheless, evaluation must be undertaken, and an *evaluation module* represents a significant aid to 'fudging' a system to try out. It is also useful for ascertaining *what* the system should say,

192

although the lack of intelligence and concatenation is likely to mean that the evaluation system is not a suitable tool for demonstration of *how* it should be said. It may even be possible in some limited cases that the evaluation system on its own is all that is required to add speech to a system, but this is likely to be the exception.

LIMITATIONS AND PITFALLS

While the *evaluation board* is an essential tool for the design of a speech system, it should not in general be expected to fulfil a larger role. The temptation is to treat the evaluation board as a low-cost version of the final product, and there is a real danger that synthetic speech as a concept for a product will be rejected if this happens. Several things encourage this:

Interaction

The acceptability of speech as an add-on to a system depends on it being an aid to communication; if the rate of speaking is too slow, or the information content is too weak, speech will jar with the consumer, and he will be happier without it. An evaluation system will not, in general, have all the interactive features of the final product, and so the messages sent will seem stilted and artificial. The machine may actually appear to be less responsive to the user's wishes than if it didn't have speech at all!

Concatenation

Systems which are driven by key-closures, or similar inputs, as most evaluation modules are, will not be able to put together complex phrases, but the final product probably will. Hence the naturalness of the entire phrase will not, in general, be as good on the evaluation module as in the final system (it will certainly be different).

Audio

An evaluation module does not usually have any audio filtering, to keep costs low and minimise the size of the unit. If a filter is incorporated it will certainly not be the best there is. Additionally, the audio amplifier is often small, or non-existent, especially on battery-powered units. The audio output stages are frequently neglected when building the evaluation system or added as an afterthought. However, they can have considerable impact on the intelligibility of the speech, and its acceptability, and hence warrant care and attention, especially if the application involves intelligibility in the presence of ambient noise.

Power supplies

Because evaluation modules are optimised for cost and size, they tend not to be optimised for power consumption. It is to be expected that the evaluation module will use up appreciably more power than the speech output part of the final product, and this should be borne in mind when performing the evaluation. Additionally, the characteristically 'peaky' current drain of evaluation boards is likely to cause some voltage fluctuation, and this in turn may cause the clock frequency to change, if a variable-resistor and capacitor arrangement has been used.

EXAMPLES

The *Tinytalker* provided by Texas Instruments, for example, is a compact, low-cost unit which includes a loud speaker on board (see fig. 12.1). Only a power supply needs to be connected and it will speak one of eight phrases as selected by an eight-way switch. This design uses the absolute minimum of circuitry since no microcomputer or intelligence is present on board. On the other hand, this implies that interfacing the module to other equipment is only possible in a rudimentary way.

Figure 12.1 The TINYTALKER evaluation board. (Reproduced by permission of Texas Instruments Ltd)

Alternatively, boards with a higher capability are available which could still be included in the category of evaluation module – the *TDS910* speech synthesiser Eurocard from Triangle Digital Services is a good example (see fig. 12.2). Physically, it is the standard single-Eurocard size (160 × 100 mm), with a standard DIN41612 connector to the outside world. Like most evaluation modules, however, the signals do not conform to any computer bus standard. It requires a single power-supply connection, and contains all the electronics necessary to make the synthesiser speak.

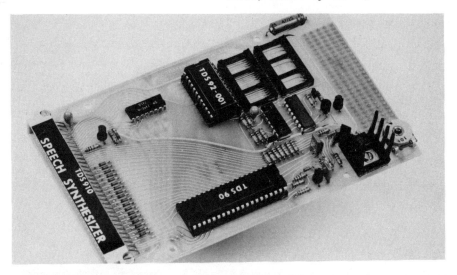

Figure 12.2 The TDS speech synthesiser Eurocard. (Reproduced by permission of Triangle Digital Services)

The TDS910 board accepts input in three different formats. The available methods of requesting the utterances of a phrase are:

(a) Contact closure
(sixteen closures/utterances provided)
(b) Parallel binary
(255 codes/utterances provided)
(c) Serial *ASCII*
(255 codes/utterances available)

Output is to an 8 ohm loud speaker at 250 mW rms from a small on-board amplifier. Only rudimentary filtering is performed. The audio output is routed to a spare pin on the DIN connector.

SPEECH DATA STORAGE

Most evaluation boards come with sockets for industry-standard 16K or 32K EPROM/ROMs, and additional memory can often be connected externally. They are usually shipped with a selection of standard phrases in ROM or EPROM, although only in rare cases will these be what are actually needed for evaluation. The manufacturer, or his agent, will usually supply speech data to the customer's script, using the techniques described in chapter 13. He will, if requested, provide it in EPROM for plugging in, in place of the standard data. In some cases, there may be limitations on how long each utterance may last, or other artificial restraints on the data which will not apply to the final product.

12.2 *Low-cost OEM boards*

In many applications it will be required that a speech synthesiser be linked directly to a microprocessor system bus, despite the fact that the volume of the end-product will be too small to justify a custom electronic design. In these cases a standard off-the-shelf PCB (PWB) product will be sought – a product that is more suited to use in a production system than an evaluation board. The key features of such an *OEM board* will be low cost, simplicity of structure and versatility of application. In this section two OEM boards, each based on the General Instrument LPC synthesiser, are described which would be suitable for medium volume speech system design.

HARDWARE EXAMPLES

The first example to be shown here incorporates an *SP0250* synthesiser with an *8039* microprocessor, and a block diagram of the board is shown in fig. 12.3. A photograph of this product is also shown in fig. 12.4. The microprocessor, operating at 9.36 MHz, accesses program memory, vocabulary storage, and control interface on its bus, and the synthesiser is connected to its Port 1. A 3.12 MHz output on T0 supplies a clock signal to the synthesiser, while the active data request from the synthesiser is sensed as a status signal on T1, and the data is strobed to the synthesiser by the *PROG* pulse (using an otherwise irrelevant *MOVD* instruction to generate the strobe). Various programmed output states on Port 2 are used to select memory chips and to enable the control data latch. Program memory in the first memory chip is read by *PSEN*, while vocabulary data (which also occupies part of the first memory chip) is read by the *RD* signal.

Since the processor in this case is dedicated to speech control, there is no need to use the synthesiser data request as an interrupt signal. *INT* serves instead as a status input for external control. The control interface provides a latch for message selection codes but might also be used for direct transfer of coded speech data independently of on-board vocabulary memory. The audio output circuit consists simply of a buffer amplifier (not needed in all applications) and a single-section RC low-pass filter. The filter, which is designed to compensate for high-frequency pre-emphasis applied to the speech signal before processing, is adequate to suppress steady-state components at multiples of 20 kHz generated by the pulse width modulator in the synthesiser.

With respect to the control interface, the circuit of fig. 12.3 looks much like an *8212* output port. A still simpler configuration is possible when an interface latch is not required. For example, data transfers

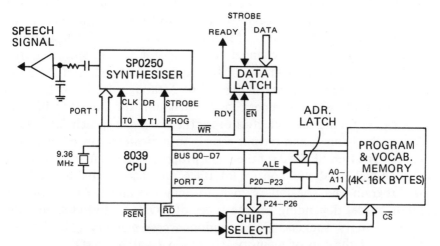

Figure 12.3 Block diagram of the M410 speech module

Figure 12.4 The M410 speech module (Reproduced by permission of the Speech Technology Corp.)

to the synthesisers may use the data bus, with *WR* as a data strobe, while still using T0 and T1 for clock and status functions. Interface commands (message selectors or direct speech data) would then be transferred via Port 1, with *INT* serving as an actual interrupt input to minimise the time needed to hold data stable at Port 1.

When a more powerful MPU, such as the *Z80A*, is used in the design of an OEM board, the processor can be used for simultaneous independent control of as many as four speech synthesisers. A much simplified block diagram for a four-channel voice response system operating from a VME computer bus is shown in fig. 12.5. A photograph of the corresponding hardware appears in fig. 12.6. Although details of the computer interface do not appear in the diagram, the interface includes input signals for message selectors or for the passing of speech data, and to select each channel, and output signals to indicate status of each voice channel. The four SP0250 synthesisers, program and vocabulary memory, a scratch-pad RAM, and control interface, are all connected to the Z80A bus. Program and vocabulary memory may use most of the 64K-byte address space, depending on the types of ROMs or EPROMs installed in the memory sockets. Fixed random-access memory (1K bytes) is addressed at the top of memory. Using a 3.12 MHz crystal, one of the synthesisers provides a buffered clock output to drive the CPU and the other synthesisers.

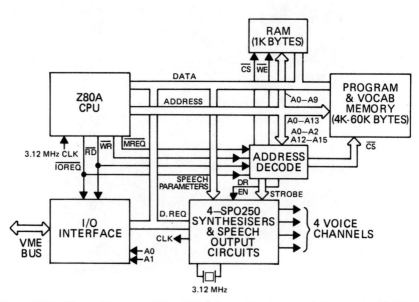

Figure 12.5 Block diagram of the M450 four-channel speech board for VME bus.

SPEECH DATA FORMAT AND CONTROL PROGRAMS
In chapter 10 it was noted that a frame of data transferred to an LPC synthesiser consists of a number of bytes (15 bytes for the SP0250, or 120 bits, including 12 coefficients) and that synthetic speech is typically

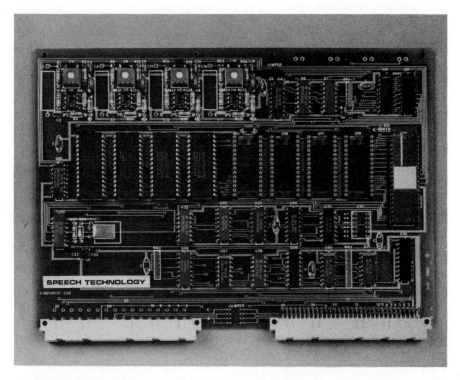

Figure 12.6 The M450 four-channel speech board (Reproduced by permission of the Speech Technology Corp.)

coded at 40 to 50 frames per second. Therefore, it is apparent that the average data transfer rate to the synthesiser may be as high as 6000 bits per second. There are, however, many ways to reduce this rate without significant degradation of speech quality, some of which were discussed in chapter 5.

Data reduction takes place automatically during most speech processing methods in the following ways:

(a) Not all coefficients require full 8-bit accuracy, and normally voiced speech can be represented by a total coefficient field of 50 to 60 bits for a twelfth-order filter;

(b) Fricative speech sounds are adequately reproduced by a lower-order filter;

(c) Silences are coded with no information other than time duration;

(d) Where spectral characteristics change slowly, filter coefficients often may be coded incrementally (delta-coded) rather than with full accuracy;

(e)　A frame may be repeated without change when there is only minor spectral variation over several pitch periods.

The result for the SP0250 is 20 to 25 frames per second of speech with an average of 80 bits per frame.

Data compression places a significant burden on the microprocessors in the circuits of figs 12.3 and 12.5. Each frame is interpreted by means of a two- or three-bit header, and the number of data fields and size of each field are scheduled by look-up tables as the data is extracted from memory. The speech parameters, expanded for direct transfer to the synthesiser, are also stored in RAM where they may be recalled for incremental coefficient coding and for automatic interpolation of amplitude and pitch (for voiced speech) over frames that are repeated. In the case of fig. 12.3, the 128-byte internal RAM of the 8039 is sufficient for this purpose. Further, part of the RAM space is also used as a storage buffer for external message selection codes in order to reduce service time from the external controller. External RAM is used with the *Z80A* in fig. 12.5, and this must be larger than 128 bytes, to hold the independent parameter and message buffers for four voice channels as well as a program stack. Typical program sizes are 750 bytes for the 8039 and 1200 bytes for the Z80A.

12.3　*Programmable speech systems*

WHAT IS A PROGRAMMABLE SPEECH SYSTEM?
In a general sense, all speech systems are pre-programmed to execute a dedicated function. In particular, in applications where voice output is expected in response to activities in the environment, the programming of system functions is essential. However, the introduction of speech systems to the mass market has generally been made via custom pro-grammed systems containing a very limited number of micro-chips essentially configured to perform in a unique product. These speech systems are not suitable for general applications of synthetic speech where the demand for the end product is low.

Programmable systems for low volume applications of synthetic speech are needed for a number of different reasons. In product development, it is necessary to have equipment which would emulate functions that are to be custom programmed eventually into low-cost micro-chips. In developing a dedicated vocabulary it is necessary to evaluate the message content in its full context prior to commitment to the final product. On the other hand, in some applications, such as aids to the handicapped or security systems, a degree of 'personalised' customisation becomes necessary. *Programmable speech systems* are therefore necessary both for end equipment applications having a low volume market and for development of customised systems for high volume production.

General systems functions

Most speech systems comprise three different functional blocks. The *controlling function* monitors the 'operating environment' and initiates the generation of appropriate output messages in response to 'events' sensed. The controlling function is not necessarily performed by a dedicated microcomputer, but can be provided by a device which is executing many other functions in a host system. The *voice synthesising function* simply 'obeys' the commands issued by the controller and proceeds to generate samples of synthetic speech. Finally, the *voice ROM* contains speech data which define the utterance being generated. Additionally, there may also be *look-up tables* located at fixed addresses to provide language independency to the system and data lists defining concatenation structures to permit the 'construction' of a message from a number of different utterances.

However, the use of a programmable speech system means that these tasks can all be undertaken in *software* rather than in a custom hardware design.

AN EXAMPLE

In this section we discuss, as an example of programmable speech system, the Texas Instruments *Superspeaker* (shown in fig. 12.7).

Design philosophy

Programmable microcomputers (usually with on-board EPROM) are readily available but in general tend to be of relatively high cost when compared with customised micro-chips. Additionally, the operation of these devices tends to be more complex than is generally required for speech control functions and generating software to 'program' a speech system will be a rigorous and costly exercise.

The approach taken in some modules, however, is to provide complete programming freedom as far as speech data is concerned and to pre-program a custom microcomputer (in the case of the Superspeaker, a Texas Instruments *TMS1100*) with the capability of executing standard synthesiser control functions and of self-configuring system functions as a result of 'system data' stored integrally with speech data. In other words, the controller, a low-cost customised device normally aimed at high volume applications, has been customised to 'obey' programmable data to comply with the system's operating environment.

Figure 12.7 The Superspeaker programmable voice computer (Reproduced by permission of Texas Instruments Ltd)

The *voice ROM* in the Superspeaker utilises EPROM and incorporates a highly optimised interface directly with both the synthesisers and the controller to reduce the number of integrated circuits used in circuit design. (In high volume applications the electrical interface is restructured to be between the synthesiser and custom voice ROM.)

This approach has made it possible to produce a speech module which can be 'bolted' to a considerable number of applications by programming standard EPROM devices with suitable *Speech* and *System* data.

System operating environment – definition
This can be simply defined as a number of *events* that occur, each of which requires a specific message to be spoken out. One of the most straightforward electrical interfaces that can be defined is a mechanical switch which either opens or closes as a result of an event. The module can be configured such that the controller scans a switch matrix activated by the host environment. The active state of each switch can be programmed as described later. In practical applications a large number of messages may be required and hence a maximum of

thirty-two switches can be configured, as well as a *paging* function, which allows the generation of up to 128 different utterances. The paging function can, for example, be used to switch the system between four different languages.

Frequently, speech subsystems need to plug into a processor-based host environment. Such a subsystem can be expected to perform all local 'housekeeping' functions and generate appropriate message output upon receipt of a simple code. A message number may be communicated from the host processor, for example, thus simplifying the software required by the host. The Superspeaker can be configured to interface with an 8-bit parallel bus to fulfil this function, with the capability to interrupt the host on completion of message.

System operation and features
Figure 12.8 shows a block diagram of the Superspeaker. The controller can preset any desired starting address value in the address counter and subsequently *READ* the data stored in the programmable memory via the synthesiser interface, which is bidirectional. The synthesiser increments the address counter either during data read operations or during speech output to gain access to sequential data in memory.

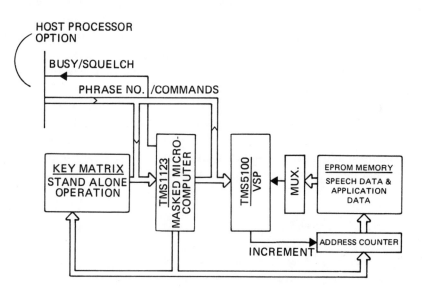

Figure 12.8 Block diagram of the Superspeaker

On power-up and initialisation of the controlling program the controller fetches system vectors from memory and configures itself to suit the operating environment. If configured to scan a switch matrix, the controller proceeds to obtain the *key-attributes* (the opening or the closing of a switch) which signal events to the controller. Finally, the address contained in the *WAKE-UP* vector is fetched, transferred to the address counter, and the synthesiser is initialised to speak. During speech the synthesiser operates independently of the controller and obtains sequential speech data from the memory whilst signalling its status to the controller. On completion of the initialising sequence the controller commences to monitor its event interface in readiness of normal operation.

Responses to events are determined by programming a *vector table* as shown by fig. 12.9. Upon sensing an event, the controller fetches the primary *phrase vectors* data from the location in memory associated with the event. One field of this data contains the *key* and *audio attribute* data. The remaining field comprises a *phrase list pointer*, which points to the start of a list of addresses of speech data. In addition to the speech address data the pointers contain *utterance type* instructions to the controller. A *NORMAL* utterance instructs the controller to proceed to the next data on the phrase list on completion of current utterance. A *LAST* utterance causes the controller to stop on completion. A *CONCATENATE and CONTINUE* code results in the controller to *CAN* (hold) an utterance indicated by a simultaneous event, before returning to processing the current phrase pointer list. Use of utterance types, therefore, permits the economical manipulation of speech data to generate multiple messages.

Audio attribute codes enable the programming of the way in which a message is generated. A *REPEAT* code will generate a message repeatedly until cancelled by a dedicated switch in the system. An *ALARM* code results in a dedicated output line from the controller becoming periodically active. This line can be used to generate a visible indication in addition to voice output. Finally, a *REPEAT and ALARM* code generates a combination of the two effects.

General features

A number of features have been designed into the system to comprehend human factors associated with speech. For example, if a number of speech-generating events occur simultaneously, or whilst a current message is being generated, the system 'queues' the unspoken events in order of priority and continues to generate messages. A *PARDON* key has also been provided to regenerate the latest message generated.

The Superspeaker is a prime example of how a programmable speech system can be designed to cater for a variety of applications at low cost.

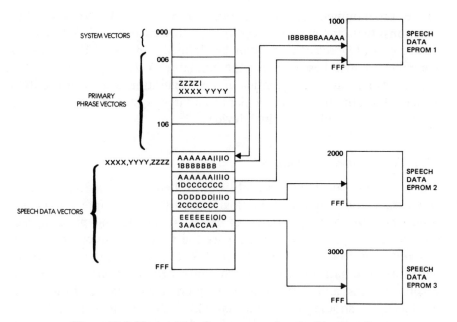

Figure 12.9 Vector table for programming the Superspeaker

It has to be conceded that using such a general-purpose system in specific applications will inevitably be a design compromise. Nevertheless, it makes speech synthesis viable in low volume applications which would otherwise be prohibitively costly.

PROGRAMMABLE SYSTEMS FOR EMULATION
One further use for programmable speech systems must be explored before leaving the subject – that of *ROM emulation*. It is necessary to check the performance of any system comprising customised voice and control functions rigorously before committing the associated EPROM data to be masked into custom devices (if high volume is planned). It is, therefore, necessary to emulate the devices destined for the target product with hardware which mimics the devices electrically and functionally at a pin level. Such hardware has to be programmable if standard modules are to be used for development and to support the interactive activities inevitably associated with product development.

Compact, low-cost emulation hardware is available for most mask programmable microcomputers. Hence, for emulating a speech system the only additional hardware required is for the speech data ROM device. For example, the *TMS6100* 128 kbit speech ROM is emulated by a single printed circuit board ROM emulator, which allows its data to be programmed by using a number of EPROMs. Various other functions that are maskable options in this particular ROM, such as an internal *chip select code*, can be defined and tested by the use of a number of switches on-board the emulator. A flying lead terminating with a header having an identical pin-configuration to that of the ROM device allows the board to be linked to a target system to test all coding aimed to be masked into a final device.

12.4 *Text-to-speech modules*

There are now available a variety of finished text-to-speech products which span most of the technologies discussed in chapters 8–11 and offer the user a broad range of trade-offs, including price, speech quality, and ease of use. To compare the various products it is useful to determine how much of the total text-to-speech function a product performs automatically, how much control the user has over the conversion process, and, ultimately, how good is the quality of the speech produced. It should be noted that although the quality of text-to-speech output can be very intelligible and natural, none of the currently available products can produce speech which would be mistaken for human. Most of the commercial products were designed to speak English, although some implementation of other languages has occurred.

CONVERSION PROCESSES

A generalised block diagram of text-to-speech conversion is shown in fig. 12.10. In each of the products available, the function of each of the blocks in the diagram must somehow be accomplished. The more accurately that the implementation of each block approximates the behaviour of a human speaker, the more natural the speech output sounds. For each new product, the designers must make decisions on the method of implementing each block. For some blocks, there are many alternatives.

Text normaliser

It is desirable to be able to use as input to a text-to-speech module the same text strings which would be normally encountered in print. Thus a string such as *1,234* should be spoken as *one thousand two hundred and thirty-four* and not as *one comma two three four* if it is to be clearly understood by the general listener. Text normalisation can also handle abbreviations and forms like *22nd* and *12:00*. Text normalisers which must make decisions must also be controllable by the user so that incorrect decisions can be rectified.

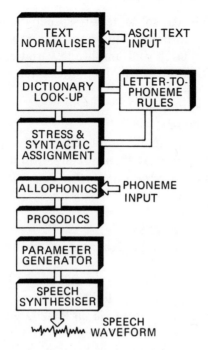

Figure 12.10 The flow of text-to-speech conversion

Letter-to-sound conversion

Accurate conversion of normalised text to equivalent sounds requires both a set of rules and a list of exceptions to those rules. Since the look-up process is usually much faster than application of the rules, no speed penalty is paid for extensive exceptions lists. The size of the memory available can be important, however.

Stress and syntactic marking

Very natural speech can only be produced if the converter knows what it is saying. But only in the most complex laboratory systems is there memory available to handle such problems as *Wind the clock* vs *The wind is blowing* or *He is present* vs *Please present the gift*. These require far more syntactic processing than can be accommodated in marketable products. However, here some processing is clearly better than none and, in general, the more the better. Any product should at least let the user enter phoneme strings with stress marks to permit specification of correct pronunciation and stress when the automatic results are not acceptable.

Allophonics and prosodics

Each sound produced by a human vocal tract is influenced by the other sounds surrounding it, so a text-to-speech product must operate similarly to speak naturally. This naturalness is enhanced by incorporation of proper pitch and amplitude variations at the clause and sentence level. These cues can help the listener identify questions, for instance.

Final speech production

Once the sound string to be produced is fully specified, it must be converted into an electrical signal. If algorithmic smoothing is used, this process includes generation of the data that drives a filter representing the vocal tract.

REPRESENTATIVE PRODUCTS

Four examples will serve to illustrate current product offerings.

Votrax Type-n-Talk

This is the most widely used of the low-cost text-to-speech converters (Dec. 82). It accepts ASCII text via an RS-232 port and uses a 3 kbyte program for letter-to-sound conversion. It uses the *SC-01* synthesiser chip also made by Votrax but does not have rules to make use of the chip's four-level inflection control. The rules produce accurate pronunciation for about 65% of input text, but more complex sets (perhaps 95% accurate) are expected shortly. No text normalisation is performed and the user must frequently and carefully prepare text to produce the desired output. Since the SC-01 chip contains a fixed sixty-four phoneme set, no allophonic processing or smoothing is possible. An on-chip formant synthesiser produces the speech.

Yahara Speech Machine

This is a board product using the Votrax SC-01 chip with a more extensive set of rules than the *Type-n-Talk*. It performs some text normalisation and has more accurate letter-to-sound rules than the Type-n-Talk. In addition, some memory is available for the user to add an exceptions list. Like Type-n-Talk, the Speech Machine has no automatic inflection control and cannot do either allophonic processing or parameter smoothing.

Street Electronics Echo GP

This product uses a letter-to-sound rule set originally developed by the Naval Research Laboratory (US), which is about 97% accurate, in conjunction with an extended allophone set to produce improved pronunciation. It also inflects at the ends of sentences. It does not incorporate text normalisation or smoothing. Its synthesiser device is the *TMS5220* produced by Texas Instruments. It is available in both board and packaged forms.

Telesensory Prose 2000

This device is representative of the more comprehensive text-to-speech systems available, and at time of writing (Dec. 82) is probably the only commercial unit which incorporates dynamic smoothing of the vocal-tract model filter parameters. It has a complex text normaliser which handles abbreviations, a variety of numerical formats, acronyms and mnemonics, and certain punctuation conventions.

The letter-to-sound algorithm consists of about 400 context-sensitive rules and over 2800 exceptions which produce accurate phonetic and stress output for about 99% of (American) English text. The user can also enter text in phonetic form should the pronunciation of certain words need to be specified. Allophonic modification is performed automatically. This product also generates clause and sentence level stress by detecting the presence and position of certain 'function' words such as pronouns and prepositions, by recognising various punctuation marks, and by measuring the length of clauses.

Because of the extensive processing performed automatically by this product, a large set of commands is provided to allow the user to change speech rate, fundamental frequency, amplitude, prosody, and a variety of text string interpretation controls. These avoid locking in automatic processes which may not be correct in all contexts.

Finally, the generation of the parameters to drive the filter, a *Klatt* vocal-tract model, is done by an algorithm which accurately reproduces the movement of formants in real speech. It is available as a Multibus board (see fig. 12.11) or in an enclosure.

PRODUCT COST

The lowest cost boards are now less than $100 in quantity and there-fore suitable for inclusion in low-cost products. However, these pro-ducts cannot be reliably used to speak to listeners who are not familiar with the voice. On the other hand, the Telesensory board, although several times as expensive as the phonemic synthesisers, is certainly very suitable for communication with untrained listeners.

EXPECTED IMPROVEMENTS AND ENHANCEMENTS

Projects now underway should produce two general results: prices will continue to fall for products at all current performance levels, and newer products will be introduced which have higher quality than is

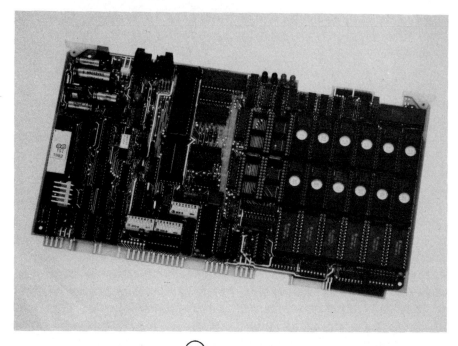

Figure 12.11 The PROSE 2000 ⒯ᴹ text-to-speech board. (Reproduced by permission of Telesensory Speech Systems)

available now. These will probably include some of the synthesis technologies which have been long available in the laboratory but never used in commercial products – diphones, demisyllables, and some of the more complex variants of linear predictive coding are candidates. Products are also beginning to emerge which can operate well in languages other than English.

12.5 *Further reading*

The number of companies currently building products based on semi-conductor synthesisers far exceeds even the list of semiconductor manufacturers given at the end of chapters 9–11. Accordingly, no attempt will be made here to mention companies involved in speech products for direct sale to the consumer. However, we will offer as a guide to the reader a short list of companies who in 1982, to the editor's knowledge, were manufacturing (not distributing) synthesis modules for original equipment manufacturers. This list only represents a small subset of the companies involved in the area, and apologies are made in advance to those who are not included.

SOME MANUFACTURERS OF BOARDS FOR SYNTHESIS-BY-ANALYSIS

Analog Devices, Norwood, Massachusetts
Applied Micro Technology, USA
Arfon Microelectronics Ltd, Caernarfon, Wales
Centigram Corp., Sunnyvale, California
Cognitronics Corp., Stamford, Connecticut
Easicomp Ltd, Norwich, England
ICS Electronics, San Jose, California
Infolink, San Diego, California
Microvoice Systems Corp., Laguna Hills, California
Mutek, Corsham, Wilts, England
Namal Associates, Cambridge, England
Perception Technology, Winchester, Massachusetts
Periphonics, Bohemia, New York
Speech Technology Corp., Santa Monica, California
Street Electronics Corp., Anahiem, California
Stynetic Systems, New York
Technology Service Corp., Santa Monica, California
Telesensory Speech Systems, Palo Alto, California
Texas Instruments Inc., Dallas, Texas
Triangle Digital Services, London

SOME MANUFACTURERS OF TEXT-TO-SPEECH MODULES

Ackerman Digital Systems, USA
Alien Group, New York
Euroka OY, Finland
Infovox, Stockholm, Sweden
Interstate Electronics, Anahiem, California
Intex Micro Systems Corp., Troy, Michigan
Street Electronics Corp., Anahiem, California
Texas Instruments Inc., Dallas, Texas
Votrax Inc., Troy, Michigan
X-com, France
Yahara, Centreville, Massachusetts

CHAPTER 13

SPEECH DATA PREPARATION

David Gilblom (13.1, 13.2),
Eugene Helms (13.3, 13.5), Larry Pfeifer (13.4),
Peter Rush (13.6)

In this chapter we discuss the important topic of the preparation of data for use with speech synthesiser chips. We concentrate here on the aspects of recording and editing which are common to most synthesis methods, and the reader should refer also to the individual description of the synthesiser he is intending to use. However, the chapter is written with the example of LPC in mind, since the majority of data preparation systems that have been offered to the public to date have been of this type.

13.1 *Choosing a speaker*

It is very important to choose a speaker who has a voice that is both pleasant to listen to and analyses well. Not all pleasant-sounding voices analyse well. A good first step is to listen to audio recordings of several candidates: if they sound bad on tape, they will sound worse when further processed. A good voice will sound 'full' (resonant), not 'thin'; pitch will sound stable rather than wobbly; and the speaker will not trail off (in pitch and amplitude) drastically at the end of phrases.

It is apparent that in general the lower the speaker's fundamental frequency, the better his or her voice will sound when synthesised. (The primary reason for this, in LPC, is that existing analysis routines severely underestimate the bandwidth of vocal-tract resonances in speakers with high fundamental frequencies.)

Fundamental frequency alone, however, is not an adequate guideline to the quality likely to be achievable in the processed speech. The particular shape of the vocal tract of the speaker may influence the result. In theory, the formant frequencies for a given sound, which result from a particular configuration of the oral and nasal cavities and define the resultant acoustic characteristics of that sound, are the same regardless of the speaker (and his or her particular F_0). However, such patterns do vary slightly with speakers so that formants may be closer together or further apart. This slight difference in the analysed formant structure can make a difference when the number of poles (and reflection coefficients) used in LPC analysis is reduced from the optimum. The decreased accuracy of the analysis program may result in its confusing two formants as one, merging them into a single peak. Therefore, some speakers' voices might sound fine analysed at high data rates, but not at low ones.

The actual facts can only be determined by specialised computational analysis. Such a degradation at low data rates may affect both naturalness and intelligibility (see chapter 14). It is interesting to notice, however, that even speech synthesised from relatively little information (e.g. female speech) may maintain fairly good intelligibility at low data rates, despite decreasing naturalness, if the speaker has a vocal-tract shape that just happens to be maximally compatible with the analysis routine.

As an example, Telesensory Speech Systems recently conducted an experiment where a male speaker whose F_0 was about 100 Hz, was compared in intelligibility with a female speaker having an F_0 of over twice that frequency, across a wide range of data rates. Although the human-sounding quality of the male speaker's speech remained greater than that of the female speaker throughout this range, the female speaker's intelligibility remained higher, and the gap widened as the data rate decreased. This is a graphic illustration that naturalness and intelligibility must be considered separately, as they may be affected differently by LPC analysis depending on the speaker.

OTHER CONSIDERATIONS

Although the technical qualifications determined by a sample analysis are necessary to permit a speaker to be used, they alone are not sufficient. Many projects can be expected to continue for some time, so speaker availability should be considered. Voice stability is also important if vocabulary additions are expected. Persons aged 25 to 45 are likely to have the best long-term stability.

Accents and mannerisms should be avoided unless they are deliberately desired. Voice quality should be matched to the intended application: stern for warning systems, gentle for assistance systems, and so forth (see chapter 2). Speakers must be able to talk from written material without inserting undesired pauses or extraneous sounds such as clicks, hisses, slurps or hums. In addition they must speak naturally, not as though they are reading. Perhaps a good test is to listen to a practice tape ten or twenty times. If you begin to get annoyed, the user of the product probably will too.

Selecting a speaker is a critical part of a large investment so no amount of care in this process can be considered excessive.

13.2 *Making a recording*

STUDIO RECORDING

It is possible to directly digitise the voice of a speaker in a studio, or to make a high quality tape recording for subsequent analysis. While the former method is obviously preferable, the latter method is often employed when comparing sample phrases from different speakers.

A sample recording for the purpose of evaluating a speaker's potential should include a brief passage of continuous speech, about twenty monosyllabic and polysyllabic words which are not run together and eight to ten sentences with five to eight syllables each. This material should represent the full range of sounds in the language.

Recordings should be made in a sound-proofed room using a professional reel-to-reel recorder (not cassette) and a high quality microphone. (A typical facility is shown in fig. 13.1.) The following specifications are well recommended:

Speed   = 7.5 ips (19 cm/s) at least.
Format   = Half track (preferred) or quarter track, monophonic
             mode, to produce identical signals on both channels.
Tape type = 1 or 1.5 mil. polyester base, high output oxide
             coating (*Maxell UD* or equivalent).

The speaker's mouth should be about 20 cm from the microphone, far enough so that stop consonants (e.g. /p/) do not produce a percussion effect. The recording amplitude can then be adjusted so that an utterance peaks between −3 and 0 on the VU meter (though it is satisfactory for some peaks to swing slightly outside this range). The setting should be made on the basis of rehearsal with a phonetically varied set of material, containing in particular all vowels.

The material the speaker is reading should be positioned so that the microphone does not pick up the sound of rustling papers.

The speaker should rehearse the material beforehand to make sure that both the content and the pronunciation are in accord with the requirements of the project.

To avoid background electrical noise, it is best to shut off any computers, air conditioning, fluorescent lights, water coolers or other

Figure 13.1   A typical recording facility (Reproduced by permission of Texas Instruments Ltd)

machinery in the vicinity of the sound booth, to the extent that this is possible. The recording should also be made away from vehicular traffic (ground and air).

PRE-ANALYSIS SCREENING

A data acquisition system must always form the 'front end' of the analysis equipment, whether a tape or a direct recording is being analysed. The analog signal is low-pass filtered (at 5 kHz, for example, for a sampling frequency of 10 kHz), an 8-pole elliptical filter being suitable. This filtering is necessary to reduce the amount of speech information processed, and has little effect on most speech sounds. Fricatives (/f/, /ʃ/, /s/, /z/) will be somewhat reduced in intelligibility by this process, since they contain essential 'noise' components at frequencies greater than 5 kHz. Female speech, which normally has much higher-frequency energy than male speech, will also be affected somewhat by the filtering.

The filtered speech is then scaled to match its amplitude to the A/D converter and digitisation is begun. To preserve enough data for 5 kHz bandwidth and twelve-pole reconstruction, the speech must be at least digitised to 12 bits at a 10 kHz sampling rate. It is interesting to note that this 120 000 bit/s data rate will be reduced by more than a factor of fifty when a typical LPC analysis is done, with little loss in intelligibility or naturalness.

When the speech has been digitised, the waveform should be examined more closely (especially for a 'new' speaker) to make sure it does not suffer from *diplophonia*. In a diplophonic waveform (most easily seen as part of a vowel nucleus) the sum of every *two* periods is approximately constant, but contiguous periods are notably different from each other, giving a long–short–long–short effect. A speaker with this voicing characteristic will sound perfectly fine to the ear, but should not be used for LPC because the ambiguity in pitch period will cause undesirable artifacts to be generated during the analysis/synthesis process.

When the studio manager is absolutely certain that a good recording has been made, it is safe to move on to the next stage. However, it must be remembered that no analysis system can make up for a bad recording.

13.3 *Speech analysis and editing*

Following the vocabulary recording session, analysis procedures must be performed on the speech to achieve data compression, the goal of analysis–synthesis techniques. The analysis of speech can take on many forms including a wide variety of techniques. In any case, the result of this analysis must ultimately be the precise set of parameters required to drive the speech synthesiser to obtain the desired acoustic output. Figure 13.2 illustrates the steps following the recording process.

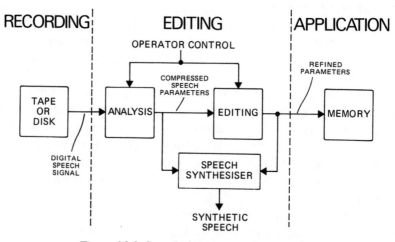

Figure 13.2 Speech data preparation overview

As a first step in the speech analysis, automatic procedures are typically used to generate initial estimates of the synthesis parameters. For synthesis techniques based on speech production modelling, estimates of parameters describing vocal-tract excitation and transmission characteristics, along with the associated time profile of signal intensity, are computed. These parameter estimates can alternatively be derived using automated interactive techniques. This allows an operator to inspect visually the time- and frequency-domain aspects of the digitised speech signal for events pertinent to the analysis method. A simple example is the location of pitch periods in the waveform. By marking significant events, better parameter estimates can generally be obtained from the analysis processing.

The improved performance that generally results from human intervention in the analysis procedure suggests that deficiencies exist in the totally automatic analysis. These deficiencies are due in large measure to violations of fundamental assumptions made about the character of the speech signal, assumptions inherent in the waveform or speech production model. The non-stationarity of the speech signal within an analysis frame is a good example. In analysis systems where no information in the signal is used to aid frame placement, gross changes can occur within frames. Rapid spectral transitions typically result in poor estimates of vocal-tract parameters. Inadequate approximations of formant centre frequencies and bandwidths will result in poor quality synthesised speech. Likewise, poor excitation parameter estimates can be obtained when, for instance, voicing transitions occur within frames. Although automatic procedures can be developed to use information in the speech signal in placing frame boundaries, the most reliable and effective approach to this remains automated interactive techniques. This is particularly true when the operator can listen to the synthesised speech immediately during the analysis to monitor the results and take corrective action when needed.

An alternative to a strictly automatic or automated interactive approach to preparing synthetic speech data is a sequential procedure that follows the speech analysis with interactive editing sessions, possibly using different computer facilities. This differs from interactive analysis in that the parameters resulting from analysis are edited in an attempt to improve speech quality. This approach has the advantage of requiring more modest processing and data storage facilities than does the analysis system. The signal processing operations and mass storage required for digitised speech signals need not be accommodated in simple editing systems. It is feasible in this approach to have a single analyis system which feeds compressed speech parameters to multiple editing systems. In such a case as this, the digitised speech is not available at the editing stage. Consequently, the editor is constrained to operate only on the compressed speech parameters.

Regardless of the analysis technique that is used, the quality of the resultant synthetic speech is strongly dependent on the original speech signal. Unfortunately, the details of this dependency are not always clear and, in general, are not well understood. Although noise conditions and signal level have a definite bearing on the outcome, these parameters are straightforward to address. Rather, it is the obscure dependencies of the synthetic speech quality on the original utterance that ultimately determines the outcome. The original speech signal is processed by a sequence of analysis steps that are typically the source of any distortions that result in the synthetic speech. Assuming the analysis procedure is fixed, problems in the synthetic speech can be addressed, outside of editing, only by modifying the original speech. This means simply using another utterance.

As stated above, the acoustic makeup of an utterance dictates the results of a given analysis procedure. Among the problems that can arise during analysis, deficiencies in modelling of spectral or temporal behaviour are among the most prominent. Speech production and waveform modelling techniques inherently perform better on some signals than on others. Signals that closely match assumptions of the model yield best results. The lack of model compatibility can be associated with single acoustic events or even extend to being generally characteristic of a given speaker's speech. Consequently, speech generated by some speakers consistently yields better quality synthesised speech than that of others.

However, a given utterance by any speaker is subject to yielding poor results from the analysis due to the severe time and frequency quantisation that is the basis of most speech modelling techniques. The occurrence of problems in the analysis is generally unpredictable from listening to the original speech utterance. The adequacy of an utterance for analysis cannot be fully assessed without reviewing the resultant synthetic speech. If there is no option for rerecording an utterance that yields poor results, the burden of correction lies totally in editing or re-analysis. The greater the capability of the data preparation system in terms of rerecording, re-analysis, or editing, the better are the results that can be expected.

The demand for synthetic speech data preparation has given rise to the development of facilities with wide-ranging capabilities. General-purpose data processing systems can be used for performing speech analysis in non-real-time on digitised speech data stored on magnetic tape or disk. Although signal processing software packages can be used to some extent in processing the speech, procedures specific to the target synthesis device must ultimately be employed in the preparation of synthetic speech parameters. Likewise, editing procedures which manipulate the synthesis parameters require some degree of tailoring. In general, analysis and editing systems developed specifically for a synthesis device or set of devices will yield best results.

Special-purpose hardware can similarly benefit the speech data preparation effort. Although the analysis of the speech can be performed with a general-purpose processing unit, a high performance unit such as an array processor can greatly speed up the operation and increase throughput. At the editing stage, the capability to listen to the synthesised speech is necessary. Ideally, the target synthesiser is interfaced to the editing system to allow the real-time generation of the synthetic speech resulting from each parameter modification step. This special-purpose hardware is preferred to real-time software synthesis because of its ultimate accuracy in illustrating how the speech will sound when generated by the target synthesis device.

Even with computer systems that are customised for speech data preparation, the editing task can be a labour-intensive effort. Removing distortions from the synthetic speech indirectly by manipulating input parameters to the synthesiser is a non-trivial and often expensive task. Numerous tools can be developed to aid the editor, relating to the visual display of the speech parameters, the facility afforded him in modifying them, and the visual and aural feedback given to demonstrate the results of the modification.

The ability of the editor to listen efficiently to the synthetic speech is critical to the editing process. Key to isolating the location of acoustic events is the easy review of the synthetic speech utterance in total and in segments. An interpretation is required of the editor as to the precise parameters which are the source of a given distortion in order for him to determine what action should be followed to correct the problem. The establishment of a causal relationship between acoustic events in the synthetic speech and specific speech parameters is fundamental to the speech editing task. Hence it is desirable for the speech parameters that are displayed and are modifiable to have easily discernable acoustic correlates.

While speech synthesis devices which use reflection coefficients or PARCOR coefficients directly offer advantages to the synthesis implementation, the properties of the parameters in the acoustic domain are obscure by inspection. This has fostered the development of editing systems which translate to intermediate parameter sets for the purpose of manipulation. For example, reflection coefficient vectors can be translated into formant centre frequencies and bandwidths for modification, as an alternative to direct editing of the reflection coefficients. Although the formant parameters must be converted back into reflection coefficients for synthesis in this example, editing is allowed to take place in a domain to which the editor can more readily relate. This serves to illustrate that editing need not take place directly on the synthesis parameters. In addition to parameter domain considerations, the parameter display is of considerable importance. The graphical display, as well as numeric display, of editing parameters can be quite useful. Parameter modification can conceivably be performed graphically as well.

In summary, synthetic speech data preparation systems can take on a wide variety of configurations, depending on the capital investment to be made, the throughput required, and the synthesis device to be used. The need for costly editing of synthetic speech parameters will likely be reduced by the development of more sophisticated synthesis devices as well as improved speech analysis techniques. In the mean time, development of systems allowing the human speaker to be involved throughout the data preparation process will offer high potential for improved synthetic speech data preparation results.

13.4 *The ILS software package*

Following the background to the features and uses of speech processing and editing systems given in section 13.3, in this section one such software suite will be described in more detail. While there are several software packages available, mainly from the manufacturers of LPC devices such as Texas Instruments, the software chosen as an example here was written by an independent consultancy, the Speech Technology Inc., California. This package, *ILS* (Interactive Laboratory System), is undoubtedly the most widely used speech analysis and editing software throughout the world at this time (January 1983).

ILS consists of a large number of computer programs designed around a standard set of files, with standardised operating procedures, and comprehensive documentation. The programs provide a set of signal processing tools which are particularly applicable for speech analysis, synthesis and recognition work, and the software runs on a variety of computers and operates in an interactive manner by means of a graphics terminal.

As outlined above, computer processing of speech usually begins with collecting speech utterances and then digitising them into disk files through an analog-to-digital converter. With ILS, digitised speech is stored in a standard file called a sampled data file. There are many different ILS programs which can operate on sampled data for speech display, speech editing, spectral processing, digital filtering, analysis and synthesis, formant tracking and more. The software also has the facility for labelling speech segments and maintaining a data base for segment sorting, retrieval and processing.

Some of the more elementary operations involve speech signal display, editing and manipulation. A display program allows any desired segment to be plotted on the graphics terminal. Parameters specified by the user allow variations in scale factor, display mode and position on the screen. The program allows either single-channel or multi-channel displays.

For applications which require speech editing, the cursor feature of the terminal can be invoked and used to mark the beginning and end points of a desired segment. Marked segments can be labelled, transferred, modified, deleted or played back through a digital-to-analog converter for listening.

For speech signal conditioning, ILS can be used to design both *FIR* (Finite Impulse Response) and *IIR* (Infinite Impulse Response) digital filters. The user can specify characteristics for classical forms of low-pass, band-pass, high-pass or notch filters. From the specified characteristics, a filter design program computes the filter coefficients and stores them in a disk file. A subsequent program can be used to compute and display the frequency spectrum of the filter. The actual filtering operation is performed by a general-purpose filtering program.

There are several ways of computing and presenting spectral analysis results. One program generates and displays a log-magnitude spectrum of any selected window of speech data. Another program computes and displays a smooth model spectrum based upon an autoregressive (linear prediction) analysis of the signal. In order to observe the dynamics of speech, it is possible to call for a three-dimensional display of consecutive frequency spectra obtained from either FFT analysis or linear prediction analysis. Figure 13.3 illustrates a three-dimensional plot of sixteen consecutive smooth linear prediction spectra. The 3-D display has full hidden line removal, which results in easy visualisation of trends and movements of resonant frequencies.

Another way of observing the dynamic behaviour of the speech signal is through a pseudo-spectrographic display, as shown in fig. 13.4. The upper box in the display contains a plot of the speech signal itself, with 10 msec time reference marks along the top of the box. The long, narrow box in the middle of the display contains a line plot of the RMS energy of the signal. The large box on the bottom half of the display shows the position of the resonant frequencies as a function of time, for each consecutive analysis window. The tick marks along the sides of the lower box represent 500 Hz intervals, increasing from bottom to top, and time increases from left to right.

STARTING FRAME = 20, NUMBER OF FRAMES = 16

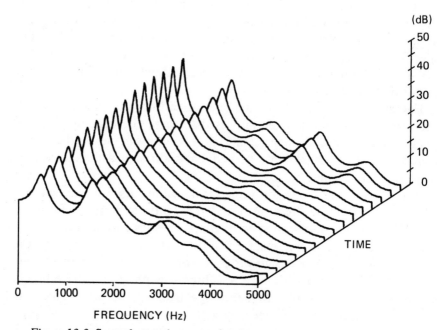

Figure 13.3 Smooth speech spectra for sixteen consecutive time windows

The short vertical lines in the large lower box represent the resonant frequencies, with the length of each line proportional to the bandwidth of each spectral peak. All information in the display is time synchronised so that simultaneous time- and frequency-domain behaviour can be observed.

The pseudo-spectrographic display of fig. 13.4 is a useful tool for locating the transitions and steady states of speech sounds, which is important in speech segmentation and labelling. The frequency, bandwidth and amplitude data for the resonant frequencies are also stored back in an ILS analysis file for future processing. For example, it is possible to run another ILS program which will take the frequency and bandwidth data and apply a formant tracking algorithm, with subsequent plotting of formant trajectories as a function of time.

ILS is frequently used in speech synthesis and speech compression applications. Besides the linear prediction analysis programs for coding speech, an automatic pitch extraction procedure is provided which uses a statistically based cepstral analysis algorithm for computing pitch periods. The speech parameters, pitch, and gain are then used by a synthesis program to regenerate an artificial version of the original

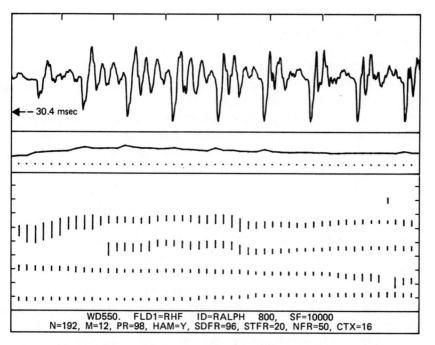

Figure 13.4 Pseudo-spectrographic display, synchronised to speech waveform

speech signal. Programs are also available for hand-marking pitch periods, with subsequent processing by pitch-synchronous analysis and synthesis programs.

The programs which have been described are but a few of the many signal processing tools in ILS which can be used for speech processing. The software is being used successfully in hundreds of installations worldwide. Because of its capabilities and wide acceptance, many speech research and development projects have been spared the costly and time-consuming task of designing and programming a signal processing software system.

13.5 *Portable speech preparation systems*

As discussed earlier in this chapter, the synthetic speech data preparation task is an expensive endeavour in terms of both equipment and time. While the capability to synthesise speech has been readily available using inexpensive chip sets for some time, the investment required to generate the speech parameters that drive the synthesis devices has been far greater. This gross cost imbalance between the cost of programming the synthesisers and that of the synthesis devices themselves surely acted as an impediment to the application of low cost speech synthesis systems.

Viewing the task of synthetic speech parameter development as the 'programming' of the synthesiser suggests that *speech development systems*, along the same line as *software development systems* for microprocessors, might be a viable approach to this problem. Indeed, low cost systems allowing totally in-house vocabulary development and flexible application prototyping would have distinct advantages over the service bureau approaches offered before, and obviate the necessity for a large computer to run a software package such as that described in section 13.4.

Motivated by the clear utility of such a system, Texas Instruments Inc. and Centigram Corp. recently developed microprocessor-based speech development systems to support their synthesis systems. These development systems consist of a microprocessor CPU, real-time speech analysis capability, parameter editing facility and speech synthesis function. The Centigram system offers floppy disk storage of speech parameters, whereas the Texas Instruments' system features an EPROM programming facility and an interface to a general-purpose host. The Texas Instruments development system consequently can be used in a variety of environments and constitutes a very flexible tool for synthetic speech development.

The TI system, known as the *Portable Speech Lab*, is self-contained in a metallic carrying case (see fig. 13.5) and is compatible with all of TI's LPC speech synthesis chips. The system's portability allows the hardware to be shared by different development teams within an organisation, and no complex understanding of speech is required in order to encode and replay speech for review. However, by interfacing the Portable Speech Lab to a dumb terminal, more experienced users find a full array of analysis, editing and EPROM programming control at their disposal. This allows quick generation of vocabularies that can be used directly in a product or evaluated in a prototype system. Going a step further, the equipment can be interfaced to a host computer that controls a speech data base. The data base can serve as an archive for encoded vocabularies. This allows previously encoded phrases to be retrieved, combined or edited, auditioned, and downloaded into EPROMs.

The Portable Speech Lab consists of five boards of the TM990 type as shown in fig. 13.6. The components are a CPU board using a TMS9900, a memory expansion board to hold up to twelve seconds of speech parameters, a speech synthesiser board for audio output, an EPROM programmer and a real-time speech processor board. All boards

Figure 13.5 The 'Portable Speech Lab' speech preparation system. (Reproduced by permission of Texas Instruments Ltd)

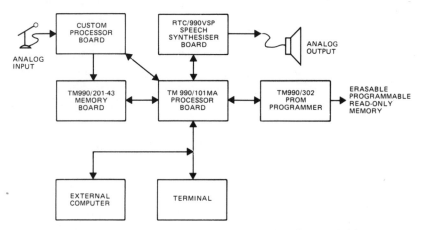

Figure 13.6 Block diagram of the 'Portable Speech Lab'

are standard TM990 parts except the speech processor, which was custom designed for this product. Its function is to perform the real-time compression of the incoming speech, in conjunction with software running on the CPU board, to reduce the data rate to about 180 bits/s from the 96 000 bits/s of the sampled speech waveform. This eliminates the need for a mass storage facility in the portable speech lab and allows for its compact design.

The low cost and ease of use of this type of data preparation equipment are obviously attractive, but of more importance is the real-time feedback of the synthetic speech to the speaker. This opens up a new dimension to the synthetic speech development effort. Many of the problems discussed in section 13.3 that develop during analysis of the speech can be addressed effectively by the speaker. By reviewing the synthetic speech, the speaker can adapt his input until the desired result is obtained. This feedback aspect not only generates better results from the analysis, but it substantially reduces the amount of editing required. It is much easier for the speaker simply to repeat a phrase than it is for an editor to attempt corrections by modifying the speech parameters. Since such real-time systems eliminate the time cost of analysis, re-analysis is made significantly more effective and attractive than editing. Accordingly, the TI Portable Speech Lab is expected to point the direction for future developments in synthetic speech data preparation.

13.6 *Configurable speech analysis hardware*

So far in this chapter various hardware and software systems have been discussed, all attempting to offer a complete package of functions which are immediately usable for speech data preparation for a given technology. In this final section, we turn our attention to configurable software and hardware which can be moulded by the user into the development tool of his choice. The example used here will be based on the *TDS900* Eurocard FORTH computer, manufactured by Triangle Digital Services Ltd (see fig. 13.7).

All digital speech analysis systems must inevitably include certain elements: a data acquisition system, an analysis computer and a synthesis system. The idea behind the *Speech Analysis Computer* offered by Triangle is to provide a 'kit of tools' which contains these main elements and a totally configurable analysis section. The kit includes:

(a) A data acquisition *front-end*, including a dynamic microphone, pre-amplifier, high- and low-pass filters and an analog-to-digital converter.

(b) A *FORTH* microcomputer board, with 80 kbytes of RAM for raw

Figure 13.7 The TDS 900 Eurocard FORTH computer. (Reproduced by permission of Triangle Digital Services)

speech data capture, for program storage and for storage of subsequently analysed speech parameters.

(c) Floppy disk storage and VDU.

(d) A digital-to-analog converter and loudspeaker, for playback from RAM.

(e) An *EPROM Emulator*, with a DIL plug for insertion into a speech synthesiser.

(f) An EPROM programmer.

The speech analysis and editing is carried out on the FORTH microcomputer board, and the user is encouraged to experiment with writing his own programs in the configurable *Fig-FORTH* language, to perform any particular type of analysis. However, to start the user off in the right direction, and to provide the analysis capability required for the *TDS910* synthesiser made by Triangle (which uses a time-domain data-compression technique) some software packages are available. Since the source code for these packages is provided, the user can change the functions to suit his purposes:

(a) *Fig-FORTH* kernal and system software.

(b) Input speech capture, playback and editing software — acts like a *digital tape recorder*.

(c) Speech analyser, editor and *assembler*, for the *TDS910* synthesiser.

The concept of an *assembler* for speech data is an unusual one and worthy of some explanation. Assembly *source code* is constructed in a file to represent parts of utterances that are stored in the file of digitised speech, and to illustrate how different sections are to be concatenated together, an example is given below:

```
;BLEACH
;P.RUSH
11 CTRL 4,.260
PHON FD,1
SILC .92
PHON FE,1
PHON FF,4
PHON FG,1
PHON FH,5
PHON FI,1
SILC .268
CTRL 3,.260
PHON AI,1
DONE
```

This fragment of source code points to the appropriate speech data to synthesise the word *bleach* on the TDS910 synthesiser. The listing was originally 'machine generated' by a FORTH program and subsequently hand-edited to make use of speech segments that had previously been stored in memory as parts of different phrases. After editing, this source code listing can be 'assembled' to produce object code which can be compressed and used in the synthesiser.

The first two statements are *comments* (just as in a microprocessor assembly listing), and the next line is a control statement defining this as the eleventh utterance, to be found in position 4 in the ROM space. The '260' defines the data capture period in μs. Each 'PHON' instruction defines that a stored segment of speech is to be played next, the first 'operand' giving the label of the speech segment and the second specifying how much of this segment is to be played. Finally, the 'SILC' instruction defines that a window of silence should be inserted. Note also that utterances defined in this way can be re-used in the definition of a new utterance, as has been done at the end of this example. In this case 'CTRL 3,.260/PHON AI,1' replays a /tʃ/ sound that has been sliced off a previous word.

Both the *assembler* technique, and the *EPROM emulator* (in-circuit emulator) are techniques derived from the familiar technology of microprocessor development. So too can the whole approach described in this section be likened to a microprocessor development system. It is hardware which can be applied in many different ways by different applications – but a thorough understanding of speech is a prerequisite.

CHAPTER 14

DESIGNING A SPEECH SYSTEM

Geoff Bristow

The preceding thirteen chapters have shown that there are many more issues involved in speech system design than simply defining the pin-out of an integrated circuit, although these issues are not beyond one all-round designer with the appropriate background and interest. This chapter is intended to tie together some of the conclusions and show how to set about a design from start to finish.

14.1 *Stages in a speech system design*

Figure 14.1 shows an idealised flow diagram of a speech project development. Of course, this is not meant as a rigid plan but rather as a guide to a suitable order in which to undertake the various activities. Note especially that the field trials are not necessarily conducted using the final electronics, but perhaps with a simple evaluation module. This means that the trials can start immediately after the conception of an idea, and also that the project can be abandoned or restructured if necessary without any wasted design effort. Each suggested design stage will now be covered in further detail, using a hypothetical example.

14.2 *Concept trials*

At the inception of a new idea for the application of speech synthesis there will inevitably be many unanswered questions in the mind of the designer, and indeed scepticism amongst the financial supporters or company management. The most fundamental question will need to be answered first: *Will it work?* In particular, will the users of the product or system react favourably or unfavourably and will they respond in the required way? If the equipment is a consumer product, will it be

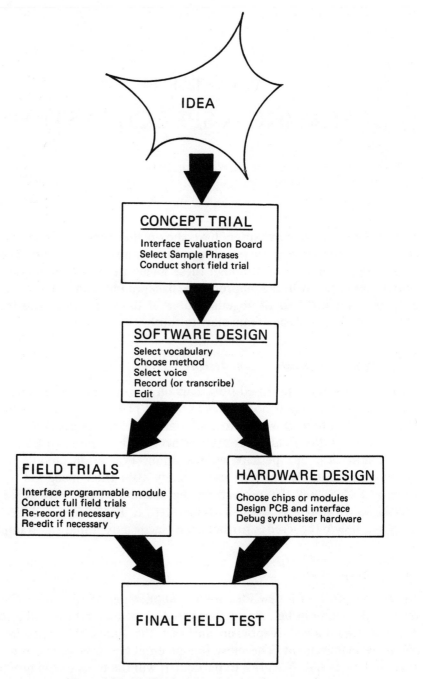

Figure 14.1 Idealised stages in a speech system design

liked and bought? Alternatively, if it is a public service system such as for train announcements at a station, will the public feel well served or will they feel patronised, alienated, or confused?

For the purpose of illustration, let us suppose our new idea is for a loudspeaking system in a doctor's waiting room, to replace a bell for inviting his patients into his surgery. The product would be in the form of a small box to sit on the doctor's desk, on top of which were a number of buttoms to initiate various messages. The box would be wired to loudspeakers in the waiting rooms, and also into the surgery office.

Upon conceptualising the product it is easy to let one's mind run on, thinking perhaps about the possibilities of concatenated phrases with different doctors' names to cope with several concurrent surgeries, but there are some fundamental questions which can be answered just using a simple trial phrase like *Next patient please*. For example, would it be important to have the *actual* doctor's voice, or would a *general-purpose* recording be sufficient? If the former is required to retain the personal atmosphere of the surgery, each box will need customising and the product will be much more expensive than a microphone and public address system. On the other hand, if an actor's voice which is friendly and comforting is found to be well accepted by the patients, the box will probably work out cheaper than a public address system. Thus, the answer to this simple question would probably give a strong indication as to whether the product would be destined for success or failure.

How would one go about finding the answer to such fundamental questions, with the minimum of investment? The answer is to use a simple off-the-shelf *evaluation board* as described in section 12.1 of this book. The simple three-word custom phrase *Next patient please* can be purchased from a speech consultant at the minimum of cost, or recorded with the appropriate equipment as outlined in chapter 13. The phrase will probably be placed in *EPROM* and plugged into the evaluation board, while the loudspeaker and doctor's push button will be wired on directly. After a minimum of expenditure and no more than a week's delay, a *concept trial* can begin.

While the form of the trial is obviously flexible and will depend on the type of product or system, the essential element is the use of a suitable cross-section of *naive* subjects. (Naivety in this sense means that they are unaware of the background to the trial, and have not become particularly acquainted with synthetic speech beforehand.) As far as possible the circumstances of the trial should match the actual situation in which the product will be used. In the case of the device for the doctors' waiting room, a concept trial would simply consist of the prototype being used in place of the usual bell (or whatever) during a normal surgery time. The doctor may then informally ask each patient's opinion in his opening conversation, or the patient may be asked to complete a simple questionnaire on his way out. Of course, the larger and more representative the sample of patients the better, but for better guidance on the size of sample to choose in any given experiment the reader is encouraged to explore the literature given at the end of this chapter, or consult an experimental psychologist or statistician.

After the concept trial, the designer will not only have decided whether to proceed with the project or not, but he will also have formulated some strong ideas about the type of voice and message which will be most applicable. His next job will be to prepare his vocabulary in detail with the correct speaker and try it out again.

14.3 *Software design*

CHOICE OF MESSAGE

At this stage the designer can make a first pass attempt at a complete vocabulary listing, making use of concatenation of words into different sentences for different occasions (where applicable). For example, for the product for the surgery, the designer may have decided on the following general purpose phrasing:

> *Would the patient with card number [43] please go through to surgery [B].*

He may also have thought of a few extra features that could be added at no expense, such as the occasional sentence like:

> *We apologise for the delay, there has been an emergency. The doctor hopes to continue his surgery in [20] minutes.*

Each of these examples takes advantage of the unique ability of speech synthesis (as opposed to magnetic tape, etc.) for restructuring a sentence by replacing a particular word or two. In other words, the bulk of the sentences needs only to be stored once in memory, along with the speech data for each of the numbers and letters. (In fact, not even all the numbers need to be stored — see chapter 6.) Also, while it is not possible to emulate this function using the simplest of evaluation boards, more complex (but nevertheless, off-the-shelf) programmable speech modules are available to do this task (see section 12.3).

CHOICE OF DATA TYPE

Although it is still very easy to buy the *hardware* required to try out this vocabulary, the investment which is now being put on *software* is considerable compared with the concept trial stage. Since most speech consultants charge for processing by the word, this new vocabulary of some sixty words represents about twenty times the financial investment made in the initial trial. Accordingly, the designer will want to be as sure as possible that he is going down the right route and that he will not have to retrace his steps. This means making the decision about type of synthesiser, so that the data he produces now will be compatible with his final electronic solution.

Many of the decisions that are to be made between types of synthesiser chip and the manufacturer to be patronised will be matters of designer preference based on the information that has been presented in chapters 8–11, and will not depend on the type of application or the outcome of the concept trials. However, some clear decisions do rest on the *vocabulary size* and *type of quality* required for the application, and to discuss these issues adequately, we must first define 'speech quality'.

Naturalness versus intelligibility

What exactly do we mean by quality? We have noted that the quality of speech is subjective rather than objective, but along what axis could it be measured? Is it sufficient to describe synthetic speech as *good* or *bad*? Most workers in the area now agree that there are two dimensions of quality, which we can call *naturalness* and *intelligibility*. In fact, it is certainly possible to generate synthetic speech which is rather more easy to understand than the natural speech from which it was derived, even though it does not sound at all like a human being. Conversely, one can process and resynthesise a speech sample to sound perfectly natural, but yet people could fail to understand it when it was played through a loudspeaker, without the normal aid of the sight of the lips moving.

It is possible to place the quality requirements of a given application on a two dimensional plot such as fig. 14.2. Although the ideal speech would generally be that in the top right-hand corner (perfectly natural and perfectly intelligible), the technology at present does not allow this at low bit rates and a judgement has to be made as to which aspect is most important. Indeed for any given bit rate there will theoretically remain such a trade-off, but as the rate is increased the performance on both axes increases towards a qualitative optimum.

Some rather gross application categories are given in fig. 14.3 to illustrate the use of this concept. Firstly, it is generally assumed that in the case of an industrial alarm, intelligibility is of the essence. For

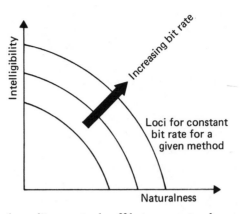

Figure 14.2 Speech quality as a trade-off between naturalness and intelligibility

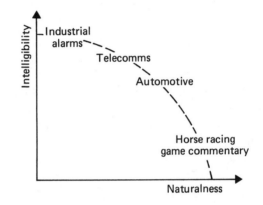

Figure 14.3 Some examples of the naturalness/intelligibility trade-off

example, during the well-reported *3 mile Island* nuclear accident there were apparently up to 100 different bells and other alarm signals ringing in the control room at the same time. It is hardly surprising, therefore, that the main reason why the incident became quite as serious as it did is attributed to operator confusion.[1] Clearly, in such a situation, distinct, comprehensible instructions are of paramount importance. In any case, as noted earlier, with that level of activity and importance of the information, the listener would be unlikely to notice the *type* of voice, only the content of the message. It may even escape his notice whether the speaker was male or female.

On the other hand, the author is aware of an application in an arcade version of a horse-racing game, where the operator watches a video graphics picture of a horse race, listens to the racing commentary, and places a bet on his favourite horse. The speech synthesis which was recorded successfully for the racing commentary was almost totally unintelligible, as indeed one often finds such commentaries to be! However, the naturalness was extremely good, as was apparently required to help the pundit to feel at home in the appropriate atmosphere.

Most applications, however, require a reasonable level of both naturalness and intelligibility, and will appear somewhere near the middle of the graph, although the emphasis will differ. For example, one may assume that intelligibility has the edge in telecommunications because there is no other communication medium available if that one fails, whilst in cars there will generally be a visual backup (and the aesthetics of the voice will also be an important selling feature in the showroom). Returning to our doctor's waiting room, we can probably assume that both naturalness and intelligibility are important, but naturalness may be most crucial to its acceptance.

Quality vs vocabulary size

Having defined the *type* and *level* of quality required, and the size of vocabulary which is ideal, a thought must be given to the target cost of the end equipment. The very highest quality, as noted in chapter 1, will be obtained with PCM, but the data storage space may be twenty times that for LPC. If the vocabulary is very small this may be acceptable, but if not, a compromise in the quality will have to be made to minimise the semiconductor memory costs.

For medium-size vocabularies most of the techniques discussed in chapters 8–11 could be used, and are likely to be of similar cost. However, for very large vocabularies a cost decision must again be taken. The data storage for LPC chips, for example, can generally be expanded indefinitely, but the cost will rise linearly with the number of words. The alternative is to move to text-to-speech. This must result in some quality degradation, but fig. 14.4 shows how, for very large vocabularies, the small overhead of memory required to run a text-to-speech system proves to be negligible compared to the savings made in word-data memory. Also, the quality of text-to-speech systems tends to be high in intelligibility, even if low in naturalness, which makes them an obvious choice for many large-vocabulary information output applications.

An illustrative comparison of the three basic methods of synthesis (see chapter 1) is depicted in fig. 14.5. Unfortunately, while variables such as bit rate and vocabulary size can be measured exactly, a good standard for quantitative comparison of speech quality has not yet been proposed in the literature, making such a decision plane necessarily qualitative in nature. Nevertheless, our doctor is certain to opt for a

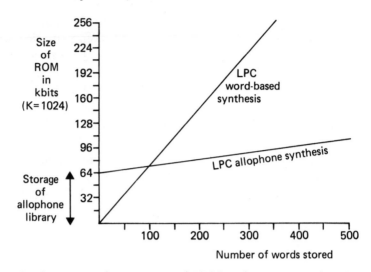

Figure 14.4 Comparison between typical LPC-based text-to-speech and word-level synthesis

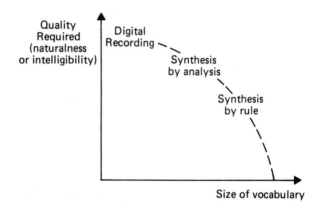

Figure 14.5 A decision plane for the three types of voice output

custom recorded phrase for his application, to ensure acceptance amongst the patients, although the quality and cost of time-domain synthesis, LPC, and word-based formant synthesis would probably all be equally suitable.

CHOICE OF VOICE
Having made the decision about synthesis method, the designer may or may not be left needing to find a trained speaker. In the case of phonetic synthesis (chapter 11) or text-to-speech (chapter 6 and section 12.4) no speaker will be required, although this could be an

advantage or a disadvantage. In the surgery design, for example, a particularly friendly and considerate voice may be specified and the freedom to choose a suitable actor may be very important.

In general the choice of voice, and indeed the choice of intonation and mood with which the phrases are spoken, is one of the most difficult and intangible parts of the system design (see chapter 2). Once again, though, the golden rule is to *try it out*; set up a trial, similar to the concept trial, using the minimum of software and hardware, and let naive listeners make a judgement. For the waiting room, we shall assume that the panel chose a lady newsreader who was accustomed to doing Sunday evening television appeals.

14.4 *Field trials*

For the field trial, all the choices will have been made and the vocabulary will have been recorded, processed, and edited to the designer's satisfaction, but the electronic design need not be ready. As far as the user is concerned, the hardware is irrelevant (provided that any prototype wiring can be conveniently hidden) as long as the user interface is realistic. The product can be tested fully at this stage, therefore, providing the behaviour of the programmable module is identical to that of the final device. The only features that this prototype will not exhibit will be the cost and size of a production unit.

During these final field trials problems will inevitably appear with the vocabulary – *software bugs* we can call them, by analogy to the development of microprocessor systems. There will be words which for some reason do not sound right when played away from the studio. Indeed the whole character of the speech will appear differently when actually in use than when being prepared. The speech for a car, for example, should certainly have been edited finally in a car using the actual speaker (see chapter 13), but nevertheless, when the engine is running and the listener is concentrating on the road the effect will be quite different. Likewise, the phrases for the doctor's waiting room will come across quite differently in a crowded room with babies crying than in a silent studio. For these reasons it is likely to be necessary to go back to the studio and change the sounds yet again.

Unfortunate effects of the selected vocabulary will also show up. For example, the effect of repetition on a captive audience can be most frustrating; one could well imagine that the field trials of the waiting room device would end with very bad reports, despite the encouraging concept trials. The intial study included only three words, remember, which may be acceptable when repeated many times.

But if you are twentieth in the queue to see the doctor, can you imagine listening to:

> *Would the patient with card number [42] please go through to surgery [A].*

> *Would the patient with card number [43] please go through to surgery [B].*

> *Would the . . .*

twenty times in a row? It would be likely that, following these field trials, the designer would amend his vocabulary to a simpler structure which can better stand the repetition, perhaps:

> *Number [42] to surgery [A], please*

However, this is of course conjecture − only a real field trial would indicate the best compromise.

14.5 *Hardware design*

Once the project is certain to proceed and the synthesis method has been chosen, the hardware design can be started in parallel with the field trials. In this case the decisions rest mainly on cost–volume trade-off, and amount to the same *build versus buy* concept which will be familiar to microsystem designers. The material cost of a customised printed circuit design is generally lower than the purchase price of a ready-made speech module, but the cost of development of that PCB design must be amortised across the number of units sold during the product's lifetime. Accordingly, the real cost per unit of a custom-designed part is extremely high for low volume products but drops dramatically with volume, whilst the price per unit of a manufactured module is relatively low for small volumes but falls only moderately with volume (see fig. 14.6).

This means that for low volume products, and even prototype runs of high volume products, the designer can complete his system around the same programmable speech module that he used for the field trials. He may care to spend some further effort on filtering or amplifier design (as discussed, for example, in section 10.4) but that is all. However, if the marketing predictions look favourable (or in any inherently high volume industry such as telecommunications) he should be ready to design some custom electronics using the technology described in chapters 9–11, or at least to interface a low-cost *OEM board* to the system as described in section 12.2. The bulk of this

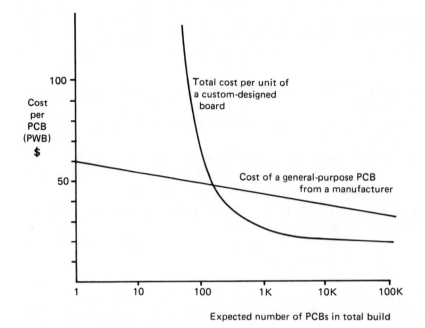

Figure 14.6 The 'build versus buy' trade-off for a typical speech board. The graph shows the total cost per unit built if the materials and labour are $20 per unit and the full development cost of the circuit is $5000. Also shown is a typical price curve available from a manufacturer for a more general board which would nevertheless serve the same purpose

hardware design is then likely to live on through successive products, and even successive upgrades of synthesiser chip – as with microprocessors, it is mainly the software that will change.

As we complete this chapter, and therefore the formal text of this book, we leave our fictitious doctor running a prototype batch of 100 surgery systems based on standard modules. He hopes to test the market for 3 months or so, by installing them in a range of surgeries and two large teaching hospitals, and then to hand over to an electronic consultancy to engineer a production unit. The reader is now encouraged to examine some further application examples in part 3, this time mostly written from the personal experience of each contributor.

14.6 *Further reading*

This chapter has referred several times to the concept of the field trial, and has pointed out the importance of good experimental design in this area. A reader who has a purely engineering background is strongly advised to consult with a psychologist to design his field trial in order to gather the most useful data for subsequent statistical evaluation, but the reader who is interested in pursuing the experimental design himself may refer to some of the following useful texts for guidance

Clarke, G.M. (1969) *Statistics and Experimental Design*. London: Arnold.

Cohran, W.G. and Cox, G.M. (1957) *Experimental Designs*. New York: Wiley.

Cox, D.R. (1958) *Planning of Experiments*. New York: Wiley.

Finney, D.J. (1955) *Experimental Design and its Statistical Basis*. Cambridge: Cambridge University Press.

Moser, C.A. and Kalton, G. (1975) *Survey Methods in Social Investigation*. London: Heinemann.

Oppenheim, W.N. (1966) *Questionnaire Design and Attitude Measurement*. London: Heinemann.

Robson, Colin (1975) *Experiment, Design and Statistics in Psychology*. Harmondsworth: Penguin Modern Psychology Series.

Stuart, A. (1976) *Basic Ideas of Scientific Sampling*. London: Griffin.

Notes

1. *The Report of the President's Commission on the Accident at Three Mile Island* (the Kemeny Report), obtainable from the Superintendent of Documents, US Government Printing Office, Washington DC 20402, USA.

PART 3
APPLICATIONS

CHAPTER 15

TALKING COMPUTERS
IN THE CLASSROOM

Tony Gray

15.1 *Speech synthesis in the classroom*

In the Student Union building at Loughborough University sits a
pin-ball machine. The game is related to the Flash Gordon story and
every half minute or so the machine berates those sitting quietly
nearby sipping their beer with the threat, *Emperor Ming awaits!* This
machine is one of the few applications of speech technology in a
British educational institution regularly encountered by a wide cross-
section of individuals.

However, things are changing and the aims of this paper are to
identify two broad types of utterance which will be commonly encountered in the educational application of speech technology and
introduce some current British work in this field.

The first application concerns the use of speech as a means of
enabling non-readers to use educational software. The second relates to
a specific use of speech which radically improves the effectiveness of
microcomputers as an aid to learning in one portion of the primary
and special school curriculum. These discussions are within the context
of educational computing in England and Wales, where although
machines are becoming common,[1] the level of speech technology
available is below that possible using larger computers and the type
of sophisticated systems being developed at the Joint Speech Research
Unit (JSRU)[2] and elsewhere. Those interested in the scene outside
the UK may like to use the reference given as a starting point for their
reading.[3]

SPEECH QUALITY

In a perfect world artificially produced speech would be high fidelity and as easily understood as the original. In education at least, such a world is yet to exist, and the technical problems of producing quality synthesised speech with a microcomputer have made it necessary to differentiate that which may be merely understandable in application from that which must be intelligible. However, it may be that this distinction will continue to be useful even when the technical reasons for its existence have disappeared. This is because speech required of an educational computer system would seem to fall into two broad categories of utterance: that which *prompts or motivates* the user and that which carries precise *didactic* content. At present these two categories carry implications for the quality of speech (and the cost of producing it). However, when speech is as much a part of computing as the VDU, the types of utterance seem unlikely to alter. Consequently, identifying and exploring this now will help our future understanding; not of how to make machines speak, but *when* they should speak and *what* they should say. Let us now examine these categories of speech a little more closely.

Using speech as a prompt is the most common and the least specialised application. Here the speech is intended to inform the user or elicit a response. For example the program might say, *These are your choices. . . ,* or *Would you like to try again?*, or *Well done! Here's another. . . .* Under these circumstances it is only important that the speech is understandable; that the user knows the meaning of what has been said. Since meaning can be gleaned from context (and software which uses speech in this way should offer a means of repeating the last utterance), the quality need not be high.

Tom Vincent of the Open University says:

> *Synthetic speech. . .not acceptable to critical ears. . .may well be acceptable if this means of communication creates opportunities that would not otherwise exist.*[4]

and in his work with blind students this is certainly the case. With sighted users, reinforcing speech with a visual prompt, when appropriate, increases the perception of meaning of that prompt.

Other types of application require a more critical approach, the speech having to be both intelligible and natural. This is because when speech has a didactic role, the precise content of the speech is important, not merely its general meaning. For example, in software intended to help pupils develop and practise early reading skills it may be necessary for the system to speak a set of *blends* or *digraphs* as examples for the pupil to learn. If this material is of poor quality, the learner will have a bad model to copy and suffer accordingly.

Consequently, before picking a speech system for classroom use, careful consideration must be given to the application and the impact this will have upon the choice and cost of hardware. The examples in this chapter illustrate this by referring to particular classroom applications.

TALKING COMPUTERS FOR NON-READERS

There are two major groups of non-readers: those who cannot accurately perceive print for reasons of visual or perceptual impairment, and those who have yet to acquire the skills. The talking computer can offer new educational experiences to these groups. Given below are three examples of the use of speech synthesis in teaching aids — two where the speech acts as a prompt in the program, and one where the speech carries essential teaching material.

15.2 *Speech as a prompt*

EXAMPLE 1

The *Open University* in the UK offers higher education to anyone who wishes to continue their studies. Tuition is mainly by correspondence, but students do attend tutorials, seminars and summer school. Computers are widely used and much interesting work is under way exploring the possibilities of computer-aided learning through modem links, light pens, teletext, and other extensions of the traditional role of the computer in University life. The inclusion of synthetic speech as an extra medium of instruction seems natural, but to the University's 200 visually handicapped students this development is essential.

Dr Tom Vincent began a project in 1980 with the aim of helping sight-impaired students, many of whom avoid courses with a large computing input simply because of the difficulties associated with using a terminal. At that time only two means of enabling a blind student to operate terminals were employed: a normal-sighted person relayed information, or an expensive device for converting optical information onto a pad of vibrating pins was used.[5] Neither method was satisfactory. Consequently, Dr Vincent began looking at the possibility of creating a low-cost synthetic speech system based upon existing technology in order that it could be available to large numbers of students. This work is being done as part of the University's *Microcomputers and Teaching* project,[6] and a description of the early part of the work has been published.[7,8] Initial findings are encouraging:

> *CAL (Computer-Aided Learning) for blind students has been shown to be possible through the use of synthetic speech. Equally important has been the use of low-cost, commercially available hardware — the lack of this feature has prevented many facilities in the area of special education being made available to potential users. With the cost of microcomputers and speech synthesisers continuing to fall, this technique should find wide-spread use for blind people who need access to computing facilities.* [9]

More recently, Dr Vincent has been pursuing the problem of adding speech output to a *Perkins Brailler* with a view to applying this to the teaching of braille and the preparation of text from braille input.

Thus, adults were able to use a computer without any visual output and, although the work is in its early stages, the future looks bright. Interestingly, the quality of speech seems not to have been a problem and consequently achieving a low-cost solution seems possible. This is a good example of understandability alone being the criterion for acceptable results, providing account is taken of the type of utterance required — in this case largely as a prompt.

EXAMPLE 2

The second example is drawn from that part of my own work which concerns the design, evaluation, and development of software for primary schools.

A major problem with mathematical courseware concerns the reading level in a program. With some pupils there is no difficulty — number, reading, and language skills develop hand in hand. However, there is a dilemma when a mis-match occurs. For example a mature poor-reader may have good computational and problem-solving skills. Alternatively, a program may offer number work at the correct level for young children, but require a reading age of nine and above. Equally, a young pupil may need to acquire particular language skills in order to proceed but be hindered by the barrier of text.

These problems can be overcome by using speech as the prime interactive medium within the program. For example the speech can reinforce written messages or be used alone to reward, explain or encourage.

However, the problem of redundancy must be born in mind. Educational software which indiscriminately uses the full power of the microcomputer can be counter-productive. An inconsidered, technically masterful cascade of graphics, text and speech may be confusing, some messages being ignored to the detriment of the learning experience envisaged by the program designer. It is better to have precise use of colour, sound and speech to emphasise particular points, draw attention to graphic information or highlight areas of text. This is particularly true of software used by children.

Another aspect to be remembered is the need to suppress some messages following the initial run. It is aggravating and disturbing to have a spoken prompt on each of the twenty-five occasions a particular point in a program is reached. If this is allowed, users again begin to ignore messages and subsequently become desensitised to important utterances which occur elsewhere.

This type of application does not require high quality speech. Indeed pupils at a special school in Goole, Humberside have been using a speech system just on the limit of understandability, and have not encountered any major difficulties in using the software written and provided for them by Keith Anderson, a local business man.

15.3 *Speech as a didactic medium* (Example 3)

Speech which carries information which is intrinsically important must be of good quality. This example outlines recent work in the Education Department at Loughborough University of Technology aimed at producing a speech system which can be used to help non-readers who have not yet acquired these skills. The thinking behind the selection of hardware and the list of essential words and sounds will be discussed.

CHOOSING THE EQUIPMENT

The best learning aid for children is a good teacher. Anything less is a compromise. In selecting equipment for classroom use, the intention must be to control this process of compromise so that teachers can still have confidence in the learning aids they are using. The following criteria emerged to guide selection.

1. Quality

The speech must be sufficiently good to allow children to make accurate associations between aural and visual representations of words. This implies high intelligibility and naturalness because in this application words often come individually or in short phrases. Less information is available consequently to enable the pupil to recognise words; and anticipate meaning and sound sequences within and between words. It is also important that a good 'model' is presented to the learner. The list of words and sounds which has been used by the project to test systems which allow 'home processing' of speech is given in table 15.1.

Table 15.1 Test list of words

and	off
about	press
apple	put
bath	queen
box	rain
bring	share
chair	she
egg	stop
feet	then
from	thing
good	this
had	type
his	use
ink	up
jam	very
kept	was
left	well
milk	yes
next	zoo

2. Control

(a) Control of speech production is vital: *word flow* is as important as the accuracy of individual word sounds. The rhythm and timing of an utterance carries a good deal of its meaning and control over cadence, intonation and pitch are necessary if the lilting flow of human speech is to be achieved. It is important to be able to avoid aggressive mechanical chanting by means of good control.

(b) A prime strength of any computer system is its ability to interact with the user. Easy manipulation of the available sounds is important, therefore, in speech devices designed for didactic use.

(c) Control is also important to the teacher. It is important that staff in schools can adapt software to suit their particular needs. A device producing good quality natural-sounding speech is of little value if small changes require enormous amounts of time, patience, and skill.

3. Content

The aim of the project is to develop materials which will help children acquire the reading skills of the average nine year old. This requires mastery of a relatively small number of words and sounds, and the impact of this fact upon the choice of equipment is considerable. Large vocabularies are either expensive or time consuming to achieve, and if only a relatively small quantity of unrepeated speech is needed, there seems little point in choosing a system which has a potentially unlimited vocabulary, particularly if speech quality suffers. However, if a limited vocabulary system is chosen, it is crucial that the available vocabulary is carefully selected in order to match the precise requirements of the application in mind.

4. Cost

Price, quality and *memory* are interlinked. One aspect of the dilemma facing those interested in artificial speech is that micros have small memories and high quality speech requires memory in quantity. Some trading-off is therefore necessary, especially if a vocabulary in excess of, say, thirty words is required. A system needing only small amounts of memory would certainly be the most attractive and since disk drives are expensive, systems which can be operated using cassette or cartridge storage are desirable. In addition, cost dictates that only readily available systems be considered.

THE CHOICE MADE

Using these criteria, systems on the market which synthesise speech from stored phonemes were decided against. This was because at the time such systems did not satisfy the above criteria of control and quality. This decision effectively limited the field to those systems which use whole words from natural speech, and this introduced the problem of memory capacity.

Systems which digitise speech more or less directly deliver good quality home-recorded speech and given that the vocabulary may be chosen by the user, the system becomes very attractive for our purposes — but for the factors of cost and memory. Such systems typically require a minimum of 48 kbytes for the data storage and control program to produce a few seconds of continuous unrepeated speech. If high resolution graphics are also employed, the problem of memory becomes acute. This makes the approach expensive because the board, additional memory and a disk drive have to be bought in addition to the standard microcomputer.

These points and the fact that unlimited vocabulary is not needed led to the decision to look for a *synthesis-by-analysis* system with a pre-recorded, fixed vocabulary, and a board was obtained with a vocabulary primarily intended for application as an industrial verbal warning device. As can be imagined this had rather limited classroom appeal. However, as a means of exploring the potential of this method of speech production, the board was useful.

Taking our criteria in turn. . .

1. Quality

Being based upon recorded natural speech the words had a reasonably 'human' sound to them. Despite the American accent (which is unsuitable for this application in British schools), and the sometimes rather eccentric stressing, the consensus amongst teachers who heard the system was that it approached an acceptable level of quality for classroom use.

2. Control

The original board met the criteria and following this lead, the project is now working with another system which allows good control of intonation, cadence and pitch. This enhances greatly the educational value of the speech and initial indications are that a truly didactic role for the utterances can be fulfilled.

3. Content

One major problem with the original board was its limited vocabulary. Since only a small number of words are needed for our purposes, around 500, work has been progressing towards the time when a large vocabulary specially designed for classroom use will be available.

4. Cost

Such boards are relatively cheap, they require no additional memory to operate and will work quite satisfactorily with cassette and cartridge storage systems.

Conclusion

All in all, the 'words in aspic' approach to synthesised speech — that of having a pre-recorded fixed vocabulary on a chip — seemed to have distinct advantages except in the matter of choice and extent of vocabulary. This being the case, a list of words and sounds considered essential to the specific application in mind was developed and this will now be discussed.

CHOOSING THE VOCABULARY

While educational experts will undoubtedly disagree about any final choice of words, it seems most expedient to base the criteria for their selection upon what may be considered 'good practice' by teachers. Consequently, the following criteria were used to formulate the word list.

The list must include words and sounds which:

(a) occur most frequently in the vocabulary of the average adult reader. This will enable their use with as wide a range of published reading schemes as possible. The work of McNally and Murray offers some guidance,[10] although this vocabulary needs bringing up to date;

(b) enable the teacher to encourage the development of social language skills. For example, those pertaining to danger, direction, instructions, road signs and others whose misunderstanding could lead to injury or inconvenience;

(c) are directly associated with the development of temporal, spatial, numerical and mathematical concepts;

(d) are the names of everyday items familiar to children, and which contain examples of sounds in use;

(e) allow the talking device to be 'civil' and 'user friendly';

(f) enable adequate positive feedback and reinforcement for children's learning;

(g) enable teachers to adopt a combination of teaching strategies with individual learners. This implies that the list should contain examples of all those sounds, blends and digraphs listed by the National Association for Remedial Education (NARE),[11] in addition to the words identified by the other criteria. Whilst including some pure phonemes the NARE list has letter sounds, blends and digraphs which are of particular relevance in the classroom. Often these units are larger than the individual phoneme.

Using these criteria, the list in table 15.2 was created. The words and sounds can be accessed and spoken in any order, to any rhythm. The arrangement is therefore designed to ease selection, not to impose sequence.

Notes on the main list

(a) Some additional words and sounds are available because they sound the same as words/sounds already present. These are given in table 15.3.

(b) All major blends and digraphs are present either as individual sounds, or in example words on the list. Table 15.4 gives those sounds available in example words.

(c) The 'extra sounds' may be added to other words. . .

    e.g. *big, bigger, biggest*

(d) Numbers of any size may be spoken by combining elements.

Table 15.2 List of words and sounds

Numbers	The names of letters	The sounds of consonant letters (& unambiguous sample words)	The sounds of vowel letters
Nought	A	b e.g. boat	a e.g. apple
One	B	c cat	a bath
Two	C	d dog	a about
Three	D	f fork	e egg
Four	E	g get	i it
Five	F	h hat	o off
Six	G	j jump	u up
Seven	H	l lot	u put
Eight	I		
Nine	J	m milk	*Vowel Digraphs*
Ten	K	n not	ar e.g. vary (hair)
Eleven	L	p pen	au haul (tall)
Twelve	M	r ran	ee green
Thirteen	N	s sit	ir bird
Fourteen	O	t top	ou out
Fifteen	P	v very	oo room
Sixteen	Q	w well	oo look
Seventeen	R	x box	oy boy
Eighteen	S	y yes	
Nineteen	T	z zoo	*Blends and Digraphs*
Twenty	U		ch e.g. children
Thirty	V		easu treasure
Forty	W		qu queen
Fifty	X		sh short
Sixty	Y		th third
Seventy	Z		th this
Eighty			ng bring
Ninety			
Hundred			
Thousand			

Words

about	above	add	after	afternoon	again	all
always	am	an	and	angry	another	any
apple	arm	as	ask	at	away	

20 words

baby	back	bad	bag	ball	because	bed
been	beginning	behind	before	below	best	better
big	bike	bird	black	blue	boat	boil
book	bottom	box	boy	bridge	bring	brother
bus	but	buy				

31 words

cafe	cake	call	came	can	can't	cap
car	cap	centi	chair	children	choose	circle
closed	coat	cold	colour	comb	come	copy
could	count	cow	cream	cup		

26 words

dad	danger	date	day	dear	did	different
dinner	divide	do	dog	doll	done	don't
door	down	draw	drink	duck	dwarf	

20 words

ear	eat	egg	empty	end	enough	entrance
equals	every	exit				

10 words

face	farm	fast	father	fell	few	fifth
find	finger	fire	first	fish	flower	fly
foot	for	fork	found	from	full	fun

21 words

game	garage	gave	get	ghost	girl	give
glass	go	going	good	got	gram	green

14 words

had	hair	half	halt	hand	hang	happy
has	hat	have	he	head	hello	help
her	here	hill	him	his	home	horse
hot	house	how				

24 words

Table 15.2 (contd.)

Words							
if	in	ink	into	is	it		6 words
jam	jump	just					3 words
keep	kept	kilo	kite	knife	know		6 words
lady	last	later	learn	least	left	leg	
less	let	letter	like	litre	little	live	
long	look	lost	lot	love			19 words
made	make	man	many	may	me	men	
metre	middle	mile	milk	milli	money	more	
morning	most	mother	mouth	mr	mrs	much	
mum	must	my					24 words
name	narrow	near	never	new	next	nice	
night	nose	not	nothing	now	number		13 words
o'clock	of	off	old	on	once	only	
open	other	our	out	over	own		13 words
palm	past	pat	pen	pence	pencil	penny	
pet	phone	picture	pie	pig	place	plate	
play	please	police	pound	press	private	pull	
push	put	puzzle					24 words
quarter	queen	question	quick				4 words
rabbit	rain	ran	read	rectangle	red	right	
road	room	round	run	rung			12 words
sad	said	same	sat	saw	say	school	
scratch	seat	second	self	set	share	she	
shop	short	should	side	sing	sister	sit	
sky	slow	small	snake	so	some	soon	
sorry	splash	spoon	spring	square	station	stop	
street	sun	sweet					38 words
table	take	talk	tall	tell	than	thank	
that	the	thee	their	them	then	these	
they	thing	think	third	this	those	thumb	
time	to	today	tomorrow	top	toy	train	
treasure	tree	triangle	try	tune	type		34 words
under	up	us	use				4 words
van	very						2 words
walk	want	was	water	way	we	well	
went	were	wet	what	when	where	which	
white	who	wide	will	window	wish	with	
woman	word	work	would				25 words
year	yellow	yes	yesterday	your			5 words
zebra	zoo						2 words

Days of the week	Extra sounds	
Monday	-ing e.g.	running
Tuesday	-th	fourth etc.
Wednesday	-est	biggest (-ist)
Thursday		
Friday		
Saturday		
Sunday		

Table 15.3 List of extra words, single sounds, blends and digraphs present as 'doubles'

Word	Present as	Sound		Present as
too	2	k	c	S*
fore	4	q	qu	D*
ate	8	ll	l	S
bee	B	ff	f	S
sea	C	gg	g	S
see	C	ss	s	S
owe	O	zz	z	S
queue	Q	ck	c	S
tea	T	ph	f	S
you	U	wh	w	S
why	Y	ai	ar	D
air	ar (sound)	aw	au	D
bean	been	ay	A	N*
bye	buy	ea (meat)	E	N
by	buy	ea (bread)	e	S
deer	dear	er	ir	D
hare	hair	er	a	vowel (about)
no	know	ew	U	N
knew	new	ie–ei	E	N
knows	nose	oa	O	N
knot	not	ie	I	N
hour	our	oe	O	N
plaice	place	ue	U	N
reed	read	oi	oy	D
read	red	or	au	D
write	right	ow (cow)	ou	D
rode	road	ow (crow)	O	N
sew	so	ur	ir	D
sum	some			
son	sun			
there	their			
weigh	way			
wear	where			
witch	which			
wood	would			

Other less common words are also present.

*S = sound, D = digraph, N = names.

Table 15.4 Sounds available in consonant blends

Final Consonant Blends:

ft, ld, lf, lk, lm, lp, lt, mp, nd, nk, nt, pt, st, sk, ang, ong, ung

Initial Consonant Blends:

bl, cl, dw, fl, gl, pl, sl, br, cr, dr, fr, gr, pr, tr, sc, sk, sm, sn, sp, st, sw, tw

Long Consonant Blends:

scr, spl, spr, squ, str

(e) The sample words given to illustrate various sounds are all from the list and aurally unambiguous. . .

    e.g.   *b* as in *boat* not *bat* (confusable with *pat*)
            sh as in *short* not *shop* (confusable with *chop*)

(f) Some words were selected for their multiple usefulness as examples of sounds, everyday objects and relationship to other words on the list. . .

    e.g.   *comb* — gives the *-mb* ending.
            hair — gives the *-ai* digraph and is related to *comb*.
            garage — gives two *a* vowels.
            car — distinguishes *-ar* from *-ar* in *vary*.

(g) Some words may be adapted. . .

    e.g.   *Mum*   + *i* = *Mummy*
            Centi − *i* = *sent, scent*

This greatly increases the vocabulary available.

(h) Particular pronunciations are required in places, advice having been sought from the BBC pronunciation unit and their written guide.[12] Also, some sounds are not included for reasons outlined below.

    e.g.   (i) *zebra* = *zeebra* (animal) not *zebra* crossing.
        (ii) *the* and *thee* both present.
        (iii) *wh* is not included as it is now rarely used.
        (iv) *w* is included as a consonant sound, but it is not usually spoken alone in natural speech. The sound is really *oo* + the rest of the word. e.g: *well* = *oo* + *ell*.
        (v) *again* — long *ai* not *agenn*.
        (vi) *after* — short *a* not *arfter*.
        (vii) *afternoon* — long *a* to give both versions of *after*.

RECORDING THE VOCABULARY

A recording of the above list has been made. The project team are indebted to Barbara Moran, a speech therapist employed in South-East Derbyshire; and John Witty, a professional specialising in voice work and broadcasting, both of whom have been of considerable help in making the final tape. With their aid, experience and expertise, a good quality recording was achieved and much learned about the process of making tapes for this purpose:

(a) The speaker should record the words in a number of short takes. This is to avoid that pattern of intonation which arises when recording a long list of unconnected words. If this is not done, the words sound unnatural when combined in phrases. In effect each word should sound as though it was in the middle of flowing dialogue.

(b) Each word should be lightly stressed, pitched consistently with the other words and, if possible, given a slight 'lift' in the middle when pronounced. The speaker should try to avoid giving the words 'colour', as neutrality increases the quality of the artificial speech arising from the recording.

(c) The speaker may find it easier to make the recording if he speaks quietly, the engineer compensating for the low volume. Low volume gives greater control over the individual sounds within words.

(d) A listener with a good ear should be present to pay attention to each word. This ensures that the speaker does not subconsciously slip in tone, pitch, volume or intonation. Also, the tapes should be reviewed to ensure absolute precision of sound production. For example, a final *d* should contain no element of *t* or redundant vowel.

   e.g.   *good* not *gooder* or *goodt*

(e) When recording consonants, the redundant vowel should be assiduously avoided. It is not part of the sound. (Unless, of course, facilities are available for editing out the vowel sound later.)

   e.g.   *p* not *pe*

(f) Some words hover between di-syllable and tri-syllable in flowing speech. The speaker should try to achieve this pronunciation.

   e.g.   *different* is neither *diff,rent* nor *diff-er-ent*
          every   is neither *ev,ry*   nor *ev-er-ry*
          question   is neither *ques,tion* nor *ques-ti-on*

(g) When recording sounds, it has occasionally been found helpful to imagine the unspoken element and voice only the required portion of the word.

e.g. *a*(*bout*) (*bout* unspoken)
th(*is*) (*is* unspoken)

Alternatively, these elements can be edited out of the whole words which contain them.

It can be seen that when speech is to have a didactic content, very precise account must be taken of the application. The work at Loughborough is continuing and soon it is hoped to have this large specialised vocabulary available for full field trials.

15.4 *Conclusion*

A considerable amount of work is being done to enable computers to speak intelligibly. Less work is being done to try and decide when they should speak and what they should say. This paper offers two broad types of utterance — speech as a prompt and didactic speech — which it is thought will play a part in educational applications.

In order to illustrate the complexity of application decisions encountered in education, the amount of work yet to be done, the advantage that could flow over the next few years and to point at another area of classroom use for the talking computer, a concluding example will be given.

At present many Asians coming to the UK are having problems learning English. The education system, already under pressure, is trying to cope with this extra burden. In addition to their problem of learning English as a foreign language, many of these people are illiterate in their mother-tongue. One cannot give them books in Gujurati to help them acquire English, they cannot read. One cannot offer them long-term personal tuition, resources are scarce. This is a classic application for computer-aided learning. A microcomputer having the prompt speech in the mother-tongue and the didactic speech in English could radically improve the lot of both tutor and student alike. Such a specialised application would require a specialised speech ROM, appropriate software and an effective evaluation project to develop the materials and the vocabulary. None of this is impossible, but financial constraints prevent the work going forward at the desired rate. Equally, as with so many projects in educational computing, the hardware is developing at a much faster rate than the teaching profession can cope with — testing new learning materials takes time.

We are at the start of a revolution (and I use the word advisedly), in the way teachers create learning environments in their classrooms. There is a need for massive continuous in-service training for teachers, and the development of tested, effective new pedagogic techniques. The talking computer is seminal to these developments, and it is only half the story. When we have speech recognition as well, we will be ready to meet the challenge of educating those young people (already in our schools) who will commence their adult life at the beginning of the twenty-first century.

References and notes

1. A government scheme has been launched in the UK which will mean that every school will have at least one microcomputer by 1983. Overview in *Microelectronics Education Programme – The Strategy*. London: Department of Education and Science Publications Office, 1980.

2. The JSRU is housed at the Government Communications Headquarters, Cheltenham, England. See, for example, Edward, J.A. (23 Jan 1981) 'Recent work at the JSRU on speech synthesis by rule'. Conference paper, *IEEE Conference: The Computer Generation of Speech*, London.

3. (a) Levine, A. and Sanders, W.R. (1979) 'The MISS speech synthesis system'. *INSPEC conference paper, IEEE International Conference on Acoustics, Speech and Signal Processing*, 2–4 April 1979, 899–902.
   (b) McCormick Piestrup, A. (1981) *Preschool Children use an Apple II to Test Reading Skills Programs*. Portola Valley, CA, USA: Advanced Learning Technology.
   (c) Elliott, L.L. (1979) 'Performance of children aged 9 to 17 years on a test of speech intelligibility in noise using sentence material with controlled word predictability'. *Journal of the Acoustical Society of America* 66(3), 651–653.
   (d) Kerns, R.L. (1980) 'When the computer speaks students listen'. *Conference paper – 12th Annual Meeting of the American Institute for Decision Sciences*, 5–7 November 1980.
   (e) See also the numerous papers concerning the PLATO project in the USA.

4. Vincent, A.T. (1982a) 'Computer assisted support for blind students – the use of a microcomputer linked voice synthesizer', *Computers and Education* 6, 55–60.

5. Opticon(R), Telesensory Systems inc., Palo Alto, CA, USA.

6. For a list of publications concerning the Open University's computer-aided learning work, contact The Open University CAL Studies Group, Institute of Educational Technology, The Open University, Milton Keynes, England.
7. Vincent, A.T. (1982a) – see above.
8. Vincent, A.T. (1982b) 'CAL for blind students: some recent developments'. *Microcomputers and Teaching Project Report*, Milton Keynes, England: Open University.
9. *ibid.*
10. McNally, J. and Murray, W. (1962), *Key Words to Literacy*. Curriculum Studies No. 3, London: Schoolmaster Publishing Company.
11. Herbert, D. and Davies-Jones, G. (1974) *A Classroom Index of Phonic Resources*, London: National Association for Remedial Education.
12. Birchfield, R. (1981) *The Spoken Word – a BBC Guide*. London: BBC Publications.

CHAPTER 16

SPEECH SYNTHESIS IN TELECOMMUNICATIONS

Peter Roe

16.1 *Role of synthetic speech in telecommunications*

Telecommunications was, until the late 1970s, almost exclusively a voice technology, but since then the transmission of data over the communication network has increased in importance. Despite the increased use of data, voice traffic has not decreased nor is it likely to do so. The reason behind this is that voice communication is still man's fastest communication method. A message containing meaning and emotion is easily conveyed between individuals, or groups, and this communication may be established over all the existing telecommunications networks with little degradation.

The parameters that are of most importance to a communications engineer are the bandwidth required and distortion that is introduced by the transmission system. Noise and distortion can be reduced by using a digital transmission system but the bandwidth is increased substantially compared to that of an analog system. A digital system that only requires the same bandwidth as an analog channel is obviously an ideal combination. The bandwidth that is allocated for voice transmission is standardised to 4 kHz in an analog transmission system and allows a voice spectrum of about 300 Hz to 3400 Hz to be transmitted. When the voice is digitised (using a *Codec*) in a digital transmission system, the bandwidth is increased to 64 kbit/s. The digital coding method uses a non-linear logarithmic law to encode 256 levels every 125 μs. This equates at an 8 kHz sampling rate into a 64 kbit/s data stream. The decoder reverses this process and reconstitutes the original 4 kHz bandwidth analog signal.

It is interesting to compare briefly the requirements of voice communication and visual communication. There is no doubt that by the use of our eyes we can input a large amount of information and indeed some information can only be effectively absorbed visually. The data that has to be transmitted to include all the information in a television picture for instance amounts to several megabits per second. Even with all this visual data available it is still surprisingly difficult to communicate visually without resorting to a representation of our spoken language. To put it more clearly we normally write down the words we say so that they can be read visually by another. Despite the fact that when we do this we tend to choose our words more carefully, we are often misinterpreted and we can lose most of the emotion which perhaps we wished to convey. Considerable skill is required to put over in the written word what we so easily achieve when we speak to one another, as any successful author will testify.

The printed word has an advantage when it comes to storing or copying some information. Even in an electronic medium, such as a telex system, the coded characters that make up the printed word are easily stored and transmitted. However, when the information has to be either input or output for humans, the transducers required impose a restriction on the written word for fast and efficient communication.

People do not go naturally with keyboards. Output from visual display or printer is expensive and generally inconvenient considering the cost and size of the equipment required. Advances in this area of technology will undoubtedly do something to help in the future but the cost and convenience of voice communication will be difficult to equal.

VOICE QUALITY IN TELECOMMUNICATIONS

Considering the continuing need for voice communication, synthetic speech must have an important part to play in telecommunication systems and yet there has been some reticence within the industry to adopt it. Why should this be so?

There is no single reason but most explanations seem to revolve around the word *natural*. At one extreme the quality of synthetic speech must approach that of natural human speech, in order to be understood easily and correctly. Yet at the other extreme the ability of a machine to speak to us with a human voice, in response to our actions, and in an intelligent manner, can be unnerving and unnatural. Strangely, a voice response from a toy or arcade game is quite acceptable, but a serious response from a piece of equipment is not nearly so. This situation will improve as synthetic speech becomes more commonplace.

One can draw a useful parallel here with the introduction of seven segment displays to the field of visible output. There was a body of opinion which declared that the distortion of printed numbers into the stylised seven segment format, which is now almost universally used, would be unacceptable. The human race has adapted to them just as surely as it will to stylised synthetic speech.

A second factor which has delayed the introduction of synthetic speech into telecommunications is the need to quantify the speech quality obtainable from a synthesis system. The communications network is very well specified in terms of audio transmission performance but generally these specifications pertain to simple parameters like frequency response, signal-to-noise ratio and harmonic distortion. In digital systems equivalent parameters are specified and considerable work has been done to evaluate the effects of quantising noise or distortion introduced by pulse code modulation in transmission systems.

Valuable though these specifications are in maintaining standards of speech transmission they are limited in their ability to ensure that synthetic speech is of an adequate quality. Other contributors have addressed this issue and in particular the reader is referred to section 14.3. In a basically speech-orientated industry like telecommunications, quality has attracted more attention than most. Ironically, as synthetic speech improves so the need to assess it in a special way will diminish. Hopefully by the time methods of fully assessing the distortion introduced by synthesis have been established there will be nothing left to measure.

APPLICATIONS FOR SYNTHETIC SPEECH

Having discussed the challenge of introducing synthetic speech into telecommunications let us examine where this can be done most usefully. The biggest impact of the technology will not be felt until voice input can be processed as easily as voice output. Even so there are a number of areas where synthesisers can contribute to the effectiveness of the network. The most popular technique used for voice synthesis in telecommunications is *linear predictive coding*, because LPC parameter extraction is also the basis of most voice compression systems. Experience gained from LPC voice output will be a valuable introduction to future voice input and voice compression systems for telecommunication manufacturers and users alike. Chapters 5 and 7 explore the advantages of LPC in these important respects.

The levels of integration that have been achieved with LPC chips mean that synthetic speech can be readily used in either a central exchange facility or in the subscribers terminal. One of the applications to be described later uses synthetic speech actually in a telephone instrument. In general the use of synthetic speech in the network is aimed either to enhance it by adding new features or, alternatively, to guide the user through the more complex facilities of existing systems. A typical network is shown in fig. 16.1 and suitable points in the system where synthetic speech can be applied are clearly shown.

If one is designing a voice response system for a centralised installation, such as an exchange, the criteria that one needs to apply have different priorities to those which apply in a subscriber terminal. In an exchange environment the cost of a speech subsystem is shared between all the subscribers connected to the exchange. The concept of shared equipment is fundamental to exchange system design because of the low percentage of time that an individual subscriber is actually using the exchange equipment. Despite the fact that a minimum of electronics is dedicated to each individual subscriber this still represents something like 75% of the cost and size of a modern exchange installation. Consequently, shared services can be added at relatively low cost. The very fact that a speech subsystem must be shared between a large group of users will in itself probably increase the size of the vocabulary required to service a wider range of requirements.

Some uses and types of message for the telephone environment are shown in table 16.1. As can be seen there is an overlap between centralised synthesis systems and individual subscriber systems that is a result of the advance of CMOS microcomputers into telephone terminals.

British Telecom introduced voice guidance into its first *System X* local exchange during 1982 using a speech subsystem incorporating digitised rather than synthesised speech. The system uses 32 kbits of storage for each second of speech, providing high speech quality close to that of a 64 kbit PCM channel, but at the expense of a lot of memory. An advantage of stored PCM data for this type of application is that it is directly compatible with the format of the subscribers digitised speech signals and can easily be inserted into digital transmission paths. Despite the continuing reduction in the cost per bit of memory, vocabularies will usually increase to cancel out any advantage gained and the size and cost of memory will remain a considerable disadvantage to PCM-based speech systems.

From a telephone administrations point of view it is desirable to have a common user interface to its network and so even a small exchange may require a significant amount of voice output. This may use many times as much memory as all the rest of the exchange software. In these circumstances the low memory requirements of synthetic speech are an attractive method of keeping a common voice interface at a low cost.

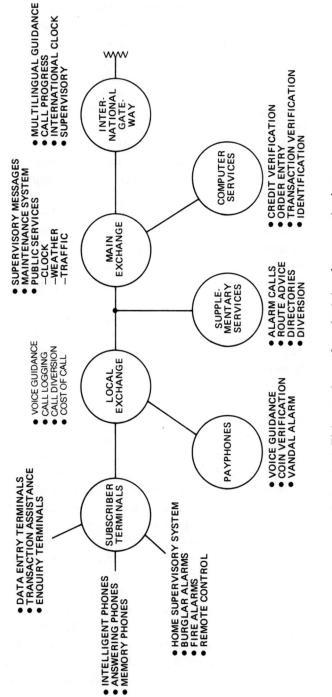

Figure 16.1 Widespread use of synthesis in telecommunications

Table 16.1 Examples of telecommunication phrases

Central office	Supervisory messages	Please replace your receiver and consult the directory
		The number you have called is busy. Please try later.
Central office	Voice guidance	Enter the number followed by a star . . . .
		Number 223 124 is stored against short code 17.
or _ _ _ _		
Subscriber terminal	Supplementary services	A reminder call is booked for 7:30 a.m.
		This is your reminder call.
Subscriber terminal	Home or business terminal	The office is closed today. Please call again.
		No one is available on this number. Please call 282 679. Thank you.

In order to compare memory size, a vocabulary of 200 words – not unreasonable for modern exchange facilities – would require around 500 kbytes of data storage using 32 kbit PCM. The total software for a small exchange may be only 100 kbytes. The storage requirements using synthetic speech may be reduced by an order of magnitude without sacrificing any flexibility and maintaining adequate speech quality. What is more, advances in synthetic speech coding can be expected to reduce the data rate even further and improve the quality.

16.2 *A multiport synthetic speech subsystem*

The schematic diagram of a synthetic speech subsystem, using components available in 1982, is shown in fig. 16.2. The system is a general-purpose multiport announcement or voice guidance system and as such is not dedicated to a switching environment but could be used anywhere in the network. Indeed the concept of a special facilities exchange which can be accessed from anywhere on the network is an attractive way of providing services without the need for upgrading each local exchange. Synthetic speech plays a major part in providing and guiding users through many of the new facilities.

The example shows a bank of synthesiser chips sharing a common data memory and providing eight analog output channels. LPC synthesiser data has a sequential structure which is ideal for sharing. The

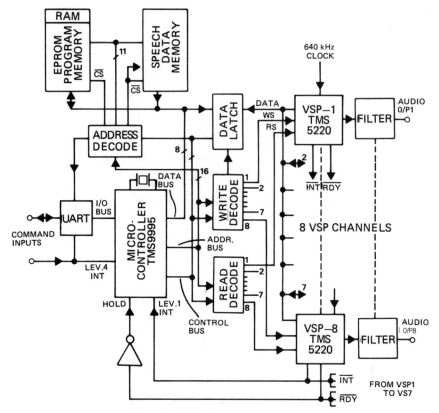

Figure 16.2 Multiport speech system

voice data is entered at a particular point and is then used sequentially by the synthesiser until an utterance is complete. It is an easy process to feed the synthesiser with data and one controller can service the requirements of several output channels. Although this may seem obvious, some speech compression techniques utilise coding which is not sequential and where instead jumps are made backwards and forwards into the coded data, making it difficult to share memory address space.

A brief description of the speech subsystem will illustrate some of the principles of operation of a multiple access system. The system comprises principally a controlling microprocessor, in this case a Texas Instruments' *TSM9995*, a bank of eight *TSM5220* speech synthesis chips, and an area of memory for the controller software and LPC speech data for the synthesisers. The rest of the logic is shown in simplified form and mainly comprises address decoding and data latches. Detailed information on LPC synthesis chips can be obtained by reference to chapter 10 and to the manufacturers' data sheets, but to aid understanding of the system the main features of the relevant chips follow.

TMS5220 VOICE SYNTHESIS PROCESSOR

The TMS5220 VSP is an 8-bit bus-orientated synthesiser made in PMOS technology. The bus interface comprises four control lines and an 8-bit data bus. The control lines are WS (*write select*) for writing data into the synthesiser, RS (*read select*) for reading data out, RDY (*ready*) timing for data transfers and INT (*interrupt*) line. The *ready* signal is used to synchronise the transfer of data in and out of the synthesiser. It will go low and remain low until data has been successfully latched into the synthesiser, or in the case of read select until valid data is available from the synthesiser. The controller must follow this hand-shake to ensure data is not lost. The interrupt is used to alert the con-troller to a change of status in the synthesiser.

The speech synthesiser is controlled from the data bus using four registers which provide access to *data-in*, *data-out*, *control* and *status*. The data written to the control register, as its name suggests, controls the synthesiser. It can be initialised and set to speak in various modes by writing control data to the register via the 8-bit bus. A useful feature of this particular chip's architecture is an on-chip 16-byte *FIFO* buffer which is placed between the data-in register and the rest of the processor. The buffer is filled with voice data by the microprocessor at high speed and emptied much more slowly by the synthesiser. It allows one controller to keep many synthesisers talking at the same time. The synthesiser status register has bits indicating *buffer-full*, *buffer-half-full*, *buffer-empty* and *talking*. The analog output of the TMS5220 is used in this application but a digital output is also provided on the chip.

THE TMS9995 MICROCONTROLLER

The TMS9995 is a good microprocessor for controlling a speech sub-system. It is a high performance 16-bit microprocessor with on-chip interrupt latches, timer/counter, a flag register and an 8-bit data bus. The microprocessor also has a capability to be placed in a *hold* state when it suspends operation under control of its hold input. This is an easy way of synchronising a fast processor to a slow synthesiser. An additional useful feature of the processor is its on-chip 256 bytes of RAM which can be treated as 128 × 16-bit registers, or in this application as pointers into the data area for eight synthesisers. There is an additional input/output bus structure which is independent from the data bus and in this application is used for communication between the speech subsystem and the main exchange hardware by a serial data link. As far as the rest of the system is concerned, the speech subsystem is an intelligent peripheral, receiving high level instructions from the main system and providing spoken messages. The degree of intelligence in the speech subsystem will depend upon the overall system philosophy. In this instance a simple peripheral command structure is implemented to turn a command of the form *speak-port – message type – data – acknowledge* into a spoken utterance of, for example, *please call number two eight two, six seven nine after six o'clock, thank you*. The message will be spoken from the defined port and completion of the message would be acknowledged to the main system.

CONTROLLING MULTIPLE SYNTHESISERS

The number of ports that can be handled by one controlling microprocessor depends upon the time required to transfer data to all the synthesisers when they are speaking together. The critical factor is the ratio of the time required to identify and fill a FIFO buffer, divided by the time required to consume a full buffer. The overhead to convert a command message to a set of pointers for an utterance is relatively small compared to servicing the synthesiser when it is actively speaking that message. The mechanism for directing a string of LPC data bits to a particular synthesiser will be described, from which the overhead required to service the whole bank can be assessed.

The block designated *decode* on the schematic is responsible for decoding and latching sixteen memory addresses into eight WS outputs and eight RS outputs. A data direction control is also decoded. Writing to one of these sixteen addresses will generate either a WS or RS to one of the synthesisers whilst at the same time switching the data latch to the appropriate direction.

As soon as one of the WS or RS synthesiser inputs becomes activated the common RDY line temporarily halts the microprocessor by taking its hold input low. When the synthesiser has completed the data transfer to or from its registers the halt condition is removed and the program is allowed to continue.

CRITICAL TIME ANALYSIS

Let us assume that all synthesisers are speaking and that their buffers are all nearing the half-empty point, at which time one will issue an interrupt. All synthesisers must be replenished with data before the last one becomes empty and stops speaking prematurely. The time available to do this is the time taken to consume a half-empty buffer of 8 bytes of data at the highest rate. In the case of the TMS5220 this is about 35 ms. The first synthesiser to be serviced will require 8 bytes to fill its buffer whilst the last device may require 15 if it is just about to run out of data.

If eight synthesisers are being serviced then in the worst case this means eight interrupts, eight passes through a polling routine involving eight reads of status on each pass and about ninety write cycles to fill up all the buffers. This makes a total of about 150 synthesiser accesses for each 35 ms loop. If we assume for now that all of the time can be spent servicing the synthesiser buffers then each complete access must take less than 220 μs.

The basic operation of moving bytes from the speech data memory involves testing a data pointer to see if any more data is to be transferred, moving the data and incrementing two counters. This can easily be achieved in less than 100 μs with the instruction set of the TSM9995, so even in this worst case situation over 50% of the processor's time is available to handle the background tasks of the system.

The software to control the operation of the system is less than 8 kbytes and 56 kbytes of address space is left for the LPC speech data. This is equivalent to a vocabulary of 200 to 300 seconds of *unrepeated* speech or 300 to 400 words, which is probably enough for a comprehensive guidance and message system. The chip count for an eight-channel voice subsystem with this size of vocabulary, controlled via a serial interface, amounts to thirty-three chips occupying just a single printed circuit board.

The addition of the voice subsystem just described to a network requires that the system should be capable of responding with speech output. This would normally be the software in the *stored program control* section of an *electronic* exchange. Until a substantial part of the network is equipped with this type of modern exchange a 'facility gap' will exist between the old electromechanically served subscribers and a subscriber with a new electronic exchange.

16.3 *Speech synthesis in telephone subsets*

One way in which the facility gap is being plugged is by so-called *intelligent telephones*, which have a microprocessor in the subset and can provide some of the facilities that an electronic exchange may offer. The type of feature that is achieved by providing the subscriber with memory to store numbers can easily be provided by including CMOS memory in the subset. The subset has its own small battery to ensure that stored numbers will not be lost if the subset is disconnected from the exchange for any reason. Features such as *last number redial, notepad memory* and small repertoires of *short code numbers* can be provided in this way. As the features increase in number and sophistication then a synthetic voice system in the subset can make the operation more 'user friendly'. It can be used for both voice guidance on how to use the features and to listen to the numbers stored in the various memories.

The main advantage of voice synthesis in this application, however, is to provide a voice message to a calling subscriber from a subset that would otherwise remain unanswered. Currently, most telephone answering machines are based on magnetic tape cassettes of various types. The philosophy behind this range of products is that the calling subscriber is answered by a pre-recorded tape announcement. The caller is usually invited to respond with a message which is recorded on tape in the machine. Unfortunately, the unreliability of the tape systems and the marked reluctance of many people to speak into recording machines means that they often leave something to be desired. One answer is to leave a message for the caller to call back again at some specific time when it is known the telephone will be answered, or alternatively to invite the caller to dial another number where the call may be dealt with.

A small vocabulary of synthesised phrases which can be quickly customised from the telephone keypad, by adding a time to call back or an alternative number, can do this much more effectively than a tape-based machine. Such an instrument can be powered from the telephone line and requires only the addition of two or three chips to add speech synthesis to an existing intelligent telephone circuit.

A suitable arrangement is seen in simplified schematic form in fig. 16.3. The centre of this system is the *TMS1304C* microcomputer, which provides the subset with all its intelligent features and controls the speech synthesis chip. It is a CMOS microcomputer with 2 kbytes of ROM program store and 128 bytes of RAM, actually organised as 256 × 4 bits, which between them can provide *last number redial* and ten *short code* number stores. The rest of the program allows the instrument to operate on either pulse-dialling or tone-dialling networks, selected by a link, using the *TCM5089* dual tone encoder. *On-hook* dialling is included to allow hands-free operation, using a low power amplifier and a small loudspeaker to monitor the progress of the call.

The low power CMOS microcomputer allows the whole instrument to be powered by the current drawn from the telephone line. A primary battery is used to back up the line current so that, should the line be broken or the telephone unplugged, the short code numbers in the

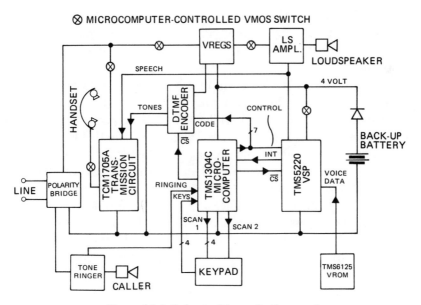

Figure 16.3 Subset with synthetic speech

microcomputer memory are retained. The current drain of a CMOS device in its halted mode is only a few microamps.

All of these features can be easily accommodated in a single microcomputer which can be used to replace a conventional dialler chip.

One of the other two chips in the telephone circuit is a *TCM1506A* tone alerter, which drives a small transducer and also provides a ringing signal to the microcomputer. The other chip, a *TCM1705A* contains the amplifiers and gain regulation circuitry for the earpiece and microphone line interface. This arrangement is only slightly more complex than a basic electronic telephone, it can be fitted in the same style case without a display and requires few additional keys. The speech synthesis chips provided for the answering machine type features can also be used to listen to the various memories, so that a visible display is not really necessary in this type of instrument.

The main purpose for including the speech synthesis chips in this application however is to allow the subscriber to program his telephone to give a *voice message* to anyone who calls in his absence. The advantage of synthetic speech is that a message can be configured from suitable phrases in a few seconds using only the keypad. The disadvantage is that only a few phrases are available and they must have been encoded previously. It is however possible to satisfy most situations by either inviting the caller to call back at a specified time or to call another number. The assumption being that most people actually prefer to speak to the person they have called rather than leave a message. There is usually no way of knowing when a tape recorded message will be heard, if at all, and often a second call is made if a message is important.

The advantage of easy programming is achieved quite simply in this application by having three dedicated keys to select a basic message. The *message* key is held down whilst the variable part of the message, consisting primarily of numbers, is keyed in from the keypad. When the *message* key is released the message will be played back to confirm that it is correct. An *unattended* key is switched on to enable the automatic message facility so that the telephone will answer itself, after it has rung for a preset time, and speak its message to the caller. The synthesised message is preceded by a fixed announcement of *this is a recorded message*, to help callers avoid the embarrassment of speaking to the synthesiser. Simple key sequences are defined so that each message can be checked, and to allow the contents of some of the memories, particularly the short code stores, to be interrogated.

This type of instrument satisfies a number of different user needs both at home and for a business, whilst for a telecommunications administration it helps to fill the facility gap and make more cost-effective use of the network, since fewer calls will be unanswered and uncharged.

16.4 *Future role of synthesis*

The synthetic speech applications outlined are simple voice output systems but communication is a two-way process. The really explosive growth will occur in the late 1980s when speech analysis can be achieved in real time to reduce the data rate of a digital communications system. When this happens all the digital switching and transmission systems will immediately see a ten times increase in capacity. If speech data requires no more data than say 2400 bits/s then it becomes economical to store that data in voice form and messages can be forwarded to the recipient when he is available in much the same way that a telex message is delivered. With such a low data rate, packet switching techniques can be used to maximise the efficiency of the network just as they are used with conventional data.

The use of voice recognition techniques is yet another example of a natural use of the technology for controlling the network. The use of dials and push buttons to obtain a connection is very crude in comparison to the potential power of a spoken command into the microphone. In effect this goes back to the origins of the telephone network when it was necessary to ask an operator to connect a call. Now, however, the operator can be just a voice-controlled computer occupying a few cards in the latest electronic telephone exchange.

CHAPTER 17

SPEECH OUTPUT
FROM COMPLEX SYSTEMS

Frank Fallside and Stephen Young

17.1 *The role of speech in information technology*

It is widely held that the next industrial revolution will be a result of *Information Technology* (IT), a combining of computing and communications, and indeed that it has already begun. This has come about largely because of microelectronics technology, which allows computer hardware to be fabricated very cheaply. This means firstly that computers are becoming more widely used in their conventional roles in science, engineering and business and secondly, and perhaps more significantly, that they are resulting in new products concerned generically with *information processing*. Early examples are word processing, the electronic office and Prestel, but these are only a beginning and many more technical innovations can be expected.

A feature of Information Technology is that it changes the way that computers are used; rather than being used by specialists only, as in their conventional role, they will become distributed throughout society to provide information processing facilities, in the way that telephone, water, gas and electricity facilities are provided now. A consequence of this wider spreading is that it becomes essential to make computers usable in more natural ways than by the conventional keyboard and display man–machine interface.

Since speech is one of the most natural communication methods used by man there is a strong impetus to develop capabilities for computers which will allow them to both understand speech and produce it themselves. There are many areas where in addition to 'corresponding' with a computer by a keyboard and display, it would be useful to 'discuss' with a computer by voice. For example rather than communicating by telephone using telephone directories of of every-increasing size, it would be much more efficient to request a connection by voice using a person's name and address.

It is possible to be quite futuristic about this but many technical problems remain to be overcome before it can come about. There is currently much research taking place or planned in this area, for example in several national initiatives – the *Fifth Generation Computer Systems* programme in Japan,[1] the *Alvey* proposals in the UK,[2] the *Esprit* initiative in continental Europe, and various programmes in the US. A common general feature of these initiatives is that they propose natural communication with computers by voice and by graphics and by plain text. This swing to natural communication is quite profound and will affect the whole form of a computer. Instead of, as now, the process being dominated by the processor with its conventional programming languages and protocols, which require a specialised user, the process will be dominated by the user, using natural communication and protocols. This will be done by providing the computer with *knowledge bases* to allow both natural communication and the problem-solving capabilities required by this usage. And one of these knowledge bases will be concerned with speech input–output. It is probable that about half of a computer system of the 1990s will be concerned with this interface and half with processing capability, compared with current systems which consist almost entirely of processing capability with a very small user interface.

For the present the major barrier to speech communication with machines is in speech recognition, which is still at a very primitive stage. As described elsewhere in this book techniques in speech synthesis are much further advanced and so speech output is more feasible. While it is likely that speech output will not become widely used, or fully developed, until speech input is possible, there are a number of early applications. In this chapter we discuss some of these briefly and then concentrate on a particular type of information system which provides speech output from a computer-controlled water-supply system.

SYSTEMS WITH SPEECH OUTPUT

The earliest information system with speech output was the *speaking clock*. This is simple but effective, providing recorded information synchronised to the time of day. A next step in computer-controlled telephone networks will be the provision of recorded messages of a wider nature, for example messages which explain what codes should be dialled to obtain special services. These provide a measure of interaction with the user via the handset keyboard. Also the technology has advanced – whereas the speaking clock uses pre-recorded analog speech, demonstration versions of the later systems use messages consisting of concatenated digitised words.

There are also several commercial systems available which provide speech output. Some of these use spoken information which is recorded in directly digitised form. Others, for example the (Thorn) Ericsson system, use recorded speech which is stored in the form of synthetic speech parameters. These types of system are accessed by the user over the telephone network. The user calls up the system by a touch tone keyboard which he also uses to request data. The information computer prompts his requests by pre-recorded messages and then provides the requested information by inserting numerical data into pre-recorded *slot and filler* messages (see later). These systems are quite widely used for giving information about, for example, commodity stocks and bank transactions. They also allow end-of-day sales returns to be entered remotely, again using spoken prompts.

These commercial systems are early pioneers. Their development will include the use of speech recognition for user input and much more flexible dialogue from the computer. A number of research systems have already been demonstrated, for example by Bell Telephone Laboratories in tasks associated with telephone directory information and a system for airline enquiries and reservations using limited speech input and output.[3]

Research into such systems is proceeding along two separate paths which will eventually converge. Firstly, research into speech recognition. Most recognisers at present work on a word by word basis for quite a limited vocabulary and so only quite simple and fixed format messages are expected or recognised. As a result the output speech has to be quite limited – prompting the user or providing fairly fixed format information output. The thrust of this work is to extend vocabulary lengths and to deal with speaker variation.

The second approach is research into natural language processing. In this work speech is not used at all, but plain text. The goal here is to understand the meaning of the input text (not just what words occur as in speech recognition at present) and also to generate output text in response. This attacks the problem in a more fundamental way, the emphasis is now on meaning and the object is to understand quite complex statements, to seek answers to queries and to construct statements in reply. This is another of the knowledge bases which will appear in fifth-generation computers. It is probable that the first information systems with flexible speech input and output will employ speech-to-text conversion at the input, natural language processing internally for message understanding, problem solving and output statement construction, and then text-to-speech synthesis at the output. This is the most direct route available although it is likely there will eventually be a blurring of distinctions, since for example message understanding, or *semantics*, is a necessary component of speech recognition and message generation is fundamentally important in speech synthesis.

In the rest of this chapter we concentrate on a particular information system.

17.2 *Speech output from a complex system*

The particular system is a computer-controlled water-supply system supplying about 0.25 million consumers in an area south of Birmingham (see fig. 17.1). In this a large, distributed plant, comprising pumping stations, reservoirs, etc., is controlled by a central computer which scans the state of the systems via a telemetry network. The computer then calculates an appropriate pump control strategy and sends this out to the system via the telemetry network to control the pumps to meet the system's water consumption demand, at minimum cost of electricity for pumping.

The control computer contains a database of information about the system. This information exists at several levels:

(a) Low-level information about the current state of the plant — which pumps are on, what the current levels of the reservoirs are, etc. This information is effectively instantaneous since the complete system is continuously scanned once every few minutes.

(b) Higher-level information about the day's operation of the plant. This includes the results of the control calculations and other calculated information. For example the control strategy is calculated once a day, at the beginning of the day, when a prediction of the day's consumption is computed and a calculation of the day's optimal pumping schedule is made based on this prediction. This part of the data base contains information which is higher-level in control terms and also of a longer time scale than (a). It includes information about the current day such as estimated consumption and pumping cost and also about previous days.

(c) High-level, longer term information about operation and planning of the plant. This information is of a strategic nature — such as, how peak or annual consumption is growing in comparison with available capacity, the planning of new resources to meet such increases and their achievement at minimum cost.

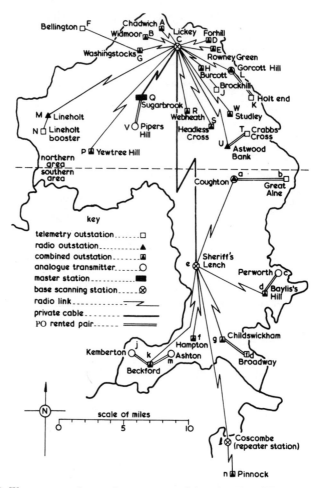

Figure 17.1 Water-network supply area served by the East Worcestershire Water-works Company

(d) Highest-level information about emergencies and alarms. Part of the computer control is concerned with emergencies such as loss of electricity at a pump station, equipment failure, or a significant departure of actual consumption from predicted consumption which may indicate a burst main, etc. This may use instantaneous data or longer term calculated data. It clearly demands the highest priority and must provide alarms for the operators.

The data base is seen to define an information world for the system and one which exists in a hierarchy of levels.

We note also that this particular system is only one example of many.

An increasing number of systems of this general type exists in which a large plant of some type — whether a water-supply network, an electricity generating station, a chemical plant, an assembly line or a steel rolling mill — is controlled by a computer, or computers. This is a conventional role for computers, for on-line control. However such systems are ultimately supervised by people, who make choices about its operation, for example dealing with breakdowns or emergencies, who have to supply information to customers about loss of supply, repairs, etc., or in management by people concerned with planning, with costs and financing. This is an example where the computer is required to provide information processing for operators and management, as well as conventional processing to provide network control. Following the logic that for information processing it is preferable to provide a more natural communication than by keyboard and display, it was decided to investigate the provision of speech output from the system. We note that in this system as in many other computer-controlled systems, much of the information required for output is already present in the control data base.

The central question in providing speech output for such systems is then *what is the best way of generating speech output from a non-textual data base*? In the following we describe one particular solution for the case of the water supply network.

The simplest solution is to use a *slot and filler* technique. In this a preformed message is provided with gaps left, into which variable data words are inserted. A simple example for alarm messages in the water-supply network would be.

	a mechanical fault		Bromsgrove	
THERE IS	an electrical failure	AT	Chadwick	STATION
	an intruder		Bellington	

There are several objections to this scheme in all but the simplest systems. One is that in systems or information worlds of any complexity a very large number of preformed messages would be required. Another is in speech quality, since for example the overall intonation contour for the message is dependent on all its parts whereas here we are linking phrases with fixed individual intonation contours.

17.3 *Speech Synthesis from Concept (SSC)*

A more general approach to this type of problem is one where the information system, in response to an enquiry, generates a message as well as speaking it. This removes the need for preformed messages and their dimensionality problem. In this approach extensive use is made of knowledge of the system. Also, although the system is physically large its information world is quite restricted. Thus there are a finite number of questions one could sensibly ask it and a finite number of types of answer it can give. This means that only quite a constrained knowledge base is required in the information system to answer questions.

The system has three main parts — an *interface* section which extracts the *concept* of the information request; a *message-generating* and *intonation-generating* part which assembles the reply information and some information for its speech synthesis; and a *speech synthesiser* section. Requests for information are made via a touch-tone keyboard which is used to enter the input concept.

The method is termed 'speech synthesis from concept' (SSC) because of its use of the input concept. Several variants have been investigated,[4,5] but for the present we consider one particular version which has been implemented.[6] This is shown in some detail in fig. 17.2. At the top the interface program extracts the input concept from the input request and the data base. This is passed to the *semantic component* which interprets the meaning of the input concept from knowledge of the water network. The *syntactic component* establishes a grammatical description of the answer sentence from grammar rules. A string of output words is now established by the semantic and syntactic components.

At this stage a text-to-speech synthesiser could be employed to output the message. However in this system synthesis by word concatenation is used. There is some advantage in this since a full parse of the message is already available from the syntactic component. The *phonological component* defines the way in which the isolated words representing the complete utterance must be concatenated. This is done by referring to a directory in which all the words known to the synthesiser are listed together with certain phonological information. The phonological component must also define the pitch contour for the utterance.

This information is passed by the phonological component to the *word concatenator*. This takes the prestored synthetic speech parameters corresponding to each word in the utterance, appends the pitch contour and, after making any adjustments required at the word boundaries, it passes the resulting synthetic speech parameters to a hardware synthesiser, which produces the output utterance. We now consider these steps in more detail.

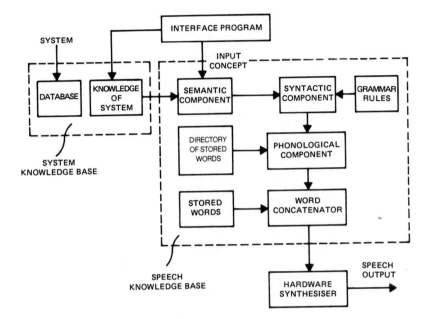

Figure 17.2 Speech synthesis from concept

DATA BASE AND KNOWLEDGE BASE ORGANISATION

Let us consider a particular information request which examples others. This is, *What is the current level of the reservoir at Gorton Hill? –* a request for instantaneous information about a particular part of the system.

It will be remembered that the data base contains a hierarchy of information at various levels. In the implementation these were divided into four levels:

level 0 instantaneous information about plant elements
level 1 calculations about the day's operations in a zone
level 2 calculations about the day's operations of the complete system
level 3 alarm information.

Also all the data within these levels have unique codes. An example of the form of the data base for level 0 is shown in fig. 17.3. This is part of a 'half-hour log' of system devices and consists of device codes and their current values. For example the code *157* refers to Gorton Hill reservoir level and *27.3* refers to its level as percentage full. Similarly, in level 1: *612, 3.96* refers to the consumption: *3.96 Ml, in the Hazy Hill zone, 612.*

date: xx.yy.zz	time: xx.yy
0203	00.04
0115	00.05
0114	00.00
0034	00.00
0147	082.3
0507	094.4
0506	083.5
0143	00.00
0157	27.30
0304	00.02
0235	00.02
0314	071.5
0335	098.3
0277	084.6
0167	095.8
0145	00.00

Figure 17.3 Part of a 'half-hour log'

The knowledge base is largely in the form of lists, part of which is shown in fig. 17.4. A device code can thus be decoded by following a list until an end-of-list symbol is encountered. Thus, for example, code *157* is decoded as: *level, Gorton Hill, tower.*

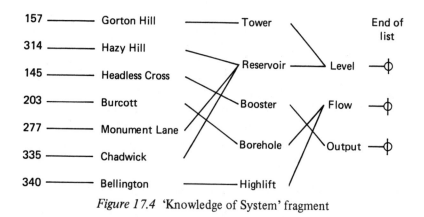

Figure 17.4 'Knowledge of System' fragment

SEMANTICS AND SYNTAX

In our current example, *what is the current level of the reservoir at Gorton Hill?*, the input concept – the meaning of the input request – can be simply coded as two numbers *157,0*; the device and the information level requested. This request is passed to the interface program which extracts the required data from the data base as *27.3*, the current percentage level. These three numbers are now passed to the semantic component. This can uniquely infer the required output information. In the present example it would recognise a simple notion of equality. The semantic program then extracts the internal information relevant to the code number *157*. In this case the device is recognised to be the *subject* of the equality notion and so a *subject group* is formed from the system knowledge base:

(*SG, level, tower, Gorton Hill*)

Similarly, an *object group* is formed from the data value:

(*OG, twenty, seven, point, three*)

Finally, the notion of equality generates a one word *verb group*:

(*VG, is*)

The syntactic component is now activated. This generates a phrase marker which describes the grammatical construction of the output utterance in a tree structure, as shown in fig. 17.5. This tree is built up from a grammar which consists of sets of rules. The rules relevant to the current example are:

$$S \rightarrow SG + VG \tag{1}$$
$$SG \rightarrow NP(+ NP)(+ AP) \tag{2}$$
$$NP \rightarrow (DT)\begin{Bmatrix}(AJ + NP)\\(N + NP)\\(N)\end{Bmatrix} \tag{3}$$

The symbols used are defined in the legend to the figure. In rule (2) the parentheses indicate an option and in rule (3) the braces indicate a simple choice between different expansions. We note that the semantic component provides only *content words*. These are words which directly convey meaning, as opposed to *function words* such as *the*, *for* and *at* which serve a syntactic purpose and have to be introduced by the grammar in general; in the present simple example no function words are required.

When the phrase marker has been completed its terminal words represent the output message. This string of words is now passed to the phonological component.

PHONOLOGY
This is responsible for defining the way the isolated words of the

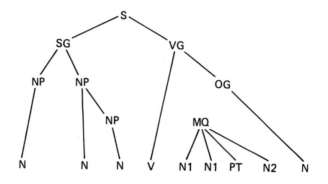

Gorton Hill tower level is twenty nine point three percent

Figure 17.5 Tree structure of the grammar used to generate the output utterance.

S	= Sentence	SG	= Subject Group
OG	= Object Group	VG	= Verb Group
NP	= Noun Phrase	AP	= Adjective Phrase
N	= Noun	V	= Verb
AJ	= Adjective	N1	= Number
DT	= Determiner	N2	= Number
MQ	= Measured Quantity	PR	= Decimal Point

utterance are to be concatenated and for specifying the shape of the associated pitch contour.

The concatenation used is based on the work of Olive[7] who pioneered work on synthesis by word concatenation. For each word stored in the directory there is a feature word which specifies the categories of the initial and final phonemes. These are used to assist concatenation in a number of ways. For instance a measure of *coarticulation*, how successive words affect each other, is provided by smoothing the word parameters at word boundaries in the presence of vowels, and in the case of combinations such as stop–stop or stop–fricatives, the final plosive burst of the first word must be suppressed.

The pitch contour is determined at two levels. Firstly, its gross shape is determined at the phrase level by the *phrase marker*, and secondly, its finer structure at the word and syllable level is derived from information stored in the directory entry of each word. As shown in fig. 17.6 the shape of each segment is determined by five parameters – the start, peak and end frequencies, the end slope and the position of the peak. These parameters are stored in a list and a continuous contour is derived by a quadratic interpolation between start and peak and a cubic interpolation beyond it.

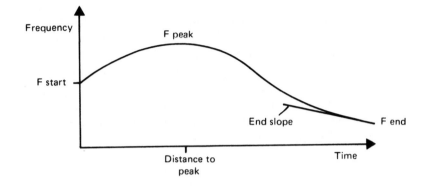

Figure 17.6 A typical pitch contour

WORD CONCATENATOR AND HARDWARE SYNTHESISER

For this application a vocabulary of about 300 words is necessary. These were pre-analysed off-line, using the autocorrelation linear prediction method, and stored in the form of reflection coefficient strings (see chapter 5). They were digitised at 10 kHz, Hamming-windowed to 25.6 ms, and analysed to twelve reflection coefficients. The parameters blocks were stored on disk and an entry made into the directory table giving the address of the word and its phonological data, such as initial–final phoneme categories.

During synthesis, referring to fig. 17.2, the word concatenator takes the prestored synthetic speech parameters corresponding to each word in the utterance and appends the pitch contour. This data is stacked in memory and any smoothing is carried out in the stack. The data is then passed pitch-synchronously to a hardware synthesiser (Cambridge Electronic Design Ltd) under interrupt control and the output utterance is produced.

RESULTS

The system was implemented on a 16-bit minicomputer with 64 kbytes of memory and a 10 Mbyte disk. In operation the time delay between an information request and the onset of speech is about one second. As mentioned, a vocabulary of about 300 words is used, requiring disk space of about 360 kbytes. The system, which was developed as a research demonstration system, performed well, producing speech of good intelligibility. A few samples of the types of utterances produced are shown in the appendix to this chapter.

17.4 Conclusions

Some of the reasons for using speech input–output in conjunction with computer-based systems have been discussed. Any major adoption of these techniques must await improvements in speech recognition and in the provision of more flexible output messages. To overcome these difficulties, considerable research will be required, and indeed has now started in several national initiatives.

A particular information system, which provides speech output from a computer-controlled water-supply network, has been described. While the water-supply network is relatively complex and provides a wide range of data, the range of messages is quite simple and well within the capabilities of the information system. It is felt that the method used – speech synthesis from concept – is a general method and may find other applications in systems which are linguistically more complex, in the future.

Acknowledgements

The authors wish to thank the East Worcestershire Waterworks Company for their cooperation in the work and Mr J L Trim, formerly of Cambridge University Department of Applied Linguistics, for much helpful advice. The work was funded by the UK Science and Engineering Research Council.

References

1. *Proc. Intl. Conf. on Fifth Generation Computer Systems* (1981). Tokyo, Japan: Japanese Info. Processing Centre.
2. *Report of the Alvey Committee* (1982). London: HMSO.
3. Rabiner, L.R. and Schafer, R.W. (1976) 'Digital techniques for computer voice response: implementation and applications'. *Proc. IEEE* **64**.
4. Young, S.J. and Fallside, F. (1979) 'Speech synthesis from concept'. *J. Acoust. Soc. Amer.* **66**, 685–695.
5. Young, S.J. and Fallside, F. (1980) 'Synthesis by rule of prosodic features in word concatenation synthesis'. *Int. J. Man–Machine Studies* **12**, 241–258.
6. Fallside, F. and Young, S.J. (1978) 'Speech output from a computer-controlled water-supply network'. *Proc. IEEE* **125**, 157–161.
7. Olive, J.P. (1974) 'Speech synthesis by rule'. *Speech Communication Seminar* Stockholm.

Appendix: Sample speech output

In addition to *level 0 logs* for particular parts of the network of the type described in the text, some other examples are (with the input data shown in brackets):

> *The predicted consumption for the Hazy Hill zone is 3.48 Ml* (611,3.48,1)
>
> *Hazy Hill reservoir level has fallen by 10.3 percent since the previous log* (314,10.3,1)
>
> *There is a mains failure at Wildmoor station* (303,100,3)

CHAPTER 18

USING LPC
FOR NON-SPEECH SOUNDS

Gerard Benbassat (18.1),
Edward Carterette, Carl Shipley and
Jennifer Buchwald (18.2)

18.1 *Making music with LPC*

The linear predictive (LP) model of speech production has been studied primarily for speech communication applications and in particular for data rate reduction. As a result, we usually associate this signal processing technique with a degradation of the sound quality, which would seem to make it quite inappropriate for musical applications. However, in the context of music synthesisers and computer music, the flexibility of the LP model itself makes it a good candidate for the *production* of musical sounds, if not for their *reproduction*. Indeed the LP model, which assumes a single pseudo-periodical source of excitation of an all-pole filter, makes the LP analysis techniques inadequate for polyphonic sounds, which limits linear prediction's application for digital recording of music.

On the other hand, linear prediction allows for independent control of the fundamental frequency, the spectral envelope (and thus, to a certain extent, the harmonic content) and the energy contour of a sound, which are the basic ingredients necessary for artificial synthesis of musical sounds. In particular, the success of LP for modelling the speech signal makes it a very attractive approach for the synthesis of singing voices.

In music the expected level of sound quality is much higher than in speech synthesis applications. The sound must be crisp and clear; all 'fuzziness', 'buzziness', clicks and pops, not unusual in synthetic speech, must be eliminated. Also, the resulting pitch must be musically accurate. All these requirements call for a slightly different use of the same basic LP model.

MORE ACCURATE MODELLING

To produce a sufficiently rich voice timbre, the bandwidth of the all-pole filter should be at least 5 kHz and could be increased as high as 12 kHz with some benefit. Consequently, the sampling rate should be set between 10 and 24 kHz and the order of the filter adjusted proportionately to keep a given simulated vocal-tract length. This leads to twelve to sixteen poles, if we keep the usual two-pole modelling of the combined glottal pulse and lip radiation effects. The number of poles can be increased to provide a more accurate modelling of the glottal pulse. Up to order fifty-five at 22.5 kHz sampling frequency has been found useful (Moorer, 1979), but very good sounds can also be produced with order twelve at 10 kHz sampling rate.

The spectral envelope of the sounds to be used in the actual synthesis can be obtained through LP analysis of real vocal music although the analysis method must be chosen carefully, especially for high-pitched voices. At high fundamental frequencies (alto soprano) the analysis tends to include the fine structure of the spectrum, as well as its envelope, in the poles. Using such a model with a different fundamental frequency might result in a totally different harmonic content, which could be disastrous. One way to reduce this effect is to use a pitch-synchronous type of analysis, with a narrow window length not exceeding two pitch periods.

The production of high pitches brings also another difficulty regarding the precision of the fundamental frequency. The fundamental is actually produced by the repetition of an excitation function (usually having a flat spectrum) every T samples, T being the period expressed as an integral number of samples. The ear is approximately sensitive to $\log T$, which implies that a useful measure of the precision of the fundamental frequency is given by the relative precision of T. If T is an integer its relative precision becomes rapidly unacceptable as the frequency reaches the female range. Two problems appear: the pitch scale becomes false (the required precision is on the order of $1/1000$) and the small pitch variations (on the order of $1/100$) cannot be smoothly represented. For example, $F_0 = 800$ Hz at a sampling frequency of 16 kHz would be represented with a 2.5% precision.

A computationally expensive way to solve this problem is to increase the sampling frequency. Another way is to use an *over-sampled* excitation function so that T can be expressed as $T' = T*K$, K being the over-sampling factor, thus increasing the relative precision proportionally. During the actual synthesis operation, the function is *under-sampled* at frequency F_s (operating sampling frequency of the filter) and with a phase shift that depends on the remainder of the integer division T'/K. This under-sampling implies that the function must have its spectrum entirely between 0 and $F_s/2$, and have no energy between $F_s/2$ and $F_s*K/2$. If such a condition were not met, the resulting sound might be very buzzy.

As a side effect, such a function has its energy more evenly distributed over the pitch period. This reduces the peakiness of the signal which is sometimes accused of giving a buzzy quality to the LPC sounds.

SYNTHESIS OF SINGING VOICES

The acoustical parameters to be controlled for generating singing voices are similar to those used in speech synthesis. The filter parameters control the evolution of the spectral content of the signal, as would the articulations of the vocal tract. The fundamental frequency of the excitation function controls the pitch of the voice according to a given melody. The gain of the filter controls the energy contour of the sounds. As a result, the basic mechanisms for constructing speech can be transposed for singing, but with various degrees of emphasis on the different features of the sounds. Particularly the control of pitch and formant positions requires specific attention.

The differences appear primarily in the sustained parts of vowels. First, the formant positions for spoken and sung vowels are different, especially for professional singers (Sundberg, 1970). This implies that the spectral shapes to be used must be obtained by the analysis vowels actually sung.

In addition, a given vowel may need to be synthesised on a very large pitch range. As a consequence it is not possible to consider that the spectral envelope is independent of the fundamental frequency, as is the case in speech synthesis. Otherwise, for certain pitch periods, the timbre of the voice can be drastically changed and become totally inhuman. In fact, an analysis of professional singers' voices (Sundberg, 1975) has shown that the formants are consistently modified as a function of the fundamental frequency, particularly at high pitch levels where most vowels seem to be merged into a single unique sound.

In practice, if the synthesiser filter is controlled by resonant frequencies, these can be automatically modified as a function of the pitch, for each vowel, according to some rules. Alternatively, different patterns can be stored for each sound, each at a different pitch.

Another aspect that requires specific attention in the sustained parts of vowels is related to small variations of pitch. If a steady tone is synthesised with a constant pitch value, the resulting sound is very dry and does not resemble any sound produced by a human being.

It is even difficult to recognise the vowel from which the spectral envelope was extracted. An analysis of real speech shows that whenever a speaker tries to maintain a constant pitch, he effectively produces small variations around the desired value. They are probably due to the non-instantaneous psycho-acoustic feedback control of vocal-cord tension, and air pressure in the lungs which must be adjusted to produce a given frequency of vibration of the vocal cords. These variations can be modelled by the addition of two or three independent random variations at different lag times (Rodet, 1981). The total maximum variation is on the order of 3–5% but it is important that it be smooth. The difference between two consecutive pitch values should not exceed about 0.5%, otherwise the variation could be perceived as being performed in steps.

A voluntary variation of pitch that is observed in singing voices is called the *vibrato* effect. It is essentially a periodic variation of the pitch, of which the amplitude can go as high as 10% and the frequency is on the order of 2–7 Hz depending on the frequency of the pitch. The amplitude of the vibrato is itself subject to random variations that can be modelled in a similar way to the basic ones.

Adding randomness and vibrato to the pitch can produce very realistic-sounding voices, even using a single spectral pattern repeated over and over.

For the production of other parts of sounds, like consonants or vowel attacks, where spectrum (and pitch) are rapidly varying, similar considerations to those made for speech synthesis are applicable. Both construction by rule and concatenation of stored sound segments (such as *diphones*) can be used. For the first approach, it is preferable that the synthesiser filter be controlled by resonant frequencies as in a formant synthesiser (Rodet, 1980). This does not rule out the use of a lattice structure since the resonant frequencies can be converted to reflection coefficients before being used in the filter. The diphone-like approach is limited by the size of the dictionary required, especially considering the need to have different patterns for different pitch periods. However, in some cases it may be sufficient to make only a small number of different sounds, vowels or consonants, so the second approach may be more efficient.

Another level of concern is related to the translation of musical notation into a realistic and acceptable interpretation. If the pitch, duration and loudness of the sounds are straightforwardly converted from the musical score, the result can be disastrous. Adequate rules must be developed to make a correct correspondence between the musical signs and the appropriate acoustical signal (Sundberg, 1982).

For instance, the loudness should be increased with the pitch, and the amplitude decreased at the end of a note. Durational contrasts are sharpened by reducing the length of the short notes. Pitch variation in *portamento* (where notes are made to flow together) must be controlled carefully according to the distance between the two tones. Vibrato has to be set progressively. Many other factors are involved, and this is a subject of current investigations.

EXTENSION OF THE RANGE OF APPLICATION OF LINEAR PREDICTION
Just as it is possible to synthesise singing voices using a music synthesis technique, such as frequency modulation (Chowning, 1982), it is possible to synthesise other types of sounds with an all-pole filter. Such a filter is mainly limited in its ability to provide an accurate control of harmonic content. Each pair of poles can only provide one peak in the spectral envelope, so a very complex harmonic structure could necessitate a large number of poles in order to be accurately reproduced. However, the spectral envelope control provided by the filter makes possible the synthesis of a very large variety of sounds, including instrument sounds.

18.2 *The speech of animals*

> **Jellicle Cats are merry and bright,**
> **And pleasant to hear when they caterwaul.**
> 'The Song of the Jellicles',
> *Old Possum's Book of Practical Cats.*
> T. S. Eliot

SYNTHESISING ANIMAL CALLS
Animal vocalisations may prove to be useful as a model for studying the prosodic features of human speech. As examples, the case for cat cries and human infant cries is made by Buchwald and Shipley (1983), and Jürgens (1979) discusses the case for non-human primates such as chimpanzee, gibbon, rhesus monkey and squirrel monkey. From an even wider view animal calls are central to the anthropologist in the study of species-specific social communication, and to the psychologist in the study of speech as well as the relationship of speech production to speech perception. Recent experimental results on perception of speech-sound categories by animals parallel findings on human infants, which suggests the possibility that the speech and hearing mechanisms originated and evolved symbiotically (Kuhl, 1979). The non-verbal component of human speech especially intrigues the neurobiologist

because 'The intonation patterns used during scolding, lamenting, caressing, or jubilating as well as nonverbal utterances such as laughing, whining, moaning and shrieking express emotional states of the utterer and thus must be homologized with animal vocalizations' (Jürgens, 1979, p. 11).

The rapid and remarkable development of human speech analysis and synthesis since about 1968 has hardly touched the study of animal vocalisations. Except for a few pioneering studies, the synthesis of animal vocalisations has been largely by the use of playback of recorded calls, resonant circuits, bandpass filtering and pure-tone mixing. Pye (1967) credibly synthesised the waveforms of bats' pulses by pulse and frequency modulation of sinusoids which were then refined by tuned filtering. In a more sophisticated approach, though apparently no birdspeech was synthesised, Greenewalt (1969) accounted for many of the acoustical properties of birdsong by a transmission-line electrical analog of a simplified model of the *syrinx* (lower larynx or 'song organ'), wherein lie two acoustical generators, one in each bronchus. These sources can be rapidly modulated independently in frequency and amplitude, thus the bird can produce two notes or phrases simultaneously.

Based on a lumped-parameter approximation of the transfer function of the human vocal tract driven by pulses or noise, Capranica (1965), in an elegant work, synthesised mating calls of the bullfrog and other anuran species. A calling male evokes the calling response of other male bullfrogs to form a chorus which draws the voiceless females inexorably to the breeding ground. Filtering and synthesis experiments showed that two concomitant formants ($L \triangleq 200$ Hz and $H \triangleq 1400$ Hz) evoked the mating call and that L and H excited, respectively, complex and simple single-unit activity in the eighth nerve. Apparently the peripheral auditory nervous system provides the neural basis for coding the mating call. Also it was found that a 500 Hz tone abolished both L activity and the evoked mating call but not H activity. These results help to explain how the bullfrog's mating call acts as a mechanism for isolating species and why heterospecific mating among anurans is rare. The male bullfrog and female bullfrog are in tune. He knows how to say it and she has ears only for him.

Lieberman's *The Speech of Primates* (1972) is a collection of studies which '. . . show that the supralaryngeal vocal tract of modern man has evolved gradually for the purpose of enhancing rapid communication by means of speech' (page 1). From anatomy, and from spectrograms and waveforms of calls of rhesus monkey, chimpanzee and gorilla, it was found that these animals' vocal mechanisms are unable to produce human speech. Essentially breathy and irregular output arose from a tube of uniform cross section. Tongue manoeuvres do not change the shape of the supralaryngeal tract. Some formant transitions are seen, but arise apparently from laryngeal, velar or lip movements. A computer model (Lieberman, Klatt and Wilson, 1969) based on the area function of the supralaryngeal vocal tract indicated that the rhesus monkey has a restricted vowel space and can not produce human speech. Lieberman and Crelin (1971) reconstructed and modelled the vocal apparatus of Neanderthal man, and compared modelled vowel triangles among adult modern man, adult chimpanzee, newborn modern man and adult Neanderthal man. Only adult modern man's vocal tract could form the abruptly changing area functions necessary for producing the vowels [a], [i] or [u], which are absent from the vowel repertoire of the chimpanzee, newborn human and Neanderthal man.

Though non-human mammals may not be able to produce the full range of human speech, they obviously can make vowel-like sounds, noisy consonantals and plosives. The expression of emotion through prosody appears to be widespread among mammals. Clearly, the development of accurate analysis and synthesis models of animal vocalisations is necessary for assessing the degree to which similarities exist in the vocal behaviour of animals and humans.

MODELLING THE VOCAL TRACT OF THE CAT

We had synthesised kitten calls as early as 1977 (see Carterette, Shipley and Buchwald, 1979) incidental to linear prediction (LP) theory analysis of vocalisation in cat and kitten. In the present paper we show that acoustical tube modelling of the vocal tract of the cat and linear prediction of the cat vowel can be done using the ideas and procedures of LP models of human speech, which are now easy to access.

A mid-saggital section of the head of a young adult cat (fig. 18.1) suggests that its vocal tract, the *oropharynx*, is a simple, uniform cylindrical tube, closed at one end, which we may call U1. Its principal resonances are given by

$$T_k = (2k-1)c/4l \qquad (18.1)$$

($k = 1,2,\ldots$) where l is the length of the tube and c the velocity of sound, which at physiological temperatures is approximately equal to $35\,500\ \mathrm{cm\,s^{-1}}$. Successive resonances (formants) are odd integer multiples of T_1.

If $l = 7.4$ cm (by actual measurement; see below) then the predicted first three resonances of the simple lossless tube U1 are given in line 1 of table 18.1.

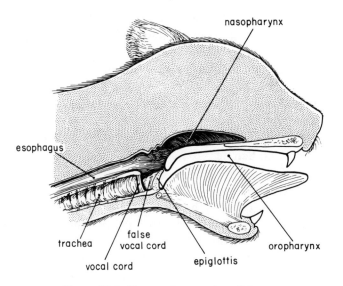

Figure 18.1 The vocal apparatus of the cat

Table 18.1 Theoretical and measured formant frequencies for a young adult cat

	T_1 (Hz)	T_2 (Hz)	T_3 (Hz)
Theoretical centre frequency	1199	3598	5997
Measured centre frequency	1688	4877	7942
Bandwidth	268	344	598
Amplitude	5324	5109	4823

Lines 2, 3 and 4 give, respectively, the first three formants, and their bandwidths and relative amplitudes, of the midcall of a young adult cat ('Georgia') obtained by LP analysis. Clearly the theoretical values T_1, T_2 and T_3 are rather different from the observed values, although the odd-integer relationship is suggested. We observe that when calling a cat's lips are much retracted, hence the vocal tract is much shortened. The equivalent length of the tract, using the theoretical F1 of table 18.1 and equation (18.1), is 5.26 cm, giving F1 = 1688, F2 = 5064, F3 = 8440, closer to the observed but with predicted F2 and F3 too high.

However, a real physiological tube is lossy. Losses owing to yielding walls tend to raise frequencies whereas viscous and thermal losses tend to lower frequencies. But since the wall losses affect lower frequencies most and the other losses affect higher frequencies most, the net result is (Portnoff, 1976, as cited in Rabiner and Schafer, 1978) that, relative to a lossless tube U1 and a radiation load of zero at the lips (a 'short circuit'), F1 is raised whereas F2 and F3 are lowered.

This would bring F2 even closer to F1. Alas, bandwidth ought to *decrease* with increasing formant frequency; just the opposite is observed. Fortunately, the radiation loss at the opening is considerable and most significant at the higher frequencies. The final expected result, taking all losses into account, is that the formant frequencies will be lowered and resonances broadened, the higher more than the lower. This pattern fits reasonably the data of rows 1, 2 and 3, above. Furthermore, the U1 + losses + radiation model well describes human speech (Rabiner and Schafer, 1978).

SYNTHESISING THE CAT CRY

The consonance of cat and human analyses gave us some assurance that LP synthesis of the cat cry would prove valid. The basic general theory we use was developed for speech synthesis structures in terms of the reflection coefficients of an acoustic tube model. The essential idea is that by doing LP analysis of the pre-emphasised 'speech' signal one obtains a z-transform inverse filter $A(z)$ whose reciprocal $1/A(z)$ is an estimate of the vocal-tract transfer function (see chapter 5). The reciprocal of $A(z)$ incorporates the glottal shaping term $G(z)$ and the vocal-tract transfer function $V(z)$, and assumes that the pre-emphasis filter equals the lip-radiation factor $L(z)$, that is,

$$A(z)^{-1} = G(z)V(z)L(z) \qquad (18.2)$$

We synthesised cat cries in two ways from a modification of an LP synthesiser (Markel and Gray, 1976), (1) by using actual vocal-tract area measurements, and (2) by means of parameters obtained from LP analysis of the call.

Calls were recorded from young adult cats using a condenser microphone (Sony ECM-20FA) and magnetic recorder (TEAC 3340S) having an overall amplitude response between 50 and 11 000 Hz of ±3 dB. Typical values were 70 dB SPL (re 0.0002 dynes cm^{-2}) recorded frontally at a distance of 10 cm, in a sound isolation chamber. After isolation bandpass filtering (Krohn-Hite 3302) between 100 and 11 000 Hz, calls were stored on magnetic disk after 12-bit analog-to-digital conversion (Analog Devices ADA-343) having an accuracy of plus or minus one-half least significant bit, at a sampling period of 4.5×10^{-7} s (22 222 Hz). All subsequent processing was done with a Hewlett-Packard HP-2100A computer.

A typical young female cat ('Georgia') weighing 3.5 kg, for whom recorded calls were available, was sacrificed. From the mid-saggital section of the head several sets of measurements were made of vertical and lateral distances in the vocal tract from the glottis to the maximal extent of the lips. The means of the measured areas in cm² (times 2) are plotted as a function of distance from glottis in fig. 18.2(g). The length of the vocal tract from glottis to lips was 7.4 cm. Note that the area at lips is about 2 cm², compared to about 5 cm² for a human uttering a neutral vowel.

EXPERIMENTAL RESULTS

From the measured areas, or from LP analyses, reflection coefficients were computed and used as input to a speech synthesis structure based on (a) a two-multiplier lattice filter, (b) pitch-synchronous interpolation of gain and pitch and reflection coefficients, (c) gain computed on error-signal energy, (d) number of coefficients $M = 10$, (e) randomly perturbed pitch period of 2.475 ms (404 Hz), and (f) 128 samples used in analysis frames.

By means of a rigid head-holder and linear resistor, the amount of mouth opening was measured, which ranged from zero at the beginning of the call, reached a maximum of 1.5 cm just before maximal call amplitude and fell to zero at end of call. Figure 18.3 shows a 500 ms portion of an unstressed call of Georgia plotted as relative amplitude versus frequency (kHz). Successive plots in the $3d$ (depth) dimension are at 10 ms intervals. Figure 18.2 shows area functions for several stages of the call: (a), (c) and (e) are derived from the LP *analysis* coefficients whereas (b), (d) and (f) are derived from the analysis of the LP *synthesis*; (g) is the measured area function and (h) is from the corresponding LP synthesis.

From these and other data, it appears that LP analysis and synthesis reflect the area changes in vocal-tract sections in a reasonable way. The first third (glottis to 2.5 cm) of the vocal tract remains constant but the anterior two-thirds of cross-sectional area increases with mouth opening from as little as 2 cm² to as much as 12 cm², a ratio of six. In computed area function just after the call peak (not shown here), area increases monotonically as in a horn with a tulip flare whose maximal cross-sectional area was reached at the lips.

Table 18.2 shows some details of a few calls and related synthesis. The labels (a) to (h) correspond to those of fig. 18.2. Data are from LP analyses as described above except that $M = 8$ so as to elicit the main theoretical resonances T_1, $3T_1$ and $5T_1$ (F1, F2 and F3, respectively). Captured in the analysis are the locations of resonances, and the relative ordering of bandwidths and amplitudes. Frequency location is good, with overprediction in the synthesis of F1 by 1.5 per cent, of F2 by 6 per cent and F3 by 5.5 per cent. Though bandwidths predicted are generally too wide, relative amplitude predictions are good.

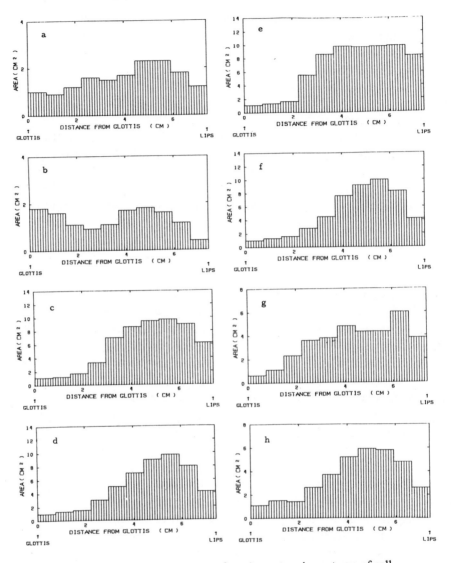

Figure 18.2 Vocal-tract area functions at various stages of call

Finally, fig. 18.4 shows graphically three 24 ms segments of waveforms. The top is from the late middle part of the call, the centre segment was synthesised from the middle of the call and the bottom segment is an LP synthesis from the measured area function. Clearly, the synthesised waveforms resemble the call but are overdamped. More accuracy may be obtained by proper matching of input and output energy. Nonetheless, the data of table 18.2 and the LP analysis plots of amplitude versus frequency in fig. 18.5 show reasonably good

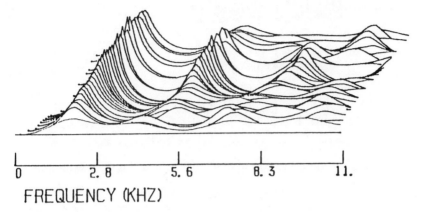

FREQUENCY (KHZ)

Figure 18.3 Spectral plot of cat call as a function of time

Table 18.2 Details of calls and their related synthesis

SOURCE	F1	F2	F3	BW1	BW2	BW3	A1	A2	A3
(a) S4	1796	4830	7533	378	1135	1932	5043	4420	4347
(b) SYN4	1816	5701	8291	748	902	1773	4731	4458	4266
(c) S30	1688	4877	7942	268	344	598	5324	5109	4823
(d) SYN30	1701	4897	7476	270	723	1297	5332	4606	4431
(e) S24	1676	4868	7798	266	480	912	5266	4854	4586
(f) SYN24	1721	4908	8061	283	693	1288	5237	4648	4477
(g) Line (h) based on vocal-tract cross-sectional area measurements									
(h) SYNGEO	1678	5058	7833	608	1070	1241	4800	4500	4400

The SOURCE column shows the relative position in the call of the LP-analysed waveform, with S4, S24 and S30 referring to early, peak and declining portions of the call. SYN4, SYN24, and SYN30 are the corresponding LP-synthesised waveforms, each based on 1280 successive samples. The columns F1, F2, and F3 give the LP-analysis values of the first, second and third formants (in Hz); BW1, BW2 and BW3 give the corresponding estimated bandwidths (in Hz); A1, A2 and A3 give the associated estimated relative amplitudes (in arbitrary units). SYNGEO was synthesised from actual measurements.

agreement between analyses and syntheses (spectra (a)–(h) correspond to area functions (a)–(h) of fig. 18.2).

DISCUSSION

This study shows the feasibility of using linear prediction synthesisers for modelling the vocalisations of cats and, by extension, the vocalisations of any mammalian species including the cries of the newborn or developing human infant. Calls having known properties can be synthesised for the purpose of studying the development of social communication and the relationship between vocalisation and hearing. Laboratory 'standard' calls can be specified by reference to analysis and

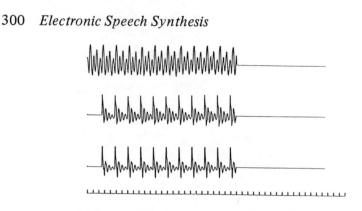

Figure 18.4 Actual (top) and synthesised cat calls as time waveforms

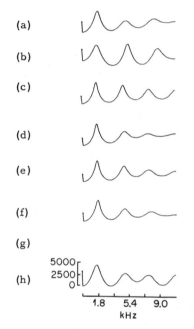

Figure 18.5 LP spectra of call segments and their respective syntheses

synthesis programs just as is now the case for human voice. Many useful neurobiological investigations may be undertaken since, especially in cat and non-human primates, a good deal is known of cortical and sub-cortical regions whose controlled stimulation elicits vocalisations (Jürgens, 1979).

Some interesting and hard problems remain. We require an explicit model of glottal excitation and study of its interactions with the vocal tract. Dynamic changes in the cat's vocal tract require charting by cineradiography. Nothing is known of consonantal, noisy calls which can drive the system into a tube open at both ends, as happens in the case of the human infant also, or of the cat's way of modulating the call by changing the length of its vocal tract by manoeuvres with lips and laryngeal muscles. Particularly difficult to assess is the extent and effect of nasal coupling, for as fig. 18.1 shows, the *nasopharynx* is a large cavity. For nasal vocalisations the transfer function of the vocal system will show zeros as well as poles, which should be seen in LP analyses as broadened formant bandwidths.

ACKNOWLEDGMENTS
This research was supported in part by grants HD 04612 and HD 05958, National Institutes of Health, and by a grant from The Regents of The University of California.

References

Buchwald, J.S. and Shipley, C. (1983) 'A comparative model of the infant cry'. In *Infant Crying: Theoretical and Research Perspectives* (Eds Lester, B.M. and Zacharia Boukydis, C.F.). New York: Plenum Press (in press).

Capranica, R.R. (1965) *The Evoked Vocal Response of the Bullfrog*. Cambridge. The MIT Press.

Carterette, E.C., Shipley, C. and Buchwald, J.S. (1979) 'Linear prediction theory of vocalization in cat and kitten.' In *Frontiers of Speech Communication Research* (Eds Lindblom, B. and Öhman, S.). New York. Academic Press, pp. 245–257.

Chowning, J.M. (1982) 'The synthesis of sung vowel tones'. *International Computer Music Conference, Venice, Italy*, Sept. 1982.

Crouch, J.E. (1969) *Text-atlas of Cat Anatomy*. Philadelphia: Lea and Feibiger.

Greenewalt, C.H. (1968) 'Bird song'. *Acoustics and Physiology*. Washington: Smithsonian Institution.

Jürgens, U. (1979) 'Neural control of vocalization in nonhuman primates.' In *Neurobiology of Social Communication in Primates*. (Eds Steklis, H.D. and Raleigh, M.J.). New York: Academic Press, pp. 11–44.

Kuhl, P.K. (1979) 'Models and mechanisms in speech perception: Species comparisons provide further contributions'. *Brain, Behavior and Evolution* 16, 374–408.

Lieberman, P. (1972) *The Speech of Primates*. The Hague: Mouton.

Lieberman, P. and Crelin, E.C. (1971) 'On the speech of Neanderthal man'. *Linguistic Inquiry* 2, 203–222. (Reprinted in Lieberman, 1972.)

Lieberman, P., Crelin, E.S. and Klatt, D.H. 'Phonetic ability and related anatomy of the newborn and adult human, Neanderthal man and the chimpanzee'. *American Anthropologist* **74**, 287–307. (Reprinted in Lieberman, 1972.)

Lieberman, P., Klatt, D.H. and Wilson, W.A. (1969) 'Vocal tract limitations on the vocal repertoires of rhesus monkey and other non-human primates'. *Science* **164**, 1185–1187. (Reprinted in Lieberman, 1972.)

Markel, J.D. and Gray, A.H., Jr (1976) *Linear Prediction of Speech*. Heidelberg and New York: Springer-Verlag.

Moorer, J.A. (1979) 'The use of linear prediction of speech in computer music applications'. *Journal of the Audio Engineering Society* **27**, (3), 134–140.

Pye, J.D. (1967) 'Synthesizing the waveforms of bat's pulses'. In *Animal Sonar Systems: Biology and Bionics* (Ed. Busnel, R.-G.). Jouy-en-Josas (France): Laboratoire de Physiologie Acoustique, CNRZ, pp. 43–64.

Rabiner, L.R. and Schafter, R.W. (1978) *Digital Processing of Speech*. Englewood Cliffs, New Jersey (USA): Prentice-Hall.

Rodet, X. (1980) 'Research in musical synthesis using a model of vocal production'. *International Computer Music Conference, Queen's College, New York*.

Rodet, X. (1981) 'Musical synthesis, evolution of the chant project'. *International Computer Music Conference, Danton-Texas*.

Sundberg, J. (1970) 'Formant structure and articulation of spoken and sung vowels'. *Fol. Phon.* **22**, 28–48.

Sundberg, J. (1975) 'Formant technique in a professional female singer'. *Acoustica* **32**, (2), 89–96.

Sundberg, J. (1982) 'A rule system for converting melodies from musical notation into sound'. *International Computer Music Conference, Venice, Italy*, Sept. 1982.

CHAPTER 19

A COOKBOOK
OF APPLICATION IDEAS

Marvin Talbott

Having read through nineteen chapters to reach this point indicates that the reader must be very excited — either about electronic speech technology itself, or anticipating completion of the course in which this reading matter was assigned. In either case, the reader is apt to be eager now to begin to apply some of the technology discussed in earlier chapters and obtain tangible results. This chapter is intended to help the reader begin applying the technology first hand.

Since each reader will be interested in different aspects of the technology, and each individual will find different applications appealing, an effort has been made to offer a representative smorgasbord of possible applications, so that hopefully there will be something of interest for everyone. Some applications are rather thoroughly laid out (such as the Talking Clock in section 19.1) to guide the reader through a complete ready-made application, but most are merely mentioned in passing with cautionary comments about the application for those readers that strike out into that area. Sections 19.1 and 19.2 deal with synthetic speech applications, as hobbyist and entrepreneural ventures. Sections 19.3 to 19.5 consider applications for the voice input systems that were described in chapter 7, and 19.6 discusses aspects of applications dealing with the handicapped.

19.1 *A synthesis project for the hobbyist*

If it's electrical you can make it talk. That's the concept that is propelling the synthetic voice industry. As a practical matter most serious hobbyists will read this book with preconceived applications in mind — and after studying the underlying theory will be more interested in actually constructing a working unit than in reviewing lists of potential applications. Therefore, this section details how to construct a talking clock from commercially available circuits.

The Talking Clock was chosen to be affordable (costing less than $80), and constructable from commercially available parts. The lack of suitable vocabularies usually tends to be the limiting factor in utilising synthetic speech in non-commercial applications. However, recently a modest amount of pre-chosen vocabulary has become available tailored to specific functional needs, so it is now possible to obtain appropriate vocabulary to implement a digital clock readout on an inexpensive ROM. That was one of the principal reasons for choosing a talking clock as an introductory example of synthetic speech usage. Similar ROMs can also be obtained with representative industrial, avionic, military and weather vocabularies. Most have male voices. The one used in this example happens to be female. The implementation detailed here is not a unique solution, nor can it be said to be optimal in any sense of the word — rather it is representative of what a hobbyist might encounter, and is presented as a reference point from which a novice in the field can launch out.

PARTS LIST

The digital clock can be obtained directly as an individual chip (National *MM5387AA*), or its pin equivalent can be found at Radio Shack already packaged and operating an LED digital alarm clock (Cat. No. 63–826). It adds about $5 to the cost by purchasing the full *Micronta* LED digital clock, but for breadboard work it is felt to be worth it as no additional power supplies or clock chip hook-up support are then necessary. (+15 volts can be picked up directly from pin 28 [V_{ss}] for supply to the input side of the *CD4050* chips, as well as establishing ground through pin 29 [V_{DD}].) The output of the clock chip can be tapped directly off the LED display input pads.

Other electronic chips needed

Part	Description	Quantity
Z-80	Microprocessor	1
74LS138	3-to-8 line DEC/MPLX	1
74LS02	Quadruple NOR gate	1
TMS2516	2K × 8 EPROM	1
74LS374	Octal D-type flip-flop	1
74LS244	Octal buffer	4
CD4050	Hex non-inverting buffers	4
TMS5220	Speech synthesiser	1

(contd.)

Part	Description	Quantity
VM71003	Vocabulary PROM (optional if software rewritten)	1
TMS4045	1K × 4 RAM	2

The optional RAM is used to store stack pointers. Although this facility would usually be removed in a commercial product, it is invaluable when experimenting in the lab, because of the flexibility that it provides.

Figure 19.1 shows the circuit diagram. The clock is interfaced to the TTL circuitry through the CD4050 chips, whose states are buffered in the 74LS244 chips. Their output ties into the system data bus which is interrogated by the Z-80, running from its code in the TMS2516. The data bus conditions are latched by the 74LS374 upon command, and then utilised to control the vocabulary chosen by the TMS5220 out of its private VM71003 vocabulary.

Most speech synthesisers that are now available as single chips were designed to drive small inexpensive speakers such as often used in modestly priced, mass-produced talking products. As such their characteristics are electrically and accoustically matched to these speakers, and surprisingly enough, they sound better when played through small, inexpensive speakers than when put through better quality audio equipment!

The microprocessor code to control this implementation can be obtained from Marvin Talbot, Corporate Engineering Centre, Texas Instruments Inc., North Central Expressway, Dallas, Texas. While lengthy, it is rather straightforward and contains numerous supplementary comments to aid in understanding. It has been the author's experience to find novice users of synthetic speech quite frustrated at the lack of detailed examples to follow in learning how to use the newer technologies. In general the difficulties do not arrive out of theoretical misunderstanding, but rather lack of experience and sufficient documentation to understand the critical timing or control sequences necessary to make the chips speak. Hopefully, this working example will help some hobbyists over these initial hurdles and guide them on to more interesting and challenging applications.

19.2 *Synthesis ideas for the entrepreneur*

Commercial utilisation of synthetic speech has been a reality for half a decade. Starting with children's educational learning devices, synthetic speech quickly found utilisation in appliances, elevators, automobiles

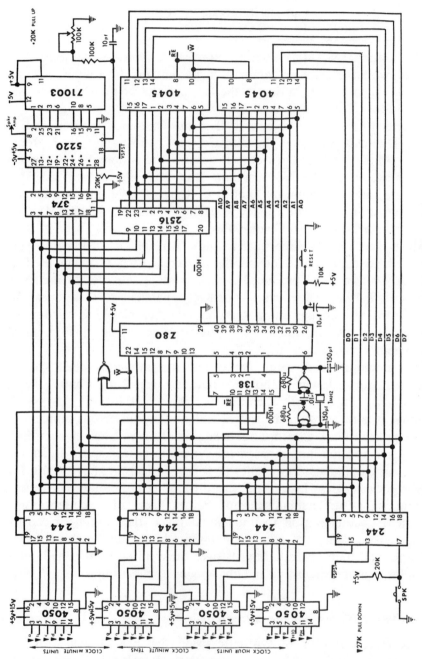

Figure 19.1 A simple 'talking clock' circuit for the hobbyist

and computer terminals. The anticipated explosive growth in toys and games did not immediately materialise, due in large measure to the depressed economic condition of the industry in the early '80s and the high price tag that such electronic gadgetry would have to carry. Opportunities still exist for commercial entries in these areas and many others, but even greater opportunities may lie in two largely untapped fields; namely alarm systems and data base readouts.

ALARM SYSTEMS

It is a proclivity of human nature that in emergencies when logical reasoning and emotional composure is most needed, it frequently is not present. Bells, whistles, sirens and similar alarm systems often evoke so much panic when heard, that the situation is exasperated rather than the danger being lessened. What has been learned from studying crisis situations (such as the near disaster in 1979 at the nuclear power plant in Three Mile Island, Pennsylvania) is that when complex actions are required to avert even more danger, and the personnel are aware of the problem(s) and actively seeking a solution, additional raucous alarms only add to the frustration level, and do not contribute to the solution.

What is ideally needed is a computer monitoring the situation, and determining from instant to instant what should be the next course of action taken. Optimum human response will then be obtained if this action item is clearly, calmly conveyed by a voice that inspires confidence! Such alarm systems lend themselves to complex technical environments – nuclear stations, chemical plants, power stations, cockpits of modern jet aircraft, etc; but are equally viable in many other environments. The interiors of many large buildings represent real deathtraps in the event of fire blocking the nearest marked exit route. A small computer monitoring such a structure would plot all available escape routes (even predicting where the fire is likely to spread to within a few minutes) and guide persons in the building out via loudspeakers located throughout the building. Again, studies show that confident audible guidance, at such times as when darkness and smoke can obscure visual indicators, could save many lives. Appropriate derivatives of such systems could be widely utilised in private homes as well. The fields of spoken audible alarms is just getting started, and lots of opportunities exist in it.

DATA BASE READOUTS

Synthetic speech offers the natural inferface between computers and the telephone. The pervasiveness of the telephone makes it an almost universally available computer terminal for any computers that are equipped with well-designed speech systems and connected to the phone system. Any data contained in a computer could theoretically be transmitted via a speech telephone interface, but obviously some types of information are much more compatible with this interface than others. In general, lengthy transmissions of numerous data values do not lend themselves to verbal readout.

There are two basic problems with verbal readout of lengthy tabular data. First, whereas visual displays allow rapid scanning across non-pertinent data entries, verbal readout is sequential by nature and may often consume unacceptable amounts of the user's time verbalising non-pertinent data prior to arriving at the desired value. Second, most users can only retain a single data value that they receive audibly (certainly no more than a few values) even if the values are relatively simple in form. This suggests that phone interfaces are best suited for single answer queries, such as. account balance?, invoice number?, shipment date?, unit price?, etc. Of course, once any single query has been verbally answered and the user has had time to record the answer, well-designed systems would allow additional queries. The challenge then lies in constructing appropriate software access mechanisms to complex data bases that facilitate rapid access to any needed data value without having to list intervening values sequentially, and that also pause to await the users' next response before proceeding.

Within the scope of large privately owned computer data bases, such as that discussed in detail in chapter 17, numerous opportunities abound for the intelligent use of synthetic speech to distribute data base information. The applications are not limited to 'system' information — field sales and service functions normally involve remote acquisition of data, and as such are naturals for using synthetic speech to handle phone inquiries. Any travelling businessman could communicate with his/her office, monitoring pertinent data through appropriately designed systems. Probably the single most limiting factor to more widespread utilisation of such data base readout systems will be the perceived sensitivity of the data being accessed. Appropriate safeguards with access codes will be absolutely necessary for any viable use of non-public data bases in the business world.

Public data bases also offer interesting opportunities for commercial synthetic speech ventures. Such information as time, temperature, foreign exchange rates, transportation schedules (fares and seat availability as well), weather forecasts, stock market and commodity prices, and sports scores, although having dynamic content, all have well-defined vocabularies, widespread interest, and lend themselves to phone inquiries. Less structured vocabularies requiring the ability to update messages in near real time are characteristic of news summaries, calendar of event announcements, promotional advertisements, etc.

The concept of telephone inquiry should not be limited to computer data. Virtually any sensor can be interrogated through such a telephone system. Remote weather sensors on mountain tops could be telephoned for readouts, storage tanks and valves could report their available capacity and flow, chemical processes could report temperature, pressure, acidity, etc. In short, wherever it would be desirable to occasionally have a human monitoring events, except that it is not feasible due to economic or environmental factors – if a standard phone can be installed it is probably now possible to provide such monitoring in a cost-effective manner.

19.3 *Voice input expectations*

Speech recognition is often cited as the coming commercial panacea by rather detached observers. The 'obvious' application, a voice-activated typewriter, has been referred to as a *talkwriter*. It is an excellent example of the unrealistic expectations attached to futuristic speech recognition systems. The root of this is based in the fact that to understand things not experienced, humans develop their expectations by comparing to what they have experienced. The fact that all the previous experience that the general public have had with speech recognition incorporates human intelligence, is generally overlooked. As a result public expectations for speech recognisers assume inherent intelligence far in excess of what can be expected in any commercial offering for years.

The common perception of the 'talkwriter', is that such a machine would replace the secretary/typist. Realistically, public enthusiasm would wane dramatically (even if errorless recognition were available) if there was a comprehension that dictation would involve explicitly 'speaking' punctuation, capitalisation and page positioning (e.g. indentation, tabbing, etc.), if not outright spelling all text! Problems such as handling the spelling of proper names, resolving ambiguous homonyms, and handling other non-standardised reduction of the spoken word to text will be paramount problems for public acceptance of initial commercial talkwriters.

Secondarily, human listeners are much more forgiving than mechanical systems will be perceived to be. Consider the frustration of an individual who finds they are not understood by a mechanical listener. Society has carefully worked out diplomatic responses that do not

imply guilt (such as *I'm sorry, what did you say?*) to handle misunder-
standings in common speech. No guilt is implied in such transactions,
as the listener may be at fault for not being attentive enough to the
speaker — when both are human! However, when a mechanical listener
becomes involved the public expectation is of a flawless attentive
listener, and anything missed — especially if it is consistently misunder-
stood — will imply fault to the human speaker, no matter what response
is given as an error message.

These concerns about user expectations are presented here because
they are not unique to the talkwriter application. Anyone seriously
considering applications involving speech recognition needs to concern
themselves with the perceived inherent intelligence of the unit by its
potential users. Many commercial venture possibilities will become
unattractive in this light, but a few might be able to use such biased
perceptions to their advantage. The amateur hobbyist obviously has
much concern in this area — making their applications more straightforward; so their potential application will be considered first.

19.4 *Voice input projects for the hobbyist*

Speech recognition for the amateur hobbyist offers unlimited opportunities, and because of the scarcity of pre-existing commercial products
involving speech recognition, almost anything that even marginally
works will be exciting, fun and novel. There are a few commercial
units available to serious hobbyists that want to invest money in prebuilt equipment. The offerings are rather dynamic, so be sure to check
out all the latest offerings if you decide to purchase such a unit. (A list
of manufacturers involved in the field was given in section 7.5.)

If after investigating available commercial speech recognition systems
you find them either inappropriate for your needs, or simply too
expensive, don't despair — you can probably build what you need,
yourself! One of the best aspects of trying to build a speech recognition
unit is the diversity of implementations open to the amateur. The only
fundamental requirement of a speech recognition system is that it be
able to differentiate reasonably well between defined alternative spoken
vocabulary inputs, as well as screening out other non-input-directed
speech and noise. There aren't too many areas left that offer so few
restrictions on system designs, so imaginative designers can have lots of
fun with this much freedom — *the sky's the limit!*

Probably the simplest screening method for any applications could
be provided by a low sensitivity, highly directional microphone — so
that it tries to differentiate anything it 'hears' and obviously screens

out all other 'unheard' comments and background noise. The key to differentiation is appropriate choice of the recognised vocabulary! It might be very difficult to design an amateur system that readily distinguishes between the words *start* and *stop*, but it would be much easier to build a unit to distinguish between *start motor* and *stop* (or *start up* and *off*). Such distinctions can be made by simply timing the length of the utterance, or counting the number of words spoken. Since you will be specifying the vocabulary as well as the recognition system, make it easy on yourself and pick a vocabulary that is spread as far apart as possible in the parametric representation of speech that your unit uses to differentiate the vocabulary. In many cases it need not be a sophisticated or complex solution. It could be speaker dependent and trained to match pre-recorded templates against current input for best match — in any parametric representation of speech. It could be a simple unit that measures instantaneous energy in the speech signal, distinguishing the words by comparing the number of zero energy crossings, or it could be as simple as a counter of syllables or words.

To show just how straightforward such a unit can be, consider fig. 19.2. The input audio channel is split, with one side going through a high-pass filter set at about 2 kHz, and the other side going through a low-pass filter, set at about 1 kHz.

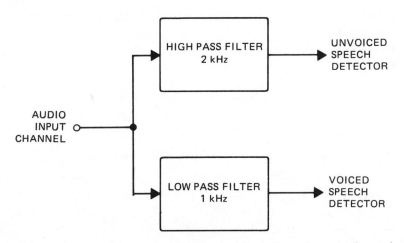

Figure 19.2 A simple 'speech differentiator' for voice and unvoiced sounds

Simplistic differentiation between voiced and unvoiced vocabulary results from this unit. Words such as *yes* and *no* can be separated easily based on the unvoiced /s/ in *yes*. Thus if the only vocabulary to be recognised is *yes* or *no*, the above recogniser should prove adequate (recognising *yes* any time the unvoiced detector is activated, and *no* any time the voiced detector is activated without the unvoiced activation following closely). This same unit would also differentiate between *one* and *two* (keying on the unvoiced /t/ in *two*), or between *on* and *off* (keying on the unvoiced /f/). While such versatility may often be desirable, this kind of flexibility requires further care and attention because the unit would not be able to distinguish between all members of such an expanded vocabulary (e.g. it can't differentiate between *yes* and *off*). This usually results in designing the unit to be a 'state-machine', and carefully excluding non-distinguishable vocabulary pairs from ever occurring in a single state of the machine (i.e. when the machine is in state A it is listening for *on* or *off* — and nothing else, while when it is in state B it listens for *yes* or *no* only).

Probably, the first application that comes to mind for most hobbyists is voice remote control. Many individuals that enjoy electronics and science hobbies relish the science fiction portrayals of voice-controlled robots in movies of the past. Such dreams are now realisable for many hobbyists. Simple voice-controlled motorised vehicles have already appeared in the commercial toy markets. The speech differentiation can be as simple as counting the words spoken in each command, with very satisfactory control using only two states. A realistic vocabulary for such an implementation is shown in table 19.1.

Table 19.1 Suitable vocabulary for a two-state, word-counting, vehicle motion controller

Word Count	States	
	Stationary	Moving
1	GO	STOP
2	BACK UP	TURN RIGHT
3	—	PLEASE TURN LEFT

More sophisticated recognisers, such as speaker-dependent, trained, template matching units, could of course easily distinguish between individual single word commands (e.g. *left* and *right*). Simple motion control would be adequate for many children's toys — vehicles, dolls, robots, etc. Electric model railways are a particularly interesting application ground in which to try out voice control. On the more elaborate model railway layouts, not only could the operator control road switches and the speed and direction of various trains, but frequently other auxiliary electrical models (e.g. lights in buildings, or moving ramps at loading platforms, etc.) are available to be controlled.

More ambitious hobbyists that want to move beyond the realm of youthful toys, may want to construct functional helpers to aid around the house, mowing and watering the lawn, fetching items, etc. The mechanical aspects of such robots may well prove more challenging than the speech recognition or electronics involved. Speech input to such a device is normally handled over a walkie-talkie link, so that orders aren't being shouted — and confused with other background noise. *How-to* books on mechanical and electronic robot construction can usually be found in computer and electronic hobby stores. Most of these robot books do not include speech circuitry, but provide the structural robotic base on which to implement interesting speech designs.

If expense is not a major concern, several fairly sophisticated operational robots, complete with closed-circuit television, are commercially manufactured. They are normally used in public relations as crowd pleasers, typically found performing at trade conventions and retail store promotions. These robots typically contain a standard audio microphone and speaker, complete with a radio link to the remote control unit. The remote control unit provides the logical base on which to build speech recognition and/or synthetic speech, but will always be frivolous as long as a human operates the remote control unit.

A little more realistic for most hobbyists is voice remote control of appliances. During 1981 a major Japanese corporation showed a television set that incorporated user-trained voice control at several major electronic trade shows, and featured it on at least one television commercial. The set responded to such words as *on*, *off* and the digits to select channels. To use it, the operator 'trained' the set by repeating each keyword several times while the set captured his/her typical vocal pronunciation of the keywords. (It is necessary that remote television voice control be speaker dependent, as it is not desirable that chance occurrence of keywords spoken over the audio channel of the set should cause the set to change channels, or turn off!) Remote appliance control via voice is a realistic goal for any enthusiastic hobbyist in this field. Probably the prime candidate to control is the morning alarm clock — after all, who wouldn't want to silence it just by shouting at it!

The newest electronic entry to the home, the home computer, may well offer the most fertile ground of all for the hobbyist. Its memory can hold templates and processing algorithms. By its very nature, these can be frequently changed and updated, to try numerous and varied approaches, without incurring major costs of new hardware components or obsolescence of the prior implementations. Since the home computer can be used to control any electrical device in the home (lights, heating, stereo, security system, etc.) it offers the potential to extend voice control to any or all such devices from a single input unit. Furthermore, since input sensory microphones can readily be routed to a home computer from any location(s) chosen in or around a home, such a system should offer the maximum flexibility for a typical hobbyist. Prebuilt equipment is commercially available to interface to many major home computers. Inquire about them and peripheral equipment where you purchased your computer. Do be careful when purchasing such equipment, and make certain it fulfills your needs as you will typically find it a sizable personal investment, with performance normally only on par with most modest recognition systems.

Voice input on home computers is often used to control operating functions and to select available options from menu screens. It typically involves voice training, that is it is *speaker dependent*. Many individuals enjoy the aspect of privacy and file-security that this can provide, while some other users will want to teach their computer to respond to several voices. Of course voice input usage in application programs is only limited by the imagination of the programmer who writes the application software. The common commercial technology now exists to differentiate vocabularies of several score words or utterances for speaker-dependent, trained systems. The problem then becomes one of remembering what the 'acceptable' vocabulary is during usage. This may sound easy enough, but practice shows that when the vocabulary exceeds a dozen or so 'non-unified' control functions (the ten digits would comprise a 'unified' set, as would the pair 'on'/'off', etc.) users do not readily retain the full vocabulary set, and either quickly confine themselves to a comfortable subset, or when necessary refer to written lists of the vocabulary.

Probably the area of voice input that offers the most near-term possibilities is in video game control. One can easily imagine numerous exciting game possibilities where both hands are busily engaged in controlling various aspects of the game, and the player excitedly shouts *next, stop, fire* or whatever relates to the game being played. Numerous opportunities exist to sell quality video games authored by individuals, and the inclusion of a voice input option would certainly be a distinguishing feature; however, anyone authoring video games solely for economic profit would be well advised to stay clear of voice input in the near future, as the available customer base having (or willing to purchase) voice input peripherals for their computers or gaming machines will be very, very small.

19.5 *Voice input ideas for the entrepreneur*

Having been cautioned about such an undertaking in section 19.3, the aspiring voice input entrepreneur should realise that commercially profitable voice input systems remain elusive, and will probably not be prevalent until dramatic breakthroughs occur in the overall performance of voice input recognition technology. However, there do exist a few anomalies in the field of speech recognition and closely allied fields that seem to offer some near-term opportunities, so these will be considered here as possible applications of interest.

The areas commonly being pursued by existing voice input systems are in situations where the use of the hands for keyboard entry of data is difficult or impossible. The most prevalently documented problem of this nature is package handling in a postal centre where automated routing of the parcels handled is available if data relating to the routing of the parcels can be entered into the system as the packages are being manually handled. Variations of this same situation routinely occur in warehouse, shipping and inventory handling in many large industrial and business operations. While not overwhelmingly numerous, their occurrence is sufficiently frequent to have attracted the interest of several commercial offerings vying for positions in the voice recognition marketplace. They have met with widely varying degrees of success, and, probably because of the lack of any other significant public applications of the technology, the history of many of these attempted applications is well documented in the technical literature. These results should be thoroughly reviewed by anyone planning on pursuing the technology seriously.

Due to the speaker-dependent aspect of voice input systems, the concept of a voice-activated security lock is a logical area for serious consideration of commercial development. The concept of security locks that don't require the owner to carry a pocketful of keys, or memorise an intricate combination, would certainly be very attractive to the general public, if competitively priced with existing alternatives. Indeed, the selectivity of voice input systems is narrow enough that it is probably reasonable to consider a voice-activated lock on an automobile that would not allow operation of the vehicle until authorised by a completely sober owner. Such a safety device, if found adequately reliable, might even be mandated for inclusion on automobiles. The narrow band of acceptance possible with voice-activated systems can virtually guarantee rejection of unauthorised usage. The problems to be worked out will tend to centre on assuring that access is consistently granted to valid requests even when there are minor vocal changes (head cold, emotional states, etc.).

The complicated transformation between the inherent meaning conveyed in audible speech, and the parametric digital representation of resultant linear predictive coding would have been a dream come true to any cryptographer a few score years ago. Even today, without working hardware synthesisers or knowledge of precise integer formats, the task of determining what is being communicated in a digital LPC string is exceedingly difficult. With even a modest degree of digital bit encryption the result is for all practical purposes a virtually impregnable encoding of the message being audibly conveyed. Industrial encoders for secure transmission of sensitive data would seem to be a realistic commercial possibility.

Finally, as a commercial voice input venture, some mention should be made of the possibility of automated language translation. There is no doubt about the value such a device would have if it were available today. It is hard enough to simulate functionally with full computers using unambiguous keyboard inputs! Such a vocal capability is clearly beyond the known technology in any meaningful sense – but the objective is desirable enough to encourage a great deal of interest. Numerous research efforts in government, universities, and industries are under way hoping to 'solve' this problem. Not surprisingly, the most intense efforts in this field centre around the multilingual domains of greater Europe, while there is much less activity in the relatively monolingual American and Japanese cultures. Serious workers in this field would do well to keep in touch with developments in the European technology.

19.6 *Speech technology and the vocally impaired*

Both synthetic speech and voice input technology offer tremendous opportunities for implementing advanced aids for the handicapped. Due to the relatively short time that these technologies have been available, both commercial companies and hobbyists will find this a rewarding field to explore – especially in view of the results accomplished for others.

Synthetic speech, as a substitute voice for the vocally impaired individual, is still in its infancy. Ideally there are four basic requirements that a user seeks in such a device:

(a) intelligibility,
(b) sufficient vocabulary flexibility,
(c) functional ease of control, and
(d) affordability.

Until quite recently, the affordability of virtually anything except pre-recorded messages (which don't offer much vocabulary flexibility) was not reasonable to the typical individual needing the instrument. The new technologies discussed in this book are beginning to have an impact in this area, and will undoubtedly continue to offer increasingly better aids for those needing assistance. The other three requirements deserve further comment.

INTELLIGIBILITY

This is simply the concern of whether or not the synthetic voice is consistently understandable. Sometimes the word 'natural' will be used in discussions about this point (as in chapter 14, for example). While there is no argument that a pleasant, natural sounding synthetic voice is desirable, there should be no question that 'naturalness' is a luxury in a voice in such a communication aid, while 'intelligibility' is a necessity. Therefore factors such as inflection, pitch, intonation, are helpful when they improve intelligibility, and desirable when sufficient intelligibility is present but they can never be traded for even slight losses in intelligibility!

Intelligibility is especially difficult to discern after you have been exposed to synthetic speech for even a short while. Our ears have a way of adapting to the speech patterns we hear, and our discernment of what is intelligible to the 'virgin ear' is correspondingly reduced. It is also important that the novice listener hears the utterances without pre-knowledge of what is to be spoken. The task of confirming that you heard an utterance that is written on a paper in front of you requires much less intelligibility than understanding the content of an utterance about which you have no prior knowledge.

The last word of caution is to make certain that the intelligibility is retained in the environment where the device will normally be used. The best example of this pitfall is the common telephone. Because the phone only passes certain frequencies of audible sound, utterances that are perfectly intelligible to listeners in the room with the speaker may not be intelligible over the phone. Most of the technologies currently in widespread usage are quite compatible with phone transmission, if any care at all is taken in developing speech with forethought to this aspect. Some devices may be developed for use in the presence of significant background noise and if so that should be carefully taken into consideration. Whatever the synthetic voice, and however it is intended to be used, it will be of no value if it can't be understood. Therefore no matter how great it sounds to you – or even to everyone else in your development laboratory – always try it out in the environment in which it's intended to operate with untrained listeners, and be prepared to modify it based on their reactions.

FLEXIBILITY

Vocally impaired individuals are constantly frustrated by their inability to express themselves adequately. Ideally they want a voice synthesis unit that is as flexible as the normal human voice. The other three factors (cost, intelligibility and ease of control) force compromises to be made. If constructive synthesis is used (see chapter 6), maximum flexibility and affordability are usually obtained with corresponding sacrifices in intelligibility and ease of control. On the other hand, if fully developed words and phrases are synthesised from original speech, then a better intelligibility and ease of control are normally achieved, at a sacrifice in flexibility. In any case, the random access now afforded via any electronic speech synthesis system certainly offers a great deal of improvement over the lack of flexibility offered by serially recorded messages.

CONTROL

This is the aspect that separates applications for the handicapped from all other mass-produced speech products. Since each impaired person has specialised needs unique to their own individual impairment, standardised methods of controlling speech units will be inappropriate for large segments of this specialised population. In essence, this has meant that the economies of scale have not been successfully applied to their needs, which means that most of the tools built for their use tend to be prohibitively expensive. The challenge may be viewed as segmenting that which can be mass produced and that which must be tailor-made for each individual. If a standardised interface could be established to link the mass-produced speech units to custom-made controllers, perhaps a first step would have been taken towards bringing the benefits of economies of scale to this community as well.

VOICE INPUT

For many handicapped individuals that lack control of various motor functions, but still retain their ability to speak, effective voice input control could bring new meaning and freedom to their lives. In these cases, since the system is solely dedicated to an individual user, speaker dependency (including extensive training) is not only permissible, but may even be desirable. (Spoken utterances that might not be readily discernable by untrained human listeners will often be consistent enough from utterance to utterance to allow a trained speaker-dependent system to 'recognise the intent of the speaker.) As was mentioned above, the key here is individuality and diversity of needs. Generalised speaker-dependent trainable voice input systems that drive general-purpose microprocessors certainly seem well suited to such tasks. The difficulty is determining how and what motor responses are controlled by the microprocessor, and being sure it has failproof safeguards so that no possible misunderstanding could result in a dangerous or harmful condition to the user. This area is certainly ripe for inventive applications, and also in need of established interface standards to facilitate cost benefits.

CHAPTER 20

APPLYING LINGUISTICS
TO SYNTHESIS

Francis Nolan

As has been pointed out many times in this book, the widespread use of speech technology will not be possible without resort to the principles of linguistics. In this chapter we explore some of the ways in which application of this discipline can enhance the capabilities of a voice output system.

20.1 *Communication beyond intelligibility*

THE NATURE OF HUMAN SPEECH
It would be ironic if the full potential of a new technology for communicating between machine and man went neglected because we were blinkered by the constraints of an old technology, yet that is precisely the danger at the present time. Speech synthesis (the new technology) has been widely regarded as a means for converting text (the old technology) into spoken sounds, and the criteria for evaluating the success of the synthesis have centred on listeners' ability correctly to identify words. But this approach to synthesis, it can be argued, undervalues the subtlety and complexity of human speech communication.

The reasons for this narrowness of approach lie in the pre-eminence in our culture of the written word, and our tendency to view writing not merely as a facet of language realised in a visual medium, but actually as a visual record of speech. But of the many kinds of information that can be carried by speech, writing is strongly biassed towards what Lyons (1977: 50) calls the 'descriptive' function of language:

'the transmission of factual, or propositional information'.

This dominance is clearly seen in any author's attempt to convey the speech of his characters; simply to record words such as *I'll try to finish it tonight* is not enough to convey much of what the reader would have gleaned if he had actually heard the utterance, and which the author has to resort to analysing and converting to factual information: . . . *he said doubtfully, in his high, plaintive voice.* or . . . *she retorted confidently, her harsh voice giving particular emphasis to the word 'tonight'.*

The written language and its particular biases has long dominated linguistics, as well as our everyday thinking about language; and paradoxically the model adopted by many *speech* researchers, explicitly or implicitly, is one which reflects the bias of written language towards factual information. A common, but oversimplistic, model of speech communication is shown in fig. 20.1.

Here, a simplex 'message' or 'meaning' is encoded first by the linguistic mechanism — the 'grammar' known by the speaker, including syntactic and phonological rules — and then the phonetic code output by the linguistic mechanism is converted into acoustic form by the activity of the vocal apparatus.

However, within linguistics interest has grown in the facilities available in speech for transmitting information beyond the factual — in *paralinguistics* in one of its many senses (see e.g. Crystal, 1975: chapter 2, and chapter 3 of this book). The definition of 'linguistics' and 'paralinguistics', of what is 'central' to the linguistic system and what 'peripheral', is not at issue here; rather, the remainder of this section will merely outline some of the kinds of information conveyed by speech, and then indicate the ways in which they are encoded in speech.

INFORMATION CONVEYED BY SPEECH

A conceptual distinction useful when considering the information conveyed by speech is that drawn by Lyons (1977: 33) between signals which are *communicative* versus *informative*:

> 'a signal is informative if (regardless of the intentions of the sender) it makes the receiver aware of something of which he was not previously aware'

whereas a signal is communicative:

> 'if it is intended by the sender to make the receiver aware of something of which he was not previously aware. Whether the signal is communicative or not rests, then, upon the possibility of choice, or selection, on the part of the sender'.

It should be noted, however, that it is not possible to categorise a 'signal' as communicative or informative by inspection of the signal

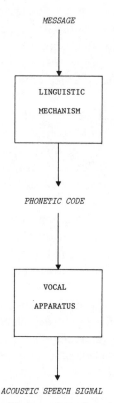

Figure 20.1 A simplistic model of speech communication

alone – as a classic instance, speaking in a whispery voice may be the result of the speaker's intention to communicate the confidentiality of what he is saying; but equally, it may simply be informative of the fact that he has laryngitis.

When a speaker produces an utterance, we may consider as under-lying it a complex *communicative intent*. Although any analytic com-partmentalisation of this communicative intent is likely to be con-tentious and certainly imperfect, the top part of fig. 20.2 gives an idea of some of its more important subparts (for a more detailed discussion of communicative intent and its mapping onto the linguistic mechanism see Nolan (in press: 2.3). Crystal (1975: 12) makes a division into *cognitive* and *effective* subparts, where cognitive refers to what Lyons (above) terms 'factual' or 'propositional' information, and affective relates to the attitude of the speaker – as, for instance, when a person speaks using a wide pitch range and specific pitch contours to communicate a friendly attitude, or speaks loudly and harshly to communicate his anger.

To these perhaps most basic subparts of communicative intent we must add at least the following: *social, self-presentational* and *regulative*.

In recent years sociolinguistics has revealed and quantified the degree to which our speech changes according to the context in which we are speaking (or more strictly, our interpretation of that context); for instance, as the context becomes more formal, so we tend often to change aspects of our speech in such a way that it becomes more like that of people we perceive to be of higher status (see e.g. Labov, 1972). We may also, depending on circumstances, 'converge' or 'diverge', making our speech more, or less, like that of other participants in the interaction (cf. Giles *et al.*, 1979), for example speaking quietly with someone who speaks quietly to us. The encoding in speech of a speaker's response to factors like these may be thought of as the result of the *social* part of communicative intent.

Again, a wide variety of information may be encoded by a speaker in order to project a personality corresponding to his self-image (in some particular context) (Argyle, 1967: 162):

> 'Certain aspects of behaviour during social encounters can be looked at as consequences of the participants having self-images. They present themselves in a certain way, adopt a particular "face", and try to get others to accept this picture of themselves.'

Personality dimensions such as extroversion–introversion, dominance–dependence and masculinity–femininity (or their perceptual equivalents) may be marked by particular ways of speaking, and these can to some extent be intentionally adopted to encode the speaker's *self-presentational* communicative intent.

Finally, participants in an interaction 'regulate' it (with more or less success) so that 'speaking turns' are allocated to each; a speaker indicates (probably through his overall pitch level, loudness and rate of utterance) whether he is approaching the end of a turn and anticipating a response, or conversely, is 'in full flow' and unwilling to yield the floor.

Clearly, however, as soon as a speaker begins to speak he produces many signals which are not communicative – intended – but merely informative. This is most apparent if we consider what a listener can infer about a speaker just from his speech. He can make a fair assessment of the speaker's sex, age, social background, and also to some extent personality and health. Notice that the cumulation of these inferences plays a large part in defining the speaker as an individual, and in the hearer's ability to recognise him as such from his voice.

Such information as this which a hearer can infer from speech and which is not under the communicative control of the speaker might

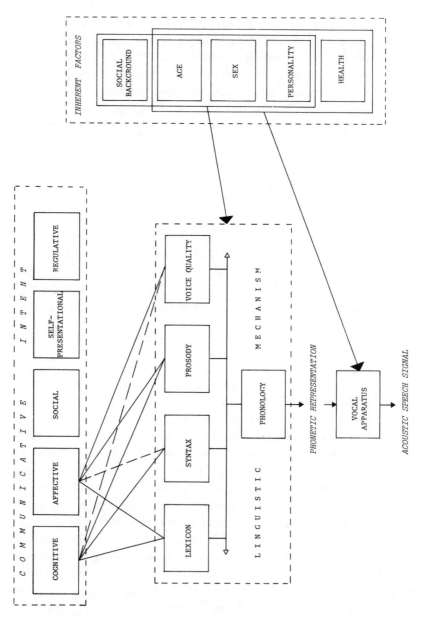

Figure 20.2 A model of speech communication

be termed *inherent*. The sources of this inherent information are shown on the right of fig. 20.2.

THE ENCODING OF INFORMATION IN SPEECH

Having now considered the complexity of information underlying speech, it is appropriate to examine how it becomes encoded in the speech signal.

Any language user may be thought of as having at his disposal a number of linguistic resources with which to realise his communicative intent. In the simplified model of fig. 20.2 these are shown as *lexicon*, *syntax*, *prosody*, *voice quality* and *phonology*.

Crudely, the *lexicon* is the speaker's 'dictionary', his stock of words complete with their semantic, syntactic and phonetic properties; while *syntax* comprises a set of rules for combining words in grammatical sequences. It is the combination of these resources which receives best representation in our writing system.

To a first approximation, the *prosodic* resource can be seen as the systematic use of fundamental frequency (pitch), intensity and duration in ways which do not affect the identity of words; most importantly it concerns the 'intonation' or 'melody' of speech. Comprehensive treatments of the prosodic resource are to be found in Crystal (1969) and Lehiste (1970).

Speakers have the possibility of making alterations to the way they speak which pervade their speech for considerable time spans, as in the case of the use mentioned above of a whispery voice to indicate confidentiality, or the complex of vocal features often adopted when talking to very small children. In some cases these volitional speech tendencies may pervade most or all of a speaker's speech production, as in the instance of someone who (for no biophysical reason) habitually speaks with heavy nasalisation, or a breathy phonation type. These medium- to long-term speech tendencies are generally known as *voice quality*.

A distinction needs to be made between the voice quality *resource*, which exploits speech parameters susceptible to manipulation by a speaker, and *intrinsic* voice quality, which derives from the organic limitations of an individual's vocal tract. Both kinds of voice quality – long-term habitual speech patterns, and phonetic effects of organic origin – contribute to the personal quality by which we can recognise a voice. Laver (1980) includes an extensive discussion of voice quality, and provides the hitherto most comprehensive framework for its phonetic description.

Finally, the *phonological* resource integrates the outputs of the other linguistic components to produce a *phonetic representation* compatible to the capabilities of the vocal tract.

The mapping onto the linguistic resources of any subpart of communicative intent is one-to-many, and varies from language to language; for simplicity, fig. 20.2 shows only the mapping of cognitive intent and affective intent.

In communicating his cognitive intent, the speaker will choose appropriate words and an appropriate syntactic form, together with an intonation pattern which may help to reinforce the syntactic form (perhaps question versus statement), and also delimit syntactic units; it is occasionally possible (dotted line) that a voice quality may be used to add to, alter, or even reverse the otherwise apparent cognitive content of an utterance (as in the case of voice quality features signalling irony).

For affective intent, if a speaker wishes to communicate for instance an attitude of deference and politeness, he may do so by selecting 'polite' words, certain appropriate intonation contours, and a voice quality also deemed 'polite' in the culture concerned; possibly too by selecting certain syntactic conventions associated with politeness.

Sociolinguistics has shown speakers to vary, according to the formality of the context, their choice of words, syntax and particularly certain phonological variables (cf. Labov, 1972); mapping onto prosody has not been demonstrated, though cannot be ruled out, while Esling (1978) has demonstrated sociolinguistic stratification in terms of voice quality and hence the potential for its exploitation socio-communicatively.

If we take as an example a speaker wishing to communicate that he is a 'competent' person, he will in particular map his intent onto the prosodic resource and the voice quality resource. Research has shown (Scherer, 1979: 186ff) that a higher mean fundamental frequency (up to a certain threshold) will elicit higher ratings from listeners on personality traits subsumed under 'competence', while it is likely that extremes of lax or tense voice quality would cause a downrating in terms of competence. Much research remains to be done in this area.

Lastly, the burden of signalling whether a speaker is approaching the end of a 'turn', or intends to continue speaking, is borne by prosodic cues – probably including a fall to a low fundamental frequency terminally – although the exact nature of these cues remains to be demonstrated.

We can turn now to the determining relationship of the inherent factors on the right of fig. 20.2 on the speech signal. This determination may take place at two levels: an inherent factor may determine the (long-term or short-term) characteristics of the vocal apparatus, or it may determine the nature of the linguistic resources available to a speaker. For instance, the health of a speaker will determine the short-term state of his vocal tract — we can infer that he has laryngitis. At the other end, a listener will infer much about a speaker's social background from various aspects of the linguistic system he uses — particularly, for English, pronunciation. But many of the inherent factors may determine both vocal mechanism and linguistic resources; old age is revealed not only by tremor and shrillness in the voice induced by organic changes, but perhaps by outdated locutions and pronunciations.

It emerges from fig. 20.2 that speech communication is a complex and sophisticated phenomenon — which, it has to be admitted, is far from perfectly understood. However, we are now in a position to consider how speech synthesis may progress from its present principally 'spoken writing' state towards a better emulation of the information capacity of speech communication.

20.2 *More flexible synthesis systems*

Although the distinction is not as clear cut as might superficially appear, we can divide applications of more flexible synthesis systems into those where the output replicates the voices of several different individuals, and those where variation in the voice of a single individual is used.

SYNTHESIS SYSTEMS REPLICATING SEVERAL DIFFERENT INDIVIDUALS
Synthesis of the voices of different individuals (D) will be equivalent principally to altering the inherent factors in fig. 20.2, though it should be remembered that some contribution to personal voice quality may result from habitual exploitation of the voice quality (linguistic) resource.

D1 *Multi-speaker information channel for different hearers*
If synthetic speech is being used to give similar information or instructions through the same channel to two or more listeners, then more efficient than explicitly cueing the attention of one particular listener would be to do this implicitly, by having him listen for a particular voice. For two listeners, a male versus female distinction would probably be the most natural to react to.

D2 *Multi-speaker information channel for different information*
Here the relevance of different kinds of information would be cued by the use of different synthetic voices; for instance in an airport different voices could be used for arrivals versus departures, and for inland versus international service.

D3   Multi-speaker output to accommodate preference of listeners

Different classes of hearer may have preferences for different kinds of voice – commercial users of speech synthesis apparently favour breathy-voiced female speakers, presumably when aiming their products at male listeners; and children may respond better to a female voice with a large pitch range than to a stern male speaker.

D4   Multi-speaker reading machine

Reading machines for the blind are already a practical proposition, but may be fatiguing to listen to for long periods; one development which might make their output aesthetically more acceptable would be the option for the user to select a variety of voices. More ambitiously, reading machines for the blind, or for aiding children to learn to read, might be programmed to synthesise different voices for different characters in plays.

D5   'Identikit' voice system for forensic purposes

Whilst identification of individuals by their voices in forensics must be approached with utmost caution and reservation (see Nolan, in press), there may be scope in forensic investigation for the use of synthesis to build up samples of a voice on the basis of a witness's description, in the same way that 'identikit' or 'photofit' pictures of faces can be constructed. The resultant synthetic voice would serve both as an aid in enquiries; and also, rather than reliance on the impressionistic and unsystematic descriptions used by the witness, the exact synthesis parameters of the sample could be checked against reference files of anlysed known voices.

SYNTHESIS REPLICATING VARIATION IN THE VOICE OF THE SAME INDIVIDUAL

Synthesis of variation in the voice of the same individual (S) can be equivalent in fig. 20.2 either to a speaker mapping some aspect of his communicative intent, or to determination at the level of the vocal tract by an inherent factor such as state of health.

S1   Prosody supporting cognitive information

A synthesis system which could reliably emulate the use of prosody by human speakers would render connected speech more natural and intelligible by giving the listener cues to the syntactic and semantic organisation of the speech. Human speakers, for instance, organise the flow of speech into intonational segments sometimes called *tone units*, which correspond to some extent with logical units of meaning, and signal the relative importance of certain words to the listener's perceptual system by giving them intonational prominence. The longer and more complex the utterances being conveyed by synthetic speech, the greater is the enhancement to intelligibility of realistic prosody.

S2   Prosody and voice quality conveying limited affective information
For some applications, a limited capacity for communicating affective information by prosody and voice quality should prove useful. For example, a pilot receiving some of his knowledge about the aircraft's state through synthetic speech would find appropriate reaction easier if urgent messages requiring immediate action were synthesised with those paralinguistic features characteristic of urgent real-speech utterances, in contrast to 'neutral' characteristics for messages requiring no urgent action.

S3   Prosody and voice quality conveying extensive affective information
If we consider the specific example of synthetic aids for the speech handicapped — cerebral palsy victims, for instance — it is apparent that, in a literate society at least, a device which does no more than convert written text into speech has little advantage over written text. Indeed, it may have a disadvantage, which is parallel to the observation frequently made that people listening to non-native speakers are less consciously aware of, and therefore less forgiving towards, intonation and voice quality errors than pronunciation errors. That is, a foreigner who mispronounces a word will simply be noted consciously as a non-native speaker, whereas when he uses an inappropriate intonation pattern, or voice quality, this is likely to escape conscious notice and be interpreted directly — giving rise to the misunderstanding that the foreigner is being rude, or aggressive, or whatever. A speech aid which produces 'machine-like' speech, or speech with a few inflexible intonation patterns, will cause an adverse response in a listener at a subconscious level which may take considerable conscious effort to overcome.

The ultimate ideal, of course, is a synthesis aid flexible enough for the user to be able to communicate his affective intent as subtly as the prosodic and voice quality resources of real speech provide for; this clearly provides immense challenges not only at the level of the synthesiser but also in terms of its control by the user.

S4   Analysis-by-synthesis of voice quality in speech pathology
A device of the following sort might be of use to the speech pathologist. It would be a synthesiser which responded appropriately to specifications

in terms of descriptive voice quality labels (such as those provided by Laver (1980) – *whispery* voice, *nasalised* voice, *palatalised* voice, and many others). The speech pathologist might make an initial auditory description of the voice, and use the synthesis specifications corresponding to this description to produce an initial synthesis sample. He would then compare this with the patient's real speech and modify the synthetic sample until an optimum auditory match was achieved. At this stage, the current synthesis parameter values would serve as a quantitative description of the voice under investigation, and could also be compared with later values to chart progress. The advantage of such an *analysis-by-synthesis* route to a quantitative description over straight acoustic analysis would be that the clinician's skill and experience at detecting voice quality abnormalities would be playing a direct role. Hypotheses made by him on the contribution of various factors to the voice would be being tested by comparing the output of the synthesiser to the real speech.

20.3 *Current feasibility*

In this section the feasibility of the applications outlined above is assessed in the context of current commercially available synthesis chips, and the assumption of limited computing power.

Two basic strategies are considered for flexible synthetic speech output. In the first, variation in the output is achieved simply by having multiple stores of *primes* (speech data sets); in the second, parameters from a single store of primes are used and modifications made to produce variation in the output.

MULTIPLE STORES OF PRIMES

A conceptual overview of this kind of approach is shown diagrammatically in fig. 20.3. When a particular 'text' or utterance is to be synthesised, this is input to a *controller* which then fetches from store the necessary primes (in parameterised form) to be concatenated – phrases, words, syllables or segments depending on the size of prime used in the particular application. These are then concatenated and forwarded to the synthesiser. Variation in output is obtained simply by having multiple stores of primes – a complete set of primes for each speaker, and each voice quality required; multiplied by the number of different prosodic patterns to be associated with each prime.

The function of the controller is very straightforward – simply to select at any moment the appropriate prime store. The system, however, is conceptually inelegant and is highly unparsimonious, the

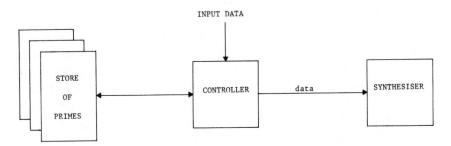

Figure 20.3 Variable-output synthesis: multiple prime stores

multiple store repeating vast amounts of redundant information. Nevertheless, when the number of primes, and the number of output variants, are small, and memory more available than computing power, this approach may allow flexibility of output simply and effectively. Subject to these limitations it could cope with types of application D1, D2, D3 and D4, and S2 above.

MODIFICATION OF A SINGLE SET OF PRIMES

In this approach, as shown in fig. 20.4, the controller no longer selects primes from different stores (there is only one) but rather forwards instructions to the synthesiser modifying its behaviour. Given available synthesis chips, these modifications would currently be of a rather crude nature, but could nevertheless bring about considerable variation in voice quality and prosodic characteristics.

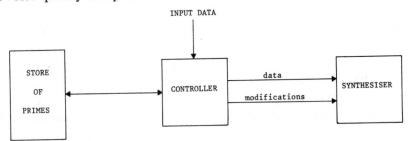

Figure 20.4 Variable-output synthesis: limited parameter modification

The kinds of modification which could be achieved include the following. Changing the synthesis sampling rate would have the effect of raising or lowering all frequencies in the speech signal, thus changing both fundamental frequency (pitch), and formant frequencies, that is the speech characteristics resulting primarily from the larynx, and the vocal tract, respectively (see chapter 4). An increase in sampling rate would resynthesise male primes to sound more like a female voice; but the limits on naturalness of this kind of procedure must be recognised.

Between real speakers with different-sized vocal tracts the different formant frequencies are not related in a linear fashion, nor are the relationships constant across different vowels, and so large changes in sampling frequency are likely to result in unnatural sounding voices. Nor is laryngeal pitch (being the product of an independent mechanism) tied to variation in formant frequencies; but this independence can be replicated by using the controller also to change the pitch coefficients of voiced segments. In this way two of the major factors affecting the quality of voices can be matched in impression of distinct (if not always natural sounding) speakers; it is likely that D1, D2, D3 and D4 above could be tackled with at least partial success.

Manipulation by the controller of the pitch coefficients, together with durational changes (by duplicating or deleting data frames), gives the potential for exploiting the prosodic resource (cf. S1), but it must be appreciated that the complexity of the relationship of prosodic patterns to the syntax and semantics of connected speech is so great as to make success unlikely without highly complex algorithms and considerable computing power. On the other hand, the kind of application mentioned under S2 would be feasible, where perhaps just two modes of utterance, one 'normal' and one 'urgent', could be satisfactorily achieved by a global increase in pitch for the intonation contour of the latter.

A third kind of modification would be to add noise to the voicing excitation source of the synthesiser, or to replace the voicing pulse excitation by noise altogether. By simulating whispery voice, or whisper, these changes would again allow for a limited replication of voice quality changes in an individual, and so perhaps be adequate for applications of type S2; but whilst this kind of modification would be part of what was required for D4, D5 and S3, S4, the variation provided would by no means be comprehensive enough.

This section has given an outline of what is achievable using the sort of synthesiser now commercially available, and very limited computing power, although using a powerful signal processor chip as the synthesis controller would considerably extend the capability for parameter manipulation (see section 10.3). The final section considers future development towards fully flexible synthesis.

20.4 *Beyond current limitations*

The model presented schematically in fig. 20.5 represents a goal for research, and which would ultimately underlie a synthesis system of sufficient flexibility to fulfil the applications outlined above.

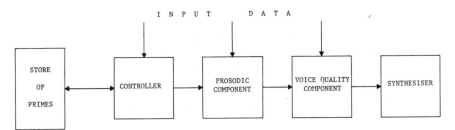

Figure 20.5 Variable-output synthesis: approaching the flexibility of real speech

Importantly, the model incorporates a component for the assignment of prosodic characteristics to utterances, and would involve the derivation of appropriate pitch contours, and the durational adjustments associated with these in the intonation of real speech. The precise nature of this component depends on the application in mind.

Supposing the system were to communicate purely cognitive information (cf. S1 above), then the task of the *prosodic component* would be to assign intonation patterns appropriate to the syntactic structures, taking account of factors such as length of phrases, supplied to it. In the case of synthesis from text (e.g. in a reading machine implementation), this syntactic structure would have to be ascertained by parsing the text (see e.g. Meli, 1981); or in the case of messages being generated from a data base in non-linguistic form, the generation process itself would be required to supply adequate syntactic structure (e.g. Young, 1978). As stressed above, the assignment of prosodic characteristics at the abstract level is a far from simple operation; whereas at the lower level of the synthesis itself, manipulation of pitch coefficients, duration, and if necessary gain coefficients, do not present a serious problem.

If, however, the communication of extensive affective information (S3 — the synthetic speech sounding angry, friendly, ironic, etc.) were to be accomplished, then information in addition to syntactic structure would have to be supplied (from 'above', in the diagram). This is precisely because, as pointed out in section 20.1, the same syntactic structure plus lexical items can convey quite different affective information. There is no way to predict for certain the correct affective content from the string of words alone. In the case of an aid for the speech handicapped, the affective information would have to be supplied by the user; he would specify not only the words of the utterance, but some indication of the manner in which it was to be spoken ('animatedly', 'gently'; or perhaps 'pleasantly', 'ironically'); and these specifications would be interpreted in terms of prosodic modifications by the prosodic component.

In the ultimate kind of machine–man synthesis system which achieved *synthesis from concept* (see chapter 17), or more comprehensively in the terminology of the present article *synthesis from communicative intent*, the system would be generating and realising as well as its own cognitive content also the affective intent with which it was to be associated and this would be the source of the specification 'from above' to the prosodic component.

It cannot be overemphasised, however, that the research task for the linguist in analysing the relation between prosody and affect far exceeds the research needed to achieve implementation at the level of the synthesis system.

Moving right in fig. 20.5 we find a *voice quality component*. This component must be extremely sophisticated if the system is to tackle the tasks of D5, where in principle any normal human voice, and S4, where even pathological voices, must be within the capability of the synthesiser.

The voice quality component would operate independently on two separate types of parameter – the laryngeal source, and the vocal-tract resonances – and in this respect mirrors the speech production mechanism. In terms of synthetic speech, the first would mean being able effectively to change the shape of the excitation waveform to obtain results parallel to those which occur when speakers make different laryngeal adjustments. Research effort in phonetics is currently being put into investigating this aspect of speech production; and the implementation of the results on a synthesiser with an excitation waveform variable under program control should prove a tractable problem.

The second, particularly if the parameters corresponding to vocal-tract resonances are linear prediction reflection coefficients, is likely to prove more troublesome. For one thing, the differences between the formant patterns of different individuals with vocal tracts of varying sizes are highly complex and phone-specific due to the shape of the vocal tract; likewise the effects of one individual modifying his vocal tract (cf. Nolan, in press: chapter 4). Secondly, it is likely that such vocal-tract dependent voice quality modifications would have to be made either in the domain of formant frequencies, or in the domain of vocal-tract shapes. In either case moderate computing power is implicated in the transformation to the relevant domain, and, after modification, back to reflection coefficients.

If it is accepted that speech synthesis should aim to exploit fully the potential of the communicative mechanism it is emulating, then two things are essential for the field. Firstly, an understanding of what the complexity and potential of that mechanism is; and secondly, concrete goals at which pragmatically motivated research can be levelled. It is hoped that this paper has at least begun to do both of these; and in so far as it has, it will also have made it clear that the attainment of the goals will require close contact between the fields of speech engineering, phonetics and linguistics – contact which should prove theoretically and practically fruitful to all three fields.

References

Argyle, M. (1967) *The Psychology of Interpersonal Behaviour*. Harmondsworth: Penguin.

Crystal, D. (1969) *Prosodic Systems and Intonation in English*. London: Cambridge University Press.

Crystal, D. (1975) *The English Tone of Voice*. London: Edward Arnold.

Esling, J.H. (1978) 'Voice quality in Edinburgh: a sociolinguistic and phonetic study'. PhD dissertation, University of Edinburgh.

Giles, H., Scherer, K.R. and Taylor, D.M. (1979) 'Speech markers in social interaction'. In *Social Markers in Speech* (Eds Scherer K.R. and Giles H.) Cambridge and Paris: Cambridge University Press and Editions de la Maison des Sciences de l'Homme.

Labov, W. (1972) *Sociolinguistic Patterns*. Philadelphia: University of Pennsylvania Press.

Laver, J. (1980) *The Phonetic Description of Voice Quality*. Cambridge: Cambridge University Press.

Lehiste, I. (1970) *Suprasegmentals*. Cambridge, Mass.: MIT Press.

Lyons, J. (1977) *Semantics*. Cambridge: Cambridge University Press.

Meli, R. (1981) 'The conversion of teletext into speech'. PhD dissertation, University of Cambridge.

Nolan, F. (In Press) *The Phonetic Bases of Speaker Recognition*. Cambridge: Cambridge University Press.

Scherer, K.R. (1979) 'Personality markers in speech'. In *Social Markers in Speech* (Eds Scherer K.R. and Giles H.), Cambridge and Paris: Cambridge University Press and Editions de la Maison des Sciences de l'Homme.

Young, S.J. (1978) 'Speech synthesis from concept'. PhD dissertation, University of Cambridge.

CHAPTER 21

TOWARDS THE FUTURE

Geoff Bristow

21.1 *The speech recognition breakthrough*

At the time of completion of this book (January 1983) speech synthesis
is already beginning to appear in man–machine interfaces of various
types. By the time the reader has got to this point, no doubt such
applications will be commonplace. So what is the next step?

Most commentators and market prediction reports agree that a
boom in design activity and sales of speech-based products will occur
during this decade, although the opinions differ as to exactly when.
For example, a recent IRD report[1] stated that the market for voice
I/O products would grow to one billion dollars by the year 1990, in
Europe alone. However, a revolution on this scale will not occur based
solely on speech output. Although the revolution has started on the
very simple principle of *display replacement*, it will be completed by
a new generation of *interactive systems* which exploit more fully the
capabilities of natural communication.

From a functional design point of view, speech output can be regarded as an interface 'element', along with cathode ray tube, liquid
crystal, light emitting diode or vacuum fluorescent displays. Considered in this light, speech output is a similar additional cost to a
system as that of a relatively complex numeric display, and therefore
many times cheaper than cathode ray tube. Of voice response systems,
speech synthesis offers lower cost and size and much higher reliability
than magnetic tape output, and the ability for concatentation of
messages out of sound elements. On the other hand, synthesis requires
much more complex data preparation methods.

A usage pattern based entirely upon this model, however, would
make poor use of the potential of voice communication, and is not

336

likely to gain the respect of the public. The man–machine interface will not be fully exploited until we have achieved true two-way voice communication. While there are times when voice output alone is essential, and times when voice input is essential, a partnership between voice input and output will always be desirable.

Table 21.1 Application categories for voice I/O

Application categories	Voice input	Voice output	Comments/examples
Telecommunications:			
— control	*	**	I/P with touch-tone keys
— store and forward	**	**	Solid state messages
Controlled environments requiring:			
— hands-free operation	**	*	e.g. stock counting
— eyes-free operation	*	**	e.g. cars/aeroplanes
— alerted interest		**	e.g. public address
— added interest	*	*	e.g. educational aids
Text input/output	*		Unskilled word-processing (with manual correction)
Aids for the disabled:			
— control by the physically handicapped	**	*	Adapted consumer products
— text I/O by the physically handicapped	**		Word processors
— control by the blind	*	**	Adapted consumer products
— text I/O by the blind	*	**	Talking books
— communication by the speech impaired		**	Speech communication aids
Language/speech training	*	**	Educational computers

*Speech function desirable.
**Speech function essential.

Table 21.1 illustrates this by dividing applications of speech technology into some gross categories and defining for each area whether speech input or output is essential, desirable or has no particular value (other than novelty value). The assumption is made that where voice input is *essential*, voice output usually is *desirable* as a partner, and *vice versa*. Only in one area are voice input and output equally essential, almost by definition, and that is *store and forward* – the technique of recording a speech message in RAM using usual speech analysis methods (such as LPC), and resynthesising at a later date. Elsewhere there is usually a definite reason why speech control is imperative (*eyes-free*, *hands-free*, etc.) but completing the feedback loop using the same communication method is a useful convenience.

Such a move towards interactive systems is inevitable. Although no sudden breakthroughs are expected in the accuracy of speech recognition, a limited capability exists now and the extent of the capability will gradually improve. More importantly perhaps, the *cost* of the state-of-the-art is falling dramatically, as happened with synthesis. Thus the use of voice input technology is currently limited only by the cost/performance requirements of a given application, and this will remain the case as the performance per dollar improves and more applications are opened up.

21.2 *Power to the user*

Most speech designers agree that the most fundamental principle in the design of talking systems is to give to the user the ultimate power of manual operation and the silencing of speech output. This is essential in the case of system malfunction (especially for voice input), and it is desirable to allow choice on the part of the user to cater for different tastes and avoid alienation or annoyance.

A good way of arranging such user control is with a user-selectable *message mask* in which each of the possible messages in a system are allocated a certain level of priority, either in software or in a hidden peg board, set of links, etc. The option of only listening to messages of a certain priority level can then be selected easily with a simple switch in an accessible position.

A typical message mask is shown in table 21.2, where four possible types of message which may be output from a domestic central heating system are presented. In this example, it is envisaged that the switch would be located on the central heating programmer panel, and would have four positions marked as *emergency messages only, routine messages level 1, routine messages level 2* and *diagnostics*. The diagnostic option would only be chosen by the central heating engineer when he was testing the operation of, for example, the room thermostats, while routine message levels 1 and 2 present two different choices for normal operation. This example assumes that under normal circumstances the house owner would usually wish to be alerted when a window has been

Table 21.2 An example message mask for a domestic heating system

Message	Emergency messages	Routine Message levels		Diagnostic messages
		1	2	
'The temperature in the baby's bedroom has dropped below 20 degrees.'	X	X	X	X
'The front bedroom is losing heat fast.'		X	X	X
'The hot water is now up to temperature.'			X	X
'Radiator 5 has just switched OFF.'				X

X = Enable this message if the mask level is selected.

left open in a room which is being heated, while he may or may not be interested to be told when the water is hot enough for him to have a bath.

On the other hand, there will certainly be times when he would not want to be bothered with any speech at all, even if he has left a window open, although even in this case he is sure to be interested if the temperature in the baby's bedroom has become critically cold! Such a rare situation would be captured using the 'emergency messages only' section. Finally, in the case where the user selects the highest priority message selection, he is likely to need the capability to hear the repeat of any important information upon re-selection of a normal message level, as discussed in section 12.3 regarding the operation of a 'pardon' button.

More complex man–machine interfaces, such as those involved in an office work station, will generally require the capability of total manual override using a keyboard and VDU in the normal way.

21.3 *Networks*

While we are by no means certain how we are each likely to react to vocal machines in our lives, the prospect of a cacophony of individual voices throughout one's environment is even more horrific.

Fortunately, however, there are some likely remedies for this. The Philips Corporation have already taken note of the need within the domestic environment to link pieces of equipment together in a very simple network. Users of remote control televisions and video recorders will already have noted the requirement to hold two separate remote control units if a common manufacturer has not been used for both products, and similar duplications of apparatus occur all around a house. The Philips solution is to include a standard domestic 'bus' interface (the 'd2B' bus) in many new products, so that they can be wired together and advantage can be taken of common facilities. Clearly, the opportunity exists in such a system to add a single 'human interface' unit, which can include voice communication (see fig. 21.1). In such a scenario the 'house' assumes an identity of its own with a particular voice. For example, the 'house' may advise you that there is somebody at the door, whereupon you could ask to communicate directly to the caller who is standing on the doorstep. After ascertaining that the caller is a person you would like to see, you may ask the 'house' to open the door, switch off the television and start the coffee percolator.

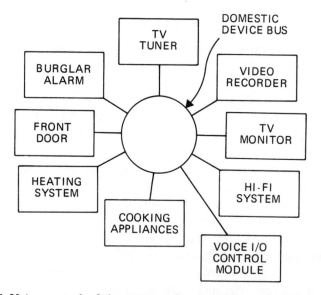

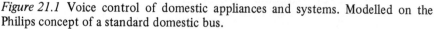

Figure 21.1 Voice control of domestic appliances and systems. Modelled on the Philips concept of a standard domestic bus.

Although such a single speaking identity is yet to be seen in the domestic environment, it is already beginning to appear in automobiles. While some early designs of speech synthesis systems for cars have included a dedicated speech box for normal dashboard operations and a separate one for vehicle warning systems, some manufacturers have already moved towards a single speech unit which is wired to a number of separate microprocessor-controlled sub-units within the vehicle.

Thus the 'car' is inevitably given a single identity and can be interrogated for information.

Turning to one's place of work, it is evident that an evolution towards a single 'work station' has already occurred. For example, manager and secretary alike need only interface to the *local area network* at one single human interface point each, which at the minimum consists of a keyboard and screen. The addition of a speech communication facility to such a work station would mean that the user is immediately able to access all the facilities available on the network, which may include communications and computing facilities as well as his own personal diary and filing system, etc. It is also pleasing to note that, when this facility is added to all work stations on a network, the disabled may be able to appear as 'full members' of the network, regardless of their particular mode of communication to the work station. For example, a user with a speech impairment may enrole himself in his speech recognition system so that his distorted pronunciations of words are nevertheless recognised by the computer; a recipient of a computer message elsewhere on the network would then receive a voice response in exactly the same way as if a user with unimpaired speech had spoken it into his own recogniser, or indeed the same as if a deaf person had typed the message into his terminal.

21.4 *Conclusion*

Wherever possible throughout this book the reader has been presented with hard facts, or at the very least a good reference as to where to find the facts. One area of conjecture, however, hangs over the whole work — that of the social desirability and public acceptance of a world in which machines communicate with man by the most exclusively human communication medium, speech. It is the opinion of most of the authors of this book, that the responsible exploitation of this powerful capability will yield great benefit in our lives. But this remains only an opinion. As shown in this book, speech synthesis has 'come of age' and it is waiting to be tested. However, it will be in the interactive link with speech recognition where the greatest potential, and the greatest dangers, lie.

Note

1. *European Speech Recognition and Synthesis Markets*, Report No. 515, International Resource Development, Norwalk, Connecticut.

INDEX